Popular Culture Theory and Methodology

A Ray and Pat Browne Book

SERIES EDITORS
Ray B. Browne and Pat Browne

Popular Culture Theory and Methodology

A Basic Introduction

EDITED BY

Harold E. Hinds, Jr.
Marilyn F. Motz
Angela M. S. Nelson

The University of Wisconsin Press
Popular Press

The University of Wisconsin Press
1930 Monroe Street
Madison, Wisconsin 53711

www.wisc.edu/wisconsinpress/

3 Henrietta Street
London WC2E 8LU, England

Library of Congress Cataloging-in-Publication Data

Popular culture theory and methodology : a basic introduction / edited by Harold E.
Hinds, Jr., Marilyn F. Motz, Angela M. S. Nelson.
    p.   cm.
"A Ray and Pat Browne book."
Includes bibliographical references and index.
ISBN 0-87972-870-1 (cloth : alk. paper)
ISBN 0-87972-871-X (pbk. : alk. paper)
    1. Popular culture. I. Hinds, Harold E. II. Motz, Marilyn Ferris, 1951–. III. Nelson,
Angela M. S., 1964–.
    CB151 .P65 2002
    306 21—dc21

                                                                        2002022303

CONTENTS

Introduction   1
    Angela M. S. Nelson

I. THE PIONEERS: WHAT IS POPULAR CULTURE?   7
  1   Masscult & Midcult   9
      Dwight Macdonald
  2   Popular Culture: Notes Toward a Definition   15
      Ray B. Browne
  3   Notes for an Introduction to a Discussion of Popular
      Culture   23
      Russel B. Nye
  4   Revolution in Popular Culture   30
      Peter Burke

II. BEYOND THE FRONTIER: POST-1960S AND '70S ANSWERS TO
    WHAT IS POPULAR CULTURE?   47
  5   The Discovery of Popular Culture Before Printing   49
      Fred E. H. Schroeder
  6   Synchronic vs Diachronic Popular Culture Studies and
      the Old English Elegy   55
      Tim D. P. Lally
  7   On the Nature and Functions of Popular Culture   62
      Gary L. Harmon
  8   Popular Culture as the New Humanities   75
      Ray B. Browne
  9   The New Validation of Popular Culture: Sense and
      Sentimentality in Academia   85
      Michael Schudson
 10   Rationalizing Genius: Ideological Strategies in the
      Classic American Science Fiction Short Story   107
      John Huntington
 11   Understanding Popular Culture   118
      John Fiske
 12   The Joke(r) Is on Us: The End of Popular Culture
      Studies   127
      Barry W. Sarchett

III. MACRO HOW-TO-DO-IT APPROACHES TO THE STUDY
   OF POPULAR CULTURE   153
   13 Notes Toward a Methodology of Popular Culture
       Study   155
       Lawrence E. Mintz
   14 A Holistic Approach to the Study of Popular
       Culture: Context, Text, Audience, and Recoding   163
       Harold E. Hinds, Jr.

IV. FORMULA: A PIONEERING THEORY   181
   15. The Concept of Formula in the Study of Popular
       Literature   183
       John G. Cawelti
   16. Formalism and Popular Culture   192
       David N. Feldman
   17. An Economic Perspective on Formula in Popular
       Culture   214
       David Paul Nord

V. POPULAR CULTURE, A UNIQUE AESTHETICS?   229
   18. Against Evaluation: The Role of the Critic of Popular
       Culture   231
       Roger B. Rollin
   19. A Critical Analysis of Roger B. Rollin's "Against
       Evaluation"   244
       John Shelton Lawrence
   20. Son of "Against Evaluation": A Reply to John
       Shelton Lawrence   260
       Roger B. Rollin
   21. With the Benefit of Hindsight: Popular Culture
       Criticism   266
       John G. Cawelti
   22. New Experimental Aesthetics and Popular Culture   271
       Dan Ash

VI. POPULAR CULTURE AND FOLK CULTURE   309
   23. The Folklore-Popular Culture Continuum   311
       Peter Narváez and Martin Laba
   24. The Bosom Serpent   313
       Harold Schechter

25. Contemporary Legends and Popular Culture:
   "It's the Real Thing"   318
   Paul Smith

26. Cultural Studies as Confluence: The Convergence
   of Folklore and Media Studies   344
   S. Elizabeth Bird

VII. POPULARITY   357
27. Popularity: The *Sine Qua Non* of Popular Culture   359
   Harold E. Hinds, Jr.

28. Popularity: How to Make a Key Concept Count
   in Building a Theory of Popular Culture   371
   Harold E. Hinds, Jr.

29. The Development and Stages of Popular Culture:
   A Case Study of Tokugawa and Meiji Japan   382
   Ling Chan Becker and Harold E. Hinds, Jr.

VIII. SELECTIVE BIBLIOGRAPHY OF ADDITIONAL WORK
   ON POPULAR CULTURE THEORY AND METHODOLOGY   407

INTRODUCTION

Angela M. S. Nelson

Even before the establishment of the *Journal of Popular Culture* in 1967 and organization of the Popular Culture Association in 1970, there was considerable interest in the academic study of popular culture. Since then the interest has only grown. *Popular Culture Theory and Methodology: A Basic Introduction* brings together a small select core of essays representing a wide variety of writings from the past forty years. Ranging in publication dates from 1960 to the present, these essays highlight academic debates about popular culture as well as diverse theoretical views.

Popular Culture Theory and Methodology: A Basic Introduction chronicles the ideas of some of the pioneers of popular culture study as well as those who have followed in their paths. Overall, it is hoped that this diverse offering of writings will fill a void by partially tracing the heritage of popular culture studies scholarship and by presenting general definitions, theories, and methods for the study of popular culture.

Popular Culture Theory and Methodology basically asks and attempts to answer two questions: (1) what is popular culture? and (2) how does one study popular culture? The volume contains twenty-six re-printed essays and three original essays. The book is divided into seven parts with a selective bibliography of additional works on popular culture theory and methodology.

The first part titled "Pioneers" asks the question: "What Is Popular Culture?" Dwight Macdonald's essay, "Masscult & Midcult," of 1960 is the first in this part and it predates all of the other selections in this volume. While this is not to say that popular culture studies scholarship began with his essay, it does provide a beginning point for the discussion of the subject in terms of what is popular culture, folk culture, and elite culture. Popular culture (or "Masscult"), according to Macdonald, is a kind of culture "manufactured for the market." His position on popular culture is summarized in these words:

Masscult is bad in a new way: it doesn't even have the theoretical possibility of being good. Up to the eighteenth century, bad art was of the same nature as good art, produced for the same audience, accepting the same standards. The difference

1

was simply one of individual talent. But Masscult is something else. It is not just unsuccessful art. It is non-art. It is even anti-art.

To be sure, if Macdonald had had the last words on the subject of popular culture, then Ray Browne would certainly never have forged ahead to found a new department at Bowling Green State University in the early seventies which now offers Bachelor's and Master's degrees in popular culture.

Ray Browne's pioneering essay "Popular Culture: Notes Toward a Definition" of 1972 follows and it provides a tentative definition of popular culture that set the stage for many conferences and journal articles in the years following its publication. According to Browne, popular culture is "all those elements of life which are not narrowly intellectual or creatively elitist and which are generally though not necessarily disseminated through the mass media."

Russel B. Nye (one of Browne's most friendly and outspoken opponents) in his article titled, "Notes for an Introduction to a Discussion of Popular Culture" of 1971, does not directly define popular culture but reviews the trends in the study of popular culture at that time. In addition, he speaks plainly about methodologies in popular culture studies concluding that no one method provides the "ultimate" procedure for gathering meaning from a popular cultural product:

Popular culture can be considered as a point at which the investigative techniques of the social sciences and the humanities may converge. . . . There is, then, no single, approved methodology for the study of popular culture, but several. . . . We should be able to choose that method of investigation which allows us to find out what we want to know. What works best is the best methodology.

Indeed, the use of multi-methodologies is a key characteristic of the field of popular culture studies.

Peter Burke's essay, "Revolution in Popular Culture," rounds out the first part of this volume. While Burke's emphasis is on the idea of revolution in popular culture (which is really viewed as "folk culture"), his review of three traditions of analysis among British historians, which trace the problems of continuity and change in popular culture, is useful. He does not simply answer the question; he documents the history of the subject and leaves the readers to develop their own conclusions.

Part II, Beyond the Frontier: Post-1960s and '70s Answers to "What is Popular Culture?" includes eight essays. Fred E. H. Schroeder, John Fiske, and Gary L. Harmon explore popular culture in ways somewhat unlike earlier explorations at the beginning of the movement. For example, Schroeder's essay on "The Discovery of Popular Culture before Printing" is intriguing because it asks and answers the question about when popular culture began. While he does not attempt to give an exact date, he does agree with Browne's belief that popular culture began with the appearance of human beings on earth, long before the printing press, industrialization, and urbanization. Schroeder notes that religion is the pivot between popular culture before and after printing because religious "cultural materials and practices were mass-produced or mass-disseminated at an early time in history."

Fiske's position on popular culture in "Understanding Popular Culture" emanates from a British cultural studies and Marxist per-spective: "Popular culture is made by subordinated peoples in their own interests out of resources that also, contradictorily, serve the economic interests of the dominant." Harmon agrees with Fiske in "On the Nature and Functions of Popular Culture" that studying popular culture involves studying people and what they believe, fear, and hope for. However, he devotes the majority of the essay to clearly defining popular culture and elite culture, clarifying their creators, participants, and outlining their functions.

Both Tim D. P. Lally and John Huntington offer unique perspectives on the popularity concept. Lally in "Synchronic vs. Diachronic Popular Culture Studies and the Old English Elegy" suggests that a synchronic-diachronic paradigm will generate a precise and optimal study of any popular culture phenomenon. Huntington, in an excerpt from his book *Rationalizing Genius: Ideological Strategies in the Classic American Science Fiction Short Story* discusses the "classic popularity" of science fiction texts and explains how "classic popularity" is a university-based critical movement.

Essays by Ray B. Browne, Michael Schudson, and Barry W. Sarchett step back and overview the field of popular culture studies offering new insights on its placement and condition in academia. Browne strongly states that popular culture studies are the "new humanities." Both Schudson and Sarchett argue in slightly different terms that there are no "low-high" or "popular-elite" cultures. Since this is the case, the result is what Sarchett declares: the "end of popular culture studies." In addition, Schudson offers a triadic methodology for the study of popular culture that privileges producers, texts, and consumers of popular culture.

Like Schudson, Lawrence E. Mintz and Harold E. Hinds, Jr., focus on the specific question of methodology as well in Part III, Macro How-to-Do-It Approaches to the Study of Popular Culture. Mintz, in his essay "Notes Toward a Methodology of Popular Culture Study," develops four questions that can be asked regarding popular culture texts, artifacts, and experiences. Hinds, stating that his essay was inspired by Mintz's essay, in effect, clarifies and augments Mintz's methodological suggestions in "A

Holistic Approach to the Study of Popular Culture: Context, Text, Audience, and Recoding." In addition, Hinds discusses the concept of "recombinant culture" and how it may occur in popular culture.

Part IV, Formula: A Pioneering Theory, highlights the concept of formula and the effect economics has on the use of formula. John G. Cawelti's essay, "The Concept of Formula in the Study of Popular Literature," was a revolutionary piece of scholarship at the time of its publication in the *Journal of Popular Culture* in 1969. Cawelti's essay called for a shift from analyzing individual myths and cultural themes in popular literature to analyzing an integrated whole that he labeled "formula." Inspired by Cawelti's theory, David N. Feldman in "Formalism and Popular Culture" demonstrates how Russian Formalism can help determine why audiences prefer one work over another. Both Cawelti and Feldman look to the text for directions on how to analyze it and essentially believe that the texts are a reflection of the audiences' values. David Paul Nord, on the other hand, in "An Economic Per-spective on Formula in Popular Culture" suggests formula in popular culture is a compromise between the producer and the audience and that formula actually reflects the producer's values rather than the audiences' values.

Part V, Popular Culture: A Unique Aesthetics? outlines the debate over whether there is or should be a popular culture aesthetic. Roger B. Rollin's opinion that popular culture should not be "judged" by the scholar-critic in "Against Evaluation: The Role of the Critic of Popular Culture" encouraged a critical analysis by John Shelton Lawrence where Lawrence strongly disagrees with Rollin. A response essay by Rollin, "Son of 'Against Evaluation': A Reply to John Shelton Lawrence" clarifies the original essay and highlights the "occasions" where Lawrence "misconstrued" his original argument. Like Lawrence, in 1971 John G. Cawelti believed that an aesthetic of popular culture could be formulated. In an essay reprinted here from 1985, "With the Benefit of Hindsight: Popular Culture Criticism," Cawelti argues for a critical approach to mass media which employs the aesthetic or generic methods developed by popular culture scholars. Finally, Dan Ash in "New Experimental Aesthetics and Popular Culture" proposes a taxonomy of popular culture that combines research about the aesthetic experience from the fields of ethnomusicology and psychology.

Peter Narváez and Martin Laba's "Introduction" to their book, *Media Sense: The Folklore-Popular Culture Continuum* provides the introduction to Part VI, Popular Culture and Folk Culture. Narváez and Laba, Harold Schechter, and S. Elizabeth Bird essentially agree and demonstrate that folk culture can become popular culture and vice versa. Bird emphasizes that a convergence of folklore and popular culture stems from cultural studies approaches that examine audiences and how they make meaning from cultural products. Paul Smith in "Contemporary Legends and Popular Culture: 'It's the Real Thing'" examines the complex interactions between popular culture and folklore through an analysis of "Coke-Lore," a "folk-generic term for the lore associated with a whole range of soft drinks."

Finally, Part VII focuses on the concept of popularity. Two essays by Harold E. Hinds, Jr., "Popularity: The *Sine Qua Non* of Popular Culture" and "Popularity: How to Make a Key Concept Count in Building a Theory of Popular Culture," focuses on popularity as a building block of popular culture theory and methodology. Finally, an essay co-written by Ling Chan Becker and Hinds tests Hinds' definition of popular culture based on the concept of popularity by studying the development and stages of popular culture in Tokugawa and Meiji Japan.

In conclusion, if popular culture is the new humanities of the twenty-first century, then a volume such as this one, *Popular Culture Theory and Methodology: A Basic Introduction* will hopefully enlighten readers about popular culture studies scholarship and provide a vehicle for courses, curricula, programs, and departments to be reevaluated, reformed, and restructured.

I.
The Pioneers:
What Is Popular Culture?

MASSCULT & MIDCULT

Dwight Macdonald

Dwight Macdonald, an early student of popular culture, views culture as divided into folk culture, mass culture (popular culture), midcult, and high culture. His essay, "Masscult & Midcult," is a seething attack on popular culture, which is labeled non- or anti-art, and on midcult, a debased amalgam of popular and elite cultures. Macdonald's critical views were typical of many early-twentieth-century cultural critics who felt that a combination of the Industrial Revolution, post-World War II prosperity, and upward social mobility imperiled traditional elite culture. An essayist, editor of cultural and political magazines, and author of numerous books, Macdonald died in 1982.

For about two centuries Western culture has in fact been two cultures: the traditional kind—let us call it High Culture—that is chronicled in the textbooks, and a novel kind that is manufactured for the market. This latter may be called Mass Culture, or better Masscult, since it really isn't culture at all. Masscult is a parody of High Culture. . . .

Masscult is bad in a new way: it doesn't even have the theoretical possibility of being good. Up to the eighteenth century, bad art was of the same nature as good art, produced for the same audience, accepting the same standards. The difference was simply one of individual talent. But Masscult is something else. It is not just unsuccessful art. It is non-art. It is even anti-art. . . .

Masscult offers its customers neither an emotional catharsis nor an aesthetic experience, for these demand effort. The production line grinds out a uniform product whose humble aim is not even entertainment, for this too implies life and hence effort, but merely distraction. It may be stimulating or narcotic, but it must be easy to assimilate. It asks nothing of its audience, for it is "totally subjected to the spectator." And it gives nothing. . . .

But a work of High Culture, however inept, is an expression of feelings, ideas, tastes, visions that are idiosyncratic and the audience similarly responds to them as individuals. Furthermore, both creator and audience

Dwight Macdonald, "Masscult & Midcult," Partisan Review *(Spring 1960).*

accept certain standards. These may be more or less traditional; sometimes they are so much less so as to be revolutionary, though Picasso, Joyce and Stravinsky knew and respected past achievements more than did their academic contemporaries; their works may be seen as a heroic breakthrough to earlier, sounder foundations that had been obscured by the fashionable gim-crackery of the academies. But Masscult is indifferent to standards. Nor is there any communication between individuals. Those who consume Mass-cult might as well be eating ice-cream sodas, while those who fabricate it are no more expressing themselves than are the "stylists" who design the latest atrocity from Detroit. . . .

It is important to understand that the difference between Mr. Poe and Mr. Gardner, or between High Culture and Masscult, is not mere popularity. From *Tom Jones* to the films of Chaplin, some very good things have been popular; *The Education of Henry Adams* was the top nonfiction best seller of 1919. Nor is it that Poe's detective stories are harder to read than Gardner's, though I suppose they are for most people. The difference lies in the qualities of Masscult already noted: its impersonality and its lack of standards, and "total subjection to the spectator." The same writer, indeed the same book or even the same chapter, may contain elements of both Masscult and High Culture. . . .

Like the early capitalism Marx and Engels described in *The Commu-nist Manifesto*, Masscult is a dynamic, revolutionary force, breaking down the old barriers of class, tradition, and taste, dissolving all cultural distinc-tions. It mixes, scrambles everything together, producing what might be called homogenized culture, after another American achievement, the ho-mogenization process that distributes the globules of cream evenly through-out the milk instead of allowing them to float separately on top. The inter-esting difference is that whereas the cream is still in the homogenized milk, somehow it disappears from homogenized culture. For the process destroys all values, since value-judgements require discrimination, an ugly word in liberal-democratic America. Masscult is very, very democratic; it refuses to discriminate against or between anything or anybody. All is grist to its mill and all comes out finely ground indeed. . . .

The historical reasons for the rise of Masscult are well known. There could obviously be no mass culture until there were masses, in our modern sense. The industrial revolution produced the masses. . . .

Up to then, there was only High Culture and Folk Art. To some extent, Masscult is a continuation of Folk Art, but the differences are more striking than the similarities. Folk Art grew mainly from below, an autochthonous product shaped by the people to fit their own needs, even though it often took its cue from High Culture. Masscult comes from above. It is fabricated by technicians hired by businessmen. They try this and try that and if something clicks at the box office, they try to cash in with similar products, like consumer-researchers with a new cereal, or like a Pavlovian biologist who has hit on a reflex he thinks can be conditioned. It is one thing to satisfy popular tastes, as Robert Burns's poetry did, and quite another to exploit them, as Hollywood does. Folk Art was the people's own institution, their private little kitchen-garden walled off from the great formal park of their masters. But Masscult breaks down the wall, integrating the masses into a debased form of High Culture and thus becoming an instrument of domination. If one had no other data to go on, Masscult would expose capitalism as a class society rather than the harmonious commonwealth that, in election years, both parties tell us it is. . . .

The mass audience was taking shape and a corresponding shift in literary criticism was beginning, away from objective standards and toward a new subjective approach in which the question was not how good the work is but how popular it will be. Not that the creator is ever independent of his time and place; the demands of the audience have always largely determined his work. But before 1750, these demands were themselves disciplined by certain standards of excellence which were accepted by both the limited public of informed amateurs and the artists who performed for them. Today, in the United States, the demands of the audience, which has changed from a small body of connoisseurs into a large body of ignoramuses, have become the chief criteria of success. . . .

Since in a mass society people are related not to each other but to some abstract organizing principle, they are often in a state of exhaustion, for this lack of contact is unnatural. So Masscult attempts to provide distraction for the tired businessman—or the tired proletarian. This kind of art is necessarily at a distance from the individual since it is specifically designed to affect not what differentiates him from everybody else—that is what is of liveliest interest to *him*—but rather to work on the reflexes he shares with everybody else. So he is at a distance.

But people feel a need to be related to other people. The simplest way of bridging this distance, or rather of pretending to bridge it, is by emphasizing the personality of the artist; the individual buried in the mass audience can relate himself to the individual in the artist, since they are, after all, both persons. So while Masscult is in one sense extremely impersonal, in another it is extremely personal. The artist is thus charismatic and his works become the expression of this. . . .

In Masscult (and in its bastard, Midcult) everything becomes a commodity, to be mined for $$$$, used for something it is not, from Davy Crockett to Picasso. Once a writer becomes a Name, that is, once he writes a book that for good or bad reasons catches on, the Masscult (or Midcult) mechanism begins to "build him up," to package him into something that can be sold in identical units in quantity. He can coast along the rest of his life on momentum; publishers will pay him big advances just to get his Name on their list; his charisma becomes such that people will pay him $250 and up to address them (really just to *see* him); editors will reward him handsomely for articles on subjects he knows nothing about. Artists and writers have always had a tendency to repeat themselves, but Masscult (and Midcult) make it highly profitable to do so and in fact penalize those who don't. . . .

Let us, finally, consider Masscult first from the standpoint of consumption and then from that of production.

As a marketable commodity, Masscult has two great advantages over High Culture. One has already been considered: the post-1750 public, lacking the taste and knowledge of the old patron class, is not only satisfied with shoddy mass-produced goods but in general feels more at home with them (though on unpredictable occasions, they will respond to the real thing, as with Dickens' novels and the movies of Chaplin and Griffith). This is because such goods are standardized and so are easier to consume since one knows what's coming next—imagine a Western in which the hero loses the climactic gun fight or an office romance in which the mousy stenographer loses out to the predatory blonde. But standardization has a subtler aspect, which might be called The Built-In Reaction. As Clement Greenberg noted in "Avant-garde and *Kitsch*" many years ago in *Partisan Review*, the special aesthetic quality of *Kitsch*—a term which includes both Masscult and Midcult—is that it "predigests art for the spectator and spares him effort, provides him with a shortcut to the pleasures of art that detours what is necessarily difficult in the genuine art" because it includes the spectator's reactions in the work itself instead of forcing him to make his own responses. . . .

There seem to be two main conditions for the successful production of *Kitsch*. One is that the producer must believe in what he is doing. A good example is Norman Rockwell, who since 1916 has painted over three hundred covers for the *Saturday Evening Post*. . . .

The other condition for success in Masscult is that the writer, artist, editor, director or entertainer must have a good deal of the mass man in himself, as was the case with Zane Grey, Howard Chandler Christy, Mr. Lorimer of the *Post*, Cecil B. DeMille, and Elvis Presley. This is closely related to sincerity—how can he take his work seriously if he doesn't have this instinctive, this built-in vulgar touch? . . .

As I have already noted in this essay, the separation of Folk Art and High Culture in fairly watertight compartments corresponded to the sharp line once drawn between the common people and the aristocracy. The blurring of this line, however desirable politically, has had unfortunate results culturally. Folk Art had its own authentic quality, but Masscult is at best a vulgarized reflection of High Culture and at worst a cultural nightmare, a *Kulturkatzenjammer*. And while High Culture could formerly address itself only to the *cognoscenti*, now must take the *ignoscenti* into account even when it turns its back on them. For Masscult is not merely a parallel formation to High Culture, as Folk Art was; it is a competitor. The problem is especially acute in this country because class lines are especially weak here. If there were a clearly defined cultural elite here, then the masses could have their *Kitsch* and the classes could have their High Culture, with everybody happy. But a significant part of our population is chronically confronted with a choice between looking at TV or old masters, between reading Tolstoy or a detective story; i.e., the pattern of their cultural lives is "open" to the point of being porous. For a lucky few, this openness of choice is stimulating. But for most, it is confusing and leads at best to that middlebrow compromise called Midcult. . . .

In these more advanced times [post-World War II], the danger to High Culture is not so much from Masscult as from a peculiar hybrid bred from the latter's unnatural intercourse with the former. A whole middle culture has come into existence and it threatens to absorb both its parents. This intermediate form—let us call it Midcult—has the essential qualities of Masscult—the formula, the built-in reaction, the lack of any standard except popularity—but it decently covers them with a cultural figleaf. In Masscult the trick is plain—to please the crowd by any means. But Midcult has it both ways: it pretends to respect the standards of High Culture while in fact it waters them down and vulgarizes them. . . .

Midcult is not, as might appear at first, a raising of the level of Masscult. It is rather a corruption of High Culture which has the enormous advantage over Masscult that while also in fact "totally subjected to the spectator," in Malraux's phrase, it is able to pass itself off as the real thing. Midcult is the *Revised Standard Version of the Bible*, put out several years ago under the aegis of the Yale Divinity School, that destroys our greatest monument of English prose, the King James Version, in order to made the text "clear and meaningful to people today," which is like taking apart Westminster Abbey to make Disneyland out of the fragments. . . .

But perhaps the best way to define Midcult is to analyze certain typical products. The four I have chosen are Ernest Hemingway's *The Old Man and The Sea*, Thornton Wilder's *Our Town*, Archibald MacLeish's *J.B.* and Stephen Vincent Benét's *John Brown's Body*. They have all been Midcult successes: each has won the Pulitzer Prize, has been praised by critics who should know better, and has been popular not so much with the masses as with the educated classes. Technically, they are advanced enough to impress the midbrows without worrying them. In content, they are "central" and "universal," in that line of hollowly portentous art which the French call *pompier* after the glittering, golden beplumed helmets of their firemen. Mr. Wilder, the cleverest of the four, has actually managed to be at once ultra-simple and grandiose. "Now there are some things we all know, but we don't take'm out and look at'm very often," says his stage manager, sucking ruminatively on his pipe. "We all know that *something* is eternal. And it ain't houses and it ain't names, and it ain't earth, and it ain't even the stars . . . Everybody knows in their bones that *something* is eternal, and that something has to do with human beings. All the greatest people ever lived have been telling us for five thousand years and yet you'd be surprised how people are always losing hold of it. There's something way down deep that's eternal about every human being." The last sentence is an eleven-word summary, in form and content, of Midcult. . . .

The special threat of Midcult is that it exploits the discoveries of the avant-garde. This is something new. Midcult's historical predecessor, Academicism, resembled it in being *Kitsch* for the elite, outwardly High Culture but really as much a manufactured article as the cheaper cultural goods produced for the masses. The difference is that Academicism was intransigently opposed to the avant-garde. . . .

Midcult is a more dangerous opponent of High Culture because it incorporates so much of the avant-garde. The four works noticed above were more advanced and sophisticated, for their time, than were the novels of John Galsworthy. They are, so to speak, the products of lapsed avant-gardists who know how to use the modern idiom in the service of the banal. . . .

A soft impeachment—but Midcult specializes in soft impeachments. Its cakes are forever eaten, forever intact. . . .

POPULAR CULTURE:
NOTES TOWARD A DEFINITION

Ray B. Browne

Ray B. Browne's pioneering essay explores and debates the differences between what he believes to be the four basic areas of culture: elite, popular, mass, and folk. Rigid distinctions are impossible between the four as each overlaps with and is affected by the others. Finally, Browne offers a tentative definition: popular culture embraces all culture except elite culture. In 1972 he argued that it was better to err on the side of inclusiveness than on that of exclusiveness, a position to which he continues to adhere. Ray B. Browne, retired Professor of Popular Culture at Bowling Green State University and editor of the Journal of Popular Culture, *is the author of numerous studies of popular culture and has played a key role in the field's development in the United States.*

"Popular Culture" is an indistinct term whose edges blur into imprecision. Scarcely any two commentators who try to define it agree in all aspects of what popular culture really is. Most critics, in fact, do not attempt to define it; instead, after distinguishing between it and the mass media, and between it and "high" culture, most assume that everybody knows that whatever is widely disseminated and experienced is "popular culture."

Some observers divide the total culture of a people into "minority" and "majority" categories. Other observers classify culture into High-Cult, Mid-Cult and Low-Cult, or High-Brow, Mid-Brow and Low-Brow, leaving out, apparently, the level that would perhaps be called Folk-Cult or Folk-Brow, though Folk culture is now taking on, even among the severest critics of popular culture, a high class and achievement unique unto itself. Most of the discriminating observers agree, in fact, that there are perhaps actually four areas of culture: Elite, Popular, Mass and Folk, with the understanding that none is a discrete unity standing apart and unaffected by the others.

Ray B. Browne, "Popular Culture: Notes Toward a Definition," in Ray B. Browne and Ronald J. Ambrosetti (eds.), Popular Culture and Curricula, *rev. ed. (Bowling Green, OH: Bowling Green State University Popular Press, 1972), 3–11. Reprinted with permission.*

One reason for the lack of a precise definition is that the serious study of "popular culture" has been neglected in American colleges and universities. Elitist critics of our culture—notably such persons as Dwight Macdonald and Edmund Wilson—have always insisted that whatever was widespread was artistically and esthetically deficient, therefore unworthy of study. They have taught that "culture" to be worthwhile must necessarily be limited to the elite, aristocratic, and the minority. They felt that mass or popular culture—especially as it appeared in the mass media—would vitiate real culture. This attitude persists today among some of the younger critics. William Gass, for example, the esthetician and critic, takes the extreme position that "the products of popular culture, by and large, have no more esthetic quality than a brick in the street . . . Any esthetic intentions is entirely absent, and because it is desired to manipulate consciousness directly, achieve one's effect there, no mind is paid to the intrinsic nature of its objects; they lack finish, complexity, stasis, individuality, coherence, depth, and endurance."

Such an attitude as Gass' is perhaps an extreme statement of the elitist critic's point of view. Luckily the force of numerous critics' arguments is weakening such attitudes. Popular Culture has a dimension, a thrust and—most important—a reality that has nothing to do with its esthetic accomplishment, though that has more merit than is often given to it.

This point of view is demonstrated by the talented young stylist Tom Wolfe, who, perhaps writing more viscerally than intellectually, thumbs his nose at the prejudice and snobbery that has always held at arms length all claims of validity if not esthetic accomplishment of the "culture" of the masses.

Susan Sontag, a brilliant young critic and esthetician, is more effective in bludgeoning the old point of view. Far from alarmed at the apparent new esthetic, she sees that it is merely a change in attitude, not a death's blow to culture and art:

What we are getting is not the demise of art, but a transformation of the function of art. Art, which arose in human society as magical-religious operation, and passed over into a technique for depicting and commenting on secular reality, has in our own time arrogated to itself a new function—neither religious, nor serving a secularized religious function, nor merely secular or profane . . . Art today is a new kind of instrument, an instrument for modifying consciousness and organizing new modes of sensibility.

To Sontag the unprecedented complexity of the world has made inevitable and very necessary this change in the function of art. This is virtually the same attitude held by Marshall McLuhan:

A technological extension of our bodies designed to alleviate physical stress can bring on psychic stress that may be much worse . . . Art is exact information of how to rearrange one's psyche to anticipate the next blow from our own extended psyches . . . in experimental art, men are given the exact specifications of coming violence to their own psyche from their own counter-irritants or technology. For those parts of ourselves that we thrust out in the form of new inventions are attempts to counter or neutralize collective pressures and irritations. But the counter-irritant usually proves a greater plague than the initial irritant like a drug habit. And it is here that the artist can show us how to "ride with the punch," instead of "taking it on the chin."

An equally important aspect of popular culture as index and corrector is its role as comic voice. Popular humor provides a healthy element in a nation's life. It pricks the pompous, devaluates the inflated, and snipes at the overly solemn. For example, such organs of popular culture as the magazines spoofed Henry James' pomposity during his lifetime, spoofed his "high" seriousness and in general tended to humanize him.

A more reasonable attitude than Gass' and one that is becoming increasingly acceptable is that held by the philosopher Abraham Kaplan: That popular culture has considerable accomplishment and even more real possibilities and it is developing but has not realized its full potential. All areas draw from one another. The Mass area, being largely imitative, draws from the others without altering much. Elite art draws heavily from both folk and, perhaps to a slightly lesser degree, popular arts. Popular art draws from Elite and Mass, and Folk, but does not take any without subjecting it to a greater or lesser amount of creative change. That popular culture has "no more esthetic quality than a brick in the street" or at least no more esthetic potential is a contention refuted by America's greatest writers— Hawthorne, Melville, Whitman, Twain, to name only four—as well as the greatest writers of all times and countries—Homer, Shakespeare, Dickens, Dostoevski, Tolstoi, for example.

Melville provides an excellent case in point. *Moby Dick* is the greatest creative book written in America and one of the half dozen greatest ever written anywhere. Its greatness derives from the sum total of its many parts. It is a blend of nearly all elements of all cultures of mid-nineteenth century America. Melville took all the culture around him—trivial and profound— Transcendentalism and the plumbing of the depths of the human experience, but also demonism, popular theater, the shanghai gesture, jokes about pills and gas on the stomach, etc., and boiled them in the tryworks of his fiery genius into the highest art.

Many definitions of popular culture turn on methods of dissemination. Those elements which are too sophisticated for the mass media are generally called Elite culture, those distributed through these media that are something less than "mass"—that is such things as the smaller magazines and newspapers, the less widely distributed books, museums and less sophisticated galleries, so-called clothes line art exhibits, and the like—are called in the narrow sense of the term "popular," those elements that are distributed through the mass media are "mass" culture, and those which are or were at one time disseminated by oral and non-oral methods—on levels "lower" than the mass media—are called "folk."

All definitions of such a complex matter, though containing a certain amount of validity and usefulness, are bound to be to a certain extent inadequate or incorrect. Perhaps a workable definition can best be arrived at by looking at one of the culture's most salient and quintessential aspects—its artistic creations—because the artist perhaps more than any one else draws from the totality of experience and best reflects it.

Shakespeare and his works are an excellent example. When he was producing his plays at the Globe Theater, Shakespeare was surely a "popular" author and his works were elements of "popular" culture, though they were at the same time also High or Elite culture, for they were very much part of the lives of both the groundlings and the nobles. Later, in America, especially during the nineteenth century, all of his works were well known, his name was commonplace, and he was at the same time still High art, Popular (even mass) art and Folk art. In the twentieth century, however, his works are more distinguishable as parts of various levels. *Hamlet* is still a play of both High and Popular art. The most sophisticated and scholarly people still praise it. But *Hamlet* is also widely distributed on TV, radio and through the movies. It is a commonplace on all levels of society and is therefore a part of "popular culture" in the broadest sense of the term. Other plays by Shakespeare, however, have not become a part of "popular" culture. *Titus Andronicus,* for example, for any of several reasons, is not widely known by the general public. It remains, thus, Elite culture.

Wideness of distribution and popularity in this sense are one major aspect of popular culture. But there are others. Many writers would be automatically a part of popular culture if their works sold only a few copies—Frank G. Slaughter and Frank Yerby, for example. Louis Auchincloss also, though his works are of a different kind than Slaughter's and Yerby's, because his subject is Wall Street and high finance, and these are subjects of popular culture.

Aside from distribution another major difference between high and popular culture, and among popular culture, mass culture and folk culture, is the motivation of the persons contributing, the makers and shapers of culture. On the Elite or sophisticated level, the creators value individualism, individual expression, the exploration and discovery of new art forms, of new way of stating, the exploration and discovery of new depths in life's experiences.

On the other levels of culture there is usually less emphasis placed upon, and less accomplishment reached in, this plumbing of reality. Generally speaking, both popular and mass artists are less interested in the experimental and searching than in the restatement of the old and accepted. But there are actually vast differences in the esthetic achievements attained in the works from these two levels, and different aspirations and goals, even within these somewhat limited objectives. As Hall and Whannel have pointed out:

In mass art the formula is everything—an escape from, rather than a means to, originality. The popular artist may use the conventions to select, emphasize and stress (or alter the emphasis and stress) so as to delight the audience with a kind of creative surprise. Mass art uses the stereotypes and formulae to simplify the experience, to mobilize stock feelings and to 'get them going.'

The popular artist is superior to the mass artist because for him "stylization is necessary, and the conventions provide an agreed base from which true creative invention springs." It is a serious error therefore to agree with Dwight MacDonald (in *Against the American Grain*) that all popular art "includes the spectator's reactions in the work itself instead of forcing him to make his own responses." Consider, for example, the reactions of two carriers of non-Elite culture, the first of popular culture, the banjo player Johnny St. Cyr. He always felt that the creative impulses of the average person and his responses in a creative situation were immense:

You see, the average man is very musical. Playing music for him is just relaxing. He gets as much kick out of playing as other folks get out of dancing. The more enthusiastic his audience is, why the more spirit the working man's got to play. And with your natural feelings that way you never make the same thing twice. Every time you play a tune new ideas come to mind and you slip that one in.

Compare that true artist's philosophy with that of Liberace, to whom the "whole trick is to keep the tune well out in front," to play "the melodies" and skip the "spiritual struggles." He always knows "just how many notes (his) audience will stand for," and if he has time left over he fills in "with a lot of runs up and down the keyboard."

Here in condensed form is the difference between popular and mass art and popular and mass artists. Both aim for different goals. St. Cyr is a truly creative artist in both intent and accomplishment. His credentials are not invalidated merely by the fact that he works in essentially a popular idiom. Given the limitations of his medium—if indeed these limitations are real— he can still be just as great a creator as—perhaps greater than—Rubenstein. It is incorrect to pit jazz against classical music, the popular against the elite. They are not in competition. Each has its own purposes, techniques and accomplishments. They complement each other rather than compete.

Another fine example can be found among the youth of today and their rebellion against what they consider the establishment. They are obviously not a part of the static mass, to whom escape is everything. Instead they are vigorously active, and in their action create dynamic and fine works of art, as examination of their songs, their art, their movies, etc., dramatically demonstrates.

It is also unfair to give blanket condemnation to mass art, though obviously the accomplishments of mass art are less than those of "higher" forms. Liberace does not aspire to much, and perhaps reaches even less. His purposes and techniques are inferior, but not all his, or the many other workers in the level, are completely without value.

All levels of culture, it must never be forgotten, are distorted by the lenses of snobbery and prejudice which the observers wear. There are no hard and fast lines separating one level from another.

Popular culture also includes folk culture. The relationship between folk culture and popular and elite cultures is still debatable. In many ways folk culture borrows from and imitates both.

Historically folk art has come more from the hall than from the novel, has depended more upon the truly creative—though unsophisticated— spirit than the mediocre imitator. "Sir Patrick Spens," one of the greatest songs (poems) ever written, was originally the product of a single creative genius. Today's best folklore-to-be, that is the most esthetically satisfying folklore which is working into tradition today, is that of such people as Woody Guthrie, Larry Gorman and such individual artists.

To a large number of observers, however, folklore is felt to be the same as popular culture. To another large number folklore derives directly from popular culture, with only a slight time lag. To them, today's popular culture is tomorrow's folklore. Both notions are gross and out of line.

Esthetically folk culture has two levels. There is superb folk art and deficient mediocre folk art. Esthetically folk art is more nearly akin to Elite art, despite the lack of sophistication that much folk art has, than to popular. Elite art has much that is inferior, as even the most prejudiced critic must admit. In motivation of artist, also, folk art is close to Elite, for like the Elite artist the truly accomplished folk artist values individualism and personal expression, he explores new forms and seeks new depths in expression and feeling. But there are at the same time workers in folklore who are mere imitators, just trying to get along—exactly like their counterparts in mass culture.

Thus all elements in our culture (or cultures) are closely related and are not mutually exclusive one from another. They constitute one long continuum. Perhaps the best metaphorical figure for all is that of a flattened ellipsis, or a lens. In the center, largest in bulk and easiest seen through is Popular Culture, which includes Mass Culture.

On either end of the lens are High and Folk Cultures, both looking fundamentally alike in many respects and both having a great deal in common, for both have keen direct vision and extensive peripheral insight and acumen. All four derive in many ways and to many degrees from one another, and the lines of demarcations between any two are indistinct and mobile.

Despite the obvious difficulty of arriving at a hard and fast definition of popular culture, it will probably be to our advantage—and a comfort to many who need one—to arrive at some viable though tentative understanding of how popular culture can be defined.

Two scholars who do attempt a definition, following George Santayana's broad distinctions between work and play, believe that "Popular Culture is really what people do when they are not working." This definition is both excessively general and overly exclusive, for it includes much that is "high" culture and leaves out many aspects which obviously belong to popular culture.

One serious scholar defines a total culture as "The body of intellectual and imaginative work which each generation receives" as its tradition. Basing our conclusion on this one, a viable definition for Popular Culture is all those elements of life which are not narrowly intellectual or creatively elitist and which are generally though not necessarily disseminated through the mass media. Popular Culture consists of the spoken and printed word, sounds, pictures, objects and artifacts. "Popular Culture" thus embraces all levels of our society and culture other than the Elite—the "popular," "mass" and "folk." It includes most of the bewildering aspects of life which hammer us daily.

Such a definition, though perhaps umbrella-like in its comprehensiveness, provides the latitude needed at this point, it seems, for the serious scholar to study the world around him. Later, definitions may need to pare edges and change lighting and emphasis. But for the moment, inclusiveness is perhaps better than exclusiveness.

Bibliography

In the briefest bibliography possible, I suggest the following references:

Gass, William H. "Even if By All the Oxen in the World." *Frontiers of American Culture*. Ed. Ray B. Browne, *et al.* Lafayette, IN: Purdue UP, 1968.

Hall, Stuart, and Paddy Whannel. *The Popular Arts*. New York: Pantheon Books, 1964.

McLuhan, Marshall. *Understanding Media*. New York: McGraw-Hill, 1964.

———. *War and Peace in the Global Village*. New York: McGraw-Hill, 1968.

Shapiro, Nat, and Nat Hentoff. *Hear Me Talkin' to Ya*. New York: Dover, 1955.

Sontag, Susan. *Against Interpretation*. New York: Farrar, Strauss & Giroux, 1966.

Williams, Raymond. *Culture and Society*, 1780-1950. London: Chatto & Winders, 1960.

———. *The Long Revolution*. New York: Columbia UP, 1961.

NOTES FOR AN INTRODUCTION
TO A DISCUSSION OF POPULAR CULTURE

Russel B. Nye

Russel B. Nye briefly suggests that the study of popular culture in the early 1970s benefited from several developments in the 1960s: greater attention to mass communication, cultural anthropology's inclusiveness, Marshall McLuhan's ideas, recognition that mass culture did not produce cultural degradation, and the "mutual absorption of culture and technology on the popular level." In particular, Nye believed new approaches to the study of popular culture were needed, although no single method could be effective in such a diverse field. Approaches he suggested include a greater emphasis on popular culture's production, distribution, or consumption; and viewing popular culture as including "everything not elite" or as satisfying a certain type of taste. Like Browne, Nye opts for inclusiveness, rather than exclusive definitions or methodologies. The late Russel Nye taught English at Michigan State University, and authored a seminal, and still authoritative, overview of United States popular culture, The Unembarrassed Muse *(1970).*

First, let us define terms. I use the word *popular* to mean that which is widely diffused, generally accepted, approved by the majority. *Culture,* an especially protean word, I use in the sense of Edward Tylor's definition as "that complex whole which includes knowledge, belief, art, custom, and other capabilities acquired by man as a member of society," a definition which, of course, needs to be focused more precisely, depending on the use of popular materials within particular academic disciplines. This is not the occasion to trace the history of popular culture, or of attitudes toward it; this has already been done with distinction by others.[1] I am more concerned at the moment with considering briefly recent trends in the study of popular culture, as observed by cultural historians, literary critics, historians of ideas, and philosophers of aesthetics. Within the last decade there has been, if I read the signs right, the beginnings of a significant shift in our attitudes

Russel B. Nye, "Notes For An Introduction to A Discussion of Popular Culture," Journal of Popular Culture *4.4 (Spring 1971): 1031–38.*

toward relationships among cultural levels and cultural values. Artists and audiences seem to be crossing borders they shouldn't; critics are asking whether the lines that presumably separate "highbrow" from "lowbrow" or "elite" from "popular" (those classic terms never quite clearly established but traditionally and uncritically accepted) ought to be so sharply defined, or perhaps ought to be there at all. People who know Beethoven and Bartok listen to the Beatles; *Time* and *Newsweek* and Leonard Bernstein have approved California and Liverpool rock; even the *New York Review of Books, mirabile dictu,* has published an admiring article on popular music. *Peanuts* is written about by theologians and philosophers; there are articles on Marvel Comics and horror movies; John Lennon and Leonard Cohen are studied the way graduate students used to study Eliot and Pound. *Playboy* has a centerfold in the ancient and honorable *Police Gazette* tradition, and also publishes essays by Leslie Fiedler and Harvey Cox. There is a rock-opera and a folk-mass; painters use soup cans and highway signs and hamburgers. Clearly, things are not what they used to be.

There are a number of reasons for this wave of interest in, and the recent re-evaluation of, the aims, audiences, conventions, and artifacts of popular culture. I should like to identify five which seem to me immediately operative, although there are probably others equally important. First, the attention given by social scientists to mass communications and media study has revealed serious limitations in the older concept of society as composed of a naive, maneuverable mass on the one hand, and a self-controlled, cultured elite on the other. The real relationships between the mass media and their various publics is proving to be much more complicated than the simplistic picture drawn by the critics of the thirties and forties. Social psychologists find that audiences resist manipulation in ways not earlier suspected; that mass communications do more than merely transmit information; that if the media do distort reality, people have compensatory built-in resistances, of which critics have never taken full account. Furthermore, it also seems clear that attempts to convince mass audiences that they ought to reject popular culture are ingenuous and ineffective, and that the critics of popular culture too may have their own biases and limitations. I do not think we can afford to overlook the importance of those explorations of popular culture now being made by the more alert social sciences.

Second, the study of popular culture has been demonstrably affected by the example of cultural anthropology and its belief that all parts of a culture are worth study. Cultural relativism, the idea that no part of a culture has—for purposes of understanding it—innate superiority over another, has provided those who wish to study popular culture with a useful, viable methodology, as well as welcome scholarly and moral support. If it is permissible to study the songs of a Bantu tribe, or the marriage customs of a Polynesian subgroup, it seems equally permissible to study the songs of teeny-boppers in California or popular stories from *True Confessions,* and for the same reasons.

Third, the insights of Marshall McLuhan—scattered, confusing, but often brilliant—have attracted the attention of a number of younger critics who are putting together a new aesthetic which includes, rather than excludes, a wider range of cultural levels than before. McLuhan has made at least two suggestions which, in their reverberations, have deeply influenced the study of popular culture. His assertion that the medium is as important as, or more important than, the message, changed the focus of cultural criticism by shifting attention from content to medium, from *what* was said to *how* it was transmitted. "Concern with effect, rather than meaning," he wrote in *Understanding Media,* "is the basic change of our electric time;" or again, "When a medium becomes a depth experience, the old categories of classical and popular, or of highbrow and lowbrow, no longer obtain;" and again, "Anything that is approached in depth acquires as much interest as the greatest matters."

Deriving from McLuhan, critics such as Susan Sontag, for example, have opted for a "new sensibility," challenging all the old boundaries between scientific and artistic, high and low, mass and elite. In addition, another seminal idea has been McLuhan's concept of modern communications as a "mosaic;" that is, he suggests that information flows in upon the individual in a random "mosaic" pattern which is unified by the individual, who experiences and orders it. If life, as McLuhan says, has "discontinuous variety and incongruity," then art may reflect and interpret it by building similar mosaic, experiential structures in imitation of life. The Beatles' *Abbey Road* album, for example, a collection of separate songs in various styles and settings, gains full effectiveness only when the listener perceives the relationship among them all or simply experiences them all as a totality. To use the current popular phrase, "putting it all together" is a simplified version of McLuhan's idea of "mosaic" disconnection and reconnection. A novel like Leonard Cohen's *Beautiful Losers* asks the reader to do just that—to put together a discontinuous series of events and characters, separated by time and space, juxtaposed in a pattern that is no longer accidental as the reader imposes his own design on the experience.

Fourth, I think we are seeing the results of having lived for two generations with mass culture. We are not afraid of it any more, and we know how to find meaning and value in it. The dire predictions of the thirties and forties about the social disintegration and cultural decay that would inevitably follow movies, radio, comic strips, television, and jazz have simply not come true. The Canadian National Film Board calculates (and the figures no doubt hold true for the United States) that today's average 18-year-old has seen 500 feature films and 15,000 hours of television, plus heaven knows how many commercials, advertisements, comics, or hours of disc-jockey music he has heard on his transistor. Yet he seems to be able to handle it with considerable sophistication and to respond to it in a number of interesting, subtle, and imaginative ways. We have lived for three-quarters of a century with mass culture, and we are culturally no worse off than before; in fact, there is reason to believe we may be better off.

Fifth, and this is important, popular culture and technology have made a unique merger, with interesting, powerful, and utterly new results. The customized car, to cite an example, is an authentic midcentury expression of the meaning of the automobile age; there are those who find similar technological and aesthetic validity in a Brabham taking the Thunder Valley esses at Elkhart Lake, or in the intricate kinetics of a freeway cloverleaf. The artist has become technician—sculptors are metallurgists, printmakers chemists, movie directors and editors highly skilled workmen in the use of cameras, lenses, lights, cutters, and other tools of the trade. Popular artists have taken eager advantage of technology, both its materials and techniques. Acrylic paints, welding torches, television cameras, and multitrack tape recorders (Apple Records uses as many as sixteen tracks) are as much cultural tools as commercial ones, and vice versa. Painters use real telephones and bathtubs; composers artificial noises; musicians instruments like the Fender bass and the Moog synthesizer. Popular music in particular has made imaginative use of electronic technology. The sound engineer's part in making music is as creative as the musician's, using reverberation, equalization, overdubbing and distortion techniques to create sounds and performances that never existed; the amplifier alone has virtually transformed the character of much popular music. By using three amplifiers on a violin, for example, the engineer can select and combine sound frequencies and levels to produce quite new and striking sounds; to cite another example, the "wa-wa" pedal, developed recently for amplified guitar, for the first time gives a stringed instrument voice-like qualities. Certainly none of this bears resemblance to what were considered culturally acceptable techniques and subjects in the arts a short generation ago. This mutual absorption of culture and technology on the popular level is an outstanding characteristic of our contemporary world.

As a result of these and other factors, real doubts have been raised about the customary division of culture into brow-levels, and about ways of judging and investigating materials drawn from popular culture. I am not at all sure that the presumed dichotomy among "cultures" is real or natural. Do the culturally elite never search for entertainment, and the so-called "masses" never seek insight? Is culture *only* a matter of class, income, and education? If you stopped *Gunsmoke* next week, would there be larger audiences for *Oh Calcutta*? As for the argument that popular culture does not impart "genuine" values, how do you measure genuine-ness? Who can say that the TV watcher gets less "genuine" value— at *his* level of experience— than the professor reading James? I have never quite understood why, if a Ph.D. settles down with a Scotch and soda to read Ross MacDonald (who was recently favored with front-page *Times* and *Newsweek* reviews) it's sophistication, whereas a tool-and-die maker from Oldsmobile who watches *Mannix* on TV with a can of beer is automatically a slob. Whose values are the more genuine? These are some of the questions raised by the current explorations of the nature and uses of popular culture, and ones that should not only be raised but answered.

There are many more. What about standards of "good" and "bad," applied to the popular arts? Should we judge a popular novel as we would Faulkner? Is Aristotle applicable to paperbacks, Northrop Frye to television? Most of our critical standards are drawn from studies of eighteenth and nineteenth-century fiction and poetry—what have they to do with twentieth century media? As a result, what a good many critics are saying about popular culture is little more than that the aesthetic forms and aims that flourished in the nineteenth century do not satisfy the twentieth, a conclusion hardly profound. Furthermore, what do we mean by *popular,* in the critical sense? Is definition in terms of consumption, or economics, or sales, valid? Is a "good" book that millions of people read "popular" or not? What are we going to do with Charles Dickens? Or Charles Chaplin? Or *Hair*? I have no answers nor is it necessary here to make precise ones. The point is, that by continuing to ask questions the range of interest in the study of popular culture may be broadened, deepened, better understood, focused with greater precision.

The study of popular culture is still in the process of finding its methodology, primarily because it is a joint scholarly venture, involving several disciplines, borrowing and gaining something from each. I do not account this a weakness. It means, in effect, that in finding out what we want to know about the culture of a society at a given place and time, we can choose the most effective tools, whether they be sociological, psychological, historical, aesthetic, or philosophical. Popular culture can be considered as a point at which the investigative techniques of the social sciences and the humanities may converge. Where such interests draw together—in examinations of social behavior, cultural patterns, communications media, social and cultural values—the study of popular culture provides a common ground where different disciplines may combine. There is, then, no single, approved methodology for the study of popular culture, but several. Since many forms of popular culture depend for effectiveness on their collective appeal (and some, like contemporary popular music, are even collectively produced), any approach to the study of them almost necessarily must be eclectic. We should be able to choose that method of investigation which allows us to find out what we want to know. What works best is the best methodology.

Borrowing from a Wallace Stevens' poem, I should like to suggest six ways of looking at popular culture, depending on what one wishes to find out and how one wants to define it. One way turns on the study of the means by which culture is transmitted. It assumes that popular culture includes those cultural elements which are not so complex and sophisticated that they cannot be effectively disseminated among a *majority* audience. This provides a useful distinction between popular and elite cultures—i.e., a painting versus a print—by focusing attention on the distributive process. A second way of approaching popular culture may be based on an examination of the differences in the production of popular cultural artifacts, distinguishing between the unique and the mass-produced—in other words, focusing on the creative *act,* and on whether or not it can be sustained or is reproducible. John Cawelti has refined this approach by defining at least a broad portion of popular culture as that which is "characterized by artistic formulas which arise in response to certain cultural needs for entertainment and escape." That is, if there exists a majority cultural need, the popular artist evolves a formula for meeting it—the Western movie, the Sinatra song style, the McKuen poem, the *True Romance.*

Third, it may also be useful to examine the product of popular culture on the basis of its function—that is, to ask, What is it used for? Comics, B movies, "listening music," the detective story—is the point relaxation or celebration? In recognizing the difference in function between Conan Doyle and Tolstoy—both masters at their craft—it is also recognized that one does not judge either by the other's standards. What this functional approach does, and very usefully, is to acknowledge gradations of aim among serious work seriously received, unserious work unseriously received, and all stages between. Basically, this view of cultural grades derives from Santayana's famous distinction between *work* and *play* as basic human activities, between what must be done and what is done by choice. While this approach is perhaps overly generalized, it is especially useful as a tool for studying popular culture before the appearance of the mass media—one cannot, I think, study pre-media and post-media popular culture in the same ways.

A fourth approach is that suggested by Marshall Fishwick's characterization of popular culture as "that part of culture abstracted from the *total* body of intellectual and imaginative work which each generation receives," which is not narrowly elitist or aimed at special audiences, and which is generally (but not necessarily) disseminated via the mass media. Popular culture thus includes everything not elite, "everything spoken, printed, pictured, sounded, viewed and intended for other than the identifiable few." Professor Fishwick's concept is particularly useful for its inclusiveness, and for its adaptability to sociological, historical, psychological, philosophical or critical investigation. Abraham Kaplan has suggested a fifth, somewhat related approach, pointing out that the distinguishing mark of popular culture is the *kind* of taste it reflects and satisfies, rather than how widely it is disseminated. Popular culture thus becomes not dependent for definition on numbers and profits, or for uniqueness or lack of it, but rather is defined on the basis of its own nature and aims. Sixth, Ray Browne has suggested that differences among various levels of culture are to be considered matters of degree rather than of substance or audience. Culture, he has written, is not to be arranged vertically from "low" to "high," but in a kind of horizontal continuum, resembling a flattened lens or ellipsis, with Elite at one end, Folk at the other, and between, largest and most visible, Popular culture. Lines of demarcation are mobile, investigatory methods variable and pragmatically chosen, the purpose to treat culture in all its phases, to exclude none and include all. Although I cannot match Stevens' thirteen, these are six ways of approaching the study of popular culture, all valid for varying purposes, all useful in investigating what is, it seems to me, the most provocatively versatile field of academic study of our contemporary day.

The value of this pioneering conference, and of others which I hope will follow, lies in asking questions, testing boundaries, stretching conjectures. What the study of popular culture requires more than anything else at this point is this loosening of divisions and broadening of perspectives. The classic definition of culture as "the best that has been done or thought," or as "the upper ten-percent of a society's best accomplishments," has been valuable—and will always be—as a means of preserving and transmitting the cultural heritage. But on the other hand, to rule out the rest of the broad spectrum of human cultural activity as an area for exploration is a far too restrictive act. Certainly, the culture of the majority of society ought to be subjected to this kind of searching, intensive investigation by historians, literary critics, and humanists in general, if we are to know our modern, pluralistic, multileveled society.

Note

1. See, for example, Leo Loewenthal's essay, "An Historical Preface to the Popular Culture Debate," in Norman Jacobs, ed., *Culture for the Millions* (Princeton, 1961), 28–42.

REVOLUTION IN POPULAR CULTURE

Peter Burke

This essay was written for a collection which explored the role(s) of revolution(s) in history, and Peter Burke in particular addresses the question of whether or not there has been one or more revolutions in popular culture. Despite this unusual emphasis, it contains a succinct overview of three analytic traditions in the study of popular culture, and especially the European contribution to these traditions. Burke both summarizes and critiques these traditions, but does not offer a guiding definition of popular culture, perhaps because there is not necessarily a common ground between one tradition which studies mass culture, a product of the mass media, and the other two which focus on the culture of ordinary people. Burke is the author of numerous historical studies, most notably Popular Culture in Early Modern Europe *(1978), and is Professor of Cultural History at the University of Cambridge and a Fellow of Emmanuel College, Cambridge.*

. . . The problems of change and continuity have been discussed in a lively and interesting way with reference to popular culture since its discovery by historians some twenty years ago. It may be useful to distinguish three approaches to the subject, three traditions of analysis which started out from very different premises. . . . The first of these traditions emphasizes the media through which popular culture has been transmitted; the second, the society in which it has been transmitted; and the third, the history of that transmission over the long term.

I. The Media and the Critics

The twentieth century has witnessed many denunciations of popular culture, or, as it was more commonly known from the 1930s to the 1960s, "mass culture."[1] These denunciations, which generally came from literary critics, such as F. R. Leavis, rested on a simple view of historical development, whether or not this view was made explicit. The past was presented

Peter Burke, "Revolution in Popular Culture," in Roy Porter and Mikulas Teigh (eds.), Revolution in History *(Cambridge: Cambridge University Press, 1986), 206–25. Reprinted with the permission of Cambridge University Press.*

as a Golden Age, the age of the "organic community" and of "folk art." As one critic put it, "Folk Art grew from below," while "Mass Culture is imposed from above"; it is "an article for mass consumption, like chewing gum."[2] The new "mass art," said another, provides "invitations to a candy-floss world" and "sex in shiny packets," in place of the old order's "real world of people."[3] "Much of what applies to the production of goods," a third critic declared, "is true also of the mass media . . . Quantity becomes more important than quality . . . What is presented must be 'safe,' unprovocative and generally acceptable. Individual preferences are ignored, because mass-production pays best when millions of copies of a few designs are turned out rather than fewer copies of more designs."[4]

These denunciations, of which it would be easy to multiply examples, were often perceptive, but they were (ironically enough, given their stress on the need to discriminate) themselves somewhat undiscriminating. That they did not distinguish between one journal and another, or one television programme and another, was inevitable, given their assumptions about "mass-production," a term which is partly, and dangerously, metaphorical. A more weighty objection to the "cultural critics," a convenient name for a group which includes F. R. Leavis, Richard Hoggart and Denys Thompson, is their failure to distinguish sufficiently sharply either between media or between periods.

A greater concern with the characteristics of specific media was shown by students of "mass communications" across the Atlantic, who noted, for example, that radio was more effective in communicating than print because "the listener gets a sense of personal access from the radio."[5] Radio is a "hot" medium, as the Canadian critic Marshall McLuhan liked to say, contrasting it not only with print but also with what he called the "cool" medium of television.[6]

A still more serious criticism of the critics mentioned so far, British and American, is that they lacked a sufficiently acute sense of history. When was the Golden Age of folk art? When did the iron age of mass culture begin? Was the transition from one to the other a gradual one, or was it "revolutionary"? Answers differed, and they were all too rarely supported by historical evidence in any detail. For McLuhan, for example, the important changes were both sudden and sharp. Television, he wrote, was "as revolutionary a medium in America in the 1950's as radio in Europe in the 1930s," and this electric age was clearly distinct from "the mechanical age now receding."[7] For Richard Hoggart, concerned with the north of England rather than with McLuhan's "global village," the important changes took place "30 or 40 years" before he wrote, beginning, in other words, about the time of his birth at the end of the First World War.[8] Other students of English culture have emphasized what has been called the "Northcliffe Revolution," the rise of the popular press in the late nineteenth century (the *Daily Mail* was founded in 1896). Raymond Williams on the other hand, a cultural critic with a more acute sense of history than most, has pointed out that the British popular press goes back further than 1896, indeed beyond the compulsory schooling imposed by the Education Act of 1870. According to him, this popular press began with the Sunday papers of the early nineteenth century, such as the *News of the World,* founded in 1843.[9] For Williams, a Marxist of a somewhat nonconforming kind, this date is no accident, He thinks in terms of a single revolution, with three main aspects ("democratic" and "industrial" as well as cultural), although he admits that the process was spread out over a protracted period, a "Long Revolution."

Since the popular press in Britain goes back to the early nineteenth century, while the Sunday school, which provoked his comment, is still older, it is not difficult to appreciate Edward Thompson's complaint that modern critics of the media "have matters out of proportion" because they "overlook the extent and character of mass indoctrination in earlier periods."[10] Even the criticisms of mass culture are part of a longer tradition than those who voice them generally realize. In a broad sense they go back to Plato (even if he was thinking in terms of the face-to-face community of the classical city-state); but even in a precise sense these criticisms are not exactly new. Although the term "mass" was at the height of its vogue in the middle years of the twentieth century, the *Revolt of the Masses,* by the Spanish critic Jose Ortega y Gasset, was published in 1930, and Freud's *Mass Psychology and the Analysis of the Ego* (bowdlerized in its English translation as "Group Psychology") in 1921. In the middle of the nineteenth century the phenomenon of mass culture had been analyzed by Alexis de Tocqueville and also by Matthew Arnold, who once wrote that "Plenty of people will try to give the masses, as they call them, an intellectual food prepared and adapted in the way they think proper for the actual condition of the masses. The ordinary popular literature is an example of this way of working on the masses . . ."[11]

Once again we find ourselves driven back to the early nineteenth century, the age of the early Industrial Revolution. Could the rise of mass culture be the result of that revolution? The question is a reminder of one more weakness in the media-based approach, a weakness neatly exposed by the Polish sociologist Zygmunt Bauman. Bauman has drawn attention to the circularity of the common assumption that "the media of mass communication are the parent of mass culture," while on the other hand "mass culture is the parent of the mass communication media." His trenchant comment is that "For culture to become 'mass,' it is not enough to set up a television station. Something must first happen to social structure. Mass culture is in a way a superstructure resting upon what we shall tentatively call 'mass social structure.'"[12]

II. The Marxists and Popular Culture

Bauman's formulation introduces us directly to the Marxist approach to the history of popular culture. Oddly enough, the works of Marx and Engels do not. They simply did not take popular culture seriously. Marx contemptuously dismissed what he called the "idiocy of rural life," while Engels described the attitudes of English workers before the rise of Chartism in terms so simplistic they now seem quite incredible. The workers were, he wrote, intellectually "dead." "They could rarely read and still more rarely write; went regularly to church, never talked politics, never conspired, never thought, delighted in physical exercises, listened with inherited reverence when the Bible was read, and were, in their unquestioning humility, exceedingly well-disposed towards the 'superior' classes."[13] These attitudes gave way to class-consciousness, according to both Marx and Engels, when industrialization led (as it had to lead) to changes in the relation of production and made the workers into a "proletariat," ready to take part in a political revolution. And afterwards? The question became a practical one only after 1917, and when it did, the Russian communists were divided. Some of them believed that political revolution would lead naturally to cultural revolution and that the proletariat would spontaneously develop a culture of its own, which they called *Proletkult*. Trotsky, however, argued that the proletariat, uneducated as it is, "cannot create a culture of its own." Culture would be brought to the people by means of education. In this respect, Trotsky sounds like almost any middle-class intellectual of the nineteenth century (even if his ideas on the kind of culture to be taken to the people were unlike most of theirs).[14]

Trotsky's argument implies that culture will not change automatically when society changes, in other words that culture is not a mere reflection of social forces, as Marx and Engels seemed on occasion to have suggested. This "reflection" view of culture was challenged in a more direct and explicit manner by some German Marxists in the 1920s and 1930s. The Frankfurt School, notably Theodor Adorno and Max Horkheimer, argued that culture was to a considerable extent autono-mous. In some ways their views resemble those of Leavis and other British critics of the media, for Adorno and Horkheimer described recent cultural history in terms of commercialization and the rise of the "culture industry."[15]

There is a similar emphasis on the autonomy of culture—within limits—in the work of Antonio Gramsci. He too challenged the view that ordinary people were, as he put it, mere "receptacles" of culture. On the contrary, he argued, everyone is a philosopher, this "spontaneous philosophy" finding its expression in language, in action ("common sense"), and in popular religion. Gramsci believed that this everyday philosophy, or popular culture, was often influenced by the ideas of intellectuals or by those of the ruling class, who often exercise a cultural "hegemony," as he called it, over the people.[16] However, he insisted that this hegemony was not so much imposed on as accepted by ordinary people. These ideas, worked out in prison and not known very widely in Gramsci's own day, have had very great influence on the intellectual left since the end of the Second World War, and especially on students of popular culture over the last couple of decades. Their influence is not confined to Marxists. Carlo Ginszburg, for example, whose work will be discussed below, acknowledges his debt to Gramsci.

To see how the Marxist approach to culture works out in practice, a useful example to take is that of England in the nineteenth century, a privileged area so far as both the quantity and the quality of recent studies are concerned, as well as one which will bring us back to the central theme of "revolution." The example was set in the late 1950s and early 1960s by Raymond Williams and Edward Thompson. Neither Williams nor Thompson was content with the traditional Marxist view of culture as mere "superstructure." Both emphasized what they variously called "experience," "tradition," "culture" or "structures of feeling." Williams, a historically minded critic who has made his own synthesis of Marxism with the moral-literary approach of F. R. Leavis, has studied English culture as "a particular way of life, which expresses certain meanings and values not only in art and learning but also in institutions and ordinary behavior," noting that the concept "culture" was itself taken up and developed in order to make sense of the profound changes consequent on the Industrial Revolution.[17] Thompson, a historian with an unusual sensitivity to literature, has concentrated on what he calls the "plebs" in the eighteenth century and the "working class" in the nineteenth. His brilliant, controversial and influential account of *The Making of the English Working Class* (1963) opens with a sharp critique of earlier historical and sociological interpretations of the Industrial Revolution on the grounds that "they tend to obscure the agency of working people, the degree to which they contribute, by conscious efforts, to the making of history." Thompson's aim was therefore, in his own memorable phrase, "to rescue the poor stockinger, the Luddite cropper, the 'obsolete' hand-loom weaver, the 'utopian' artisan, and even the deluded follower of Joanna Southcott, from the enormous condescension of posterity."[18] He interprets the rise of working-class consciousness in the period 1792–1832 as a reaction to (and also against) economic and political pressures, but he emphasizes that this reaction was far from being an automatic one. It was shaped by what he calls a "moral culture," a "popular tradition." Hence his book is concerned not only with the factory system and the repressive measures of Tory governments in the age of "Peterloo," but also with Methodism (interpreted, in a famous controversial chapter, as a form of "psychic exploitation"), and with the values of liberty, equality and community expressed in popular ballads, in festivals, in democratic institutions (from taverns to trade unions), and in different forms of popular protest.

Thompson's later work has gone back behind 1780, thus implying that the making of the working class was an even more protracted process than he had originally suggested. His "Moral Economy of the English Crowd," for example, is a study of English food riots as moral protest, and it opens with a characteristic challenge to what he describes as the "spasmodic view" of popular history, which reduces riots to a crude response to the stimulus of hunger.[19] Thompson has written in similar terms about charivaris, about poaching and its repression, and about anonymous threatening letters, emphasizing in each case the growing conflict between the customs of traditional village communities and the rise of capitalism.[20] Despite a famous essay on the "poverty of theory," directed primarily against the French philosopher Louis Althusser, he has added to his conceptual baggage. Like Raymond Williams, he has moved closer to Gramsci, or at least made more explicit use of his ideas. The essay "Patrician Society, Plebeian Culture," which sums up the argument implicit in the more specialized studies, suggests that ruling-class control in eighteenth-century England was "located primarily in a cultural hegemony." The plebs were far from deferential: on the contrary, they were much given to protest, to acting out "a theatre of threat and sedition." However, they were not revolutionary.[21]

Neither Williams nor Thompson likes to use the phrase "popular culture." Williams rejects it because his view of culture is holistic, associated with a region rather than with a social group or class. Thompson rejects it for the opposite reason, not so much because it is too narrow as because it is too wide, and prefers the term "plebeian," in the sense of proto-working class. All the same, Williams and Thompson, together with Eric Hobsbawm, who takes Europe rather than England for his province, have been the models for the many recent studies of nineteenth-century English popular culture written from a broadly Marxist perspective.[22]

This body of work, much of it sensitive and sophisticated, is now so large that it cannot be discussed here in any detail.[23] In any case, despite areas of controversy, a common vocabulary and a common framework have developed. There is, for example, general rejection of the concept "superstructure."[24] There is a suspicion of the "history of leisure" approach on the grounds that it is too narrow and that popular culture should be sought in a whole way of life, including work. (All the same, less attention has been paid in Britain than in Germany to the historical conditions for the emergence of the new ideas of "leisure" and "free time.")[25] There is also suspicion of the term "social control," used by other historians to describe a movement which this group interprets as the attempt by one class, the bourgeoisie, to control another.[26]

Central to the approach of these historians—Raphael Samuel, Peter Bailey, Hugh Cunningham, Gareth Stedman Jones, Steven and Eileen Yeo, Robert Storch, and a number of others—is the idea of conflict, confrontation, or contest; a kind of cultural warfare with its offensives, counter-offensives, and struggles for territory.[27] On one side is ranged the middle class, concerned with the "taming" of popular festivals (diagnosed as irrational and disorderly) in the name of "discipline" and "rational recreation," together with the police, who are presented as allies of the bourgeoisie or even as "missionaries" of bourgeois values.[28] On the other side stand the working class, defending their traditions, resisting change, defining themselves by their opposition to the middle class.

These formulations have considerable value as a kind of historical shorthand, provided that this is what they are seen to be. They draw attention to the many specific local examples of cultural conflict, of resistance to the many attempts made by the authorities to abolish particular popular festivals and recreations (the suppression of street football in Derby in the 1840s is one example among many).[29] They make it easier to place these local struggles in a much wider context, to link them to large-scale processes of social change such as urbanization (via the competition for the use of public space), and the rise of capitalism (via the need for discipline at work and also for a regular work rhythm incompatible with the traditional pattern of holidays).

However, if the conflict model (and more especially the class-conflict model) of cultural change is to avoid the dangers of oversimplification and overdramatization, it has to take account of a whole series of distinctions.

In the first place, there are the distinctions between different groups who were trying to "tame" the working class and their different aims. Municipal authorities concerned with public order, temperance and dissenting groups concerned with public morality and promoters of "rational recreation" were not necessarily the same people. Indeed, they did not always work in harmony. The "discipline," "conversion," and "improvement" of the working classes were not the same ideals. Indeed, they may not always have been compatible with one another, since the encouragement of ordinary people to read and think for themselves may in the long run have rendered them less obedient to the authorities in Church, state, or factory. It is also necessary to find a place in the model for the middle-class entrepreneurs who were coming to realize the profits to be made from publishing Sunday papers or building chains of variety theatres. It would be stretching the language of warfare too far to include these entrepreneurs in the army concerned with public order or popular salvation.

In the second place, distinctions need to be drawn between different working-class reactions to the suppression of traditional recreations, or to the more general (though less visible) attempts to transform their whole culture. Resistance to suppression there certainly was, but it was not unanimous. Some members (or even some "fractions") of the working class accepted some of the new values, such as temperance or "respectability." In mid-nineteenth-century Derby, for example, trade unionists denounced the traditional popular pastime of street football (while to make matters still more complicated, some members of the middle class supported it). In short, the conflict model needs to be qualified to take account of instances of what Gramsci called bourgeois "hegemony," as opposed to coercion. However, the idea of hegemony would itself be an over-simplification if it were to be seen in rather mechanical terms as a filtering down of middle-class values which themselves remained unchanged. It might be better to follow the lead of a recent study of Edinburgh and talk of the selective appropriation of middle-class values which were reinterpreted and modified in the course of their assimilation into the working-class cultural tradition. The process is sometimes described as one of "negotiation."[30]

In a similar way, it has been argued that the material culture of the working class, or that of the eighteenth-century plebs, the values they expressed by their particular mode of conspicuous consumption (when they could afford it—and sometimes when they couldn't) were more in harmony with capitalism than the conflict model allows.[31] The new consumer goods, from gin to curtains, could be assimilated without too much difficulty into the working-class style of life.

This last argument raises the thorny question of the relation between popular culture and capitalism, or, more generally, between historical forces which are under human control and those which are not. It may well be the case that Thompson and his followers, in their desire to give back their human dignity to the poor stockingers and others, have underestimated the constraints and pressures on working-class culture. It is of course hard to talk about "capitalism" without reifying or fetishizing it, turning it into a superhuman force.[32] Perhaps the Marxist "Grand Theory" of Adorno, Horkheimer and others, discussed above, is vulnerable to this criticism. Yet the Frankfurt School's picture of the commercialization and industrialization of popular culture does contain elements missing from the new wave of Marxist studies, despite the sounder empirical basis of the latter. The next assignment is surely to investigate in more detail the relationship between those changes which can be accounted for in terms of the intentions of individuals and those which cannot, among them the shift from participatory entertainments to performances by professionals to relatively passive audiences.

Such a change of emphasis would help modify a somewhat misleading impression given by some recent studies of nineteenth-century British popular culture, the impression that the changes of that period were, if not "revolutionary," at least rather sudden. For it has not been very difficult to show, on one side of this "great divide," that some traditional cultural forms, such as the Lancashire wakes, were resilient enough to survive the Industrial Revolution; and on the other, as Thompson's more recent work shows, that important changes were taking place well before 1780, when *The Making of the English Working Class* begins.[33]

Again, attempts to suppress (or better, perhaps, to "reform") traditional popular culture go back well before the nineteenth century. It has recently been shown, for example, that the critique of popular recreations by the supporters of the temperance movement in nineteenth-century Cornwall followed the lines of an earlier Methodist attack. Indeed, both movements may be said to have followed the general lines of sixteenth- and seventeenth-century attempts to reform English popular culture.[34] To understand the nineteenth-century phase of cultural change—to decide whether or not it was truly revolutionary—it is necessary to see it in perspective, the perspective of the long term.

III. The "Annales School" and Popular Culture

The phrase "the long term" (*la longue durée*) is, of course, one of the slogans of the French historians associated with the journal *Annales: Économies, Sociétés, Civilizations*. It is taken from an article published in 1958 by Fernand Braudel, still (in 1985) the leader of the so-called "*Annales* School."[35] The term "school," incidentally, should not be taken to imply a uniformity of approach—the historians associated with *Annales* differ from one another even more than contemporary Marxist historians do, and range from quantitative economic historians concerned with changes on a grand scale to ethno-historians whose world may be no larger than a village (it is a measure if the versatility of Emmanuel LeRoy Ladurie that he combines the two approaches or, more exactly, practices them alternately).

This group has a long-standing interest in the history of culture. The founders of the journal, Lucien Febvre and Marc Bloch, were rebels against the domination of history by past politics, a protest still expressed in the subtitle "économies, sociétés, civilizations." So far as the *civilization* part is concerned, their distinctive approach was and remains the study of what they have called *mentalités collectives,* in other words attitudes, assumptions and feelings rather than ideas in any precise philosophical sense of the term. They were interested in the anthropological approach to "primitive" thought by Émile Durkheim and Lucien Lévy-Bruhl, and tried to adapt it to the study of medieval and early modern Europe. Bloch's *Royal Touch* (1923) studied the beliefs surrounding the practice of touching for the "king's evil," while Febvre's *Problem of Unbelief* (1942) discussed whether or not it was possible to be an atheist in the sixteenth century. The answer was in the negative.[36]

Although they defined the history of mentalities widely enough to include the attitudes of ordinary people, neither Bloch nor Febvre occupied himself very much with specifically popular beliefs, while Braudel has shown little interest in mentalities, to which he prefers the study of "material culture" (*la civilization materielle*).[37] The study which really introduced the *Annales* group to the subject was Robert Mandrou's *Popular Culture in the Seventeenth and Eighteenth Centuries.*[38]

Mandrou, a pupil of Febvre's, focused his attention on the so-called *Bibliothèque bleue,* a series of booklets produced by small publishers (in the town of Troyes, in Champagne, in particular), and distributed over much of France by itinerant peddlers. The booklets were cheap and they appear to have been bought by the better-off peasants and read aloud on winter evenings. On this assumption Mandrou analyzed the contents of some four hundred and fifty of these texts as a means of reconstructing the popular mentality of the period.

This analysis led him to two main conclusions. In the first place, he argued that the function of the "Blue Library" was to provide escapist literature, which emphasized extraordinary and supernatural events, but had little room for practical books (with the exception of a few medical texts and, to a lesser extent, almanacs). In the second place, Mandrou suggested that these little books expressed conformist values; indeed, that they represented the diffusion downwards to the peasants of cultural models created by the clergy and the nobility, and respectively expressed in lives of the saints and romances of chivalry. In other words, the French peasants of the old regime have to be imagined as excited by the exploits of Ogier the Dane, or sympathetically concerned with the persecution of St. Geneviève.

At much the same time as Mandrou, Albert Soboul (a Marxist historian but one who, like his master Georges Lefebvre, was not far from the *Annales* approach) published an article on the *sans-culottes* of the French Revolution, in which he noted their apparent familiarity with the ideas of Rousseau and raised the question of the way in which these ideas could have reached them. His conclusion was that the means of diffusion was popular literature, such as almanacs and song-books.[39] Taken together, the studies of Mandrou and Soboul might suggest a neat and simple conclusion, to the effect that a revolution in popular culture accompanied the events of 1798. Ogier the Dane went out, and Rousseau came in.

However, matters were not so simple. One romance of chivalry, *The Four Sons of Aymon* was still being read aloud, by Bretons at least, in the trenches in the First World War.[40] In any case, *sans-cullotes* were not peasants but craftsmen, who sometimes owned their own businesses.[41] Other qualifications and distinctions need to be made when discussing popular literature, and Mandrou has been criticized quite sharply in the last few years for failing to make them. For example, some of the items in the *Bibliothèque bleue* may not have been really "popular," while some popular literature of the period did not appear in the *Bibliothèque bleue*. The audience of these booklets cannot be assumed to have been confined to the peasants, but can be shown to have included townspeople and even members of the upper classes (women in particular). It cannot be assumed that the readers interpreted the stories in the same ways as we do, or that they agreed with the particular moral or message they found there. To attempt to reconstruct the mentality of ordinary Frenchmen and women of this period from the contents of the *Bibliothèque bleue* is rather like discussing the attitudes of the British working class today on the basis of nothing but television programmes and tabloid newspapers, as if individuals did not make critical remarks about the programmes or tell one another that "you can't believe what you read in the papers," a remark so common in the Yorkshire of Richard Hoggart's youth that it has some claim to be regarded as a modern proverb.[42]

Since Mandrou's book first appeared in 1964, the historians associated with *Annales* have been increasingly concerned with popular culture, which they have approached in a number of different ways. Jean Delumeau, on the fringe of the group but someone who has learned a good deal from Lucien Febvre, has concerned himself with popular Catholicism in France and Italy, and the extent to which magical, animist, and generally "pre-Christian" attitudes survived into the age of the Counter-Reformation and even beyond.[43] Georges Duby, one of the leading medievalists in France, has interested himself in cultural diffusion down the social scale, the phenomenon described by German folklorists of the early twentieth century as *Gesunkenes Kulturgut*. However, Duby has learned from Althusser (to whom he acknowledges a debt) and others to analyze this process not as the simple diffusion of cultural models, but rather as a form of adaptation or assimilation.[44] Again, Robert Muchembled's general study of French popular culture in the early modern period attempts to combine a Durkheimian analysis of structure with a Marxian account of change, in which his major theme is the repression of popular culture by the ruling class, while the *Bibliothèque bleue* is interpreted as the opium of the people, a sort of "tranquilizer" as the author puts it. Muchembled makes considerable play with the notion of "acculturation," taken from social anthropology. All the same, his account of cultural conflict in the seventeenth century is curiously reminiscent of accounts of the nineteenth century given by British Marxist historians.[45]

Other French historians practice a rather more distinctive approach which derives from an intellectual movement which in fact developed under the eyes of the *Annales* group at the École des Hautes Études and at the Collège de France; in other words, structuralism. It is not easy to offer a satisfactory definition of the aims of this movement, which is no more homogeneous than Marxism or the "*Annales* School," but it is held together—however loosely—by a concern with culture as a system, in which the relation between the parts is more significant than the individual items. Like language, which provided the model in the first instance, myths, food, clothes and so on are interpreted by Claude Lévi-Strauss and his followers as systems of signs, with an emphasis on binary oppositions such as "raw" versus "cooked" and "naked" versus "dressed," and more generally between "wild" and "domesticated" thought, terms which replace the more traditional contrast between "primitive" and "civilized."[46]

Rather different was the approach to systems of thought practiced by the late Michel Foucault; indeed, Lévi-Strauss asserted that Foucault was not a structuralist at all. Actually Foucault does resemble Lévi-Strauss in his stress on the intellectual system, or on "discourse," at the expense of individual thinkers, while differing from him by pointing to fundamental "epistemological breaks" in the history of Western thought (around 1650, for example, and around 1800), breaks which, he argued, affected not only disciplines such as linguistics and economics, but also attitudes to insanity, poverty, crime and sex.[47]

What has all this to do with the history of popular culture? Or, indeed, with history *tout court*? A question which has been debated with some heat in France and elsewhere, with attacks on both Lévi-Strauss and Foucault as "unhistorical," the former because he shows little interest in change, the latter because he refuses to explain it.[48] However, historians cannot afford to ignore Foucault's provocative work. His theses about breaks in the history of thought, breaks which in some ways resemble Thomas Kuhn's scientific "revolutions," demand to be confronted and discussed.[49] Foucault also took a perverse pleasure in turning traditional views upside-down, in interpreting the rise of the modern clinic (asylum, prison, etc.), not in terms of increasing humanitarianism (as the conventional wisdom has it) but of changing forms of repression. His major works are not concerned with popular culture, at least not directly, but they do have implications for its interpretation. It would not be difficult to imagine a history of popular culture written along Foucaultian lines, in which the most effective form of repression was not Muchembled's tranquilizers, or even the rational recreation movement, but the romantic cult of the people, which involved treating them as picturesque objects.

As for the ideas, or the "discourse" of Lévi-Strauss, it is obviously harder for a historian to come to grips with such an all-embracing system, but it could be argued that a major theory of culture is something which cultural historians cannot afford to ignore. Some French historians would add that the concepts of "wild" and "concrete" thought have helped them (as the ideas of "primitive" and "pre-logical" thought once helped Bloch and Febvre) to develop the history of mentalities; popular mentalities in particular.

It may be possible to be a little more precise. One of the best-known concepts formulated be Lévi-Strauss is that of *bricolage*; in other words, the process by which traditional or "second-hand" elements are reconstructed to form a new cultural system, or new elements incorporated in an old system.[50] This idea has the advantage of offering historians a way of discussing cultural continuity and change without exaggerating the importance of either tradition or revolution. It is, perhaps, particularly useful for the study of popular culture (or, more generally, of "dominated" cultures), in which it is relatively easy to see how "foreign" elements are reinterpreted in the process of incorporation.[51] We are not so far from the idea, already discussed, of "negotiation," as if different groups of historians are converging on the same goal by different routes.

It might also be argued, ironically enough, that *bricolage* well describes the reaction of French historians to structuralism. They are attracted not so much by the system, which seems ahistorical (if not anti-historical), as by the possibility of appropriating some elements from it and incorporating them in a more dynamic system than their own. Lévi-Strauss offers a new way of reading myths, so historians such as Jacques Le Goff and Emmanuel Le Roy Ladurie offer an interpretation of a medieval legend (that of the mermaid Melusine, for example) in Lévi-Straussian terms, before utilizing the results in a more traditional framework.[52] Roger Chartier has returned to the *Bibliothèque bleue,* which he reads in a more complex and a more structuralist manner than Mandrou did. As a result he has come to doubt the utility of the distinction between "learned" and "popular" culture, like the distinction between "creation" and "consumption," because he has found so many cultural "exchanges" which are more exactly transformations.[53]

Notes

1. For a useful collection of studies see *Mass Culture*, eds. B. Rosenberg and D. M. White (Glencoe, 1957).

2. D. MacDonald in *Mass Culture*, 60.

3. R. Hoggart, *The Uses of Literacy* (London, 1957); the quotations form the titles of chs. 4, 7, and 8.

4. *Discrimination and Popular Culture*, ed. D. Thompson (Harmondsworth, 1964), 10–11.

5. P. Lazarsfeld *et al.*, *The People's Choice* (New York, 1944), 129.

6. M. McLuhan, *Understanding Media* (New York, 1965), 299.

7. McLuhan, 314, 4–5.

8. Hoggart, preface. Cf. R. Williams, *The Country and the City* (London, 1973), on the way in which the great divide always seems to go back one generation before the speaker.

9. R. Williams, *The Long Revolution* (London, 1961).

10. E. P. Thompson, *The Making of the English Working Class* (London, 1963), 378n.

11. M. Arnold, *Culture and Anarchy* (London, 1869).

12. Z. Bauman, "A Note on Mass Culture" in *Sociology of Mass Communications*, ed. D. McQuail (Harmondsworth, 1972), 61–62.

13. F. Engels, *The Condition of the Working Class*, quoted in R. Johnson, "Three Problematics," in *Working-Class Culture*, ed. J. Clarke, C. Critcher and R. Johnson (London, 1979), 206.

14. L. Trotsky, *On Literature and Art*, quoted in A. Swingewood, *The Myth of Mass Culture* (London, 1977), 46.

15. T. Adorno and M. Horkheimer, *The Dialectic of Enlightenment* (1944).

16. The relevent texts from Gramsci are assembled and provided with a running commentary in *Culture, Ideology and Social Process*, ed. T. Bennett *et al.* (London, 1981), 191–218.

17. Williams, *Long Revolution*, 57.

18. Thompson, *Making of the Working Class*, 12.

19. E. P. Thompson, "The Moral Economy of the English Crowd," *Past and Present*, 50 (1971), 76–136. He took the phrase from Andrew Ure, *The Philosophy of Manufactures* (London, 1835), but inverted it to mean "economic morality."

20. E. P. Thompson, "Rough Music," *Annales: ESC*, 27 (1972): 285–310; *Whigs and Hunters* (London, 1975); "The Crime of Anonymity," in *Albion's Fatal Tree*, ed. D. Hay, *et al.* (London, 1975), 225–308.

21. E. P. Thompson, *The Poverty of Theory* (London, 1978), the title essay; "Patrician Society, Plebian Culture," in *Journal of Social History*, 7 (1973–74): 382–405.

22. E. J. Hobsbawn, *Primitive Rebels* (Manchester, 1959) is particulary concerned with popular culture.

23. Among the more important contributions are P. Bailey, *Leisure and Class in Victorian England* (London, 1978); H. Cunningham, *Leisure in the Industrial Revolution* (London, 1980); G. Stedman Jones, *Languages of Class* (Cambridge, 1984); *Popular Culture and Class Conflict*, ed. E. and S. Yeo (Brighton, 1981); and *Popular Culture and Custom in 19th-Century England*, ed. R. D. Storch (London, 1982). J. M. Golby and A. W. Purdue, *The Civilization of the Crowd: Popular Culture and Custom in England 1750–1900* (London, 1984), appeared too late to be discussed here.

24. A recent discussion in the introduction to Storch.

25. A recent example of the approach is J. Walvin, *Leisure and Society 1830–1950* (London, 1978). Recent critiques include G. Stedman Jones, *Languages*, ch. 2, and the Yeos, *Popular Culture*, 144f. On the idea of free time, W. Nahrstedt, *Die Entstehung der Freizeit* (Göttingen, 1972), a study focused on Hamburg but with much wider implications.

26. G. Stedman Jones, *Languages*, ch 2; the Yeos, *Popular Culture*, 130f.

27. E. P. Thompson writes of the cultural "battlefield"; Peter Bailey of the "contest for control," the Yeos of "'struggle," "counter-offensive" and "battle for territory."

28. R. Storch, "The Policeman as Domestic Missionary," *Journal of Social History*, 9 (1975–76): 481–96.

29. A. Delves, "Popular Recreation and Social Conflict in Derby," in the Yeos, *Popular Culture*, ch. 4. For more general study in this framework, R. W. Malcolmson, *Popular Recreations in English Society 1700–1850* (Cambridge, 1973), esp. chs. 6 and 7.

30. R. Q. Gray, *The Labour Aristocracy of Victorian Edinburgh* (Oxford, 1976), ch. 7. An influential study of contemporary popular culture in its relation to the "hegemonic" culture is *Resistance through Rituals*, ed. S. Hall and T. Jefferson (London, 1976).

31. H. Medick, "Plebian Culture in the Transition to Capitalism," in *Culture Ideology and Politics*, ed. R. Samuels and G. Stedman Jones (London, 1983), ch. 5.

32. A danger noted by the Yeos in *Popular Culture*.

33. J. K. Walton and R. Poole, "The Lancashire Wakes in the Nineteenth Century," in Storch, *Popular Culture*, ch. 5. For Thompson see notes 21 and 22 above; cf. Malcolmson (note 30).

34. J. Rule, "Methodism, Popular Beliefs and Village Culture in Cornwall," in Storch, *Popular Culture*, ch. 3; cf. P. Burke, *Popular Culture in Early Modern Europe* (London, 1978), ch. 8.

35. F. Braudel, "History and the Social Sciences," in *Economy and Society in Early Modern Europe*, ed. P. Burke (London, 1972), ch. 1.

36. M. Bloch, *Les rois thaumaturges*, Eng. trans. *The Royal Touch* (London, 1973); L. Febvre, *Le problème d'l'incroyance au 16e siècle: la religion de Rabelais*,

Eng. trans. *The Problem of Unbelief* (Cambridge, MA, 1983). The history of this approach is sketched in P. Burke, "Reflections on the Historical Revolution in France," *Review*, I (1978): 147–56.

37. P. Burke, "'Material Civilisation' in the Work of Fernand Braudel," *Itinerario*, 5 (1981): 2, 37–43.

38. R. Mandrou, *De la culture populaire aux 17e et 18e siècles* (Paris, 1964). At this point the phrase *culture populaire* sometimes meant bringing high culture to the people. Even in 1973, when a conference on popular culture—in the English sense—was held at the University of East Anglia, the French participants only discovered the difference in usage on arrival.

39. A. Soboul, "Classes populaires et Rousseauisme," *Annales historiques de la Révolution Française* (1964), reprinted in his *Paysans, sans-culottes, et jacobins* (Paris, 1966), 203–22.

40. P.-J. Helias, *Le Cheval d'orgeuil* (Paris, 1975), Eng. trans., *The Horse of Pride* (London, 1978).

41. A. Soboul, *Les sans-culottes*, Eng. trans. Gwynne Lewis, *The Parisian Sans-Culottes and the French Revolution* (Oxford, 1964).

42. P. Burke, "The 'Bibliothèque bleue' in Comparative Perspective," *Quaderni del seicento francese*, 4 (1981): 59–66. Hoggart, *Uses*, ch. 9. Cf. R. Darton, *The Great Cat Massacre* (New York, 1984), esp. ch. I.

43. J. Delumeau, *Le Catholicisme entre Luther et Voltaire* (Paris, 1971), Eng. trans. Jeremy Moiser, *Catholicism from Luther to Voltaire* (London, 1977).

44. G. Duby, "The Diffusion of Cultural Patterns in Feudal Society," *Past and Present*, 39 (1968): 1–10; "Histoire sociale et idéologies des sociétés," *Faire de l'histoire*, ed. J. Le Goff and P. Nora (Paris, 1974), vol. 1: 147–68.

45. R. Muchembled, *Culture populaire et culture des elites* (Paris, 1978).

46. Of the many works of Lévi-Strauss, particularly relevent to this argument is *La pensée sauvage* (Paris, 1962), Eng. trans., *The Savage Mind* (London, 1966).

47. M. Foucault, *Histoire de la folie* (1961), Eng. trans., Richard Howard, *Madness and Civilisation* (London, 1967); *Les mots et les choses*, Eng. trans. as *The Order of Things* (London, 1973); *Surveiller et punir* (1975), Eng. trans. *Discipline and Punish* (London, 1977); *La volonté de savoir* (1976); Eng. trans., *The History of Sexuality* (New York, 1980).

48. O. Revault d'Allones, "Michel Foucault: les mots contre les choses," *Structuralisme et marxisme* (Paris, 1970), 13–37, one of the earliest and most penetrating critiques.

49. This is not altogether coincidence. Foucault admitted a considerable debt to two French historians of science, Gaston Bachelard and Georges Canguilhem, both of them concerned with epistemological discontinuities.

50. Lévi-Strauss, *Savage Mind*, ch. 1.

51. Burke, *Popular Culture*, 123.

52. Both interpretations appeared in *Annales*, 1971. Le Goff's is translated in his *Time, Work and Culture in the Middle Ages* (Chicago, 1980), 205–22.

53. R. Chartier, "Intellectual History or Sociocultural History? The French Trajectories," in *Modern European Intellectual History*, ed. D. LaCapra and S. Kaplan (Ithaca and London, 1982), 13–46.

II.
Beyond the Frontier:
Post 1960s and '70s Answers to What Is Popular Culture?

THE DISCOVERY OF POPULAR CULTURE BEFORE PRINTING

Fred E. H. Schroeder

Fred E. H. Schroeder, even though he asserts that "mass production, mass distribution and mass communication are the primary distinguishing features of popular culture," believes that popular culture originated in some places well before the traditional beginning points favored by most scholars, who point to the invention of printing or the advent of the Industrial Revolution. In presenting his case, Schroeder in particular focuses on the following: "second-hand cultures," urbanization, taxation, efficient communication, mass production, conquest, public works, religion, and molds, patterns, and formulas. Fred E. H. Schroeder, retired Professor of Humanities at the University of Minnesota, Duluth, has written or edited a number of seminal popular culture studies, especially Outlaw Aesthetics *(1977),* 5000 Years of Popular Culture *(1980), and* Twentieth-Century Popular Culture in Museums and Libraries *(1981).*

My discovery of early popular culture occurred at the Chicago Museum of Natural History. Like many students of popular culture, I had come into this field of study by way of twentieth-century American mass-distributed media entertainment, and I was tantalized by the problem of how far back into history one could extend the mass production of cultural artifacts, which at the time I believed to be the essential distinguishing characteristic of what we might rightly call popular culture. And, like many visitors to the Field Museum, I had come into the basement gallery to look at the remote and the exotic culture of ancient history, archaeology and Egyptology. What I discovered, though, was a clay mold from which small ushabti figurines were mass-produced for funerals and for popular religious worship. On the same visit, I later observed similar molds from Tibet, and it became clear to me that I had found a technological connecting link to Sony radios, Coke bottles, penny-dreadfuls, the Bay Psalm Book and the Gutenberg Bible. I had discovered ancient popular culture. . . .

Fred E. H. Schroeder, "The Discovery of Popular Culture Before Printing," in Fred E. H. Schroeder (ed.), 5000 Years of Popular Culture: Popular Culture Before Printing *(Bowling Green, OH: Bowling Green State University Popular Press, 1980), 4, 7–11, 12–13.*

At this point, one may begin to ask whether there are any limits to popular culture: Did my "discovery" in the Field Museum not only set me free, but make me run berserk? What sort of definition of popular culture could admit such a gamut of disciplines, arts and histories?

Definitions of popular culture abound, and to those who have arrived at a satisfactory working definition, the subject is wearisome. Certainly there is common-sense agreement among active students of popular culture that they know what they are talking about. Or more likely, they know what they are *not* talking about, which is the elite, cultivated tradition of arts, thought, discourse and life styles. Underlying the cultivated tradition, I would venture, is leisure, but it is leisure that is tied to a class system. What comes first, we may never know, but when wealth falls to a leisure class, there is time to select the best, to explore refinements of thought, expression, action and object. Leisure, refinement, contemplation, cultivation, patronage: all are intertwined into that which we [c]all [sic] polished; civilized; urbane.

At the other end of the cultural spectrum is the folk tradition, and this also is what is *not* meant by popular culture, regardless of how much folk culture is a culture of the people. The folk tradition is a local phenomenon, and in its purest form, it is mainly governed by personal, one-to-one relationships. Parents, grandparents, wise ones of the tribe are the transmitters of the culture; learning is effected by means of direct demonstrations by immediate persons. Contact with other cultures is restricted or almost nonexistent. Authority is not remote, and, except for supernatural forces, it is visibly embodied in real persons. Above all, pure folk cultures are illiterate.

In simple terms, then, we know that we will not find popular culture among the isolated mountain tribes of New Guinea, nor are we to look for it in the court of Renaissance Urbino, where Castiglione set standards for conscious, literate, cosmopolitan civilization. Aside from the extremes, however, clear definitions are impossible, and the cultures of both extremes feed into the popular tradition, and we are left with a network of nagging questions. Is popular culture a reflection of the palace culture? Or is popular culture a development of folk cultures as they are increasingly influenced by outside cultures? Or is popular culture a third entity, an independent outgrowth of economic, political and technological factors?

The truth, I think, lies in the combination of all three, but I tend to believe the last named factors are most important. In other words, I have not abandoned my original belief that mass production, mass distribution and mass communication are the primary distinguishing features of popular culture. Indeed, if we focus on this definition, a surprising similarity between the elite and folk traditions is brought to light. They are both characterized by immediate personal relationships. Among the elite, the artists, the tastemakers, the leaders and thinkers are known directly rather than by media and middlemen. The courtiers in Urbino did not look at copies of Raphael's paintings; they walked up and talked with Raphael. The "Beautiful People" and "jet setters" did not read of Jacqueline Bouvier Kennedy Onassis and of Henry Kissinger in *Newsweek;* they traveled and partied with them. The *salons* of Gertrude Stein and Madame du Pompadour, the coffee houses of Dr. Johnson, David Garrick and Sir Joshua Reynolds, the intriguing palaces of Elizabeth I, Haroun-al-Raschid, Montezuma and the Ptolemies, the discussion of clubs associated with Confucius, Petronius and Socrates are not second-hand cultures. They are immediate and personal, just as immediate and personal as cultures of the campfire and the kiva. Lest I be misunderstood, let me reiterate the immense differences. The elite cultures are literate, rich and above all, cosmopolitan. The folk cultures are illiterate, merely subsistent and local. But neither receives the bulk of its culture second-hand.

Popular culture emerges along with taxes, most of all. Taxation implies a political structure, an economic system and an ideology that transcends the natural units of family, tribe and clan. It also implies extended lines of communication (and with them, non-local authority, maintenance and policing). And it implies the metropolis. This does not mean that popular culture is itself an urban culture. The farmer in the wheatfields of Saskatchewan who reads the Sunday paper, the cotter of medieval Northumbria who attends his parish church, the carpenter of Nazareth who returns to his birthplace for the imperial census are all participating in popular culture; not to the same degree as a Toronto teenybopper, a Canterbury pilgrim or a Roman bathhouse entertainer, surely, but it is popular culture just the same. Nonetheless, it does seem inconceivable to have popular culture emerging directly from a rural economy. The dependence of rural life styles on the natural cycles builds in a resistance to the arbitrary and necessary imposition of consistent schedules from the metropolis. The word *metropolis,* we should note, means "mother city." The metropolis does not necessarily require large size to produce its spawn or to exercise its influence over its subject hinterlands and colonies. It requires means of imposing consistency. Three means have already been mentioned: taxation, efficient communication and some sort of mass production technology. But what lies behind the concept of metropolis and its need for imposing consistency upon subjects and offspring? The answer is to be found in conquest and in public works. Frequently these are coexistent and large public works projects follow military conquest, as in the cases of the Hellenistic and Roman worlds. Sometimes conquest appears to operate without major public works projects, as in the Spanish conquests of Mexico and Peru. But even there where we tend to see only the destruction of cities, temples, highways, canals and records by the Spanish, there is a phoenix-like raising of missions, forts, docks and mines. In other places, it is reasonable to suppose that public works extended the influence of the metropolis without what we ordinarily regard as conquest. Irrigation and drainage projects in particular are peaceful means of extending the culture into previously uninhabited regions, but even mercantilistic colonial enterprises are not always warlike. Mesopotamia and Egypt provide examples of the former, Greece and Phoenecia suggest examples of the latter. The significance of these factors in the development of popular culture may yet seem remote, especially as we look forward to the articles in this collection. But if we recognize that the factors of conquest and public works projects produce masses of people who are beyond immediate authority, and that they also produce economic structures that cannot tolerate non-conformist individual actions, it should be clear that conquest and public works projects must produce mediate or surrogate authority, and machinery to guarantee conformity in behavior. For these reasons, it would be quite shortsighted and provincial for us to regard the popular culture phenomenon as a modern invention.

Nevertheless, there are decided differences between modern and older popular culture. The invention of movable type printing in 1450 (and the development of cheap papers) spurred the protestant reformation, and along with it, popular literacy. The span of time between Gutenburg and a genuinely modern popular literature varies from place to place but it would be safest to think in terms of one or two centuries. Luther's popular influence begins a good seventy-five years after Gutenburg, and the Italian inventions of italic type, pocket editions and printing of music are parallel in time with the Reformation. Popular, mass-produced *visual* arts, however, are Northern European occurrences that antedate the printing of books, primarily in the forms of playing cards and religious souvenirs.

Religion is the common ground, or the pivot between popular culture before and after printing. Religious cultural materials and practices were mass-produced or mass-disseminated at an early time in history, because of the desirability of consistent value and conforming behavior among constituent, colonial or subservient peoples. Hence my discoveries of mass-production molds for religious artifacts in ancient Egypt. Following the Gutenburg revolution, however, the almost exclusive religious, political, economic and military dimensions of popular culture have given room to entertainment popular culture. If you mention "popular culture" to a typical person today, the immediate associations are with mass entertainment: comic books, television comedies, movie westerns, paperback mysteries, junk foods and the like. In large part, this is due to the popular definition of *culture,* which does not include such anthropologically significant elements as banks, supermarkets, schools, churches and the army. But even more sophisticated academics will forget their anthropological and sociological training when confronted with the term "popular culture," and make the narrower, and therefore easier, association with entertainment. The reason, I suspect, is to be found in the new preponderance of secular, recreational mass production. New, that is, in preponderance, for the increase has accelerated exponentially world-wide, and it becomes an insoluble puzzle to many persons when they are asked what the populace did for entertainment before television, movies, radio, vaudeville and newspapers. The answers are partly given by folk studies: even today we continue to have self-generated traditional uses of leisure time, such as are provided in street games, traditional rhymes and melodies. But folk studies have not addressed mass entertainments, institutionalized activities, or written popularizations of either elite or folk cultures. Ordinarily, non-folk cultural historians have concerned themselves with the other end of the spectrum, singling out the masterpiece for study. Thus, although we know a good deal about the audiences of Elizabethan England, it is primarily because of interest in Shakespeare rather than in the mass audience and their popular entertainments. . . .

We should accustom ourselves to looking for the existence of molds, patterns and formulas. Molds are the most obvious and least ambiguous of mass-production techniques. They are indicators of the alienation of creator from the product, and producer from consumer, and they are indicators of a metropolitan (i.e. "mother-city") value system. There are ambiguities in molds, though. The lost-wax process of sculpture, for example, is an ancient mold process, but hardly suitable for extensive mass-production. Signature seals and stamps, such as those with which Mesopotamian merchants and bureaucrats signed clay tablets are, of course, individual. These instances are not exceptions to the general statement that molds are indicators of popular culture; rather, they are cautions to be precise in our understanding of the functions of molds in the cultural setting.

Patterns and formulas extend the scope of popular culture beyond material artifacts, but they also increase the ambiguities and the necessity of precision in our studies. As any folklorist would know, the creative process in a non-literate, local culture is in large part a manipulation of memorized formulas. This is true not only for the refrains and phrases in ballads, but for the conventions of oral traditions that underlie the great literary epics such as *Beowulf* and *The Iliad*. The decorative arts of folk cultures are also the products of patterns; one thinks immediately of pottery and cloth designs. These patterns, however, are usually executed freehand, and thus, although the folk artist may lack originality, or even "creativity," his product is not a mass-duplication to the same degree as it would have been had he used a template or a patternbook, or had he learned his song from a broadside sheet. Patternbooks and broadsides, of course, connote printing and literacy. But the very existence of any written patterns and formulas are indicators of popular, rather than folk, culture. One thinks, for example, of the vast number of ancient Egyptian memorials (e.g. *The Book of the Dead*) in which the only individuation is in the fill-in-the-blank spaces for such things as the names of the dead person, donors or places. Or one might think of the grid-pattern papyri according to which parts of Egyptian stone and wood sculpture might be carved by different artisans at different locations. Similarly, from classical Rome, we have Vitruvius' *Ten Books on Architecture,* which, it is true, were addressed to the imperial court, but which are certainly based on Greek and Roman technical manuals and patterns. Written patterns and formulas, in other words, do not require mass distribution or universal literacy to become instruments of popular culture and consistent metropolitan styles.

SYNCHRONIC VS. DIACHRONIC POPULAR CULTURE STUDIES AND THE OLD ENGLISH ELEGY

Tim D. P. Lally

Tim D. P. Lally believes that popular culture theory is underdeveloped. He argues for "a new paradigm by which we first view all culture as one expression of a given society's leisure needs and opportunities, and then distinguish degrees of popularity along two axes: synchronic and diachronic." The synchronic would focus on popularity of a text or other item in a specific and limited time and place, the diachronic on a broader temporal and cultural context. Lally also makes a case for the concept of "fictive audience," i.e., the audience implicit in an author's creation, which is not necessarily the same as a work's real audience. For Lally, fictive audience is a useful analytic concept, but one which does not imply that values expressed in a popular work must be identified with by the real audience. Lally is a Professor of English at the University of South Alabama.

The exact state of theory in popular culture studies is difficult to discern. Although some attempts to define popular culture tend to leave the question open, it is probably fair to assert that the most commonly used theory defines popular culture as the leisure activities which the working or middle classes of industrial society enjoy.[1] Popular culture is what you do when you are not working or politicking or going to religious meetings, and it is particularly those things you do which a large number of people like yourself also enjoy. The difficulties which surround any popular culture theory are legion, not the least of which is continuity: what is popular today is very often passé tomorrow. Popular culture viewed over a decade or even fewer years offers a bewildering variety of phenomena for study and reflection; surely this plethora of evidence is one cause for the high incidence of what I would term *synchronic* popular culture studies. I use this term advisedly, in that the problem is as much with cultural contexts as it is with a

Tim D. P. Lally, "Synchronic vs. Diachronic Popular Culture Studies and the Old English Elegy," in Fred E. H. Schroeder (ed.), 5000 Years of Popular Culture: Popular Culture Before Printing *(Bowling Green, Ohio: Bowling Green State University Popular Press, 1980),* 203–09.

given time-frame. For instance, MacDonald's "'The Foreigner' in Juvenile Series Fiction, 1900–1945" covers several decades of popular fiction which the author claims projects "the picture of a detached and self-assured America."[2] The study makes no attempt to put this literature into a cultural context—to correlate this fiction with other kinds of fiction or entertainment that the same audiences might also have enjoyed, or to assess or speculate about how this more or less static picture of America could appeal to audiences whose other experience included two world wars and a depression. MacDonald's essay is similar to obscure antiquarian studies about out-of-the-way places now largely forgotten—work of interest to the narrow specialist (which of course has genuine though limited value) but not to the historian whose interest is to discover and interpret significant evidence and ideas. In a case like R. Serge Denis-off's "Death Songs and Teenage Roles," an interesting idea is mentioned but never closely examined: "Coffin songs . . . may have . . . lessened the dysfunctional psychological costs of passage for the adolescent."[3] This notion offers a perspective on the songs which claims for them an importance beyond mere synchronic popularity; Denisoff's study does not quite achieve the status of a *diachronic* popular culture study which it might if this larger cultural context were examined and coffin songs of great popularity related to other sorts of experience which were enabling in the same way for adolescents.

Lest my attitude seem unduly harsh, let me acknowledge that we owe much to antiquarians and that they should be encouraged in their work—they have and will preserve evidence which others once thought worthless but now find valuable. We owe the existence of many medieval English manuscripts to antiquarians who saved them during the dissolution of the monasteries in the sixteenth century. (About some poems in one Anglo-Saxon manuscript, more later.) The contemporary popular culture scholarly endeavor will be instrumental in preserving and cataloging the records and artifacts of commonplace leisure activities of industrial society. But the development of a theory or theories about this mass of evidence and about popular culture in general is necessary; otherwise we will have a storehouse without a proper set of keys.

Theorists have taken some pains to distinguish popular culture from other forms of culture—elite, mass and folk cultures usually round out the paradigm.[4] These distinctions are not very convincing, at least to me, because they do not take into account the fact that one person may participate in all sorts of cultural activity. Indeed, it could be argued reasonably (though this is not the place to do so) that the complete citizen of a given society would be able to enjoy all forms of culture (perhaps this is what a liberal education really provides). In this regard we need popular culture studies of a demographic nature which demonstrate the range of cultural activity of all or some part of the United States. It is possible— though perhaps not politically practicable—that a few questions on the census forms would provide at least a rough estimate of our total national cultural profile. My assumption is that people get as much of and as various a cultural experience as possible; the limitations are not so much personal as institutional or questions of access. For instance, there are the recent popular exhibits at museums: grave goods from the People's Republic of China and from Egypt, and a new and popular exhibit about Pompeii in Boston. Under the leadership of Thomas Hoving, New York's sleepy Metropolitan Museum has become the city's number one tourist attraction. This is not to say that many, indeed most of those who enjoy the museums do not also watch their fair share of TV, follow professional sports, listen to the Top Fifty songs, and read sensational novels with zeal.

Perhaps part of our difficulty in using the paradigm of elite/popular/mass/folk culture is that we have to tinker with it every time we use it—we define and redefine these four pigeon-holes so that we can sort things out to suit ourselves. It is not embarrassing to say that our paradigm of culture looks like a Rube Goldberg cartoon if we recall that Thomas S. Kuhn, in his seminal works *The Copernical Revolution* and *The Structure of Scientific Revolutions,* reminds us that the paradigm provided by a Ptolemaic idea of the universe was an embarrassment to scientists long before the Copernican paradigm gained its popularity.[5] Although I cannot claim Copernican insight (nor is popular culture theory so grand a conception), I do suggest that we consider a new paradigm by which we first view all culture as one expression of a given society's leisure needs and opportunities, and then distinguish degrees of popularity along two axes: synchronic and diachronic. The optimal study generated by this paradigm would attempt to be precise about popularity and to see the phenomenon under consideration in *both* a synchronic and a diachronic context.

For instance one calculation which such a paradigm could provide would contrast two cultural phenomena which can be proven highly popular in quite different ways: a highly synchronic popular phenomenon such as the film *Star Wars* or the novel *Uncle Tom's Cabin,* and a highly diachronic popular phenomenon such as Homer's *Odyssey* or the Bible. It is quite possible that more people attended movie houses to view *Star Wars* for a certain period of time than read the *Odyssey* in that same span. Yet I think it is reasonable to assume that the total readership of Homer's poem since it was written down (it would probably be exponentially larger if we include all its audiences for oral delivery) will equal or even exceed the audience of the movie. Not only that, but these two phenomena have different futures: I assume that *Star Wars* will drop out and claim *per se* only antiquarian interest as a strictly synchronic cultural phenomenon, while the

Odyssey will continue to draw a steady if unspectacular audience. This example suggests others, for instance, a play of Shakespeare compared to the once-popular TV show *Gunsmoke.*

Another aspect of popular culture studies in which we could improve is the question of audience. It is profitless to read an analysis of popular culture in which the scholar attempts to discover the character of the audience which does in fact enjoy that certain form of leisure. For a hypothetical example or two, you do not have to be a racist to laugh at a racist like Archie Bunker, any more than you have to be demonic to be fascinated with Milton's Satan in *Paradise Lost.* It is true in both cases that your taste—your preference for certain kinds of culture—must include some provision for representations of evil in various settings (Queens Borough and Hell respectively). Although you do not have to be evil yourself, you have to recognize evil and accept representations of it in your leisure activities.

But in any case it is impossible to prove that the writers who created Archie Bunker or the John Milton who created a memorable Satan sized up a specific real audience. In a recent seminal article, Walter Ong's "The Writer's Audience Is Always a Fiction," literary study has been freed from a useless notion about audience and provided with a potentially powerful one.[6] To simplify Ong's idea, in addition to other aspects of the work of art, the author creates a possible audience for his work which is implicit in it. As readers, it then follows, part of our act of attention is to identify this audience, or as much of it as we can, although we do not necessarily have to identify *with* it. In so far as we can accommodate our taste—our own culture—to this fictive audience, we can enjoy the work of art. Such identification and accommodation does not necessarily imply approval of the values implicit in the work of art. For instance, it is entirely possible that someone may have sat through all nine hours of the recent TV marathon narrative *Holocaust* and still maintained anti-Semitic values, although it was plain (at least to this observer) that the fictive audience was supposed to be pro-Semitic. Be that as it may, the notion that literary works, and by extension all works of art, large and small, contain an implicit fictive audience as an integral part of their structure, possesses great potential for cultural studies, including popular ones.

On the basis of a fictive audience we may sketch out a few differences between a synchronic and a diachronic popular culture phenomenon. For instance, a synchronic phenomenon will have a fictive audience with topical or contemporary features—an interest in World War II, or the Trojan War. A diachronic phenomenon will have a fictive audience that includes both a topical and an aesthetic feature which expands the topical feature to typical or mythic proportions. (Here I postulate Brecht's notion that the mythic is the typical.) In other words, the diachronic cultural phenomenon contains a fictive audience which, while focused on a topic, perceives this topic in some larger context or contexts—philosophical, moral, social, intellectual, political, religious and so forth. It is possible to speculate that there may be some direct connection between the complexity of the contextual relations of a diachronic phenomenon and its popularity—why Homer is more popular than Pindar, why Dickens more than Henry James, why T. S. Eliot more than Ezra Pound, could so be explained. These works of durable popularity might be described by the Latin word *altus,* which means both high and deep. If in the case of a synchronic phenomenon the contextual relations are weak, then the attraction of the fictive audience will be directly related to the currency and novelty of its topic. If, as in the case of *Gunsmoke,* the contextual relation was with a simple law-and-order morality, the topic of cowboy life will soon be stale, and another will be sought to replace it. The cowboy will be replaced by the policeman, although the contextual relation may still be to a simple law-and-order morality. In this case, the diachronic study of TV shows will reveal an interesting similarity between the synchronic cowboy and cop shows—a shared feature in both fictive audiences, a link between two decades of TV programming. And of course, from this point, some popular culture studies would begin to make inferences about the morality of the TV audience, as if the fictive and the real audiences were identical, which would be a serious error. Only an aesthete like John Ruskin would hazard the notion that if you tell me what you like I will tell you who you are; it is an interesting weapon in polemics, one of Ruskin's special skills to be certain, but is not useful in careful scholarly studies. Some connections can be made, of course, between a fictive and a real audience, but these connections are difficult to identify and require vast interdisciplinary skill which we have yet to develop.

In the case of the largely synchronic phenomena which appear on TV, we need to be very aware of the features of even the least distinguished program's fictive audience because they tell us a good deal about the mediators. Analysis of fictive audiences can reveal with some precision the attitudes of the mediators. There is already some provocative theoretical thinking on the role of the mediators in mass media—those in charge of writing and producing the TV, radio and film programs, although much the same could probably be perceived about the editors and writers of the newspapers and magazines.[7] One must recognize that, in the case of print media, the real audience is always much more independent than with film, radio and TV. There is a vastly larger selection of reading material than there is of visual stuff; the reader is much more in charge of his cultural schedule than the viewer, or will be so until the cost of video production and portable video recorders lowers considerably.

Even so, given the pressures which are applied to TV programming, and taking into account Ong's insight about the fictive audience, a rather interesting picture of the TV audience begins to come into focus. This image contrasts with the cliché of the TV viewer as a mindless automaton, since it suggests a sophisticated awareness for many viewers. Since the preoccupations of the mediators will be reflected in the fictive audiences they create for their shows, and since the mediators will be preoccupied to some degree with meeting the demands of the powerful corporations which support the entertainment industry through advertisements, the TV audience is able to identify the values of the powerful members of their society (the ruling class, if you will) through the fictive audiences of the TV shows. There is an operation here analogous to allegory. That the ruling class might like the real TV audience to *identify with*—to become—the fictive audience is probably true, since the real audience would become much more manageable. But there is no evidence which demonstrates that the real audience has given up its own variety of identities for the fictive one. This does not exclude the possibility that the TV shows are a means—perhaps a principal one—by which the ruling class and the ruled classes communicate. If this is true, the official ratings of TV show popularity provide a kind of response to the messages contained in the fictive audience.

In this case, diachronic studies of TV would focus on a wide selection of synchronic successes—all public order shows, all situation comedies, all quiz shows, all news shows, etc. We could begin to trace out this indirect means of communication, showing what the powerful wanted to communicate and to some degree which part of their message the TV audience accepted.

An assumption that lurks behind any argument for including, say, Shakespeare in the popular culture camp is that his plays enjoyed initial synchronic success. Shakespeare, it is well known, was a successful businessman as well as an accomplished artist. Similar assumptions apply to Dickens; for poems composed in an oral-formulaic tradition (Homer's epics and *Beowulf,* for example) there is growing evidence that poetic composing ability is popular rather than 'elite' in those societies where it thrives.[8] Yet a good number of diachronic popular works had a rather modest beginning: John Donne's poetry, *Moby Dick,* the paintings of the Impressionists, and of course anything interesting you reclaim from a gravesite—no one in China or Egypt was supposed to stroll through the tombs of the wealthy to enjoy the magnificent artwork!

Although the causes for the eventual diachronic success of these slow-starters are complex and deserve full treatment elsewhere, it seems obvious that in every case a so-called elite not only discovered the artwork but also promoted its popularity rather than keeping the treasures to themselves. While the specialists in literature, art and archaeology can tell us much about metaphor or brush-stroke or the construction of a jade funeral gown, it is the specialists in popular culture who can explain why twentieth-century audiences were able to recognize the fictive audiences of these works; such a task probably requires expertise in the subject to which the work belongs as well as in the theory or theories of popular culture, which are still evolving. . . .

Notes

1. See essays by Bigsby, Williams, Barbu, Burke, Kress, Hodge and Craig in *Approaches to Popular Culture,* ed. by C. W. E. Bigsby (London: Arnold, and Bowling Green, OH: Bowling Green State University Popular Press, 1976); see essays by Browne and Rollin in *Theories and Methodologies in Popular Culture,* ed. by Ray B. Browne, et al. (Bowling Green State University Popular Press); and see essays by Browne and Nye in *The Popular Culture Reader,* ed. by Jack Nachbar and John L. Wright (Bowling Green State University Popular Press, 1977).

2. J. Frederick MacDonald, "'The Foreigner' in Juvenile Series Fiction, 1900–1945," *Popular Culture Reader,* 125–39.

3. R. Serge Denisoff, "Death Songs and Teenage Roles," *Popular Culture Reader,* 116–24.

4. Ray B. Browne, "Popular Culture: Notes Toward a Definition," *Popular Culture Reader,* 1–9; Russel B. Nye, "Notes for a Rationale for Popular Culture," *Popular Culture Reader,* 10–16.

5. T. S. Kuhn, *The Copernican Revolution: Planetary Astronomy in the Development of Western Thought* (Cambridge: Harvard University Press, 1957), and *The Structure of Scientific Revolutions* (International Encyclopedia of Unified Science, Vol. II, No.2) (Chicago: University of Chicago Press, 1962; 2d enlarged edition, 1970).

6. Walter J. Ong, S.J., "The Writer's Audience Is Always a Fiction," *PMLA,* 90 (1975): 9–21.

7. Raymond Williams, "Communications as Cultural Science," *Approaches to Popular Culture,* 27–38, and Stuart Hood, "The Dilemma of the Communicators," *Approaches to Popular Culture,* 201–12.

8. *The Making of Homeric Verse: The Collected Papers of Milman Parry,* ed. by Adam Parry (Oxford: Clarendon, 1970); Albert B. Lord, *The Singer of Tales* (1960; rpt. New York: Athenaeum, 1965); Jeff Opland, "*Scop* and *Imbongi:* Anglo-Saxon and Bantu Oral Poets," *English Studies in Africa* 14 (1971): 161–78, and "*Imbongi Nezibongo:* The Xhosa Tribal Poet and Contemporary Poetic Tradition," *PMLA,* 90 (1975): 185–208; F. P. Magoun, Jr., "Oral-Formulaic Character of Anglo-Saxon Poetry," *Speculum,* 28 (1953): 446–67; and S. B. Greenfield, "The Formulaic Expression of the Theme of 'Exile' in Anglo-Saxon Poetry," *Speculum,* 30 (1955): 200–06.

ON THE NATURE AND FUNCTIONS OF POPULAR CULTURE

Gary L. Harmon

Harmon defines popular culture by comparing and contrasting it with elite culture. What is the essence of each? How do their creators and consumers differ? Yet, he argues that there is a cultural continuum stretching from the strictly popular on one end, through cultural products sharing, in varying degrees, characteristics of the popular and elite, to the strictly highbrow. Finally, Harmon lists and briefly discusses the many different ways that popular culture "help[s] people enjoy life and refine it." Harmon is Professor of Language and Literature at the University of North Florida.

The study of any subject requires an understanding of its nature and functions. This is especially true of efforts to describe, explain, analyze, and interpret the meaning and importance of any popular culture experience.[1] Though Americans spend billions of dollars on popular entertainments and products, and though millions share popular experiences, stories, and beliefs, only in the last fifteen years or so has popular culture become the object of serious study for college and university scholars and students. Perhaps this neglect has resulted from widespread attitudes that popular culture is "mere" entertainment or "just" a commercial enterprise or "only" a phenomenon without "depth" or "seriousness"—and thus is not worthy of the kinds of critical thinking that colleges and universities are supposed to foster. Too often, even scholars have succumbed to the easy temptation to judge popular culture in elitist aesthetic, moral, or political terms that are anathema to objective analysis.[2]

While much of popular culture does entertain, is commercial, or lacks "depth," this does not mean that its serious study shares these traits. Because of the sheer popularity of popular culture, its study helps students and scholars learn what Americans are thinking, their hopes and fears, dreams and anxieties. What people are willing to share and consume is a key to their views and values, and to their unconsciously held beliefs and tensions. To study popular culture is therefore to study what we are as a people as well

Gary L. Harmon, "On the Nature and Functions of Popular Culture," Studies in Popular Culture *6 (1983): 3–15.*

as what we as individuals absorb from the culture at large. Such study is as complex and serious an enterprise as any available in academia.

This essay is an effort to provide an explanation of the nature and functions of popular culture as understood by many scholars in this emerging field. The goal of popular culture study is a better understanding of what we as participants in mass culture believe, fear, hope for, and gain or lose as a result of that participation and of how we "process" and use popular culture in our private and public lives. Thus, when anyone studies some part of popular culture, whether it is a comic book hero, a fad, a sports event, or an advertisement, several questions repeatedly arise: What is its meaning and importance? "Why do people do, make, sell, and buy popular culture? . . . How are [popular culture products and activities] structured? How are they done, made, or consumed? What is their history and development?"[3] Asking such questions leads to insights into the values, convictions, or patterns of thought generally dispersed through and approved by society.

The Nature of Popular Culture

Popular culture may be defined as consisting of the arts, rituals and events, myths and beliefs, and artifacts widely shared by a significant portion of a group of people at a specific time.[4] These basic ingredients of a culture include language (even gestures), customs, mores, values, attitudes, ideas, knowledge, and other acquired capabilities, for these embody beliefs and are often expressed in rituals, artifacts or the arts. They are typical experiences. They are what a large number of people generally use, purchase, enjoy, or practice. To study particular popular artifacts or events is a way of examining the broader culture itself. Whenever anyone watches TV, goes to a pro football game, reads an advertisement to select soap or suit or salt, helps elect a homecoming queen, dates, eats at McDonald's, reads a best seller, makes a common gesture, shops in a mall, attends a rock concert or a circus, he or she is participating in some form of popular culture. To study such an experience, one may focus on the people who share the experience, on the features of the phenomenon itself, or on its possible effects upon participants.[5]

Popular culture is usually contrasted with its assumed nemesis (since the eighteenth century) elite culture, and with its non-commercial counterpart, folk culture. Both popular and elite culture differ significantly from folk culture, which we can sort to the side by identifying its major characteristics. First, folk culture is non-commercial and created by anonymous amateurs. Second, folk culture is circulated orally, if it is not material; if it is, the knowledge of how to create that material is passed on orally. Third, the purpose of folk culture is mainly to improve on the living situation, whether the item is a song, a saying, a musical instrument, a farming tool, a quilt or a piece of clothing, or a story. Fourth, the folk involved are often "unschooled" in the ways of elite or popular culture or resist them (though folk culture has been mainly rural, now urban folk culture—among blacks or immigrant sections of a city—also abounds). Fifth, the standard used to judge a folk object or song or custom or saying is simply whether it is adopted and circulated among the folk by the folk. Finally, the creators of folk culture are generally unconscious of creating something others will use, though they generally work within the traditions of a group of which they are a part. Some key words to describe "folkstyle" are: oral, traditional, "un-schooled," continuous, homespun, earthy, improvised, community-oriented. While this description is incomplete, it serves to differentiate folk from popular and elite culture.

The features of popular culture and elite culture clarify each other, mainly because of the historical development of a popular culture from the late eighteenth century as a reaction to an elite culture, for in that period an increased technology, literacy, and standard of living generated a middle class that made popular culture possible. While the division of society and its arts into "upper" and "lower" had existed from the early days of Greece, the eighteenth century, with its burgeoning population that spread from Europe to America or concentrated in the cities was the basis for a "huge market for entertainment, with identifiable desires and responses."[6] After the revolution diluted the authority of the upper classes, education and literacy among the middle class begat an audience that began to develop its own tastes and standards. "Control of the means of cultural production and transmission passed from the previously privileged elite to the urbanized, democratized middle classes."[7]

Evolution toward a society dominated by a literate middle class has not been abated, and with that evolution have come more leisure time and more disposable income to expend on popular culture. Modern technology, from cheap, high-speed printing to radio, film, TV and computer-transmission of light and sound, has brought about not only ever-larger audiences but also more creators of popular culture experiences. Those new artists and producers for the popular market have adapted devices and patterns from both folk and elite sources to fulfill the desires of the general public. The arrival of popular culture also entailed a shift from the patronage provided by the upper classes to "the support offered by a huge, virtually unlimited, middle class audience, within the context of great technological, social, and political change."[8] Because of its clear importance to modern society and because it reflects people's (mostly) unconsciously held values and beliefs, serious study of this important democratized, urbanized, industrialized culture is vital.

Though popular and elite culture interact strongly today, there remain significant differences between them:

Popular Culture	**Elite Culture**
• more formulaic, standardized, mass produced, mainly commercial	• more "inventional," often implicitly critical of popular formulas through irony or satire; is both commercial and noncommercial
• standards of excellence not well-defined: success measured by popularity	• standards of excellence defined by persons with credentials (education, taste, etc.); success measured by critical or scholarly reception
• purpose is more to entertain than to enlighten—to meet audience needs and desires	• purpose is more to edify, enlighten, criticize, raise consciousness than to entertain—to meet refined needs and desires of an audience

MacDonald's restaurant architecture and food, the western TV series *Gunsmoke,* the film *Star Wars,* or light beer are all thus part of popular culture. Elite culture counterparts for these examples include, in turn, a one-of-a-kind fashionable French restaurant, the western novel *The Ox-Bow Incident,* Ingmar Bergman's film *The Seventh Seal,* or a fine wine whose year and region are bases for its selection. *Gunsmoke* entertains and light beer meets people's "needs" (to slake thirst without too noticeable a taste or alcoholic or calorie content). This is true even though some social "enlightenment" about right and wrong enters into that TV series and even though beer connoisseurs claim to detect taste differences among the various beers. By contrast, *The Ox-Bow Incident* takes the standard law and order issue of the formula western plot and twists it until ambiguous questions of justice and the death of an innocent man at the hands of "good" citizens become the central features of the book. Though this book was somewhat widely read, its "inventional" character (reversing the standard western formula), its positive critical reception among critics and scholars, and its primary purpose to enlighten while trying to entertain identifies it as an example of elite culture. Finally, a fine wine is designed to satisfy a demanding taste, one that depends on knowledge and experience (education)—unlike popular light beer.

The creators of popular and elite culture, like their creations, contrast in several ways:

Popular Culture Creator	**Elite Culture Creator**
• usually aware of receivers' predispositions and seems to reinforce or appeal to them	• usually aware of receivers' predispositions, sometimes to criticize and dislodge them
• professional, in comparison to folk creators who are amateurs; often a member of a "team" of experts	• professional, working more as an individual team than as a "team" member

It is important to consider the motivations and aims which figure in the creation of a cultural artifact. If the creator of a beer advertisement wants to make that beer popular to women, he will try to appeal to them by reinforcing a need associated with most women in the market group—perhaps a wish to remain slim and attractive yet join men in the beer drinking. The creator's packaging and marketing strategy will tend to appeal to such "needs."

Mystery novelists know that readers expect to be puzzled and confused at the outset of the crime novel, and then to be enlightened by the detective whose superior, magician-like intelligence organizes details and stabilizes the society (and the readers' minds) once again. Readers come to understand unconsciously that the logical, rational mind is the "best" one and that the criminal, often a rich person, is aberrant or depraved or even unhappy because of the leisured life money brings. Our commonly held prejudices and predispositions are thus reinforced. On the other hand, an elite work of fiction such as Joseph Heller's *Catch 22,* presumably a novel about war and how it is conducted, fits no formula for war novels. Its story pattern and its action are radically critical of American popular ideas about a range of topics, from war to military to love to capitalism to patriotism. Heller is quite conscious of our common sentiments on such topics and writes to criticize and dislodge them. Still, *Catch 22* is an example of a novel that, while exhibiting elite culture characteristics, became popular when millions of readers found that its critique of American society matched their own feelings.

Still another aspect of popular culture involves its participants:

Popular Culture Participants	**Elite Culture Participants**
• diverse, without a special sense of location in a social hierarchy	• self-conscious of who and where they are, particularly in relation to education, taste, and lifestyle
• a large number—a significant part of society	• number is relatively small percentage of the population, in most cases
• educational level varies; participant can enjoy the experience at different levels of sophistication	• educational level is relatively high, required to enjoy the experience at all of its levels

These characteristics suggest that the participants in popular culture might well include the aerospace engineer, the professor, the insurance executive, or the lawyer, who join the construction worker, the secretary, the plumber, and all their children to enjoy comics, circuses, a TV melodrama, a bowl football game, a wrestling match, or "Pac-Man." People from all "taste groups" *can* share in a popular culture event because it requires little preparation or sophistication to appreciate. Popular culture can thus refer to culture that "crosses class lines to become part of the lifestyle of all classes or subcultures in a particular society."[9]

One can also think of popular culture participants as members of non-elite sub-cultures, such as middle-class culture, teenage culture, counter culture, or working-class culture. All such cultures are taste cultures that "consist of values" and their forms (consumer goods, music, art, designs, news) embody political and aesthetic values.[10] The study of sub-cultures, important to students and scholars, may lead one to examine a best-selling novel or a fad that is popular with middle-class culture but not to other cultures because of cost or educational levels that the novel or fad requires. By carefully noting the cultural group associated with the object of study, the analysts will limit their conclusions about the meaning and importance of the phenomenon to that group.

Elite culture participants, by contrast, are fewer, less diverse, and more sophisticated in their approach to different cultural events or phenomena. Whatever their occupational, educational, or economic origins, these persons may eschew rock or country music for classical music, the opera, or progressive jazz; they may enjoy backgammon or bridge tournaments, games requiring skills and mental acumen, a novel by William Gass, an avant-garde ballet, or a lecture on classical myths. Thus, the diversity, size and sophistication level of their respective participant groups will differentiate elite and popular cultures from each other. The contrast may be so great that an untutored observer might think, wrongly, that a) there must be a "high" culture and a "low" (bad) culture, one that raises human consciousness on the one hand and lowers it on the other and b) that these cultural modes serve different purposes.

In fact, many of us can and do engage in a range of experiences along the cultural continuum, sometimes as part of a large heterogeneous mass audience and sometimes in the more restricted company of participants in elite culture—or in a sub-culture. This continuum might be visualized as follows:

Popular Culture	**Elite Culture**
A coke bottle	*Catch 22*
"I Want to Hold Your Hand"	*The Nutcracker Suite*
Mickey Mouse	*The Ox-Bow Incident*
MacDonald's architecture	*King Lear*
The Sound of Music	*The Sound and the Fury*
Disney World	Ruins of ancient Rome
Tarzan of the Apes	*Le Coq d'Or*
The Mary Tyler Moore Show	Rheims Cathedral
A Fistful of Dollars	Henry Moore's "Family Group"
Disco	*Le Sacre du Printemps*
M.A.S.H.	Grecian Urn

The point of this continuum is a significant and simple one, often missed: We participate in a complex culture that contains a variety of taste cultures. Moreover, in such participation, we use *all* modes of culture to satisfy our particular needs, desires, and tastes at a given moment. That any particular cultural experience can be shown to be qualitatively "superior" to another, then, is extremely doubtful. Contrary to widespread opinion, no reliable evidence exists to show that popular culture does harm to its adult participants. As Herbert J. Gans argues, it probably "goes in one eye and out the other." While it probably does no harm, it can do a great deal of good. By and large, experiences in both popular and elite taste cultures generally function in similar ways; they help people enjoy life and refine it.

Functions of Popular Culture
In virtually all discussions of popular culture items or experiences, scholars and students explore their subjects' functions. Their implied ques-

tion—How does X function in the lives of its participants?—is fundamental. Still, no full-length examination of popular culture functions exists. The subject is perhaps too ambitious, for one thing: Cultural experiences are so many and so diverse, and they function in so many ways that they elude the analysts' firm grasp. One can nevertheless identify several major functions of culture, whether popular or elite. While popular culture functions in many ways in our lives, it is not, as more and more scholars are recognizing, merely "entertainment"—amusement, distraction—though entertain it quite often does. What is more, like elite culture, which also entertains, popular culture functions in a number of positive ways, which too many people have overlooked.

Few would deny that popular culture reflects popular mores and attitudes. In so doing, it serves to *reinforce the existing cultural attitudes and lifeways,* thus functioning as a form of social control. Melodramas, for example, have as one of their main features an implied morality that reflects middle America's moral conservatism. They show forth "the essential 'rightness' of the world order."[11] Mystery and detection stories reinforce those logical thinking processes so important to an industrial society.

Popular culture also *provides role models.* Society's standards for good and bad behavior or for the best selves that persons might be are acted out in our books, TV shows, advertising, films, comics, sports, and arts. Social stability and positive behaviors are thus encouraged in the millions who, without role models, would have difficulty identifying with the values and practices that make a mass society work. Sports heroes, news announcers, film stars, major politicans, and the like, when they become genuinely popular figures, find that they must live role-model lives or suffer the consequences. Sensitive to changing mores, popular culture is also a means by which society can *introduce new role models.* For example, it was through the various mass media that many Americans were first introduced to the idea of the liberated woman and began to understand her better as a role model.

Each age produces its own real and fictional heroes: "Lucky Lindbergh" at the end of the twenties, Superman and Batman in the Depression, "Ike" Eisenhower in the forties and fifties, *M.A.S.H.*'s "Hawkeye" during the sixties and seventies. By its attention to hero-figures, popular culture becomes a major means for *introducing new values, attitudes, or lifestyles.* It is easy to think that new attitudes toward family or community, for example, just "happened naturally," but it is through popular culture that the emphasis upon "togetherness" or companionship has been promoted in an age that has increasingly isolated the individual. Such ideas as those of interracial cooperation, "small is beautiful," or living within nature rather than continuing to abuse it have been promulgated rapidly throughout our culture by means of various popular culture carriers. Popular culture thereby not only reflects our values and beliefs but makes us aware of new ones, thus creating opportunities for increased collective and individual growth and development.[12]

Another way in which popular culture often helps the individual as well as society is through what might be regarded as its consciousness-raising capacity. Certainly, much of popular culture *edifies with information or through imaginative constructs* that mirror a real world of one kind or another. Anyone can recall TV shows, magazines, tours of houses or museums, novels, films, events such as circuses, or attractions such as Sea World that (consciously or unconsciously) introduce its participants to ideas, attitudes, myths, or phenomena. The mythic power of Sea World to inspire awe and even gratitude in spectators as they witness man's mastery over raw nature in the form of the killer whale and the porpoise is but one example of how imaginative constructs are constantly a part of commercial entertainment. Theme parks, EPCOT, Cape Kennedy, Disneyland—these too edify the participants in various conscious and unconscious ways. Popular fiction often contains information that is accurate and useful: John D. MacDonald, for example, has included within his Travis McGee novels well-researched information, ranging from CPR methods to an exposé of the menace of religious cults.

Another consciousness-raising function of popular culture, particularly notable in science fiction, is its tendency to *project possible futures* based on present behaviors and practices. H. G. Wells' *War of the Worlds,* for example, tells the story of the result of a projected Martian invasion, but, by implication, predicts apocalyptic disasters if Western countries continue their imperialist practices. Hundreds of such novels, films, and TV shows project possible futures to excite our imagination and to enlighten our consciousness so we might consider the possible disastrous consequences of present practices and attitudes.

Popular culture consciousness-raising sometimes involves *simplifying complex issues* for an audience that otherwise would not even be aware of an issue or might not be interested in following its finer points; nuclear catastrophe, the effects of religious cults on the young, how the world makes oil and who controls it—all have been treated in popular culture. The "popularization" of complex matters is a process often (and easily) maligned by experts, but in a world where no one can be an expert in everything, such popularization often represents the only opportunity most people have to try to understand the issues and events that affect them. The kind of simplifying, edifying, or predicting popular culture provides may help society survive with greater social stability and harmony through shared consciousness.

Popular culture can also offer a kind of comfort and security to the individual, thus performing a *therapeutic function.* Personal and social *tensions and misunderstandings that arise from ambiguous attitudes can often be resolved* by popular culture. For instance, the western novel, through its action of "legitimized" violence, not only affirms the ideology of individualism but also resolves tensions between the anarchy of individualistic impulses and communal ideals of law and order. It does so by making the individual's action an ultimate defense of the community against the threat of anarchy.[13] Another therapeutic use of popular culture is to *mediate between the unwelcome contradictions of our lives,* as the Tarzan character mediates between nature and the demands of civilization or as TV's Columbo mediates between, among several things, the conspicuous consumption represented by the villains and the implied fear of impoverishment which we all feel.[14]

Other therapeutic functions of popular culture include the sort of *aid to emotional and social growth* that, as an example, children's fairy tales, provide. Many such tales help children move from one level of consciousness, guided by "the pleasure principle," to a more adult level, guided by "the reality principle."[15] Then, too, some popular literature, art, and events *provide a guilt-free release of our repressed aggressions.* Our culture offers many examples, from Dirty Harry films to the organized violence of boxing or football or Dick Tracy comics where, amid a simplistic moral universe, Tracy solves crimes by the violent removal of the evil.[16]

Not far removed from this cathartic function is the one in which popular culture helps participants to *"explore the boundary between the permitted and the forbidden and to experience in a carefully controlled way the possibility of stepping across that boundary."*[17] Such has always been the function of popular erotica, from stag movies to spicy novels. For example, the popular novel and film by James M. Cain, *The Postman Always Rings Twice,* explores the dangerous ground of illicit love and a murder to establish it free and clear of social restrictions. Characters in such formulaic literature express and explore actions which are taboo, but which are strongly tempting to many individuals. In this way, certain kinds of popular culture experiences can *put us in touch with our repressed selves,* with that side of our physical personality that society would deny or cause us to suppress, at possible risk to our mental health.[18] Horror films such as *Dracula,* violent detective stories, even mildly titillating films, books, and magazines can accomplish the same purpose. They function as expressions of and socially acceptable stimuli for the full range of emotions we contain.

In spite of the many positive uses it shares with elite culture, questions about the effects of popular culture continue to be raised. Critics still ask "Isn't popular culture harmful because it drives out 'good [elite] stuff'?" They seem to fail to notice that all the "high" arts, from opera to ballet to sculpture to the publication of poetry are flourishing now, in the era of popular culture, as never before. Obviously, a large and complex society needs many sources of edification, attitude reinforcement or changing, issue presentation, and the like. Though much of the discussion in this essay has stressed the consciousness-altering functions of popular culture, through its capacity to project powerful myths or to edify with information and imaginative constructs, much of popular culture still serves to *criticize or put in perspective* various behavior and attitudes. The critique may not always be deep or broad when given expression in popular novels, hit movies, comics, or situation comedies, as examples, but it is criticism nevertheless, and serves to increase the scrutiny of the real and the ideal.

The nature and functions of popular culture then can be various and complex. The study of popular culture can be seen to offer revelations about matters such as the myths that drive us: the unconscious tensions and contradictions that bedevil us: our assumptions about the human condition, the nature of man and society, and the nature of the good life: the ways we are moved from one level of knowledge, awareness, or consciousness to another; and the kinds of messages our society communicates to our unconscious. Understanding such matters helps us comprehend how the individual and society interact and evolve. Popular culture can thus be life-affirming and life-enhancing. And its study can be a productive response to the Socratic admonition—"Know Thyself"—and to its corollary—"Know Thy Society."

Notes

1. This goal is carefully worded. See for background Roger Rollin's "Against Evaluation: The Role of the Critic of Popular Culture," *Journal of Popular Culture,* 9.2 (Fall 1975). As Rollin asserts, "The only possible functions of the teacher and serious student of Popular Culture are *description* and *interpretation*—'illumination,' in short." This, an effort to avoid personal moral, aesthetic, or political preferences in scholarly examinations of popular culture, led to further arguments in two articles: John Shelton Lawrence's "A Critical Analysis of Roger B. Rollin's 'Against Evaluation'" and "Son of 'Against Evaluation': A Reply to John Shelton Lawrence," *Journal of Popular Culture,* 12.1 (Summer 1978): 99–113 and 114–17.

2. A fine discussion of the mass culture critique appears in Herbert J. Gans' *Popular Culture: An Analysis and Evaluation of Taste* (New York: Basic Books, 1974). Another, more sharply worded account of elitist aesthetics appears in Ray B. Browne's "Up from Elitism: The Aesthetics of Popular Fiction," *Studies in American Fiction,* 9.2 (Fall 1981): 217–31. A third, more oblique account of mistaken assumptions in popular culture criticism is Leslie Fiedler's *What Was Literature? Class Culture and Mass Society* (New York: Simon and Schuster, 1982).

Also, see Thomas M. Kando's "What Is Popular Culture and Is It Good Culture?" *Leisure and Popular Culture in Transition* (St. Louis: C. V. Mosby, 1975), 39–62. No review of such discussion would be complete without reference to Russell B. Nye's "Notes for an Introduction to a Discussion of Popular Culture," *Journal of Popular Culture* (Spring 1971): 1032–38.

3. Russell B. Nye, "Notes for a Discussion of Popular Culture," unpublished manuscript.

4. See extended discussion of the definition in the "Introduction" to the *Popular Culture Reader,* edited by Jack Nachbar, Deborah Weiser, and John L. Wright (Bowling Green, OH: Bowling Green State University Popular Press, 1978); in Ray B. Browne's "Popular Culture—The World Around Us," *Popular Culture and Curricula* (Bowling Green, OH: Bowling Green State University Popular Press, 1974); in John G. Cawelti's "Recent Trends in the Study of Popular Culture," *American Studies: An International Newsletter* (Winter 1971): 23–37; and in the Herbert J. Gans and Russell B. Nye works cited in the note Two.

5. The important matter of methodology is the focus of Lawrence J. Mintz's helpful essay later in this issue.

6. Russell B. Nye, "The Popular Arts and the Popular Audience," *The Unembarrassed Muse: The Popular Arts in America* (New York: Dial Press, 1970). This source includes a short history of popular culture. Another, more extended source is Leo Lowenthal's "An Historical Preface to the Popular Culture Debate," in Norman Jacob's *Culture for the Millions* (Princeton, NJ: Princeton University Press, 1961), 23–42.

7. Nye, "The Popular Arts and the Popular Audience."

8. Ibid.

9. John G. Cawelti, "Recent Trends in the Study of Popular Culture," 24.

10. For a valuable extended discussion of taste cultures, see Herbert J. Gans' *Popular Culture and High Culture,* 9–15.

11. John G. Cawelti, *Adventure, Mystery, and Romance* (Chicago: University of Chicago Press, 1978), 45.

12. For a cogent discussion of how myth works in stimulating action in a culture, see Cecil F. Tate's "American Cultural Home," *Smith's Virgin Land, The Search for a Method in American Studies* (Minneapolis: University of Minnesota Press, 1973), 47–54, which is a critique of Henry Nash Smith's apparent assumptions about the working of myth in a culture in his *Virgin Land: The American West as Symbol and Myth* (1950).

13. For this function and example, I am indebted to John G. Cawelti's *Adventure, Mystery, and Romance,* 36.

14. A discussion of this function appears in Gary L. Harmon's "Tarzan and Columbo, Heroic Mediators," *The Hero in Transition,* Marshall Fishwick and Ray B. Browne, eds. (Bowling Green, OH: Bowling Green State University Popular Press, 1983).

15. See, for an example, Bruno Bettelheim's *The Uses of Enchantment: The Meaning of Fairy Tales* (New York: Alfred A. Knopf, 1975).

16. For an exemplary discussion of this function, see Arthur Asa Berger's *The Comic Stripped American* (Baltimore, MD: Penguin Books, 1973) in the essay on Dick Tracy.

17. John G. Cawelti, *Adventure, Mystery, and Romance,* 35.

18. An inimitable discussion of this function appears in Leslie Fiedler's "Giving the Devil His Due," *Journal of Popular Culture,* 12.2 (Fall 1979): 197–207. The best example of this idea at book length is Fiedler's *Freaks: Myths and Images of the Secret Self* (New York: Simon and Schuster, 1978).

POPULAR CULTURE AS THE NEW HUMANITIES

Ray B. Browne

What constitutes "the humanities" is a topic contested not only by academics, but also by politicians. Ray B. Browne makes a passionate plea for the incorporation of the popular arts, the "democratic" or people's arts, into the humanities. For, if the plethora of benefits derived from the popular arts' consumption and study are denied, a democratic society is weakened. Browne uses a very inclusive definition of popular culture in this essay, which increasingly has been adopted by the Popular Culture Association as well: by popular culture "we generally mean all aspects of the world we inhabit . . . It is the everyday world around us . . . [it] is the voice of the people."

The winds of change that swept across America during the Sixties finally breezed through academia and blew the dust off some of the concepts of what constitutes the ideal educational curriculum, and in so doing demonstrated the importance of the study of popular culture for both the academic and the non-academic worlds. This discovery was needed because now perhaps for the first time on so large a scale both groups are coming to realize that, like it or not, the popular culture of America is the force that has overwhelming impact on shaping our lives. The so-called "elite" or "minority" culture may have some influence according to the degree it is brought to the people and made applicable to their everyday lives. But the popular culture is already *with* the people, a part of their everyday lives, speaking their language. It is therefore irresistibly influential. What it is, the way it works and its relation to the other humanities need to be understood if we are to appreciate its overwhelming influence in our lives.

By the term "popular culture" we generally mean all aspects of the world we inhabit: the way of life we inherit, practice and pass on to our descendants; what we do while we are awake, the dreams we dream while asleep. It is the everyday world around us: the mass media, entertainments, diversions, heroes, icons, rituals, psychology, religion—our total life picture.

Ray B. Browne, "Popular Culture As the New Humanities," Journal of Popular Culture *17.4 (Spring 1984): 1–8.*

Although it need not necessarily be, it is generally disseminated by the mass media, particularly since the middle of the nineteenth century.

Most important, the popular culture of a country is the voice of the people—their likes and dislikes, the lifeblood of daily existence, their way of life. In America presumably popular culture is the voice of democracy— what makes America the country she is. The culture may be manipulated in our day by the media barons—who may react too slowly to the voice of democracy (as revealed in the peculiar showings of the Nielson ratings)— or by the society which may demand too much for the people who create their culture for them. Like it or not, every American owes it to himself and his society to make a great effort, through formal or informal study and analysis, to understand the culture around him or her. Often the student will discover, if he can rid himself or herself of blind prejudice, that much of the popular culture is to be appreciated.

Actually, of course, there is nothing new in studying popular culture, that is, the culture of the times. As the editors of the *Literary History of the United States* asserted: "Each generation must define the past [as well as the present] in its own terms." And if there is opposition to the new way of looking at the phenomena of life, that is only natural, as John G. Cawelti (in *The Six-Gun Mystique*) quite properly observed: "Whenever criticism feels the impact of an expanded sensibility [which often is tied in with a political thrust] it becomes shot through with ideological dispute."

The political thrust is particularly sensitive at this time. The humanities as the football of political bias and self-interest generally continue to get redefined according to the political attitude running the show. Apparently not knowing or caring about real or objective definitions, the National Endowment for the Humanities, for example, the one institution in the United States that has a vital role in the humanities, has always bent its definition to fit that of the chairman and the politician in charge of the White House. Three administrations ago, Ronald Berman, as Chairman, was an avowed snob despite the fact that he had been the speech writer for Spiro Agnew, who made much political hay railing against the effete elitists of the East Coast; Berman obviously pleased president Nixon, again in a strange way since Nixon was so strongly against the Eastern elite group. The next Chairman, Joseph Duffy, reflecting the political attitude of Jimmy Carter, tried to redefine the humanities in a somewhat different way. As a graduate of Yale University he had been trained into forswearing his West Virginia coal-mining background, but he finally learned that there is no reason to find his childhood antithetical to a true meaning of the humanities. In his speech before the Congress at his nomination, Duffy said that he felt "There need be no issue of a separated elite as against popular participation" in the humanities. "The work of the humanistic conversation should by its nature be spread into every part and region of the country."

The present Chairman, William J. Bennett, however, has swung decidedly back to the elitist side. Mr. Bennett is either confused about proper definitions or depends entirely upon his own interpretations. For example, in a speech last year to the National Federation of State Humanities councils, he laid down four commandments. He allowed that "in pursuing the goal of fostering a better understanding of the humanities on the part of the public, there are boundaries that may not be crossed, no matter how imaginatively." Two of the commandments are paradoxical:

1. "You may not ignore the humanities."
2. "You may not trivialize the humanities."

To call efforts to broaden and modernize the humanities movements to trivialize them is a peculiar attitude that only an intellectual could take. These two commandments are mutually contradictory and they lead to negative and far-reaching results. For example, now in 1984 the National Endowment for the Humanities is calling upon the academic community to study the Constitution and America in a Bicentennial Celebration. One would think that this interest in the impact of the Constitution upon American life would include all levels. But apparently not. The NEH Bicentennial Commission told one person who applied for a grant to hold a convention on the impact of the Constitution on American Popular Culture that this kind of material was not worthy of support; the people in Washington interested in the Constitution and this Bicentennial Celebration are Constitutional lawyers and serious historians, and they are not interested in the America of common people.

The fifty local state humanities councils which have been created to bring the Humanities to the state level vary sharply among themselves in the matter of definitions and projects they encourage and support. Though confused by the signals that come from Washington they tend to be a little less elitist than the national office. All, however, both the Washington headquarters and the state offices are more elitist than the National Endowment for the Arts, though uninformed logic would tend to suggest that the NEA should be far more elitist than the NEH. Perhaps the political manipulations of the humanities, since the humanities are hard to define, are understandable, something we have to live with.

It is more difficult, however, to understand the attitudes of some academics in well-established disciplines and areas of study who at least profess interest in forming the cutting edge of thinking and innovation.

Ideologically based and apparently thoroughly rationalized, the academic groups when off the mark can be mischievous. They often masquerade as "friends" to re-evaluated and relevant definitions when in fact they are antagonists and adhere to old, elitist and questionable definitions and attitudes that do the humanities much harm.

This attitude takes all kinds of turns in different directions, sometimes aided and abetted by the NEH and other foundations. For example the summer NEH seminars for "Humanities in the Schools: Programs for Teachers and Administrators" for 1984 contain disturbing aspects. The announcement—and remember this is for public school teachers—is pretentiously presented with the cover elaborately displaying quotations from Plato—in *Greek*—Cicero—in *Latin*—and Thomas Jefferson. Roughly translated Plato's dictum says, "Knowledge depends on what you study," or perhaps more accurately, "If you don't understand what has gone before in context you remain uneducated." Cicero's statement says something like "Understand in context what happened before your time if you do not want to remain naive." Jefferson's quotation is the often-used, "If a nation expects to be ignorant and free, in a state of civilization, it expects what never was and never will be." No one would disagree with the aptness of the quotations, though Plato, we should remember, was the elitist who referred to the common people of his time as "oxen," and the Greek and Latin phrases are pretentious for most public school teachers; they would surely have been more effective in English. But apparently the purpose of the humanities, at least as seen by the NEH, is to mystify and impress more than to enlighten and lead. And undoubtedly there have been people since the Romans, other than Jefferson, who had apt things to say about the humanities.

Further, some of us might well disagree with the NEH's definition of the humanities relevant for American school teachers and through them children of the 1980s as revealed in the seminars that are to be held in 1984. Some of the subjects are "The English Heritage from Chaucer to Pope," "Shakespeare: The State of the Art," "Shakespeare in Production" and "An Institute on Homer's *Odyssey*." I would suggest that anybody outlining these courses as the most appropriate in the humanities for our public schools in this decade is going to have a hard time steering our humanities programs between the Scylla and Charybdis of elitism and conservatism and will, deliberately or not, lose us, as Odysseus was lost, in the eastern Mediterranean of old and dead ideas.

That there are stirrings of discontent and questioning can be seen in various statements by directors of the state NEH groups. One of the more cogent is that of Alan J. Shusterman, who writing an essay called "Plain Folks and Fancy Reading" in *College English* pointed out the damage done by authors of so-called "signature" art in their willful effort to write away from its general public. His hesitant conclusion leans toward an enlightened attitude about the new humanities: "Provided that a popular text is not made into an object for categorization or scorn, a skillful and unassuming teacher can use it to move to analysis of culture, dramatic method, historical analogues, or sometimes critical techniques." Such an attitude is surely a suggestion in the right direction.

As an antidote to such poison many critics of today, on the bases of some commonsense observations and assumptions, are modifying their attitudes toward the arts and culture. Susan Sontag, for example, in an often-quoted statement observed in *Against Interpretation,* "One cheats oneself as a human being if one has respect only for the style [and the content, presumably] of high culture." Roger Rollin, writing in the *Journal of Popular Culture,* argued against any form of evaluation. To him the only real authority about beauty and excellence is not the critic but the people, especially in the popular arts. In literature, he points out, the rule is "one person—one vote." Popular culture represents the triumph of the democratic esthetic. Mark Twain, Rollin might have reminded us, was proud of the fact that whereas Henry James wrote for the select few, he, Mark Twain, wrote for the millions.

All works of art—from the least pretentious to the grandest "elite" — differ not in kind but in degree. All exist on a continuum that can perhaps be best described as a flattened ellipsis somewhat like the CBS logo. On the right end is folk art, on the left end (both politically and creatively) is the so-called "signature" art. Between the two—occupying perhaps 80% of the scale—is popular art. Between the three types there are no clear lines of distinctions, only grey areas overlapping each other, one growing out of and merging into another. In all areas along this continuum, there is a vertical scale of esthetic accomplishment. Some folk creations are strong and effective, some are weak. In "elite" there are some strong statements and some weak.

Undoubtedly the largest range of strengths and weaknesses lies in the popular area, because there are far more attempts here by people with widely varying ranges of talent. But it is a grave mistake to assume that all creators of the popular arts achieve no worthwhile standards. Many do indeed. Stephen Foster's songs, for example, to a large majority of Americans are more nearly immortal than are those of Frederic Chopin. Huck Finn's path in life will always be of much greater significance than Lambert Strether's, *Uncle Tom's Cabin* a more moving statement about the downtrodden than William Dean Howell's *Annie Kilburn* is or ever was.

Students of popular culture and the popular arts keep constantly in mind the function of the democratic arts, a point which sometimes disturbs "elite" critics. The popular arts are almost always pragmatic and functional.

Alan Gowans, in *The Unchanging Arts,* perhaps says it most succinctly: "To know what art is, you must define what it *does*. You can define art only in terms of function. High art historically grew out of low art, and the functions of low art have remained unchanged throughout history." The function is to get something done—to convert the sinner, to explicate the human form, to say something about human experience—yes, to sell soap. Debating about esthetic accomplishments without keeping these purposes and functions in mind is to center on only part of the object's purpose and accomplishment.

The popular arts are more and more being equated with the humanities, or what could more properly be called "The New Humanities," as the realization grows that the conventional humanities have probably not succeeded in their function, and because acceptance of popular culture as the "New Humanities" arises from the ever-widening belief that in a democracy the democratic institutions, as well as the ordinary people, should be a main focus of attention and study. The humanities must include the arts. Historically, many academics—as well as non-academics—have looked upon the humanities and the study of a whole culture from an elite point of view. They have insisted that the humanities teach us how to live life most fully but have treated the humanities as though they were designed exclusively for the educationally and financially privileged and were to be denied to the ordinary taxpayer.

The "New Humanists" believe that this traditional elitist point of view is tunnel-visioned and myopic, and that it is misleading to study artistic creations as though the creators lived in a vacuum, oblivious to and unaffected by the society around them.

These "New Humanists" are or ought to be all-inclusive in their interests, then, because popular culture by definition has wide parameters and multiple purposes, and can comment on virtually every aspect of life. Russel Nye, for example, states, in *The Unembarrassed Muse,* a major study of the popular arts in America: "The study of popular culture, done seriously and with proper purpose and methodology, can open up new areas of evidence which can contribute greatly to what we know about the attitudes, ideas and values of a society at a given place or time; in so doing, we find a broader and deeper understanding of our society."

In studying and trying to understand a culture—drawing forth its humanities—the act of comprehending the precise and literal details in which the creator worked tends to clothe and enrich the object, giving it in the real sense of the word the humanistic truth that it could not otherwise have. Many of the works of popular culture may not be esthetically pleasing, to be sure. Neither are many elite works, especially until age and custom and elite persuasion have made them familiar and valuable. But in cultural studies esthetic value is irrelevant, beside the point. Esthetic value must be looked upon as a pleasing bonus if it is present, but by no means necessary. In fact, sometimes esthetic value can be the cause of much danger. D. G. Griffith's *The Birth of a Nation* (1915), for example, became a dangerous movie, with overwhelming aftereffects of racism, because it was esthetically pleasing. Contemporary so-called Plantation Novels, in the tradition of *Mandingo,* have no esthetic qualities, to most people at least, yet apparently they satisfy some deep-felt need of many present-day readers, which though it might be repugnant to most of us, is obviously of value to them, and we need to be aware of that appeal. The fact is that both so-called "signature" and popular artists are, each in his or her own way, merely trying to pin their names to the bulletin boards of history. They are striving not to be forgotten after death. The question of the esthetic value is then the total effect of the item itself—and its value involves far more than its esthetic quotient.

The Popular Humanities do most of the job of perpetuating a culture, as T. S. Eliot recognized years ago in crying out against popular books: "I incline to come to the alarming conclusion," he wrote in *Essays Ancients and Modern,* "that it is just the literature that we read for 'amusement' or 'purely for pleasure' that may have the greatest . . . least suspected . . . earliest . . . influence upon us. Hence it is that the influence of popular novelists, and of popular plays of contemporary life, require to be scrutinized." It is both ironic, and somehow appealing, that, like Shakespeare in the electronic age, Eliot has come to be known and appreciated most widely by the people he feared and despised in the stage production of his work *Cats.* Richard Hoggart, one of today's leading English social observers, comments, in a typical British understatement, "Literature at all levels has the unique capacity to increase our understanding of a culture." It is an attitude increasingly recognized by people of all esthetic bias. For example, Thomas Hoving, former executive director of the New York Metropolitan Museum of Art and chief editor of *Connoisseur* magazine, told Nancy Shulins, an AP newsfeature writer, in an article dated March 11, 1984, "There's a role for it [popular culture], no question. It's not the culture I care much about. But if we had examples of it from Pericles' Athens, we'd certainly be better off."

The so-called works of amusement and pleasure, as Eliot referred to them, exert their overwhelming influence because all of us come unavoidably into contact with them daily. They present in simple and therefore usable ways the ideas of the time. Often the ideas are over-simplified and may be relatively unimportant singly and individually. We therefore are inclined to look down upon them, despite the fact that we all at least pay lip service to the hypothesis that in order to live most fully we need to include as much of life as possible. Yet we frequently concentrate on—or claim to be interested in—only what we call or have been told is the important. As A. O.

Lovejoy remarked in his book *The Great Chain of Being,* many of us are not interested in ideas unless they come to us dressed in full warpaint, when in fact it is the small ideas or the accumulation of them that is important.

Actually in the seeming gap between what might be called "elite" and "popular" humanities there is no break whatsoever, as Robert Coles, psychologist and Pulitzer Prize winner, recognizes: "The humanities," he says, "belong to no one kind of person; they are part of the lives of ordinary people, who have their own various ways of struggling for coherence, for a compelling faith, for social vision, for an ethical position, for a sense of historical perspective," for a meaning—*a raison d'etre* in life.

Richard Hoggart, speaking in a larger context, said essentially the same thing: "The closer study of mass society may make us have sad hearts at the supermarket, but at the same time it may produce an enhanced and tempered sense of humanity and humility, instead of the sense of superiority and separateness that our traditional training is likely to have encouraged."

Leslie Fiedler perhaps pushes this reasoning to its logical conclusion because he believes that popular culture can achieve man's greatest challenge, that of bringing us all together again. The popular culture—or popular humanities—then, given their way, can unite us into a community which existed before people became separated by class, education, interests and desires. This function might be especially appropriate for television, with its completely democratic audience, which tends to relegate Gutenburg obsolete and to promote visual culture, the oldest kind, and with it an oral community which is broader and more democratic than the world of print, with its few but real limitations. In this world John Ball's lines in his speech at Blackheath to the men in Wat Tyler's rebellion have a ringing pertinence: "When Adam delved and Eve span/ Who was then a gentleman?"

A late voice to speak out on the need for a new look at education and for the humanities—and generalists—was Ernest L. Boyer, former U.S. Commissioner of Education, in "Toward a New Core Curriculum" (published in the *NEA Advocate,* April/May 1978). He addresses the point that Hoggart was discussing, coming down hard on those educationalists who speak about "liberal versus vocational" education to the disparagement of the latter. "Education," he insists, "has always been a blend of inspiration and utility, but because of tradition, lethargy, ignorance and snobbery, mindless distinctions are made between what is vocationally legitimate and illegitimate." In a reversion to what must seem to many a dangerous respect of Ben Franklinism, Boyer insists that the work ethic should play a strong role in the true meaning of liberal education. His remarks obviously parallel and attack the assumed distinctions between "elite" and popular humanities.

With or without Boyer's emphasis on the work ethic, no one in the New Humanities would suggest that investigation of popular culture replace the traditional humanities where those can be demonstrated to be valuable, where they can prove their worth. Or that the study of popular phenomena and culture be blind in celebration rather than keen analysis. Such studies must deserve the same care and precision as any other area in the humanities. Any other attitude would be non-intellectual and bound to defeat the purpose of education.

But, on the other hand, there is no question that it is imperative that the old concepts be tested and modified to incorporate new approaches, new definitions and new areas of subject matter. Otherwise the Humanities—in all their ramifications—will be proved misguided and generally inadequate to present-day needs and possibilities. Maybe it will be found that the "eternal truths" that the Humanities are supposed to reveal will be found to have more effective spokespersons in sources that have not been recognized in the past.

This means that there should be no sacred domains among the old humanities. They must periodically be asked to revalidate themselves, and if they cannot they must be retired until rejuvenated. Doubtless many of the workhorses should be given sabbaticals. The present-day classroom—and research desk—is the one place that cannot afford to become a museum of dead ideas and concepts. None of us ought to be willing to go "back to basics" in anything, as the blind cry of conservatives is today, or *back* to anything, especially to the humanities. At least we should insist on going *"forward"* to new basics. *Basics* to any kind of life move irreversibly forward.

Such a statement need not get anybody's back up. It is not a condemnation of what we have done in the past, it does not invalidate anybody's life's work, anybody's literary or artistic loves, even anybody's evaluations of esthetically commendable or contemptible materials. Rather it is a call for intellectuals and other people interested in studying and understanding American life and culture, in its broadest and richest sense, to become broader-viewed, more openminded and less exclusive. Nobody says one has to approve or like all the "great" works of the arts of the past or of the present; we have our personal Nielson-like ratings evaluating them from 1–10. Only people in the humanities or the arts act under the assumption that we must like what we work on and work on only those things we like; the scientists, to our betterment, do not restrict their interests to the "good" things in life. It is foolish for us to pull an ostrich-like hiding of the head and be unaware of the winds that sweep our bodies while the thinking part is in the sand. Such an attitude is not only self-defeating; it is dangerous to one's own and the culture's well-being, because in truth American culture continues to grow and develop in its own way pretty much irrespective of intellectuals' approval or disapproval, though sometimes the progress is in spite of the disapproval. Intellectuals may long for the return of the train as a romantic way to travel, and the typewriter as the perfect machine to write on, but the satellite is flying well and the word processor is on many kids' desks.

The academic's tendency is to be rather open-minded while he doesn't know much and doesn't have much to defend. But as he or she gets more and more specialized he tends more and more to be proprietary and protective over what he knows, apparently in developing such an attitude fulfilling a deep-felt need within himself to justify what he is doing. Often we turn off our listening button and on our broadcast button too soon. We learn to "profess" exclusively while we should still be learning while professing. Such a one-way activity is indeed dangerous, for it is self-defeating. We should remember that Josh Billings, one of our insightful humorists of the 19th century, reminded us: "It ain't the things we don't know that makes such fools of us, but a whole lot of things that we know that ain't so." We should always keep an open mind about the valuable things we know and the worthwhile attitudes we hold. Otherwise we insult our intelligence and jeopardize the natural and peaceful development of culture and mankind.

To paraphrase Lincoln, the Elitists can fool some of the people all of the time and all of the people some of the time, but they cannot fool all of the people all of the time. As they try to fool society in general, the only ones they really fool are themselves. They are like the emperor who struts around making people think that his clothes are superior when in fact he is not wearing any. Although Elitists through time continually change their statements about their clothes, history always recognizes the fraud and convicts them of indecent exposure.

The regrettable aspect of the process is that history moves slowly and is mainly accurate in retrospect only. The preachments of the elitist should be recognized contemporaneously for what they are. We cannot wait for the future to inscribe what we already know—that the elitists were pushing points of view out of self-interest and that these points of view represented generally only what they believed or pretended to believe; such nonsense surely did not represent a consensus.

A society that reads its present and future exclusively or mainly by looking backwards through a mirror needs to re-examine its orientation. Instead a society needs to look around at the various aspects and trust in their contemporary world. For academics a proper examination is the numerous other fields of inquiry going on around them. There is a symbiotic relationship between popular culture and these many other fields of investigation. It is the obligation and opportunity of all fields to discover the potential richness to be found in this symbiotic relationship and to exploit it.

THE NEW VALIDATION OF POPULAR CULTURE:
SENSE AND SENTIMENTALITY IN ACADEMIA

Michael Schudson

For Michael Schudson, popular culture includes both folk and mass culture. He believes that intellectual developments, primarily of the 1970s and 1980s, have provided a new legitimacy for the study of popular culture. In particular, he focuses on studies which examine the producers, texts and consumers of popular culture. Finally, he poses a question, which for him remains unresolved: if the same analytical methods can be productively applied to both elite and popular culture, are divisions between them and rankings of them by academia justified? Michael Schudson teaches in the Department of Communications at the University of California, San Diego. He is the author of several monographs. The ideas in this essay have been further developed in Chandra Mukerji and Michael Schudson (eds.), Rethinking Popular Culture *(1991).*

In the past generation, popular culture has attained a new legitimacy in American universities. Popular culture is now studied more often, in more different courses, in more departments, and with more sympathy than before. In literature, serious scholars can write on science fiction or on detective fiction or on romance novels, in short, on what is still often labeled as "trash." In history, the attention to popular culture has moved even further; the attention to the beliefs and practices of ordinary people actually has displaced studies of political, diplomatic, and military elites as the leading edge of historical writing. In the interpretive social sciences, now rubbing up against and taking inspiration from the humanities, there is also a new freshness and new importance to the study of popular culture forms.

The concept of popular culture has been revised entirely, and revitalized, by these developments. The result has been, in my opinion, a salutary new valuation of popular culture combined with an undiscriminatingly sentimental view of it. In the pages that follow, I describe the main intellectual

Michael Schudson, "The New Validation of Popular Culture: Sense and Sentimentality in Academia," Critical Studies in Mass Communication *4.1 (March 1987): 51–68. Used by permission of the National Communication Association.*

lines that have produced this change, and I suggest that the new study of popular culture now offers a serious challenge to the identity of the modern university.

Popular culture can be understood broadly as beliefs and practices, and the objects through which they are organized, that are widely shared among a population.[1] These include both "folk" or "popular" beliefs, practices and objects rooted in local traditions, and also "mass" beliefs, practices, and objects generated from political and commercial centers. Until recently, scholars have tended to praise folk culture for its authenticity and decry mass culture for its commercial origin, its ideological aims, or its aesthetic blandness. Today the picture is more complex with scholars finding that authentic folk traditions often have metropolitan or elite roots and that mass culture often is authentically incorporated into ordinary people's everyday lives. It is therefore more hazardous than it used to be to make a rigid distinction between folk and mass culture. I will lump both categories under the general term, popular culture.

Conventionally, objects taken to be part of popular culture are *readable* objects, written or visual materials for which there are available traditions of interpretation and criticism. In recent years, the range of what is considered readable has expanded vastly: now spatial arrangements, household objects, advertisements, food and drink, dress, and youth cultural styles are all parts of readable cultural systems. The special task of interpretation, for many years left to the humanities, has become a more general subject to which anthropology, sociolinguistics, and psychoanalysis have contributed, creating a new convergence of the social sciences and humanities.

The study of popular culture can be broken down as the study of (a) the production of cultural objects, (b) the content of the objects themselves, and (c) the reception of the objects and the meanings attributed to them by the general population or subpopulations. In all three dimensions—the study of the production of culture, the study of texts, and the study of audiences— intellectual developments of the past generation have provided a new validation for the study of popular culture. This development raises a fundamental question that I will take up later in the essay: what rationale remains for distinguishing "high" or "elite" culture from popular culture? If popular culture is valid for serious study, is there still a high culture that is *more* valid? That is, what justification remains for teaching—and thereby legitimating, even enshrining—some texts rather than others in university courses in the humanities? There is new thinking on this question, too, that has come out of historical and sociological accounts of the development of popular and high culture traditions and the evolution of a distinction between them. But let me begin with an examination of changes in the study of the producers, texts, and audiences of popular culture.

Producing Culture: The Sociological Eye

In the 1960s, and 1970s, the study of the mass media in sociology changed in a way that has had influence well beyond the discipline. In sociology, there were two lines of discussion of popular culture dating to the 1940s and 1950s. One line of empirical studies, in both political science and sociology, looked for specific influences of mass media content on the attitudes or behavior or voting preferences of citizens. Growing out of a concern over propaganda in the 1930s and 1940s and, to some extent, out of a concern to make propaganda *effective* during World War II, these studies came to a surprising conclusion: the effect of the mass media on popular opinion was very small. People inherited voting inclinations from their parents or had their party preferences shaped by their occupational situations and their networks of friends and co-workers. Moreover, they attended to material in the mass media most likely to reinforce views they already held. Even when they came upon opinions contradicting their own, they tended to misperceive them, very often as supportive of their own views. In the face of this selective attention and perception, the power of the media to persuade seemed much less than researchers had imagined.[2]

A second line of thought came out of European social criticism, especially the Frankfurt School work, rather than out of the American tradition of empirical social research. This body of thought developed a concept of "mass society" within the context of Nazi Germany but with an urgent sense that all of modern industrial society was vulnerable to "massification." Theorists of mass society saw the modern individual as alienated, isolated, lonely, and privatized. They saw institutions of social solidarity, the family, the neighborhood, the church, and the party, to be weakening, while the state and its connection to individuals through the mass media was growing steadily more powerful. Without local social institutions to fall back on, the individual became more and more susceptible to the siren song of the mass media and any demagogue who could control mass communication. In one of he most radical statements of this position, Max Horkheimer and Theodor Adorno (1972) argued that popular entertainment, music, the movies, and the comics, spoke in a unified voice, drowning opposition to capitalism in the United States. The "culture industry," a term they coined for the whole array of entertainment industries, was an agent of mass deception, and they repeatedly drew parallels between the propaganda of Hitler and Goebbels and American commercial entertainment.

The one tradition, then, looked hard to find evidence of "media effects" and found little; the other tradition developed a coherent theoretical stance that imagined overpowering ideological influence. In the period from the mid-fifties until the late sixties, American sociologists and political scientists largely stopped studying the mass media (although studies continued in the relatively new departments of communication or mass communication in major universities in the Midwest). Only with the rise in public concern over the news media during the Civil Rights Movement and especially during the war in Vietnam, and with the involvement of a good many social scientists themselves in these movements, did research on the mass media revive. When it did, it returned with people whose personal experiences or personal convictions made them think the media were quite powerful. The difficulty, however, was to say *how* powerful or powerful *in what way.*

There have been both theoretical and empirical answers to these questions. A theoretical effort has been to replace the notion of an overwhelmingly powerful mass culture with the more subtle, and more slippery, notion of "hegemony." The term comes from the work of Italian communist Antonio Gramsci who held that the state achieves its power not only through force but through defining a reality that citizens freely accept, a reality whereby the natural or inevitable right of the ruling class to rule is popularly taken for granted.[3]

Empirical studies have taken another road to the media effects question; many scholars have abandoned efforts to answer it directly and ask, instead, how mass media content is created, not what influence it has. This work can be seen as a different kind of reaction against the mass culture theorists. As Paul DiMaggio (1977) has suggested, the left wing critics of mass culture implicitly assume that mass culture is produced in a monopoly situation: The public will absorb whatever the culture offers because only one product is available. The right wing critics of mass culture, on the other hand, implicitly assume a situation of perfect competition where the public gets whatever it desires (mass culture is of a miserable quality because the public is uncivilized). DiMaggio argues, instead, that the central features of mass culture are the "attributes of industries, not of societies" (437). Some mass culture industries *are* in monopoly situations—the television industry (before cable) or public school textbook publishers. Other mass culture industries—trade books, records, movies, and magazines—create objects for specialized audiences, and their situation more closely resembles free competition. The diversity or innovativeness of the culture materials available to the public, DiMaggio concludes, has "more to do with the market structures and organizational environment of specific industries than with strongly felt demands of either the masses or their masters for certain kinds of homogeneous cultural materials (448).

DiMaggio and the others in sociology and political science who have contributed to "production of culture" studies helped turn the social sciences toward the simple observation that cultural objects are *produced* by specific individuals and organizations under specific legal, economic, political, cultural, and organizational constraints. This obvious truth has had a number of far-reaching consequences for an understanding of culture.[4]

First, the insight has drawn attention to the role of *organizations* and *markets* in determining production. It has thus radically subsumed the sociological study of culture under the sociology of economic life and organizations. To the extent that paintings or novels or films are things made by people and organizations as part of their effort to earn a living, they are not unlike automobiles and hardware and widgets. Important recognitions follow from this. For instance, once a cultural object is seen as an *organizational* product, some of its formal features and thematic content can be traced not to individual minds but to organizational interactions and constraints. For instance, over time, a newspaper's front page devotes about an equal measure to metropolitan, national, and foreign news. This is done not because an editor determines that they are of equal weight in the greater scheme of things. It is done because the news organization is divided into metropolitan, national, and foreign desks, each with an editor who vies for front-page play and whose demands must be satisfied by a managing editor. One of the things a managing editor manages is not news but people in their organizational roles (Sigal, 1973).

Second, if cultural objects such as romance novels or comic books or B movies are organizational products, are not fine fiction published by Farrar, Straus or experimental films made by independent film makers also organizational products? The *balance* of commercial motive and respect for artistic integrity may be different, but commercial motive is rarely absent in the production of high culture, and respect for artistic integrity often has a place in the production of popular culture.

The sociologizing influence of production of culture studies, then, has succeeded in democratizing or relativizing an approach to the study of culture. If Norman Mailer is distinguishable from Sidney Sheldon or Pablo Picasso from Leroy Neiman, it is not on the basis of craftsmanship versus crassmanship.

One factor that has boosted this sociological insight is that more of the arts have become *collective* than was once the case. For the most part, the novel is as much an individual enterprise today as in the 1800s; to some extent, it has even become more individual and less institutional since a writer can write at his or her own pace without the institutional constraints of having to come up with a serial installment for a daily newspaper as Charles Dickens did. But the rise of *film* as a central modern art, and then its off-shoots in television and video, has made the notion that art is the result of idiosyncratic individual effort difficult to maintain. We *do* maintain it, and the whole point of "auteur" theory in film criticism is to rescue the concept that film, like the novel and like painting or sculpture, can be seen as a traditional art expressive of individual genius. Surely there is *some* truth in this. But with film, it is apparent that other candidates for genius arise, not just the director, who has been lifted by critics to the central role, but also (to name just two) the cinematographer and the leading actors.

Further, some of the modern arts, and particularly those connected to film, require not only a collection of skilled people for production but require a great deal of money, much more than the funds required to support a single artist. It may be, then, that the producer or fundraiser for film or for modern theater deserves some of the credit for authorship. It is certainly true that there is a more coherent critical community for fiction, where most skillful aspiring authors can find a publisher, than there is for film, where the aspiring film maker may very well not find the funds to support the equipment to do technically good work or, finding the funds, may not find a way to exhibit the product.

Some voices in literary theory now question the whole idea of "authorship," and people speak of the death of the author. Changes in the character of artistic production along with the recognition that, even with individual authors, art making happens within a social and institutional context have contributed to a sociologizing of the idea of authorship and some radical questioning of taken-for-granted distinctions between high culture and popular culture.

Cultural Texts: The Anthropological Eye

One of the most stunning intellectual developments of the past generation came in the advances made by linguists in studying the structure of language. The advances of Noam Chomsky's structuralist revolution are today hotly debated inside linguistics, but the lesson for people outside has remained clear and constant: All human languages are equally complex. No language is closer to nature than the next. All have complicated, rule-governed arrangements for sound, syntax, and meaning. Even pidgins and creoles and dialectical variations are not degradations of a pure form of language, sloppy in adherence to rules, but new ruled systems of their own.

This insight served in some cases as inspiration for and, in most cases, can serve as metaphor for the relativizing trend in the social sciences and humanities for what objects are deserving of study. It is not that the humanities *needed* Chomsky or Jakobson or Levi-Strauss; they had, after all, a tradition of rhetorical studies on which they might have drawn. Rhetoricians saw the entire range of human verbal productions as appropriate objects for study. Aristotle drew special attention to political, legal, and ceremonial speech, but a 20th-century descendant, Kenneth Burke, was just as ready to examine aphorisms and advertisements. Yet the tradition of the humanities and especially literary study in the universities generally ignored

Burke and others who sought to democratize the range of study-able texts and, instead, took it as their responsibility to define a canon of classic texts. This has been as true in art as in literature. Not simply students of art, university humanities departments have been promoters of their favorite artists and authors. More than most departments in a university, humanities departments are, perhaps necessarily, employers of scholars *engagé,* people deeply involved in *making* the very thing—elite culture—that they study. Barbara Herrnstein Smith describes the process with respect to Homer:

> . . . the value of a literary work is continuously produced and reproduced by the very acts of implicit and explicit evaluation that are frequently invoked as "reflecting" its value and therefore as being evidence of it. In other words, what are commonly taken to be the *signs* of literary value are, in effect, also its *springs.* The endurance of a classic canonical author such as Homer, then, owes not to the alleged transcultural or universal value of his works but, on the contrary, to the continuity of their circulation in a particular culture. Repeatedly cited and recited, translated, taught, and imitated, and thoroughly enmeshed in the network of intertextuality that continuously *constitutes* the high culture of the orthodoxly educated population of the West . . . that highly variable entity we refer to as "Homer" recurrently enters our experience in relation to a large number and variety of our interests and thus can perform a large number of various functions for us and obviously has performed them for many of us over a good bit of the history of our culture. (1984, 34–35)

This is the kind of observation that literary scholars in recent years have begun to accept as they adopt a loosely sociological view of their own institution, understanding it as a hierarchical social structure with larger social functions. Frank Kermode (1983), for instance, writes of literary studies as an institution, that "professional community which interprets secular literature and teaches others to do so" (168). It has authority (not undisputed, he observes) "to define (or indicate the limits of) a subject; to impose valuations and validate interpretations." It is, he says, "a self-perpetuating, sempiternal corporation" (169).

This skeptical stance toward the academic institution as an imposer of valuations has enlarged the number and kinds of texts acceptable for study in the humanities. More kinds of literary texts have been added to the reading lists. Further, the whole concept of textuality has been applied to materials not previously regarded as textual at all, and here anthropology has made the most notable contribution.

The field of anthropology long has been concerned with texts in the collection of oral tales and myths of primitive peoples. Different anthropologists, studying the same group at different times and working with different informants, naturally picked up different variants of stories and folk tales. Piecing together from different variants the most authentic one, or concluding that *each* variant is authentic by its own light, anthropologists have worked with texts, the written-down versions of the orally transmitted tales, in understanding cultures. But anthropology has gone far beyond this still conventional understanding of the text to look upon rituals, games, and performances as interpretable texts that people *make,* and intend as meaningful objects that should be interpreted.

The most widely known instance of this kind of work is the essay by Clifford Geertz on the cockfight in Bali (1973). This essay shows the ways the Balinese cockfight represents and heightens the importance of social solidarities and social divisions in Balinese society. It also shows how the cockfight represents and heightens important psychological tendencies in Balinese personality, especially those surrounding the relationship between the Balinese man and his "cock." Geertz treads familiar ground here in connecting a cultural object to its social and psychological moorings, but he refuses to reduce the cultural object to its underpinnings. He insists that the cockfight is textual in that it is not only a reflection of a social setting or a psychological predisposition but an articulation and production of meaning. The cockfight does not express what Balinese society is but what, in a kind of collective thought-experiment, Balinese society might be if certain emotional tendencies were taken to their logical extreme. The cockfight is a safe way, culturally framed, to test out what happens when certain tendencies in the social order go unchecked, just as, Geertz argues, *King Lear* is a collective thought-experiment about what happens when fathers and daughters do not show appropriate love and respect for one another. Geertz holds that an observer can *read* the cockfight as a text just as a critic can read *King Lear* as a text.

Another anthropologist, Victor Turner, also emphasizes the readability of performances and the centrality of performances in social life. He looks especially at what he calls "social dramas," be they in a court of law or an assembly of elders or in some other ritual mode for dramatizing social conflict. Like Geertz, Turner (1984) argues that the social drama does not re-state or mirror underlying social structure but acts as a performance in society's "subjunctive" mood. Ritual, carnival, festival, theater, and other cultural performances express "supposition, desire, hypothesis, possibility" rather than fact. All of these cultural forms can be seen as ways a culture thinks out loud about itself. Barbara Babcock (1984, 107), for instance, discusses Southwest Indian clown performances as a kind of acted-out philosophizing, a meta-language and commentary on social life that "disrupts and interrupts customary frames and expected logic and syntax and creates a reflexive and ironic dialogue, an open space of questioning."

The anthropology of performance is linked closely to conventional literary criticism since, of course, there long has been attention to the performative genres of theater and, to a limited extent, poetry. A performance, like a literary work, is an activity in which the author is oriented to and intends to have some effect on an audience. This attention to performance has not only added something to the conventional notion of text but acts back upon it as sociolinguists, anthropologists, and folklorists have urged the reintegration of the study of texts into their social and often "performed" contexts. Studies of oral poetry leapt ahead when scholars showed that the structure and form of works such as the *Iliad* and the *Odyssey* derived from their roots in an oral, memorized, improvised, and performed mode of composition (Finnegan, 1977).

In this regard, one might go so far as to say that the literary text, as conventionally understood, is a peculiar form of a cultural performance where the author does not relate to the audience face to face and where the relative permanency of the mode of recording separates the performance also from the immediacy of even the author. A literary text, on might say, is a performance that has a life of its own.

Anthropologists have gone further still. With respect to texts and performances, there is always the supposition that the cultural act or object is a somewhat self-conscious commentary on social life. With some aspects of culture, there may be a symbolic system operating at an identifiable level but one of which people are so little conscious that they may even deny its existence. Mary Douglas (1982) has "deciphered" the meaning of a meal, seeing food as a system of cultural communication and the meal as an organized, structured text that comments on social organization. She also has examined consumer goods as a medium through which culture is constituted. Commodities, in her view, are not so much good for consuming as they are "good for thinking; treat them as a nonverbal medium for the human creative faculty" (Douglas, 1979, 62). Vast areas of human activity then become expressions of human creativity, texts that can be deciphered, structures that have interpretable forms: not only staged performances or culturally framed rituals but the performances and rituals of everyday behavior that Erving Goffman studied so well—etiquette, public displays, the small interactions at a bus stop or in nearly any interactional setting where a person communicates messages about him or herself to others nearby.

Compared to this radical extension of the notion of textuality, the inclusion of new literary forms into the acceptable canon for literary studies seems a minor footnote in intellectual history. Of course, it has not been experienced that way. The universities are conservators of tradition, protectors of what they regard as the best and most valuable monuments to human invention and creative expression. It is therefore in some ways easier to accept the cockfight for study than the popular romance or the codes of fashion than television soap operas. The cockfight is sufficiently exotic to be beyond our own culture's status ranking of cultural forms. The romance and the soap opera, in contrast, hold a place—a very low place—in this society's established hierarchy of literary taste.

Now that sociologists and literary scholars alike hold up for examination the social processes whereby hierarchies of taste get established, should the hierarchies be granted any remaining authority? If the "lower" forms of culture deserve study, not just as data for social science but as literary texts meriting the same attention one might give Shakespeare, does this change what the university is supposed to be about? Does it call for a radical change or extension in what we take the mission of the university to be? This is a thorny and a fundamental issue. On the one hand, nothing that is human should be foreign to the "humanities" in a university, and African or Asian or American Indian literature should have as much place as Shakespeare or Dickens in a university education; on the other hand, American universities are, and intend to be, carriers of and promoters of Western traditions of art and thought, and their curricula cannot and should not be encyclopedic. They must be pedagogic. That is, the selection of materials presented, let alone the ways of presenting them, are a vital part of the university's educational endeavor. Selection is *the* vital part, in the view of Bartlett Giamatti (1980), who argue that the main task of the teacher is the task of *choosing* where to begin and what to begin with. On the one hand, it seems perfectly appropriate to study formulaic literatures, romances or detective stories, to see how they work, to think about *why* so many people respond so eagerly to them, and to contemplate the meaning of form and formula and genre in literature generally. On the other hand, there is justification for a critical tradition that pays greatest tribute to work that challenges form, breaks or becomes self-conscious about formula, blurs the boundaries of genres, or seems to surpass the limits of meaning possible within a genre. Watchers of baseball are more interested in learning lessons from Pete Rose than from Joe Schmo, and people who enjoy eating pay greater attention to the Sunday dinner that someone takes hours to prepare than the Wednesday leftovers dumped on the table. The making of distinctions and the making of judgements of better or worse, more or less complex, more or less memorable or enduring or pleasing were not invented by power-hungry elites or greedy institutions (though elites and institutions certainly have taken advantage of their power to make *their* judgements the reigning judgements).

It may be—it certainly remains the common-sense intuition—that different qualities of art reside in the thing itself: some paintings or performances or poems are better than others. But it is now argued with equal vigor that the quality of art lies in how it is received, or in how it is created within the context of reception, rather than in some quality intrinsic to the art object itself. Roland Barthes argues we have moved from an emphasis on the Work (the pristine object with intrinsic quality) to engagement with the Text, something that is produced by reader as much as by writer, by critic or interpreter as much as by author. The quality of *reading* rather than the quality of the object then takes center stage and the critic is more producer than evaluator or consumer. Indeed, for Barthes, as long as a person reads passively, it matters little if the reading matter is Shakespeare or subway graffiti. The task is to read *playfully,* playing the text "in the musical sense of the term" (Barthes, 1979, 79). And the task for the humanities in the university, I would infer from this, is not to create hierarchies of Works but to educate readers in reading. If this can be done with Shakespeare, fine; if it is better achieved with newspaper cartoons, that's fine, too. The task is to diminish the distance between writer and reader, writing and reading, and encourage students to be players.

The notion of the ideal reader as a "player" is not the only model of how a reader should read. Perhaps a more common understanding is that a good reader reads *critically,* reads "against the text" in the terms of one critic or reads "as a process of inaugurating disbelief" according to another (Altieri, 1984, 60–61). Charles Altieri urges that good readers read through a text, submitting to "its provisional authority" as a work of art. Without abandoning a sense of critical reading, this position comes close to Barthes' notion of play and recommends to the reader an attitude that the anthropologists cited earlier would recognize as resembling the "subjunctive" mood.[5] It emphasizes gaining familiarity and facility more than distance and perspective but nontheless a kind of facility that presumes perspective.

Suppose that the university sees its task as one of educating students to read against texts and to be players of texts. At some point, the question will still arise about who is a better player and who a worse player and who is to judge and what rules of play need to be observed. The radical democratization that appears when the Work is demoted to the Text does not do away with the desire for distinctions; the university must still determine, in a redefined context, what values it should be promoting.

The Audience: The Text's Vulnerability

The movement in literary studies that Barthes identifies as a shift from Work to Text has parallels in a different field of inquiry, the sociology of ideology and the sociology of culture. The audience, in social science studies of the mass media and popular culture, has been (like the weather) something that everybody talks about and nobody does anything about. And yet in recent years a number of scholars have finally paid attention to how audiences use the media and how they employ popular culture, while reshaping it, in their own lives.

One exemplary study is sociological without having come from sociology: Janice Radway's *Reading the Romance* (1984), a study of romance novels and their readers. Feminist literary critics have begun to pay some attention to "women's literature" meaning, by that, literature frequently read by women. Most critics, including Radway, find the romance novels to be politically reactionary, generally suggesting in very predictable and stylized plots that a woman's fulfillment in life comes from capturing a man, a man with repressed emotions and a somewhat brutal attitude toward women who, nonetheless, because of some prior suffering in his own life, can learn (through the guidance of the heroine) to express true love. Not infrequently, romance novels even rationalize or explain away the hero's rape of the heroine.

What more, then, needs to be said to condemn romance novels? Radway interviewed at length some 20 women who read large quantities of romance fiction. She learned a number of very interesting things about them. First, she learned that there is not one generalized mass public for romances but that different women respond to and seek out very different kinds of romantic fantasies. (The women she interviewed devour novel after novel but look down contemptuously upon women who watch television soap operas.) Second, she learned that the women interpret the novels very differently from feminist critics. They read *more literally.* When the narrator says that the heroine was a beautiful, bright, and independent woman, and then presents incident after incident that deny her independence (and shed some doubt on her intelligence), the romance readers see the story as one of a strong woman who makes the best of her life in the midst of great adversity. The feminist critic, in contrast, takes the initial description of the independent woman to be ironic in the context of the heroine's actual behavior. Third, whatever ideological message the women may take from the novel, they use the *act of reading* the novels as a bid for independence in their home lives. Most of the women Radway interviewed were high school, or in some cases, college-educated women with part-time or full-time work outside the home and a full set of wifely and motherly chores inside the home, too. In many instances, opening their novel and propping up their feet to read signaled to husband and children that these women were temporarily unavailable and should not be disturbed. It was an assertion of independence and of a right of their own time that apparently was effective in protecting them from demands of the domestic scene.

Of course, there is a lot more one would like to know about these women and their reading. But the point Radway makes most provocatively is that the presumptuousness of the critic to say what a work means has to be questioned and can be questioned, in part, on the basis of empirical studies of what readers get from books. This is an empirical or sociological enactment of the theoretical developments in criticism that suggest that readers and critics construct texts in the act of reading. This does not necessarily mean, however, that the readers construct the texts creatively or playfully or critically. Their responses, while not determined by the text of the romance novel as a prefabricated and autonomous entity, may be shaped by other prefabricated texts, the ideologies and fantasies of popular culture at large that serve as background for reading the romance.[6]

The view that readers construct their own texts (whether critically and creatively or not) is supported by a long line of psychological research on selective attention and selective perception. There is, for instance, a study by Neil Vidmar and Milton Rokeach (1974) that found that the message of *All in the Family* was read differently depending on people's preconceptions. Highly prejudiced viewers enjoyed the show because they could applaud Archie Bunker's sentiments and see him portrayed as a likeable hero. Tolerant viewers enjoyed the show because they could sympathize with the other characters and see Archie Bunker as the butt of jokes, his own prejudices coming back to haunt him or tie him in impossible contradictions.

There is also support for this view in sociological studies of working class culture and youth culture, which demonstrate that people outside the dominant power structures of society can turn commercial products, including music, movies, and television, to their own use, creating a mocking vernacular out of the culture that comes down to them from on high. Whether it is working-class "lads" creating a culture of resistance inside the British school system (Willis, 1977) or hot rodders turning mass-produced vehicles into individual signatures of machismo and power (Moorhouse, 1983), sociologists are finding significant instances where the conventional meaning of a standard product has been altered, reversed, or upended by small or local groups and subcultures with traditions and agenda of their own. (There are also important instances where an authentic subculture uses a mass culture industry as its own medium—Southern black blues musicians in the 1920s preserved and spread their art through the popular record industry [Levine, 1977].)

Are these audiences, then, playful? Able to read against or through texts? Or are they, alternatively, egocentric, making their own meanings from the text not because they have read through them expertly but because they have not learned to truly read? Are Radway's romance readers *good* readers? Do they see the novels as displaying possible strategies for coping with women's subordinate role in patriarchal society? Is romance reading in their experience a "collectively elaborated female ritual through which women explore the consequences of their common social condition as the appendages of men and attempt to imagine a more perfect state where all the needs they so intensely feel and accept as given would be adequately addressed"? (Radway, 1984, 221). If so, then these readers are, as Radway sometimes suggests, very good readers indeed. But do the women experience reading this way? Why do they read the books' endings before buying them? Why do they insist that sad endings are unsatisfactory? Why are they uneasy with genres (like the television soap opera) that do not come to conclusions? Why do variations in the basic, prefabricated, predictable plot line and character line of romances make them uncomfortable? Have they really played with the novels or simply drifted under their spell? Have they submitted to the provisional authority of the work or given it, momentarily, absolute authority? And what would be the measure of their quality as readers?

Think of the readers of Eugene Sue's serialized melodramas in 19th century France: many of them were very active readers, even to the point of writing letters to Sue to implore him to change the plot or to protect a particularly lovable character from harm. Sue, in fact, altered his writing to accord with some of these requests. Other readers treated Sue's characters the way some television soap opera viewers treat the characters they follow so avidly—as real people, not engaging fictions. Sue was asked, for instance, to release one of his evil-fighting heroes to deal with actual crimes (Brooks, 1984,164).

Here the space between writer and reader has narrowed, but is this the kind of reader Barthes or anyone else would want to encourage? These readers, we might say, are active but *not* playful; they do not understand that fiction is play, and, consequently they do not learn to play with fiction. The first lesson about reading is probably that reading can be useful (you can read instructions) or that it can provide a measure of independence (you can entertain yourself in the absence of mother or father) or that it can be fun and exciting. Sue's readers knew all this. But the second lesson about reading is that a written text is not, or not only, a window on the world but is an imaginative construction. I agree with Peter Brooks that critics have spent too much energy on the second lesson—how is a text constructed to do its task—and not enough on the first: Why do people want to know what happens next? But is a person genuinely a reader if he or she remains unaware of the second lesson?

The study of specific audiences should be linked also to the study of the emergence of audiences historically. There has been important work recently on the development of the distinction between high culture and popular culture in the United States and the cultivation of an audience for high culture. Lawrence Levine's study of Shakespeare performance in 19th century America (1984) and Paul DiMaggio's study of the creation of a sphere of high culture in 19th century Boston (1982) both demonstrate that creating high culture was as much a task of shaping an audience as of consolidating a canon of legitimated works. In the early 19th century, Shakespeare was part of general popular culture in America. By 1900, this was no longer true. In part, the nature of Shakespeare's work matched other cultural currents and inclinations more closely in 1850 than in 1900; it better fit a population that delighted in and responded to oratory, melodrama, and heroes who could be seen as "architects of their own fortunes" (Levine, 1984, 53) than it did a population grown used to utilitarian uses of language and grown more interested in heroes and anti-heroes struggling in complex social and institutional webs. But also, in part, an upper class that felt threatened by a growing and ethnically diverse group of upwardly mobile seekers sought out certain features of culture, especially English language culture, that it could assign special moral and aesthetic value and keep safe and apart. After 1900, Shakespeare no longer belongs to the general public but to Culture, capitalized. To attend Shakespeare not only costs money but requires an educated audience, educated to appreciate the plays and to behave properly in the theater. Shakespeare audiences in 1850 were players, not consumers, of theatrical presentations (Would Barthes have approved?) and would respond vocally and demonstratively to the action on stage. We have very little comparable to this today in film or theater except among the audiences for certain cult films such as *Rocky Horror Picture Show* and, perhaps among audiences for professional wrestling. Audiences for sporting events today are probably closest to the Shakespeare audiences of 1850.

The audience itself, then, not just the products created for cultural consumption, is a social construction, a product of a sort in its own way. This is true for the audiences of elite culture as much as for audiences of popular culture, although the two audiences are cultivated and maintained by two very different organizational forms—mass culture industries for the popular audience and private associations supported by private philanthropy and some governmental subvention, plus the institutions of higher education, for the elite audience. While social scientists have begun to study the audiences that differ from middle class expectations of audience behavior, they so far have paid only scant attention to the social processes that create the standard audience for high culture. The work of Pierre Bourdieu (1984) has begun to open up this area, but there is much to be done to understand how the rules of audience behavior and etiquette are arrived at, how the norms of polite conversation and comment following a play or concert are constructed, or even what the regulations of appropriate behavior in the school classroom mean.

Audiences, including the audiences for high culture, are not born but made. If anything, this is even more true in the age of modernism and its successors than it was before. Most justifications of the humanities tend to rest on the virtues of their study for moral education, for an enlargement of the individual's vision of what the human condition is and can be. But it is not clear to me, at any rate, that this rationale can be connected to many of the leading experiments in art, music, and literature in our time. Many of these developments seem to focus on the formal properties of art, music, and literature themselves; their subject turns out to be art making, music making, or writing as activities. They may comment on but do not intend to comment on the human condition except insofar as art making *is* the human condition (a contention they do not explore). Many of the leading movements in modern arts posit or hope for a degree of autonomy of the aesthetic sense unprecedented in human experience. The equivalent in popular culture is the emphasis on "special effects," in films, in theme parks, or in 4th of July celebrations. Audiences may enjoy the dazzle or they may engage in the intellectual detective work of trying to figure out how a special effect was achieved, but they are not likely to be looking to these effects for moral guidance or commentary on the human condition.

Sense and Sentimentality

So far, I have reviewed, generally approvingly, intellectual developments of the past two decades that have profound implications for our understanding of culture. First, I have reviewed the sociological insight that cultural products are created by groups as well as by individuals and that, even with individual artists, cultural products are oriented to a small or large degree to a marketplace and to a socially constructed "art world." This insight relativizes or democratizes works of art and raises questions about the distinction that universities have made between high culture and popular or mass culture. Second, I have reviewed developments in the study of texts that vastly enlarge the range of texts appropriate for serious study. This trend suggests an equivalence across texts whereby judgements of quality do not have pride of place and may not have much of a place at all. Third, I have looked at changing views of the audience that give credit to the audience, any audience, as a privileged critic or reader, even, *creator* of the texts it reads or watches. Once again, the tendency is to relativize the concept of culture, to whittle away at the props that maintain some elements of culture as higher than others.

There is a lot of justifiable excitement about these developments. Barriers to the halls of academe are breached by cultural objects that never before had seen the inside of a classroom; hallways between departments where professors did not know one another existed are now well worn.

There has been a real liberation in all of this, based, in my view, on very good intellectual sense.

But with each of the intellectual movements I have reviewed here, there is a corresponding danger. With the sociological approach to artistic production, there is the threat of cynicism; with the democratization of the number and kinds of texts worthy of study, there is a danger of obscuring the special features of *written* texts; and, most of all, with the recognition of the active role of audiences in constructing the works they engage, there is a danger of romanticizing and sentimentalizing audiences as they exist in certain inhumane social conditions.

Production. While it is true that all art is produced by someone or some ones, not all production aims to manufacture or manufactures art. Some organizations produce toothpicks or ball bearings or toilet paper, not textbooks or soap operas. And producing the textbooks or soap operas *is* different. Certainly useful things (toothpicks) may have meanings and just as surely meaningful things (soap operas) may be useful, but for most things there is no difficulty in distinguishing whether utility or meaning is the primary feature. That there are university departments and international conferences and bibliographies overflowing on William Shakespeare, who produced plays, and not on Clarence Birdseye, who produced frozen foods, is not just an accident nor just a prejudice of people who disdain mass culture. The difference between meaning and utility remains important; the sociologizing trend in the understanding of artistic production does not erase it but asks that it be understood more carefully.

Texts. The fact that an anthropologist or literary critic can read an evening meal or a fast food advertisement or the names of athletic teams or the design of Disneyland as a commentary or meta-commentary on culture does not mean that participant natives also read the text that way. There is some danger that the recent trends in the study of popular culture may inadvertently romanticize the semiotic process itself; the academy's professional interest and pleasure in the act of interpreting can be self-indulgent, and the readings of meals or ads may be only academic *etudes* if these objects are not privileged as signs by the general community. Anthropologist Bruce Kapferer has recognized this problem:

Most anthropologists argue that rituals make metacommentaries, and thus are reflexive upon the non-ritualized, paramount reality of everyday life. But the anthropologist is in a position that would lead to such an observation: the anthropologist is never completely part of the culture being studied, but always apart from it. The subjects of research, the people, are also objects; and this is demanded by the nature of the anthropological discipline. The anthropologist, in a sense, assumes the role of a critic, for particular events are placed in the context of other events, are interrelated, contrasted, and evaluated. Therefore, while rituals might typically be regarded as reflexive events by anthropologists, it does not necessarily follow that they will be similarly regarded by participants. (1984, 203)

There is something democratic about opening up the range of things taken to be textual and accessible to interpretation, but it is as presumptuous to offer critical readings of popular artifacts as it is to interpret high culture artifacts without reference to what the actual audiences may be thinking. Sometimes, as Kapferer suggests, the artifact may be one in which the natives invest a great deal of interpretive energy themselves; sometimes, however, it will be an object that the people in question do not, in fact, think with. Vincent Crapanzano (1986) has made this point about Geertz's celebrated cockfight, that Geertz offers no evidence that the Balinese themselves see the cockfight as a text to be read, no evidence that the cockfight is marked in Balinese culture as a cultural object to be interpreted. Geertz' own interpretive virtuosity, without such support, may then be an instance of the academy's semiotic aggrandizement.

But do we not think with *all* the objects in our environment? Yes, at some level we do. But cultures do not invest all objects with equal amounts of meaning. For urban Americans, say, the power of the distinctions among street/road/avenue/court/place is much greater than that among elm/oak/maple/spruce, even though both sets of categories are part of the culture. These natives may find it worthwhile to interpret both the Sunday comics and the Sunday sermon, but they will most likely find disagreements over the sermon more troubling and the task of interpretation more significant and the value of skilled interpreters correspondingly greater.

Moreover, there is with some objects in the culture a tradition of interpretation that is cumulative and, for this reason, has acquired a sophistication or refinement that everyday interpretation does not attain. While such cumulative traditions exist with respect to a number of kinds of objects, they are especially noteworthy with respect to *written* materials, and, not incidentally, the interpretations themselves are carried on in writing. Written texts provide something that most other objects do not: the possibility of a tradition of criticism that makes an enormous difference in developing and elaborating reflective thought (Goody, 1977). It is not that analysis and reflection are impossible or even unlikely without writing, but a *sustained* tradition of reflection *is* unlikely. Certainly there can be a connoisseurship with respect to cockfights or culinary arts that exists primarily in oral culture. But with all its richness, oral culture also has its limits. The celebration of cockfights and culinary arts and clown dances in the university is all to the good so long as we do not forget that the medium of that celebration, the medium that makes thinking about these objects so interesting and enables an enlargement of our vision about what human cultures are about, is still the written word.

Audiences. It is right to observe that audiences do not absorb culture like sponges. The popular audience is selective, reflective, and constructive in its use of culture. But this is not to say that the popular audience is always critical or creative in its responses any more than elite audiences are. Even within an individual, a person responds differently to different cultural experiences. Very critical and searching readers of fiction may let music wash right over them at a concert; a discerning reader of poetry may not be able to stand before a painting in a gallery for more than a few seconds. Some people who are discriminating consumers of theater may rely on "name brands" for dance. Such people know very well, or should know, that they are more active, playful, critical, or creative in responding to some cultural objects than in responding to others.

If we can recognize such distinctions for individuals, then why not for groups? If we know, further, that in many of the areas where we *are* critical readers we have gone through a process of education, formal or informal, why can we not conclude that processes of education are central to critical and playful readings in general? And if we can say this, can we not also say, indeed, must we not affirm also that one of the tasks of education, not only in the schools and universities but in the structure of society as a whole, is, as Raymond Williams put it, "to deepen and refine the capacity for significant responses" (1983, 62)? The fact that popular audiences respond actively to the materials of mass culture is important to recognize and understand, but it is not a fact that should encourage us to accept mass culture as it stands or popular audiences as they now exist. The fact that different subgroups in the population respond in different ways to common cultural objects or have developed refined critical temperaments with regard to some local or provincial cultural form unrecognized by elites is important to understand and should lead us to recognize a wide variety of connoisseurships and a plurality of educational forms that lead to them. But this is not or should not be to admit all cultural forms equal, all interpretations valid, all interpretive communities self-contained and beyond criticism.

The celebration of popular culture and popular audiences in the universities has been a political act; it could not have been otherwise. The challenge popular culture now presents the university is not a call to erase all boundaries to what is to be treated in the classroom. Rather, it is to force a self-conscious and sociologically self-aware defense of the boundaries the university draws. The challenge is not to deny a place for judgement and valuation but to identify the institutional, national, class, race, and gender-bound biases set deep in past judgements and to make them available for critical reassessment. The new validation of popular culture should not lead higher education to abandon its job of helping students to be critical and playful readers, helping to deepen and refine in them a capacity for significant response. Instead, it should enhance these efforts with new respect for how, in some spheres and in some ways and despite some limits, students (and others) have been critical and playful readers all along.

The essay should end there. It would have, if I thought I had resolved the problems I presented.

I do not. I end up caught between a belief that the university should be a moral educator, holding up for emulation some values and some texts (and not others), and a reluctant admission that defining the basis of moral education is an unfinished, often unrecognized, task. I know, of course, that the university is a moral educator whether this is intended or not. Students learn from teachers what we value, by what values we "profess" to work, and what turns of mind or character we approve. But if we learn to be self-conscious about the implicit hierarchies of taste and value we live and teach by, will we locate adequate grounds for our moral claims? What ground can we stand on, especially when the trends that favor relativism are so much more powerful and cogent (to my own mind) than the rather arbitrary and ill-defended hierarchies of value they so pointedly confront?

If there is sentimentality on one side—would-be populists waving the banner of people's culture—there is piety on the other—ardent champions of a traditional curriculum wailing at the decline of literacy, values, morals, the university, or their students' ability to write (or even recognize) a good English sentence. Neither side seems to me very clear about the pass we have reached. We can all carry on, nevertheless: Departments and professional associations will sustain the structures for individual careers; institutional and personal investments in things as they are will keep us from looking too closely at the intellectual crisis we have come upon. But if we ever come to separating sense from romance and standards from nostalgia in all of this, it is not going to be easy.

Notes

1. This definition and some of the framework for this essay are adapted from Mukerji and Schudson (1986).

2. A review and critique of much of this literature is Sears and Freedman (1971). Another critique that takes a broader look at the conclusion that the media have limited effects is Gitlin (1978).

3. Gramsci's views and the uses of his concept of hegemony are well reviewed in Lears (1985).

4. There is now a large literature on the production of culture within sociol-

ogy. For a sampling, see Peterson (1976). An early and influential essay in this vein is Hirsch (1972). Some of the work is reviewed in Peterson (1979). A related approach coming out of fieldwork and symbolic interactionist traditions is well represented in Becker (1982).

5. On the subjunctive mood as a feature of literature generally, see Bruner (1986).

6. I am grateful to Richard Terdiman for this observation.

References

Altieri, C. "An Idea and Ideal of a Literary Canon." *Canons.* Ed. R. von Hallberg. Chicago: U of Chicago P, 1984. 41–84.

Babcock, B. A. "Arrange Me in Disorder: Fragments and Reflections on Ritual Clowning." *Rite, Drama, Festival, Spectacle.* Ed. J. MacAloon. Philadelphia: Institute for the Study of Human Issues, 1984. 102–28.

Barthes, R. "From Work to Text." *Textual Strategies: Perspectives in Post-structuralist Criticism.* Ed. J. Harari. Ithaca, NY: Cornell UP, 1979. 73–81.

Becker, H. S. *Artworlds.* Berkeley: U of California P, 1982.

Bourdieu, P. *Distinction: A Social Critique of the Judgment of Taste.* Cambridge, MA: Harvard UP, 1984.

Brooks, P. *Reading for the Plot.* New York: Vintage, 1984.

Bruner, J. *Actual Minds, Possible Worlds.* Cambridge, MA: Harvard UP, 1986.

DiMaggio, P. "Cultural Entrepreneurship in Nineteenth-century Boston: The Creation of an Organizational Base for High Culture in America." *Media, Culture & Society* 4 (1982): 33–50.

———. "Market Structure, the Creative Process, and Popular Culture: Toward an Organizational Reinterpretation of Mass-culture Theory." *Journal of Popular Culture* 11 (1977): 436–52.

Douglas, M. *In the Active Voice.* London: Routledge & Kegan Paul, 1982.

———. *The World of Goods.* New York: Basic Books, 1979.

Finnegan, R. *Oral Poetry.* Cambridge, MA: Cambridge UP, 1977.

Geertz, C. "Deep Play: Notes on the Balinese Cockfight." *The Interpretation of Cultures.* Ed. C. Geertz. New York: Basic Books, 1973. 412–53.

Giamatti, A. B. "The American Teacher." *Harper's* July 1980: 24–29.

Gitlin, T. "Media Sociology: The Dominant Paradigm." *Theory and Society* 6 (1978): 205–53.

Goody, J. *The Domestication of the Savage Mind.* Cambridge, MA: Cambridge UP, 1977.

Herrnstein Smith, B. "Contingencies of Value." *Canons.* Ed. R. von Hallberg. Chicago: U of Chicago P, 1984. 5–40.

Hirsch, P. "Processing Fads and Fashions: An Organization-set Analysis of Cultural Industry Systems." *American Journal of Sociology* 77 (1972): 639–59.

Horkheimer, M., and T. Adorno. "The Culture Industry." *Dialectic of Enlighten-ment*. By M. Horkheimer and T. Adorno. New York: Seabury P, 1972. 120–67.

Kapferer, B. "The Ritual Process and the Problem of Reflexivity." *Rite, Drama, Festival, Spectacle*. Ed. J. MacAloon. Philadelphia: Institute for the Study of Human Issues, 1984. 179–207.

Kermode, F. *The Art of Telling: Essays on Fiction*. Cambridge, MA: Harvard UP, 1983.

Lears, T. J. J. "The Concept of Cultural Hegemony: Problems and Possibilities." *American Historical Review* 85 (1985): 567–93.

Levine, L. W. *Black Culture and Black Consciousness*. New York: Oxford UP, 1977.

———. "William Shakespeare and the American People: A Study in Cultural Transformation." *American Historical Review* 89 (1984): 34–66.

Moorhouse, H. F. "American Automobiles and Workers' Dreams." *Sociological Review* 31 (1983): 403–36.

Mukerji, C., and M. Schudson. "Popular Culture." *Annual Review of Sociology* 12 (1986): 47–66.

Peterson, R. A., ed. *The Production of Culture*. Beverly Hills: Sage, 1976.

———. "Revitalizing the Culture Concept." *Annual Review of Sociology* 5 (1979): 137–66.

Radway, J. A. *Reading the Romance: Women, Patriarchy, and Popular Literature*. Chapel Hill: U of North Carolina P, 1984.

Sears, D. O., and J. L. Freedman. "Selective Exposure to Information: A Critical Review." *The Process and Effects of Mass Communication*. Ed. W. Schramm and D. F. Roberts. Urbana: U of Illinois P, 1971. 209–34.

Sigal, L. *Reporters and Officials*. Lexington, MA: D. C. Heath, 1973.

Turner, V. "Liminality and the Performance of Genres. *Rite, Drama, Festival, Spectacle*. Ed. J. MacAloon. Philadelphia: Institute for the Study of Human Issues, 1984. 19–41.

Vidmar, N., and M. Rokeach. "Archie Bunker's Bigotry: A Study in Selective Perception." *Journal of Communication* 24.1 (1974): 36–47.

Williams, R. *The Year 2000*. New York: Pantheon, 1983.

Willis, P. *Learning to Labor: How Working Class Kids Get Working Class Jobs*. New York: Columbia UP, 1977.

RATIONALIZING GENIUS:
IDEOLOGICAL STRATEGIES IN THE CLASSIC AMERICAN SCIENCE FICTION SHORT STORY

John Huntington

"Popular," as in popular works, John Huntington observes, may mean several quite different things: works aimed at the popular classes, works which enjoy contemporary commercial success, and those which find long-term acceptance. This latter he labels "classic popular texts," or those texts which are repeatedly read yet do not become part of the literary canon. Huntington critically reviews three important efforts to define and analyze classic popular texts: (1) John Cawelti's Adventure, Mystery, and Romance; *(2) David Bordwell, Kristin Thompson, and Janet Staiger's* The Classic Hollywood Cinema; *and (3) Will Wright's* Six-guns and Society. *Each of these fails his litmus test: "The problem is to find a way to discuss classic popularity while retaining a mode of selection unbiased by aesthetic presumptions." His solution as applied to science fiction follows. Regrettably space limitations allow us only to lay out his basic selection and argument. The fuller analysis in his book-length study is well worth perusing. Huntington is Professor of English at the University of Illinois–Chicago.*

. . . In aesthetic debates the term, derived from *populus,* will be opposed to "high" art and will denote the class that consumes this nonhigh art. In its strictly economic and sociological aspects the popular denotes specific commercial markets which came into existence in the eighteenth century with the proliferation of a reading bourgeoisie and a technology that allowed for relatively cheap printing.[1] The distinction implicit in the term is not as clear as it used to be. In this century, what Pierre Bourdieu would call the dominated segment of the dominant class has repeatedly, in the name of "art," transgressed the borders between high and popular culture.[2] We have even had the anomaly of a high artistic mode which calls itself "pop art." Clearly this last, while it is arguably more intellectually accessible than such a modernist trend as abstract expressionism, is not economically popular in a sense a sociologist would recognize. In order to avoid such confusion, some critics use the term "mass culture" to refer to cheap, mechanical production that can be distinguished from expensive "artistic" or "elite" culture.[3]

A more recent sense of the term emphasizes not the class basis, but by argument from the class's size, the aspect of being well and broadly liked (e.g. "a popular person"). While one can easily understand how this second meaning could have developed from the first, it nevertheless poses a very different criterion for selection. If popular in the original sense of populus defines a literature directed toward a certain class, popular in the second sense of being liked defines a literature that is spontaneously enjoyed and thus perceived as in opposition to a more difficult literature that supposedly entails an unpleasant exercise which is, somehow, "good for you." Shakespeare, Dickens, and Twain are frequently invoked as instances of the popular in both meanings of the term: although they may be considered high and serious, they are appreciated by a wide variety of people. Such moments in which both definitions of popular are fulfilled are important, but, as the continuing debates about popular and high literature show, such moments are exceptional. One cannot help but suspect that in these cases the ambiguity of the term popular is rendered almost invisible because of the indubitable sanction the canon gives these authors.

When as critics we focus on noncanonic works, we find that not only are the first two definitions of the term popular quite incongruous, but that the second—well liked—can be taken in two quite different senses. One can, to be sure, determine what is popular at this moment by looking at production and consumption figures, and a best-seller list of one sort or another can be constructed for any period. The works on such a list usually have their moment of glory and a long eclipse. One concept of the history of popular culture sees its task to recount the activity of such ephemera.[4] But in any genre there are also works that become popular in a third sense in that their popularity is not limited to a single historical moment. There grows up something like a canon, a list of "classic popular texts." This list of popular works is quite different from the list of specific works of popular art "approved" by the aestheticians of high art, which is really just a subsection of the traditional canon itself. The works that constitute the list of classic popular texts are acknowledged as classic without ever becoming canonic. *Gone With the Wind,* both as novel and as film, is paradigmatic of this phenomenon. And within the various generic fields there are inevitably special groups of texts which are seen as important and as generically paradigmatic quite apart from their aesthetic value. Sometimes, as with *Gone With the Wind,* this third form of popularity is at least in part a result of the work's popularity in the second sense. One imagines *Star Wars* will be popular in the third sense just because its initial popularity was such a remarkable historical phenomenon itself. But more commonly this third kind of popularity grows and changes in time. The popular "classics" of the detective genre, apart of course from the work of Conan Doyle, are for the most part texts that were not particularly remarked on when they first appeared.

"Classic popularity" is in large part the creation of a university-based critical movement that has been active for the last half-century and whose culminating and summarizing text is John Cawelti's *Adventure, Mystery, and Romance.*[5] In the traditional aesthetic defense of individual works, the critic defends his or her selection of a popular work on the ground that it is art. When a whole genre is being studied, the isolation of a particular text becomes problematic. When the individual work that is studied is put forth as an "example" of the genre, the term example, while it disavows rigor can subtlely turn into a paradigm.[6] Cawelti derives the structural rules for the form from such "examples" and then defines the whole form in terms of these high paradigmatic instances. Since he has, even if not explicitly so, something like a canon in mind, the circularity of his paradigmatic examples is not a problem for him. What he is interested in proving is that in these works the popular genre through its formulas achieves "art." The actual popularity, in senses one or two, of the works he studies does not matter. Poe's "The Purloined Letter" is catalogued as popular by a very loose standard: famous as it is in the academy, it is honored as "popular" only by the genealogical accident that the popular detective story can be said to trace itself back to it. Therefore "The Purloined Letter" is a bona fide member of the popular form, whatever its actual popularity was. The popular form and the canonic story work together, each contributing to the aesthetic argument what the other lacks. Cawelti defines a field which resides at the intersection of canonicity and popularities one and two.

When we approach works and forms whose primary interest for us is not their artistic value, but their popularity, such hermeneutic circles become a difficulty. The selection of the works for study may claim to be aesthetically value free, yet, just because it is a selection, aesthetic value is implied. In the last decade we have seen a number of attempts to deal with the problem the sample presents. One solution is for the critic to choose texts for study by an aesthetically neutral process. At the pole opposite to Cawelti's *Adventure, Mystery, and Romance,* which selects its exemplary texts by aesthetic intuition, is a study like David Bordwell, Kristin Thompson, and Janet Staiger's *The Classic Hollywood Cinema,* which in an effort to avoid any aesthetic bias sets up a rigorously random method of text selection by which to define the field.[7] Starting with a list published in 1961 of the almost 30,000 feature films released in the U.S. between 1915 and 1960 the authors deleted all films not made by American studios, and then, using a random number table, they made a short list of 841 films. They then "located" 100 of these (many have been destroyed or just simply lost) which they call their "unbiased sample": "Our selection procedures represent the closest a researcher can come to random sampling when dealing with historical artifacts. The point remains that our choices were not biased by personal preferences or conceptions of influential or masterful films" (388).

It is important that we understand what Bordwell, Thompson, and Staiger have accomplished by this elaborate method. They are seeking to define what they call "the concept of *group* style." Such a concept, while it encompasses various specific subgenres as defined by theme, imagery, plot, et cetera, is a generic concept analogous to a style of art. In order to interpret what Bazin calls "the genius of the system" of production itself, they assume that "Hollywood films constitute a fairly coherent aesthetic tradition which sustains individual creation" (4), and they establish a set of stylistic "historical norms" which characterize and define the "classic Hollywood film." The project aspires to a structuralism which, while it is repeatedly forced to acknowledge the historical evolution of the form, seeks ultimately to discover a set of universal principles which will define the deep structure of the style even as it points to the various "functional equivalents" (5) by which different eras adapt the core. Cawelti always defines the form in terms of its paradigmatic instances, but Bordwell, Thompson, and Staiger argue that "No Hollywood film is the classical system, each is an 'unstable equilibrium' of classical norms" (5).

The elaborately neutral process by which the authors of *The Classical Hollywood Cinema* have selected their texts is a necessary defense against the charge, which would cripple their structural generalization, that by their selection the critics have pre-determined the character of the genre they are attempting to define. Their sample is intentionally ahistorical, and their goal is to define the structural unity of a style that characterizes the whole period from 1917 to 1960. Even when, in addition to their unbiased sample, they discuss almost 200 other films chosen for their "quality or historical influence" (10), they do so not to develop historical lines of change, causality, and influence, but to "test the conclusions" derived from the unbiased sample.

The problem raised by this mode of selection is that while the process frees the choices from the bias of the critics, it also frees them from what we might call the bias of popularity, in senses two and three. Even more than the high arts, the commercial media and genres are influenced by individual works. The influence may be due as much to crass economic envy as to artistic anxiety, but it is nevertheless powerful. Some films have been more popular than others. Bordwell, Thompson, and Staiger's structuralist rigor, by ignoring the element of popularity and its influence, blinds itself to the dynamics and meaning of the history of the form.

The complexity of the term popular means that to correct this blindness we cannot simply claim to select texts on the basis of popularity, because whatever aspect of popularity we satisfy entails disregarding another. We can see the difficulty if we turn to a study that attempts to use popularity itself, however ambiguous the term, as the criterion for selection. Will Wright's *Six-guns and Society: A Structural Study of the Western* selects its texts by the simple device of limiting the study to westerns that have grossed at least $4 million in rental receipts.[8] The advantage of such an economic rule is that it defines a field entirely on a numerical register of popularity and frees the critic from any claim of asserting his own *aesthetic* standards in place of popular appeal.

Though the procedure by which Wright selects his films looks unambiguous in its mechanicalness, that simplicity is deceptive. The very number, $4 million, means different things in different periods. As a scale against which to judge the cost of a film, $4 million is high in the thirties and fairly low in the sixties. The comparatively large number of "professional plot" westerns Wright discovers in the sixties must certainly be at least in part a result of inflation. And it is thanks to this distortion that Wright's field looks symmetrical, with roughly equal numbers of the two main plots. The point of bringing up such a difficulty is not to disqualify Wright's process, but to show that even a mechanically economic definition of a popular field, though it may appear admirably unprejudiced by ideological and aesthetic presuppositions, is still deeply ambiguous and in need of further interpretation.

The categories generated by Wright's method of selection do not in themselves explain the element that makes these films popular. The difficulty becomes evident when, in an unguarded moment, Wright violates his method and rejects *Charge at Feather River* because it is an "awful western" whose "success was solely due to its big release as a three-dimensional film at a time when this gimmick was new and exciting" (30). What is revealing here is not Wright's deviation from his economic mode of selection, but his denunciation of it at this point. Wright's problem is that he is trying to be loyal to two different conceptions of popularity. What I have called popularity of the second type, contemporary commercial success, would require him to include *Charge at Feather River* in his list, but popularity of the third type, "classic popularity," requires him to reject the film. In the case of *Charge at Feather River,* Wright feels secure in his understanding that nonstructural issues made the film commercially popular. But we may also suspect that there are numerous westerns whose contemporary popularity is not at all due to their narratives, but which nevertheless remain on his list. Most obviously, many westerns are popular because of the stars who appear in them. Whatever the plot, a film with Gary Cooper or James Stewart is likely to be more successful than one with, say, Buster Crabb. Moreover, though this may change between the thirties and the sixties, directors like John Ford and Howard Hawks may be in themselves good box office. The process by which a film or a work of literature becomes popular may be in some way functionally related to the theme and structure of the work itself, but that relation is at best oblique in a world of extraordinary promotion. We can argue that elaborate promotion does not justify excluding the film, both because such promotion characterizes many films, and because it is not at all certain that a film so promoted is not still, perhaps even especially, revealing about the expectations and desires of the audience.

A third problem arises not so much from Wright's method itself but from the fact that its simplicity seems to blind him to other interpretative issues. It must strike us that Wright, for all his economic rigor, finds his generic category unambiguous. He seems to accept the industry's marketing categories. He disregards such western oddities as *Son of Paleface,* and such generic neighbors of the western as *Young Mr. Lincoln*. And he ignores the generic issues his own categories of "classical," "vengeance," "transition," and "professional" plot might raise. A mechanical register of contemporary popularity can block reflection on what a slightly different approach would consider important generic distinctions. For Wright the western is as pure, as isolated from the larger literary system, as a biological genus is from the whole of nature. He disregards the extent to which any genre mingles with others and breaks from itself.[9]

The problem is to find a way to discuss classic popularity while retaining a mode of selection unbiased by aesthetic presumptions. There may be no simple method by which to solve this dilemma. A purely economic selection, at least given the kind available to Wright, fails to indicate the basis of popularity or to begin to interpret the field. Other modes of selection, while perhaps more sensitive to ideological issues, are either biased or insensitive to popularity.

As a start, the solution to the problem of bias in the selection may be not to create a sample at all, but to find one. One of the first things a developing science seeks to find is the illuminating anomaly. . . .

For the specific case of science fiction, we can envision how a small, representative selection of popular works might look and how it should be handled. The basic selection should be as undetermined as possible by the critic's own aesthetic or historical principles. At a late stage in the study the critic may be in a position to reinterpret the original field of study and redefine it on what are now seen as intrinsic principles, but such authority is earned by the process of analysis. Such principles cannot be the basis of initial definitions of the field. And, as a corollary of this rule, we must insist that what appears as an anomaly in the unbiased sample must not be rejected as eccentric. On the contrary, it is a validation of the interpretation that it can account for what on the first view looks to be anomalous. And finally, the laying out of the field, while it is the first part of the analytic exercise, can never be final. It is intrinsic to the analytical process that it work dialectically so that at each stage of its achievement it uses the insight it has achieved to question the assumptions that originally determined the field of study.

We need to begin by finding an extraordinary situation which will yield information about common events that one could never get by simply studying the common phenomena. The book, *Science Fiction Hall of Fame,* is just such a lucky eccentricity. It is an anthology, first published in 1970 and still in print, of pulp science fiction originally printed between 1934 and 1963 and chosen as the "best" SF by a vote of the members of the Science Fiction Writers of America. The process of selecting the stories is free from the kinds of distortion, both aesthetic and economic, we have just observed.[10] First, it is not critics or scholars, but working writers who voted on the selection, and while their motives for selection are obscure—whether "best" means money-making, optimistic, beautiful, ingenious, or most profound is not at all clear—that very ambiguity prevents the selection from promoting one kind of story, one version of the genre at the expense of others. The editor, Robert Silverberg, has exercised some minor discretionary power, so that the selection is not simply a record of votes, but his hand would not seem to have seriously violated the neutrality of the selection process. The decision to give no single writer more than one story can be seen as a flattening device that slightly obscures the exceptional popularity of some writers. By focusing on individual popular stories rather than the popularity of specific oeuvres, such as those of Bradbury or Clarke, the selection process distorts one aspect of what makes works popular. And yet, by preventing the domination by a few widely recognized authors, such flattening insures a representation of a wider range of work than might a selection more in awe of a few major lights. Since all the stories are reprints, their choice is in some way a response to a tried popularity, not the expression of some booster's splurge. Here is a found version of classic popularity, chosen by "market forces" rather than by any single analyst with a bias, and relatively free from the defining preferences of a single magazine or a single editor. And finally, though one presumes the twenty-six authors may derive some profit from the reprinting of their stories, one can claim that the selection is not particularly subject to significant economic distortion. Thus *Science Fiction Hall of Fame* offers a field of stories free from the most immediate personal and economic biases that are common in the selection of popular literature.

Science Fiction Hall of Fame contains these stories:

1. Stanley Weinbaum, "A Martian Odyssey" (1934)
2. John W. Campbell, "Twilight" (1934)
3. Lester del Rey, "Helen O'Loy" (1938)
4. Robert A. Heinlein, "The Roads Must Roll" (1940)
5. Theodore Sturgeon, "Microcosmic God" (1941)
6. Isaac Asimov, "Nightfall" (1941)
7. A. E. van Vogt, "The Weapon Shop" (1942)
8. Lewis Padgett, "Mimsy Were the Borogoves" (1943)
9. Clifford Simak, "Huddling Place" (1944)
10. Fredric Brown, "Arena" (1944)
11. Murray Leinster, "First Contact" (1945)
12. Judith Merril, "That Only a Mother" (1948)
13. Cordwainer Smith, "Scanners Live in Vain" (1948)
14. Ray Bradbury, "Mars Is Heaven!" (1948)
15. C. M. Kornbluth, "The Little Black Bag" (1950)
16. Richard Matheson, "Born of Man and Woman" (1950)
17. Fritz Leiber, "Coming Attraction" (1950)
18. Anthony Boucher, "The Quest for Saint Aquin" (1951)
19. James Blish, "Surface Tension" (1952)
20. Arthur C. Clarke, "The Nine Billion Names of God" (1953)
21. Jerome Bixby, "It's a *Good* Life" (1953)
22. Tom Godwin, "The Cold Equations" (1954)
23. Alfred Bester, "Fondly Fahrenheit" (1954)
24. Damon Knight, "The Country of the Kind" (1955)
25. Daniel Keyes, "Flowers for Algernon" (1959)
26. Roger Zelazny, "A Rose for Ecclesiastes" (1963)

This is a reasonably short selection of certifiably popular stories that in some way satisfies both the demands of contemporary and classic popularity.

The question one has, then, is how *representative* is this collection? Since no selection limited to twenty-six works can help but omit some important stories, the main question is, how can we determine how eccentric is the present selection? To give some statistical sense of how well the anthology represents the whole field during this period, I have compiled two lists (see Appendices 1 and 2) [not reproduced here due to space limitations]: the first shows the popularity of the individual stories in relation to other stories by these authors written during the same period; the second shows what significant stories of the period the anthology has omitted. The first chart lists for each of the authors who appear in *Science Fiction Hall of Fame* all of the stories that have been anthologized four or more times (*Science Fiction Hall of Fame* is included as one of the anthologies). I have chosen four as a number large enough to weed out the odd story that a single, prolific editor might eccentrically reprint a number of times, and yet not so large that it will exclude important but for some reason seldom reprinted stories. Using statistical information derived from William Contento's *Index to SF Anthologies and Collections,* I arrive at a list of 319 stories.[11] Of the particular stories in *Science Fiction Hall of Fame,* only Van Vogt's "The Weapon Shop" does not make the list.[12] Thus, the evidence in Appendix 1 argues for the representativeness of Silverburg's selections.

Using a similar method, we can begin to ask what has *Science Fiction Hall of Fame* neglected? The second chart (Appendix 2) lists two categories of authors not appearing in *Science Fiction Hall of Fame.* The authors in the first category have four or more stories first published after 1930 and before 1963 (the date of the last story included in *Science Fiction Hall of Fame*) that have been anthologized four or more times (thereby making them what we can call "significant authors"). The other authors have one story that has been anthologized seven or more times (thereby making them "significant stories"). This chart includes five significant authors not included in *Science Fiction Hall of Fame,* Volume 1. . . . While there are significant stories on this second list, there are plausible reasons why they may not have made the original *Science Fiction Hall of Fame.* . . . One could argue for the importance of a number of these stories for a thorough history of SF, but I do not think anyone would claim that to omit any of these popular stories is to distort the field in an important way. . . .

As I chose the stories in *Science Fiction Hall of Fame* as my sample, I am aware that I still have many further choices to make and that these will be open to the accusation of bias. Twenty-six stories may be an enormous reduction from the approximately eight thousand stories listed in the Contento *Index,* but it is still too large a number to analyze in depth without creating an unwieldy and unfocused study. Even twenty-six stories can lure one toward the encyclopedist fallacy of believing that the larger the number of references, the more acute the analysis. On the contrary, according to structuralist principles, three stories—representing the early, middle, and late periods—might show all the issues, techniques, and developments one can find in twenty-six. What such a formally elegant demonstration would lack, of course, is the very convincing power that comes from a proper sample. No three stories could ever be accepted as accurately representative.

The dilemma of the representative sample cannot be solved: twenty-six stories are, at the same time, too few and too many. Insofar as they are too few, I have compensated by making free reference to certifiably popular works outside *Science Fiction Hall of Fame.* Insofar as they are too many, I have made interpretative choices of focus. I have, however, tried to diminish arbitrary bias by enforcing the rule that all the stories in the anthology will be treated in some layer of the analysis. I thus, finally, will be treating *Science Fiction Hall of Fame* not simply as a sample but as a book itself, composed in 1970, depicting a vision of earlier SF's history and interests. As in the conventional literary interpretation of, say, a novel, in which the analysis is the more persuasive the more of the novel it accounts for, I have found most useful an analysis which explains the presence of elements that would otherwise seem out of place or irrelevant. Such a principle of value has operated both in the analysis of the individual stories and in the final analysis of the whole anthology. Since *Science Fiction Hall of Fame* is itself an interpretation, the final interpretative act of this study has been to look at the book against the background of 1971, the year it was published. *Science Fiction Hall of Fame* is not just a reconstruction in brief of "the golden age"; it is an argument, made at an identifiable moment in American history, about the form, place, and value of SF.

Notes

1. Leo Lowenthal, "The Debate Over Art and Popular Culture: A Synopsis," *Literature, Popular Culture, and Society* (Palo Alto: Pacific, 1961), 14–51.

2. Pierre Bourdieu, *Distinction: A Social Critique of the Judgement of Taste,* trans. William Nice (Cambridge: Harvard UP, 1984), passim.

3. Alan Swingewood, *The Myth of Mass Culture* (Atlantic Highlands, NJ: Humanities P, 1977), argues that the very category, whether invoked by conservative critics or by Frankfurt School Marxists, has a conservative aesthetic prejudice embedded in it. See also Bourdieu, *Distinction,* 483.

4. Henry Nash Smith's chapters on nineteenth century dime novels seem to me central to all serious consideration of popular literature. ("The Western Hero in the Dime Novel" and "The Dime Novel Heroine" in *Virgin Land: The American West as Symbol and Myth* [1950; rpt. New York: Vintage, n.d.], 99–135.) And Louis [*sic,* Russel] Nye's encyclopedic *The Unembarrassed Muse: The Popular Arts in America* (New York: Dial, 1970) was a necessary groundbreaking to which all later studies of noncanonic art must be indebted.

5. John Cawelti, *Adventure, Mystery, and Romance* (Chicago: U of Chicago P, 1976). Cawelti's defense of the formula was important for liberating literary scholarship from its concentration on single texts. As I turn back toward the individual text, I do so with an appreciation of the power of the formulaic background that Cawelti has explicated.

6. Jeffrey Sammons, *Literary Sociology and Practical Criticism: An Inquiry* (Bloomington and London: Indiana UP, 1977), 19, makes a similar point.

7. David Bordwell, Kristin Thompson, and Janet Staiger, *The Classical Hollywood Cinema: Film Style & Mode of Production to 1960* (New York: Columbia UP, 1985).

8. Will Wright, *Sixguns and Society: A Structural Study of the Western* (Berkeley: U of California P, 1975).

9. Cf. Frederic Jameson, "Generic Discontinuities in SF: Brian Aldiss' *Starship*," *Science-Fiction Studies,* 1.2 (1973), 57–68.

10. *Science Fiction Hall of Fame* (New York: Avon, 1970). Page references are to the paperback edition. In his preface to *Science Fiction Hall of Fame,* Robert Silverberg acknowledges choosing to include a story that came in one vote behind another story by the same writer and a story by a writer with four nominated stories over a very slightly more popular story by a writer with no other nominated stories. These minor deflections from a rigorously democratic procedure do not, to my mind, constitute an appreciable intrusion of aesthetic or theoretical distortion of the sort one finds in Wright.

11. William Contento, *Index to SF Anthologies and Collections* (Boston: Hall, 1978).

12. Contento has omitted Keyes's story, "Flowers for Algernon" from his list for *Science Fiction Hall of Fame,* but the slight change in numbers resulting from this mistake does not lead to any change in the rankings.

UNDERSTANDING POPULAR CULTURE

John Fiske

Popular culture, from John Fiske's neo-Marxist, post-structuralist, and British cultural studies perspectives, is not composed of the products of the mass culture industries in patriarchal capitalist societies. Rather it is that culture produced by subordinated and disempowered people as they consume dominant culture. This culture is a mix of (1) the ideology of the economically and ideologically dominant and (2) those resources embedded in dominant culture which ordinary people use in everyday life to erode, subvert, or refashion hegemonic culture to their own needs. Thus Fiske shifts analysis from production to consumption. Furthermore, he argues that a politics of popular culture can be progressive, especially at the micro-level, even if rarely revolutionary at any level in society, and thus his theory explains change, unlike many more traditional Marxist and structuralist theories. John Fiske is Professor of Communication at the University of Wisconsin-Madison, and author of several other books on aspects of popular culture, most notably Television Culture *(1987) and* Understanding Popular Culture *(1989), a companion volume to* Reading the Popular.

Popular Culture

This book consists of a number of analyses of popular culture in practice. In their various ways they all, I hope, shed some light on the meanings and pleasures we generate and circulate as we live our everyday lives. Culture is the constant process of producing meanings of and from our social experience, and such meanings necessarily produce a social identity for the people involved. Making sense of anything involves making sense of the person who is the agent in the process; sense making dissolves differences between subject and object and constructs each in relation to the other. Within the production and circulation of these meanings lies pleasure.

Culture making (and culture is always in process, never achieved) is a social process: all meanings of self, of social relations, all the discourses and texts that play such important cultural roles can circulate only in relationship to the social system, in our case that of white, patriarchal capital-

John Fiske, Reading the Popular *(Boston: Unwin Hyman, 1989): 1–12.*

ism. Any social system needs a cultural system of meanings that serves either to hold it in place or destabilize it, to make it more or less amenable to change. Culture (and its meanings and pleasures) is a constant succession of social practices; it is therefore inherently political, it is centrally involved in the distribution and possible redistribution of various forms of social power. Popular culture is made by various formations of subordinated or disempowered people out of the resources, both discursive and material, that are provided by the social system that disempowers them. It is therefore contradictory and conflictual to its core. The resources—television, records, clothes, video games, language—carry the interests of the economically and ideologically dominant; they have lines of force within them that are hegemonic and that work in favor of the status quo. But hegemonic power is necessary, or even possible, only because of resistance, so these resources must also carry contradictory lines of force that are taken up and activated differently by people situated differently within the social system. If the cultural commodities or texts do not contain resources out of which the people can make their own meanings of their social relations and identities, they will be rejected and will fail in the marketplace. They will not be made popular.

Popular culture is made by subordinated peoples in their own interests out of resources that also, contradictorily, serve the economic interests of the dominant. Popular culture is made from within and below, not imposed from without or above as mass cultural theorists would have it. There is always an element of popular culture that lies outside social control, that escapes or opposes hegemonic forces. Popular culture is always a culture of conflict, it always involves the struggle to make social meanings that are in the interests of the subordinate and that are not those preferred by the dominant ideology. The victories, however fleeting or limited, in this struggle produce popular pleasure, for popular pleasure is always social and political.

Popular culture is made in relationship to structures of dominance. This relationship can take two main forms—that of resistance or evasion. Evasion and resistance are interrelated, and neither is possible without the other: both involve the interplay of pleasure and meaning, but evasion is more pleasurable than meaningful, whereas resistance produces meanings before pleasures.

Making popular culture out of television news, for instance, is possible and pleasurable only if the subordinate can make their meanings out of it, otherwise the news would be part of dominant, hegemonic culture only. So the news of a snow storm or of Israeli troops quelling an uprising by Arab youths can be made popular only if it offers meanings that are relevant to the everyday lives of subordinate people, and these meanings will be pleasurable only if they are made *out of* the news, not *by* the news. These productive pleasures of making one's own sense are different in emphasis from the evasive, offensive pleasures of the body.

Popular culture is always in process; its meanings can never be identified in a text, for texts are activated, or made meaningful, only in social relations and in intertextual relations. This activation of the meaning potential of a text can occur only in the social and cultural relationships into which it enters. The social relationships of texts occur at their moment of reading as they are inserted into the everyday lives of the readers. Shopping malls are different texts for women and for unemployed youths, because their social relationships differ in each case: for women, malls are legitimate, unthreatening public places, that are opposed to both the street and the home; for unemployed youths, they are a place to trick "the system," to consume the images, warmth, and places of consumerism, without buying any of its commodities. The meanings of shopping malls are made and circulated in social practices.

But they are also made intertextually: bumper stickers announcing, "A woman's place is in the mall," coffee mugs decorated with the words "mall rats," or T-shirts that proclaim the pathology of the "shop-a-holic" can be used defiantly, skeptically, critically, and variously, according to their many uses—a father giving a T-shirt to his teenage daughter would set up a series of meanings that would differ significantly from those generated by it as a gift from one of her friends. The culture of shopping malls, as of Madonna, as of the beach, cannot be read off the primary texts themselves, but only in their social uses and in their relationships with other texts. The postcards we send are as much a part of the meaning of the beach as our use of it to expose ourselves to the sun and sight of others; Madonna's posters are as much a part of her meanings and pleasures as her songs and videos. The fan decorating her bedroom with Madonna icons, the wanna-bes (Madonna look-alikes) striding down the sidewalk, are agents in "Madonna culture," their texts (the bedroom, their bodies) as signifying as any of Madonna herself. The meanings of popular culture exist only in their circulation, not in their texts; the texts, which are crucial in this process, need to be understood not for and by themselves but in their interrelationships with other texts and with social life, for that is how their circulation is ensured.

Popular Productivity and Discrimination
The art of popular culture is "the art of making do." The people's subordination means that they cannot produce the resources of popular culture, but they do make their culture from those resources. Commodities make an economic profit for their producers and distributors, but their cultural function is not adequately explained by their economic function, however dependent it may be on it. The cultural industries are often thought of as those

that produce our films, music, television, publications, and so on, but all industries are cultural industries to a greater or lesser extent: a pair of jeans or a piece of furniture is as much a cultural text as a pop record. All commodities are consumed as much for their meanings, identities, and pleasures as they are for their material function.

Our culture is a commodity culture, and it is fruitless to argue against it on the basis that culture and profit are mutually exclusive terms—that what is profitable for some cannot be cultural for others. Behind such arguments lie two romantic fantasies that originate at opposite ends of the cultural spectrum—at one end that of the penniless artist, dedicated only to the purity and aesthetic transcendence of his (for the vision is a patriarchal one) art, and at the other that of a folk art in which all members of the tribe participate equally in producing and circulating their culture, free of any commercial taint. Neither of these fantasies has much historical basis, and neither of them is any help at all in understanding the popular culture of capitalist societies. The culture dimensions of industries are where their dominance is at its shakiest: they know that people have to eat, to wear clothes, to be able to transport themselves, but they are much less sure in determining what or why they want to eat, wear, or travel in. The cultural industries, by which I mean all industries, have to produce a repertoire of products from which the people choose. And choose they do; most estimates of the failure rate for new products—whether primarily cultural, such as movies or records, or more material commodities—are as high as 80–90 percent despite extensive advertising (and the prime function of our enormous publicity industry is to try to ensure the cultural circulation of economic commodities—that is, to exploit the cultural dimension of commodities for the economic profit of their producers). But, despite all the pressures, it is the people who finally choose which commodities they will use in their culture.

These pressures are not merely economic. The beach, for instance, is not a commodity to be bought and sold, and neither are the public rest areas of shopping malls or the view of Sears Tower from the freeway. But the absence of economic power does not mean the absence of social or hegemonic power. Attempts to control the meanings, pleasures, and behaviors of the subordinate are always there, and popular culture has to accommodate them in a constant interplay of power and resistance, discipline and indiscipline, order and disorder.

Much of this struggle is a struggle for meanings, and popular texts can ensure their popularity only by making themselves inviting terrains for this struggle; the people are unlikely to choose any commodity that serves only the economic and ideological interests of the dominant. So popular texts are structured in the tension between forces of closure (or domination) and openness (or popularity). So popular culture is full of puns whose meanings multiply and escape the norms of the social order and overflow their discipline; its excess offers opportunities for parody, subversion, or inversion; it is obvious and superficial, refusing to produce the deep, complexly crafted texts that narrow down their audiences and social meanings; it is tasteless and vulgar, for taste is social control and class interest masquerading as a naturally finer sensibility; it is shot through with contradictions, for contradictions require the productivity of the reader to make his or her sense out of them. It often centers on the body and its sensations rather than on the mind and its sense, for the bodily pleasures offer carnivalesque, evasive, liberating practices—they constitute the popular terrain where hegemony is weakest, a terrain that may possibly lie beyond its reach.

Popular texts are inadequate in themselves—they are never self-sufficient structures of meanings (as some will argue highbrow texts to be), they are provokers of meanings and pleasure, they are completed only when taken up by people and inserted into their everyday culture. The people make popular culture at the interface between everyday life and the consumption of the products of the cultural industries.

The aim of this productivity is, therefore, to produce meanings that are relevant to everyday life. Relevance is central to popular culture, for it minimizes the difference between text and life, between the aesthetic and the everyday that is so central to a process- and practice-based culture (such as the popular) rather than a text- or performance-based one (such as the bourgeois, highbrow one). Relevance can be produced only by the people, for only they can know which texts enable them to make the meanings that will function in their everyday lives. Relevance also means that much popular culture is ephemeral—as the social conditions of the people change, so do the texts and tastes from which relevances can be produced.

Relevance is the intersection between the textual and the social. It is therefore a site of struggle, for relevances are dispersed, and as divergent as the social situations of the people: the popular text, therefore, has to work against its differences to find a commonality between divergent social groups in order to maximize its consumption and profitability.

There is also a struggle over relevance itself, particularly in the function of news in popular culture. Though there are many similarities between entertainment and information, and hard-and-fast distinctions between them are as useless as they are popular among TV schedulers, power does work differently in each. There are few who now believe that it is in the national interest to control the entertainment of the people so as to improve their taste (which means, in practice, to do away with popular tastes and reduce them all to bourgeois ones), but there are much more solidly grounded arguments that there is information the people *need* to have if democracy is to flourish. A politically ignorant or apathetic electorate will be unable to produce high-caliber politicians. So television news, for example, is caught in the tension between the need to convey information deemed to be in the public interest and the need to be popular. It attempts to meet these contradictory needs by being socially responsible in content, but popular in form and presentation and thus runs the risk of being judged boring and irrelevant from one side, and superficial and rushed from the other. It is caught between competing relevancies at the national (or global) level and at the local level of everyday life, and can be judged to be successful only when it manages to merge the two into one.

Politics

Popular culture is the culture of the subordinate who resent their subordination; it is not concerned with finding consensual meanings or with producing social rituals that harmonize social difference, as the liberal pluralists would have it. Equally, however, it is not the culture of subordination that massifies or commodifies people into the victimized dupes of capitalism, as mass cultural theorists propose. Different though these two arguments are, they both find in popular culture only those forces that work in favor of the status quo—the liberal pluralists may define this in terms of a consensus, and the mass culturalists in terms of the power of the dominant classes, but neither argument allows popular culture to work as an agent of destabilization or as a redistributer of the balance of social power toward the disempowered. They are therefore inadequate.

Popular culture is structured within what Stuart Hall (1981) calls the opposition between the power-bloc and the people. The power-bloc consists of a relatively unified, relatively stable alliance of social forces— economic, legal, moral, aesthetic; the people, on the other hand, is a diverse and dispersed set of social allegiances constantly formed and reformed among the formations of the subordinate. The opposition can also be thought of as one between *homogeneity,* as the power-bloc attempts to control, structure, and minimize social differences so that they serve its interests, and *heterogeneity,* as the formations of the people intransigently maintain their sense of social difference that is also a difference of interest. It can be thought of as the opposition between the center and the circumference, between centripetal and centrifugal forces, or, more belligerently, as the conflict between an occupying army and guerrilla fighters, as de Certeau (1984) and Eco (1986) characterize it. But the relationship is always one of conflict or confrontation; the hegemonic forces of homogeneity are always met by the resistances of heterogeneity.

These resistances take various forms that differ in their social visibility, in their social positioning, and in their activity. It could be argued that the least politically active are the bodily pleasures of evasion, the dogged refusal of the dominant ideology and its discipline, and the ability to construct a set of experiences beyond its reach. Surfers and video game players "lose" their socially constructed identities and therefore the structure of domination-subordination in their moments of *jouissance* when the intensity of bodily concentration-pleasure becomes orgasmic. Other evasive, offensive pleasures are those of the carnivalesque, of exaggerated, liberating fun that inverts social norms and momentarily disrupts their power.

There are arguments that such evasive or carnivalesque pleasures are merely safety valves that finally serve to maintain the current structure of power by providing licensed, contained, controlled means of expressing resentment. There are similar arguments against the political effectivity of semiotic or interior resistances that occur within a realm of fantasy that is constructed outside and against the forces of ideological subjection. These arguments hold that because such resistance occurs within the realm of the individual rather than that of the social it is defused, made safe, and thus contained comfortably within the system. But what these arguments fail to take into account is the politics of everyday life that occur on the micro rather than macro level; they fail equally to account for the differences and potential connections between interior, semiotic resistances and sociopolitical ones, between meanings and behaviors, between progressiveness and radicalism, between evasive and offensive tactics. These are the issues and relationships that are central to the politics of popular culture, and theories that fail to address them can never offer us adequate insights.

Theories of ideology or hegemony stress the power of the dominant to construct the subjectivities of the subordinate and the common sense of society in their own interests. Their power is the power to have their meanings of self and social relations accepted or consented to by the people. At the most basic level, evading this power or inverting it is an act of defiance, for any expression of meanings that establish conflictual social differences maintains and legitimates those meanings and those differences. The threat to the power of the dominant is evidenced by their constant attempts to control, delegitimate, and disparage the pleasures of the people. But despite centuries of legal, moral, and aesthetic repression, the everyday culture of the people, often transmitted orally, has maintained these evasive, resistant popular forces without which more active resistances would have no base and no motivation. Evasion is the foundation of resistance; avoiding capture, either ideological or physical, is the first duty of the guerrilla.

The basic power of the dominant in capitalism may be economic, but this economic power is both underpinned and exceeded by semiotic power, that is, the power to make meanings. So semiotic resistance that not only refuses the dominant meanings but constructs oppositional ones that serve the interests of the subordinate is as vital a base for the redistribution of power as is evasion. The ability to think differently, to construct one's own meanings of self and of social relations, is the necessary ground without which no political action can hope to succeed. The minority who are active at the macro level of politics can claim to be the representatives of a social movement only if they can touch this base of semiotic resistance of people "thinking differently." Without this, they can all too easily be marginalized as extremists or agitators and their political effectiveness neutralized. The interior resistance of fantasy is more than ideologically evasive, it is a necessary base for social action.

But such action does not occur only at the organized macropolitical level; it occurs, too, in the minutiae of everyday life. Indeed, the politics of popular culture are much more effective and visible at the micro than macro level, for this is their most sympathetic terrain.

Semiotic resistance results from the desire of the subordinate to exert control over the meanings of their lives, a control that is typically denied them in their material social conditions. This, again, is politically crucial, for without some control over one's existance there can be no empowerment and no self-esteem. And with no sense of empowerment or self-esteem there can be none of the confidence needed for social action, even at the micro level. So Radway (1984) found a woman romance reader whose reading empowered her to the extent that she felt better able to resist the patriarchal demands made upon her by her marriage, and d'Acci (1988) found women fans of *Cagney & Lacey* of all ages who reported that the sense of self-empowerment produced by their fandom enabled them to promote their own interests more effectively in their everyday lives. So the provocation offered by Madonna to young girls to take control of the meanings of their femininity produces a sense of empowerment in one of the most disempowered of social groups that may well result in political progress in their everyday lives—in their relationships with their boyfriends or parents, in their refusal to give up the street to men as their territory.

Such political gains in the specificities of everyday life are progressive rather than radical. They enlarge the space of action for the subordinate; they effect shifts, however minute, in social power relations. They are the tactics of the subordinate in making do within and against the system, rather than of opposing it directly; they are concerned with improving the lot of the subordinate rather than with changing the system that subordinates them.

This is controversial territory, for there are those who would argue that such tactics finally serve to strengthen the system and to delay any radical change in it. If this argument is followed to its extreme, it would propose that the more the subordinate suffer the better, because their suffering is more likely to provoke the conditions for radical reform. This may well be theoretically correct, but it is hardly popular. It also rests upon a caricature of capitalism, that the system is not only unfair in its distribution of power and resources (which it *is*), but also totally inhumane in its exploitation of the weak (which it is not, in general, although U.S. capitalism does treat certain groups such as those who are both poor and mentally sick with something close to total inhumanity).

The reverse side of theories proposing that popular culture is at best a safety valve and at worst an opiate is the implication that a different sort of culture could provoke radical social reform. Such assumptions, unstated though they frequently are, are utopian. It is material historical conditions that produce radical reform; evasive and semiotic resistances can maintain a popular consciousness that can fertilize the growth of those conditions and can be ready to exploit them when they arise, but they cannot in themselves produce such conditions. But the resistances of popular culture are not just evasive or semiotic: they do have a social dimension at the micro level. And at this micro level they may well act as a constant erosive force upon the macro, weakening the system from within so that it is more amenable to change at the structural level. One wonders, for instance, how effective the attempts to improve the legal status of women would have been if it had not been for the constant erosion of millions of women working to improve the micro-political conditions of their everyday lives. It is arguable that the needs of the people are better met by progressive social change originating in evasive or interior resistance, moving to action at the micropolitical level and from there to more organized assaults on the system itself, than by radical or revolutionary change. Western patriarchal capitalism has proved remarkably able to prevent the social conditions that provoke effective radical action, and to contain such radical attempts that have been made upon it. It appears to be much more vulnerable to guerrilla raids than to strategic assaults, and it is here we must look for the politics of popular culture.

References

D'Acci, J. *Women, "Woman" and Television: The Case of Cagney and Lacey.* Unpublished dissertation, U of Wisconsin—Madison, 1988.

de Certeau, M. *The Practice of Everyday Life.* Berkeley: U of California P, 1984.

Eco, U. *Travels in Hyperreality.* London: Picador, 1986.

Hall, S. "Notes on Deconstructing 'The Popular.'" *People's History and Socialist Theory.* Ed. R. Samuel. London: Routledge & Kegan Paul, 1981. 227–40.

Radway, J. *Reading the Romance: Women, Patriarchy, and Popular Literature.* Chapel Hill: U of North Carolina P, 1984.

THE JOKE(R) IS ON US:
THE END OF POPULAR CULTURE STUDIES

Barry W. Sarchett

Barry Sarchett's erudite and provocative essay rejects "the popular," since there are no justifiable grounds to distinguish popular culture from "serious" culture. Using an analysis of the 1989 film Batman, and also much of contemporary critical thought on literary studies and cultural studies, he concludes that rather than employing different critical approaches to "low" and "high" cultural texts, since there are no intrinsic differences between them, a "symmetrical" critical approach should be used to study all cultural texts. Thus both "Popular Culture Studies" and "a formally exclusionary 'Literary Studies'" are obsolete. Sarchett is Professor of English at the Colorado College in Colorado Springs.

The inflationary theory market of the eighties gave rise to a proliferation of "theory guides" designed for the undergraduate classroom and teacher, so it was perhaps inevitable that the relatively successful displacement of Literary Studies by Cultural Studies in the early nineties would create a market for introductory guides such as the three that lie on my desk as I write: Graeme Turner's *British Cultural Studies: An Introduction,* Bob Ashley's *The Study of Popular Fiction: A Source Book,* and John Storey's *An Introductory Guide to Cultural Theory and Popular Culture.*[1] Each of these primers quite usefully addresses what is perhaps the crucial issue in contemporary literary study, and, for the last several years under the aegis of the many "Posts," we've all heard the news: traditional cultural hierarchies have collapsed. What Jan Cohn has called the "weary" distinctions between highbrow and lowbrow, elite and popular (25), authentic art and mass culture can no longer be self-evidently maintained under the pressure of both cultural mutations (postindustrial, postmodern, postcolonial, post-Culture culture) and theoretical interventions (poststructuralism, postmarxism). As Andreas Huyssen wished, critics have quickly caught on to

Barry W. Sarchett, "The Joke(r) Is On Us: The End of Popular Culture Studies," Arizona Quarterly *52.3 (Autumn 1996): 71–97. Reprinted from* Arizona Quarterly *52.3(1996), by permission of the Regents of the University of Arizona.*

the fact that we are living after the modernist discourse of the "Great Divide" between high art and mass culture has collapsed (viii–ix).[2]

What interests me most about these guides, however, is a certain self-defeating contradiction between strategy and theory. Storey claims, for example, that the intention of his book "is to provide an introduction to the academic study of popular culture" (xi). However, if the category of elite art is menaced culturally and theoretically, then, given the diacritical relationship of binaries, the category of the popular is also necessarily menaced. The end of elite art ("Literature," in this case) as an ahistorical, essentialized category entails the end of the essentially "popular" as well. Ashley in particular is acutely aware of this problem: noting that "the popular-serious distinction . . . is a theoretical minefield" (2), he must therefore allow that "the very notion of a method for the study of popular fiction may be questioned" and that "the ideal to work towards is one in which analysis is directed at 'fiction' with no need of qualitative adjective" (5–6). The question then remains—what could the project of theorizing and institutionalizing "the study of popular culture" possibly mean, if the category of the popular, like the category of literature, is in fact so difficult to locate?[3] Storey declares that "popular culture is in effect an *empty* conceptual category, one which can be filled in a wide variety of often conflicting ways depending on the context of use" (1). Like John Frow, then, I choose to reject the category of the popular, which "is equally . . . a refusal of the category 'high' culture" (81).[4] This further entails the proposition that, in the context of the academic study of cultural texts, the use of the term "popular culture studies" to denote any discreet disciplinary or sub-disciplinary arena can no longer be convincingly sustained in either institutional or theoretical terms.

Most analyses of postmodernity claim that such global distinctions as high and low cultures, when "conceived as unified blocs" (Ross 28), are now hopelessly blurred. We are thus left with a dynamic cultural field of multiple, contingent, and fluid differences: microcultures which are themselves sites of multiple "subject positions"—themselves fragmented, multiple—which may simultaneously inhabit other more or less different microcultures with more or less different agendas/interests.[5] To make matters worse—or better, as I would have it—this morass of multiple relational "positionalities" seems to imply, as Jim Collins has forcefully argued in *Uncommon Cultures,* that an "official" or "dominant" culture is "increasingly difficult to identify in contemporary societies" (2). Steven Connor puts this another way: much "theory of contemporary popular culture . . . is locked into an oppositional logic of dominant and marginal which does not allow for the blending of the two categories. For, after all, what is dominant in contemporary culture is the projection of a universe of multiple differences" (*Postmodernist Culture* 189).

For my money, Collins' and Connor's analyses have the ring of empirical truth. If we therefore regard "official" and "dominant" as relational concepts rather than reified entities, then it seems that they have always been mobile signifiers in a binarized cultural field. If high culture has traditionally identified itself (at least since the eighteenth century) as transcendent Truth or Spirit (the "saving remnant") in opposition to an emerging dominant but benighted mass culture, it is also true that populist valorizations of "folk" or "popular" culture (whether these are regarded as dichotomous or not)[6] have claimed Authenticity or Truth in opposition to an inorganic, more or less violently imposed official High Culture. Historically, both sides—Platonist elites and Jacksonian cultural populist—have appropriated the (modernist) privileged space of the enlightened, alienated, marginalized Other resisting the merely self-interested power of some perceived dominant and/or official force, be they barbarian hordes, utilitarian Philistines, "Culture Industry" cabals, or paternalistic elites.

Of course the same tropes govern the usually overheated rhetoric of our recent Culture Wars, in which each side—the so-called canonbusters and the so-called traditionalists—repeatedly tries to position itself as besieged victim and the other as dominant. The cultural right may be winning the war in the mainstream press at least in part because they have successfully constructed their opponents as *simultaneously* barbarians, cultural czars, *and* effete elites (e.g., the Republicans' attack on Hollywood and the music industry, an unintentionally ironic version of Frankfurt Schoolism). However historically naïve and question-begging their arguments may be, one has to marvel at the efficacy of the conservatives' strategy: they have positioned themselves as *both* besieged Platonists and besieged Jacksonians.

My analysis takes the post-Great Divide cultural situation as a given and questions the viability of popular culture studies through two interrelated strategies: first, a reading of Tim Burton's 1989 film, *Batman,* particularly the famous but critically ignored museum scene, which thematizes the (post) cultural position of the film itself—a simultaneous and self-conscious habitation in and invocation of heterogeneous cultural spaces; second, an unashamedly theoretical intervention which clarifies and justifies my contention that popular culture studies simply cannot exist in any *theoretically* convincing way.

The museum scene in *Batman* occurs just at the narrative center of the film and otherwise suggests its centrality for those interested in cultural hierarchies because it is an overt scene of cultural transgression. It begins in the hushed, genteel temple of official culture, Gotham City's Flugelheim

Museum, through which waft the soft and tasteful tones of Mozart ("Eine Kleine Nachtmusik," a wry comment on the Batman milieu). The museum suddenly becomes a bizarre gas chamber as purple gas infiltrates the heating ducts, killing all except Vicki Vale (Kim Basinger), who has come to the museum because the Joker (Jack Nicholson) has tricked her, then anonymously provided her with a gas mask at her lunch table. At this point, the cultural mayhem begins. The Joker and his crew, one of whom holds a beatbox on his shoulder, enter the museum (significantly, in subjective camera), and upon the Joker's ironic Arnoldian cue—"Gentlemen, let's broaden our minds"—they gleefully proceed to vandalize the artworks while dancing to Prince's "Partyman."

At first glance, it all seems clear enough: the scene may be construed as a more malevolent version of the Marx Brothers' cultural carnivalism in *A Night at the Opera*. The Joker is the seditious, nihilistic destroyer of beauty, order, and art, replacing the spiritual, European Mozart with the sensual, ethnic Prince.[7] According to the zero-sum economy of High Art acolytes, the bad necessarily drives out the good, and so the Joker—purveyor of the popular—logically destroys the sacred Rembrandts, Degases, and other masterpieces. Just as the street-culture has invaded high culture, so too is Gotham threatened by the various punks, thieves, and murderers who have made the streets unsafe for the law-abiding (white) bourgeoisie. This allegorical framework coincides with conventional "leftist" readings of the Batman figure as the vigilante defender of hegemonic bourgeois order (see Uricchio 206–7 and Ross 30–35).

However, the museum scene and the Joker's function within it cannot be so easily reduced to a political allegory. Burton's Joker resists readings which position him in opposition to some privileged cultural norm. Given Batman's well-known doubleness and his complicity with the famous villains (Reynolds 67–68)—fodder for many campish oneliners about him and Two-Face in the recent *Batman Forever*—it would hardly be surprising that the film radically complicates the Joker's cultural position. He simultaneously signifies heterogeneous cultural spaces, thus becoming not a figure *different from* an assumed norm, but a figure of difference/figuration itself, the Joker in the deck—that which assumes multiple and even contradictory positions, a mask or trace without positive identity.

This becomes clear when we take into account the entire museum scene, including the Joker's puzzling conversation with Vicki Vale. His antics put into play an array of conflicting semiotic grids of aporetic force. For example, in contra-distinction to his role as art-vandal, his Prince-inflected costume—the oversized beret, purple tails, string tie—both parodies and embodies the bohemian artist/dandy, the representative figure of the besieged alienation of modernist high culture. Likewise, many of his remarks

to Vale employ common modernist tropes of the artist as privileged reposi-
tor of truth and value: he tells her that "we mustn't compare ourselves to
regular people—we're artists," and he invites her to join him "in the avant-
garde of the new aesthetic."

This could of course be read as the film's sly "post" comment on the
exhaustion of the avant-garde and the institutionalization of modernism.
After all, the Joker's vandalism of the paintings, by means of graffiti and
spray paint, could just as easily be perceived as dadaist, anti-art art—the
Joker as Marcel Duchamp. Most forms of high modernism, in effect, made
cultural transgression the virtual ontotheology of art and putatively opposed themselves to what the Frankfurt School called the merely "affirmative culture" of mass or popular culture (Marcuse 88–113). The Joker takes
this transgressive position to its logical conclusion when he defines his
"new aesthetic": "I make art until somebody dies. I am the world's first fully
functioning homicidal artist." Murder somebody, then call it art.[8]

But this still cannot contain the Joker's meta-semiotic (the term
is Eco's, cited by Collins ["Batman" 170–71]) position, for at other times
he assumes the mask of the supposedly benighted masses—the "regular
people" he himself denigrates. When he first sits down with Vale, for
example, he plays the "Theme from *A Summer Place*" on his box, the epit-
ome of middlebrow, sentimental musical tastes (at other points in the film
he listens to "Beautiful Dreamer"). Or he may, in clichéd philistine fashion,
conflate aesthetic value with commodity capital, as when he points to
Gilbert Stuart's famed unfinished portrait of Washington and gleefully remarks, "the one-dollar bill," simultaneously foregrounding his own (high)
cultural illiteracy. Likewise, his allusive language and actions are often
apposite references to the intertextual arena of mass entertainment: in addition to his Prince-like wardrobe, he borrows phrases from Chuckles the
Clown of *The Mary Tyler Moore Show* ("A little song/A little dance/
Batman's head/On a lance") and the Wicked Witch from *The Wizard of Oz*
(he cries "I'm melting, I'm melting" when Vale throws a pitcher of water
on him). Finally, when he peruses Vale's portfolio (she is a professional
photographer), he calls her slick fashion photos "crap" but admires her
Time magazine war photojournalism, thus making his cultural standards
even more ambiguous. He ends his critique of her work with the cliché most
commonly attributed to the philistine mass audience: "I don't know if it's
art, but I like it."

We could thus easily argue that the Joker synecdochically represents
the film itself, a pastiche of prefabricated styles and quotations in true post-
fashion. Collins (1991) has discussed *Batman* as an example of what he
calls "hyperconscious narratives" of meta-popular culture. That is, as a global
blockbuster heavily marketed through the strategies of vertical integration,

Batman must "circulate throughout disparate cultures" (disparate enough to hail audiences through Mozart, Prince, and Percy Faith), yet it also reflexively displays its "own status as a mobile signifier" ("Batman"167). Collins further contends that such texts "evidence a highly sophisticated understanding of their semiotic environments," so much so that they manifest "a far more elaborate form of self-reflexivity" than the meta-fictional novels of recent art culture (171). Collins' argument thus contributes further to our general understanding of the destratification of cultural arenas and practices in contemporary life, where mass culture increasingly adopts formal and rhetorical strategies from on high (Huyssen ix).

But what I want to emphasize via the museum scene is that the Joker's array of cultural preferences and competencies—the result of simultaneous conflictual subject positions—seems to be so eclectic as to be undecidable, arbitrary. Therefore *if* one were asked to account for his decentered aesthetic values or tastes—an "account" being an attempt to wrest a provisional decidability from undecidability—common sense would probably locate them within the contingent and local domain of the Joker's own psychology or desires rather than in some set of "objective" aesthetic criteria. For example, the Joker stops his henchman, Bob, from slashing the last work of art slated for destruction by simply stating, "I kinda like this one, Bob. Leave it." The painting is one of Francis Bacon's screaming figures. The Joker's remark, and the nature of Bacon's art, could seem to justify an argument that his preferences are the result of his own pathologies, somehow sympathetically allied with the particular obsessions Bacon thematizes in his work (this would also account for his attraction to Vicki Vale's corpse-strewn war photos). In other words, as this commonsense position would have it, the Joker is not making objective or rational aesthetic judgements (the Bacon is "good"); he is simply stating subjective (and often untutored and morbid) preferences, no matter which of the many cultural masks or languages he assumes, barbarian, philistine, or elite.

This commonsense move should be familiar to those of us who study popular culture because it is based precisely on the traditional means used to distinguish the different formal *nature* and superior *value* of elite texts as opposed to the popular. That is, those who value or enjoy "authentic" art do so because they have access to some objective, universal standards which are immanent in the style and structure of the works themselves, while those who do not appreciate such works or who claim to enjoy works without such intrinsic value do so because of deficiencies in their particular psychophysiological makeup or in the particular sociocultural environment into which they were "unfortunately" born and out of which they should be "educated." In a book of utmost importance for popular culture studies, *The Contingen-*

cies of Value, Barbara Herrnstein Smith has characterized this as the "key move and defining objective" of arguments advocating objective standards of value—what she calls the "axiological tradition": "the privileging of the self through the pathologizing of the Other" (38). Tony Bennett makes this same point in Foucauldian form when he discusses "discourses of value" as producing a "valuing subject" which is at the same time a *"valued* subject":

> To the degree that discourses of value address the individual as always-ready, either wholly or in part, the valuing subject they produce and require, they constitute a means for the individual's valuation of self as both subject of discernment and ultimate valued object. Their structure is thus narcissistic. (*Outside Literature* 151)

Smith locates the fatal flaw in the axiological tradition (Derridians would refer to this tradition as logocentrism) in what she calls its "asymmetrical" system of explanation.

> Certainly any theory of aesthetic value must be able to account for continuity, stability, and apparent consensus as well as for drift, shift, and diversity in matters of taste. The tendency throughout formal aesthetic axiology, however, has been *to explain each in a quite different way:* specifically, to explain the constancies of value and convergences of taste by the inherent qualities of certain objects and/or some set of presumed human universals, and to explain the variabilities of value and divergences of taste by historical accident, cultural distortion, and the defects and deficiencies of individual subjects. (36, emphasis added)

She in turn has appropriated the concept of asymmetrical explanation from Barry Barnes and David Bloor, practitioners of what is sometimes called the "strong programme" in the sociology of science. In their article, "Relativism, Rationality, and the Sociology of Knowledge," they examine the *dualism* (read binarism) of traditional philosophy of science (rationalism), which holds on to the "distinctions between true and false, rational and irrational belief and insist[s] that these cases are vitally different from one another" (25). Barnes and Bloor advocate instead an "equivalence postulate" which holds that

> All beliefs are on a par with one another with respect to the causes of their credibility. It is not that all beliefs are equally true or equally false, but that regardless of truth and falsity the fact of their credibility is to be seen as equally problematic. The position we shall defend is that the incidence of all beliefs without exception calls for empirical investigation and must be accounted for by finding the specific, local cause of this credibility. (23)

In other words, the rationalist (or axiological or logocentric) tradition explains the credibility of so-called true or rational statements on formal and/or universal grounds:[9] they simply *are* true by virtue of the nature of Reason, Induction, Logic (they are what *any* rational being would hold), by virtue of some Kantian "conditions of possibility" for knowledge itself, or by virtue of an inherent correspondence to reality.[10] However, the credibility of other statements (usually derogatorily referred to as "mere" belief) must be accounted for by local, historical, social, psychological, or other contingent factors.[11] Herrnstein Smith appropriates Barnes' and Bloor's critique of rationalist dualism for her study of evaluative standards by noting the homological structure of axiological explanations of value and rationalist explanations of truth. Thus, she advocates replacing an asymmetrical account of value with a monist or equivalent account in which all human preferences would be explained symmetrically.

In accord with such an account, evaluative divergences and the exhibition of so-called bad taste would be seen as the product of the *same* dynamics—the playing out of the same variables, but with different specific values—that produce evaluative convergences and the exhibition of so-called good taste. (39)[12]

I have, of course, distilled the main points from the complex, nuanced arguments offered by Herrnstein Smith and Barnes and Bloor. This is not the place to rehearse or defend such arguments in detail.[13] Instead, I simply want to note that what they offer us are principled and rigorous versions of what we now commonly call antifoundationalism and which all three writers refreshingly and unapologetically call relativism. For cultural analysis, such theoretical work makes a difference: simply put, when accounting for any particular array of cultural hierarchies and values, one *can* (and, from my point of view, should) *always* explain all preferences—normative and deviant, high and low, canonical and non-canonical, elite and popular—symmetrically. None are disembodied or context-free and thus all may be described as functions or interactions among several contingencies and variables such as *particular* psychophysiological mechanisms and *particular* physical environments and social communities (Smith 38).

The traditional binary privilegings of elite culture in relation to popular culture are *all* open to the charge of asymmetrical explanation. Whether "art" has been described as the classical realm of the Spirit or Intellect—as opposed to the *merely* corporeal and fleeting pleasures of the popular, whether it has been attributed to the Romantic "unique" sensitivity of the "artist" who (paradoxically) transcends all locality—as opposed to the *merely* mass-produced and overdetermined "formulas" of the popular, whether it is seen as a Kantian intrinsically rewarding experience of the aesthetic (produced or consumed "for its own sake")—as opposed to the *merely* commodified and utilitarian production and consumption of the popular, whether it is described as the realm of *jouissance* or the sublime—as opposed to *plaisir* or the *merely* representational—all of these dualisms (and more) assume one set of preferences/values which are self-evidently "rational," "transcendent," and/or "authentic" and another set which are *merely* personal, contingent, and/or artificial, pathologies in need of diagnosis, correction, or redemption.

One of the most persistent formalized distinctions used to argue for the artificial, decadent, and/or politically retrograde nature of popular or mass culture has been based on its visual immediacy and sensationalism—its spectacularity. From classical writers such as Salvianus and Tertullian to contemporaries such as the Marxist Guy DeBord or neo-conservative liberals such as Daniel Boorstin and Christopher Lasch, the "spectacle" or "spectacular relations" have been invoked, as Patrick Brantlinger reminds us, by both the right and the left to denote the substitution of "the phony for the real, untruths for truths" (256). Brantlinger further notes that aversion to spectacularity "echo[es] Platonic doubts about physical appearances and about all the arts as third-hand reflections of the ideal." Thus the visual has come to be associated with the artificial and superficial: "Because the invisible surrounds and in some sense transcends the visible, the reduction of experience to visual imagery . . . will seem to liquidate essence" (260–61).

In *Batman,* the Joker's antics offer a sustained commentary on popular culture, the media, and spectacularity. In fact, all three recent Batman films have been obsessed with the powerful effects of the mass media. Like the Riddler in *Batman Forever,* the Joker creates and maintains his power by appropriating the airwaves. And with this rictal face, the Joker, like other malformed Batman villains such as the Penguin and Two-Face, provides an occasion for considering the vagaries of the visual image. The Joker, in effect, occasions a critique of the spectacularity of the mass media. Due to his beauty-product tampering, the glamour of Gotham City's newscasters is demystified as pure "image": without their makeup, they are haggard and ordinary. However, as in the museum scene, the Joker does not seek to replace the "merely" superficial with any sort of "natural" or precommodified image. Instead, with all of Gotham's beauty products poisoned, he offers his own "new and improved Joker products," which transform consumers into visual replicas of himself. The Joker, as maker and unmaker of art(ifice) and as consummate capitalist, demonstrates that visual codes—here, beauty codes—are contingently perceived and valued. Under capitalism, indeed, all value floats. What signifies as normative or natural is a matter of cultural construction and demographic dominance—if everyone looks like the Joker, then his rictus will be coded as natural; he will have revolutionized the hegemonic discourses of the body.

This in turn implies that the mass media and spectacularity contain no *inherent* political valence. That will depend *in part* upon who "owns" access to media representations, which is why revolutionary regimes often make a first priority of appropriating, in Althusserian terms, the modes of the Ideological State Apparatus, particularly media and educational institutions. Depending on contexts of production and consumption, they may operate either (relatively) hegemonically or (relatively) counter-hegemonically.

But it is the realm of consumption that critics of the spectacle from the left and right usually base their objections by positing a passive and malleable mass audience, more or less willing victims of the vicarious pleasures afforded them by spectacularity. And *Batman* might indeed be read, at least on this score, as a film which posits mass media spectacle as a powerful tool to warp consciousness, and the mass audience as duped and uncritical, much like the masses brainwashed by the Riddler in *Batman Forever*. Nowhere is this more obvious than in one of the last scenes in the film, the Joker's Macy's-like parade for Gotham's 200th anniversary celebration. This is pure spectacle—loud music (Prince again), glaring searchlights, loudspeakers, and colorful giant balloons, all designed to excite and yet control the mass audience. The scene seems at first glance an ideal opportunity to read the film through an anti-spectacle lens, for the Joker plans to gas the entire duped populace of Gotham after furnishing them with not only "circuses," but also the proverbial "bread"—he throws money at them like confetti to further induce their compliance.

At this point in the film, the Joker's use of spectacle clearly recalls fascism, and we may feel compelled to read the film as satirizing the duped public's willingness to settle for the pleasures of spectacle even as they are destroyed by their stupidity and greed. The Joker's exaggerated speech to the crowd reinforces this reading:

And now comes the part where I relieve you, the little people, of the burden of your failed and useless lives. But, as my plastic surgeon always said, "If you gotta go, go with a smile."

He then proceeds to poison the crowd by releasing the gas installed underneath the balloons, all cartoonish figures with smiles frozen horrifically on their faces. The pleasure of spectacle, then, is associated with deadly danger. Batman's dour disposition becomes the sign of self-reflective seriousness and virtue.

But such a reading can only succeed by repressing the film's meta-semiotic strategies. That is, *Batman* is itself a (meta)spectacle. The visual appeal of the film—special effects, grand and spectacular (no other word seems to do) sets, exaggerated costumes and dialogue—these are the very stuff of the Hollywood "spectacular," that particular embodiment of the technological sublime with which we are all so familiar. From the standpoint of production, spectacle may in fact be constituted as much by a kind of playful, infantile pleasure as by any overt desire to "manipulate." Thus, if the Joker is jealously fascinated by what he calls Batman's "toys," we should remember that the movie studio may well be Burton's own sublime toy set. In Orson Welles' famous words, as he looked upon RKO studios as a twenty-four-year-old, "This is the biggest electric train a boy ever had" (quoted in Giannetti 272).

From the standpoint of consumption, the effect of the film as spectacle is equally difficult to stabilize politically. Is it in fact an anti-spectacularity metaspectacle which invites us both to identify with the pleasure of spectacle as much as it invites us to distance ourselves from its possible effects? Or might we take a cue from Baudrillard and retheorize the nature of spectacle itself? In his formulation, the masses' demand for spectacle is in itself a resistance to an elite class's (in this case, intellectuals') imposition on them of "the imperative of rational communication."[14] The spectacle, then, becomes the masses' anarchical "refusal of meaning" (Modleski 31), and consumption, as in Certeau's formulations, becomes a possible site of tactical resistance. Thus, to invoke an old commonsense distinction, many people utilize popular culture for "entertainment," resisting the "virtuous," "serious," or "socially responsible" act of reading or viewing what is for them coded as "message" texts.[15]

I am not endorsing Baudrillard's particularity sanguine view of popular culture. I simply refer to it to reinforce the point of my reading of *Batman* as metaspectacle: there can be no formal or rational calculus which can hierarchize popular texts as spectacle in binary relation to "serious" non-spectacular texts in terms of their aesthetic, cognitive, or political value or effects. All these things will depend on complex and mobile factors such as production practices, consumption practices, and what particular constructions of "pleasure" or "truth" are being endorsed, or what particular practices different people regard as constraining, oppressive, or conversely, emancipatory. Thus, preferences and judgements either for or against spectacularity can be analyzed symmetrically: both are enabled and constrained by the same variables, even though they will be played out in terms of different specific values.

For some time now, many people in cultural studies have been busily applying various strategies of symmetrical (or postaxiological or poststructuralist) explanation for cultural hierarchies. We might call this work, *pace* Nietzche and Foucault, "genealogical" in its agenda: it seeks to trace the historicity and contingency of the normative, thus relativizing those putatively fixed, abstract, and universal standards or "touchstones" against which deviation could be identified and pathologized. At the risk of ignoring much groundbreaking and justifiably admired work by Raymond Williams, Edward Said, Pierre Bourdieu, Michel de Certeau, Susan Stewart, Jane Tompkins, Janice Radway, Andrew Ross, and many others, I will cite a relatively typical example: at the beginning of his 1988 study, *Highbrow/Lowbrow,* Lawrence Levine states this broad methodological agenda in blatant terms: he wants to examine "how and when . . . the cultural categories I had been brought up to believe were permanent and immutable emerge[d]" (6).

Rationalist or universalist claims in fact always contain the philosophically suspicious move of formulating a merely descriptive rule, then inferring from it a prescriptive rule. Cultural critics who attempt to trace the contingencies of elite categories eventually notice how axiological accounts of value smuggle in, more or less overtly, prescriptive rules in descriptive language. Levine, for example, immediately complains that "the adjective 'popular' has been utilized to describe not only those creations of expressive culture that actually had a large audience . . . but also, and often primarily those that had questionable artistic merit" (31). Jan Cohn has also noted the "faulty definition" of the elite based on notions of what is better or best (25). She then goes on to provide a social and historical account, as a symmetrical account must, for the emergence of both categories, elite and popular (25–26).

Yet, however much work such as this has served to demystify elite cultures and clear some space for competing critical discourses (a project which, as Collins reminded us, can also animate popular/ mass culture as well [*Uncommon Cultures* 2–16]), it is necessary to remember that asymmetrical and privileging accounts do not always line up on the side of "official" or elite culture. As Herrnstein Smith notes, axiology has also "been invoked repeatedly to *challenge* established evaluative authority and to claim, through a duplicate or mirror logic, an 'equal' legitimacy for officially substandard or deviant tastes" (73). Most of us who study popular culture have long been wary of the self-defeating move which claims that popular texts are "just as good as" canonical ones. But forms of "cultural populism" still abound, particularly in studies of a structuralist bent, which posit some immanent qualities in the popular, which then becomes the sign of an "authentic" expression of the "real" *Zeitgeist* embodied in the "folk" or "the people" or the working class. This of course simply mirrors the axiological logic of the defenders of the tradition and reinscribes the old dichotomies by pathologizing elite culture as merely artificial, contingent, local, and self-interested.

Cultural populism is in fact fraught with all the contradictions and political quagmires of any form of populism. For one thing, it has rarely been recognized that most practitioners of (Popular) Culture Studies, especially those influenced by the Birmingham School, while positioning themselves as resisting the traditional canon and the privileging of high culture, surreptitiously reinscribe forms of elite taste and canonicity directly along modernist aesthetic lines. John Frow has commented upon "a kind of inversion" in much Cultural Studies "in which certain elite popular culture forms have been privileged, while other popular forms—'the easy listener and light reader and Andrew Lloyd Webber fan,' for example—are not" (6–7).[16] More importantly, when intellectuals invoke populist rhetoric, they are likely to engage in a double repression: first, of their own construction of an Other assigned the name of "the people," and, second, of the politically volatile act of "speaking for Others" in postmodern culture.

As a category, "the people" is no less problematic than "the popular" itself, even though the former implicitly claims, as origin, to stabilize the latter. However,

> "the people" is not a given entity which precedes cultural forms, but is rather entirely the product of cultural forms: . . . it is a fact of representation rather than an external cause of representation. (Frow 84)

For some time we have been dealing with the vertiginous cultural implications of this particular dynamic of "the politics of representation"—intellectuals' traditional representation of ourselves as transparent, which enables and suppresses our own role in constructing the Imaginary Other of the "subaltern" for whom we claim to speak or, in the more "radical" populist form of this construction, who we claim can speak adequately for itself (see Spivak). The former claim of transparency simply ignores the effect of the enunciative position of speakers on meaning and truth, while the latter simply reduces all meaning and truth to the position (or social identity) of speakers. Neither takes into account the multiple and mobile determinants which make all utterances subject to an open-ended chain of contextual effects upon meaning.[17]

In order to surmount the theoretical and political problems of the binarisms inherent in either elitist or populist accounts, I would recognize that, as Jim Collins says in another form of the symmetrical account, "*all* cultural production must be seen as a set of power relations that produce *particular* forms of subjectivity" (*Uncommon Cultures* 16, emphasis added).

Thus, in accounting for the particular pleasures, attractions, or appropria-
tions of *any* cultural texts or set of texts—that is, in accounting, in the radical sense of the word, for the *popularity* of texts, whether for one person
or for millions of people, whether texts are categorized as high, low, or anywhere in between—the same explanatory procedures and categories can be
applied as would be applied to any other text or set of texts. This does *not*
mean, as the cultural right would have us believe, that all cultural distinctions are or will be collapsed. This objection misrecognizes the very nature
of difference and distinction. They never disappear; they are simply always
in various processes of contestation, renegotiation, and imbrication. As
Stanley Fish says of the new literary theories and methods, they "do not
deny the difference of literary works but inquire into the production and revision of that difference by social and political forces" (33).

Antony Easthope, for example, argues for differences between what
he calls "modernist textuality" (or the "high") and "popular textuality"
through close readings of *Heart of Darkness* and *Tarzan of the Apes*. But,
echoing Collins, he further claims that both texts " have a *common origin*
in textuality of which the way each hails the reader is an effect" (90). This
"common origin" enables him then to make what is in effect symmetrical
analyses of both high and popular discourse and thus deconstruct that opposition. That is, Easthope explains the local and contingent social and psychological factors which account for the pleasures of both kinds of discourse as they hail subjects through "different economies of desire" (96).
The crucial point here is that Easthope does not deny difference, he simply
accounts for those differences through the same explanatory procedures
and categories.[18]

Of course, any specific historical inquiry into the production, maintenance, and revision of these differences, may—and from my point of view
should—take into account the play of power relations, hegemonical discourses, distribution of cultural capital, and other *material* factors which
Fish notoriously avoids. However, in terms of the theoretical project undertaken here, such "political" accounts only beg the (no less material) question of value formation itself because any particular political preferences
are no less contingent or embodied than any other values. That is, both how
one accounts for and analyzes material "forces" and what particular position one takes in regard to political/social struggles are always open to the
same deconstructive, symmetrical analyses as are any other assumptions
and preferences. If there is no ontology of Literature, there is likewise no
ontology of Politics, no ground from which to launch a politics that is itself
not contestable, and thus not always already "political."[19] The coal miners'
famous question—"Which side are you on?"—is no different in relation to
the dynamics of value formation than the question which in many ways

provides the focus of this paper—"Which texts do you prefer?" This is emphatically not to deny the specificity of any particular social or cultural hierarchies or the exclusions maintained by asymmetrical distributions of financial and cultural capital; it is simply to insist on the unavoidable difficulties involved in (rationally) privileging any political practices—including reading practices—or cultural texts, whether they be (contingently) coded complicitous or subversive, dominant or resistant, hegemonic or counter-hegemonic.[20]

At this point, therefore, I need to be very clear about the relatively modest claims I am making in relation to literary and/or cultural studies. Simply because the "literary" or the "aesthetic" are not essential or ahistorical categories or simply because literature or literary value cannot be described in immanent terms (at least for those of us who find poststructuralism the most compelling explanatory and conceptual apparatus), it does not therefore follow that literary or aesthetic considerations are mere illusions of "false consciousness" or are themselves, as some materialist critics or Cultural Studies advocates would have it, reducible to the ideological reinforcement of a bourgeois status quo. The former claim seems to me an obvious reverse axiological move, and the latter simplifies the complex mediations of (polysemic and heteroglot) language, literature, history, and ideology. I am, in fact, making no claims about any intrinsic ideologically complicit *or* emancipatory qualities in the "literary," the "popular," or in literary studies or in cultural studies for that matter. Indeed, I think such claims make no sense (and that they have often resulted in a kind of puritanical scholasticism which demands that we take the political temperature of our texts and institutional practices hourly). I am only claiming that, whether one treats cultural texts of any type—high or low, "literary" or nonliterary—as cultural artifacts or as privileged works of art or both (as does Stephen Greenblatt[21]), each preference involves values which can be explained symmetrically, and thus can carry no formally privileged epistemological or methodological status.

Let me take as an illuminating example the New Historicist Brook Thomas' recent and carefully articulated attempt to "risk privileging literature" (162). Departing from Greenblatt's claims for the historical value of "great art," Thomas acknowledges that "literary works are clearly not alone in registering historical complexity" (159). Furthermore, Thomas acknowledges that "there is no intrinsic difference between literary and nonliterary language," that we must "abandon the effort to define literature formally," and that therefore literature is a "socially defined . . . institution" (162–64). In other words, Thomas' antifoundationalist credentials are in good order.

Yet Thomas properly insists that all this "does not mean that there is no such thing as literature," not the least because "if literature is one social institution among others, it is also a different social institution with a different social function from others" even though its function may "change over time" (163).[22] However, Thomas prefers to risk privileging literature for the following reason:

It is in examining the way in which literature (or the literary) can put at risk privileged ideologies, including our own, that I risk privileging literature. For me the way in which the play of literary texts can challenge fixed historical beliefs is at least as important as how they work to fix them. (162)

This formulation, of course, is not particularly original; in fact one could argue that it is a latter-day version of Matthew Arnold's claim that literature is a "criticism of life." But for my purposes, Thomas' passage deserves to be carefully unpacked. First, apropos of Arnold, we should mark the liberal humanist invocation of emancipatory thought, what Stanley Fish calls the "claim of Reason to be independent of ideology." I would merely repeat Fish's objection:

To this suggestion I would pose a simple question: if you propose to examine and assess assumptions, what will you examine and assess them *with*? And the answer is that you will examine and assess them with forms of thought that themselves rest on underlying assumptions. (17–18)

That is, as Fish never tires of telling us, whether you propose to challenge *or* to fix "historical beliefs" (and what other sort of beliefs are there?), the challenging or fixing will depend on fixed beliefs which are not and can not be put on the table in the process of challenging or fixing. Thus "challenging fixed historical beliefs" itself is a fixed value or preference which may be itself challenged, but only from a ground that itself rests on preferences and values which must remain at the level of (historical) assumption. Neither challenging or fixing can claim intrinsic epistemological status as a criterion for privileging or critiquing literature—they are "values" which *may* be (a preference I am recommending) accounted for symmetrically.

Thomas' recommendation for privileging literature in fact acknowledges this. His use of first-person personal pronouns—"I risk"; "for me"— carefully qualifies his assertions as contingent preferences grounded in an (inter)personal economy. However, even if one were to agree with his preferences, I would still claim that his privileging of the literary cannot provide a basis for excluding popular texts. To do so would require a further— and familiar—argument along the lines that the popular simply collapses into ideology, whereas the "truly" literary escapes into the free and unconditioned realm normally associated with the aesthetic. This inevitably becomes a formalist assertion that some texts intrinsically challenge or decenter readers while others simply reaffirm readers' ideological predispositions. Tony Bennet has described this as

the assumption of a correlation between the determination of an aesthetic and of a politics [which] has supported the view that a text's political effects can be read-off from, or calculated solely on the basis of, an analysis of its formal properties. This assumption lies behind those debates whereby one is expected to decide, in an abstract way, either for or against realism or modernism, for or against texts of *plaisir* or texts of *jouissance*. ("Marxism and Popular Fiction" 253)

I maintain that such distinctions inevitably simplify the problematic semiotic process "concerning the extent to which effects can be inferred from form"(Bennett, "Marxism and Popular Fiction" 254) and thus they ignore the particular and contingent relationships of particular readers to texts. They also would have to ignore much work on popular culture which has demonstrated its possible subversive, oppositional effects."[23]

Therefore I am *not* arguing (in a reverse axiological move) that the "literary" is merely a benighted concept which can or should be eliminated from English departments in order to replace it with the more philosophically or politically emancipatory program of what has become known as Cultural Studies. Personally, I prefer a loosely "cultural" approach to literary studies wherein, as Vincent Leitch says, "criticism" should include critique as well as explication (167). But I further maintain that both Literary Studies and Cultural Studies are premised on ethicopolitical and (inter)personal preferences which can be accounted for symmetrically, and that, therefore, neither can claim intrinsically privileged status. Furthermore, even inside the discourse of Literary Studies, any hierarchical arrangements of the truly literary as opposed to the merely popular can also be deconstructed as tastes which may be accounted for symmetrically. Given the oft-noted demographic diversity of the "new academy," in which there exist different taste cultures and different purposes that motivate different people to read cultural texts, I would agree with K. M. Newton that "English Studies will find it impossible either to discard questions of aesthetic and literary value or to avoid taking account of theoretical, historical or ideological factors" (157).[24]

Finally, in postaxiological "literary" studies, there simply is no convincing theoretical rationale for the distinct or discrete discipline of "popular" culture studies. And for those of us who read and teach popular texts this should be the happiest of news; I simply mean that in academic departments whose business it is to study and produce knowledge of cultural texts—and that obviously includes more than English departments—there simply no longer remains any basis for privileging elite art or excluding the popular which can marshal hegemonic opposition to the serious theoretical arguments generated by poststructuralism. This further means that the category "popular" *makes no difference* in postaxiological literary studies, except as one more category among others to be interrogated. The "end" of Popular Culture Studies is only another way of denoting the "end" of a formally exclusionary "Literary Studies." Let me repeat that this does not entail the end of study/research that is (loosely) "literary" in its focus and which will necessarily give way to study/research that is (loosely) "cultural." Whether literary or cultural or both, our practices can incorporate graffiti as well as the epic, television as well as the art-film, Zane Grey as well as Henry James, Ian Fleming as well as D. H. Lawrence, Barbara Cartland as well as Toni Morrison. And any hierarchies of value which emerge from such study (or which claim the superior value of literary over cultural studies or vice versa) may be explained symmetrically and thus cannot claim universality or intrinsicality. In other words, the study of popular culture has arrived, not exactly in the way many "populists" expected, but much more forcefully than traditionalists, who desperately shrug off the whole enterprise as a corrupt fad, dare admit.

It is again the figure of the Joker who helps make this situation clear. At the end of the museum scene, when Vicki Vale throws a pitcher of water in his face and he mimics the Wicked Witch of the West, he holds his hands over his face as he screams, "I'm melting!" Throughout this scene, the Joker has been without his customary whiteface clown makeup: he's "going natural" it seems. But when he pulls his hand from his face after being doused with water, we find that it has washed off the natural face to reveal—what else?—A "mask" of whiteface. For the Joker, the natural consists only of another mask, another construction, another form of textuality. For the Joker, the mask of the elite is therefore "equivalent" to (but not the same as) the mask of the popular or even the philistine, insofar as they are all constructed and contingent categories. The joke is therefore not simply *on* us, it *is* us: the Joker's identity—that which is continuously and contingently (re)valued—describes the world of texts and institutional practices which inhabits and is inhabited by The English Department.

The Colorado College

Notes

1. For an interesting analysis and critique of the theory guides, see Parrinder, who discusses Raman Selen's *A Reader's Guide to Contemporary Literary Theory,* K. M. Newton's *Interpreting the Text,* and others. He makes the important point

that, even though all the guides putatively subscribe to poststructuralist notions of language and narrative, each one narrativizes the move from traditional forms of literary study to more theoretically "informed" study as a self-evident "advance" in practice. Such a teleological narrative from blindness to insight of course contradicts the poststructuralist premises which drive the guides. My readings of the Cultural Studies guides confirm the same contradiction at work in them, in addition to the contradiction I discuss immediately below.

2. The exhaustion of the discourse of Literature (as it is opposed to the residual and degraded categories of popular or mass culture) is superbly analyzed by Huyssen, Bennett ("Marxism and Popular Fiction," *Outside Literature*), Easthope, and Guillory. Perhaps the most influential announcement of the End of Literature is the last chapter ("Conclusions: Political Criticism") of Terry Eagleton's ubiquitous *Literary Theory: An Introduction.* Preceding Eagleton, less influential, no less passionate, and more interesting for students of American literature, is Leslie Fiedler's *What Was Literature?*

3. Bennett's "Marxism and Popular Fiction" is a crucial influence on the guides. A productive and careful mixture of deconstruction and Marxism, his essay asks us "to think outside" (239) the Literature/Popular binary and concludes that "there is no necessary reason why a space should exist within Marxist theory for the concept of Literature" (251). But Bennett's next move (from my point of view, the proper one) then calls into question the *raison d'être* of any guide to popular culture studies: "Nor is the development of a fully-fledged theory of popular fiction an appropriate response, for this axiomatically concedes the theoretical and political pertinence of conventional constructions of relations of difference and similarity in the sphere of writing" (256). In effect, I premise my essay on the undesirability of this concession.

4. But Frow correctly qualifies this rejection: "What is being rejected is not the heterogeneous space of texts and practices covered by the term [popular], nor is it the political impulse to recover and give value to the domain of everyday culture." Frow's rejection, like mine, "is only of the categories, or more precisely the *structure* of the categories used to construct and describe this space" (80–81).

5. For a sanguine but lively discussion of such a dynamic cultural field, see Clayton. See also Collins (*Uncommon Cultures*) and Connor. For a postMarxian analysis of the political implications of these cultural and theoretical developments, see Laclau and Mouffe's influential and widely debated *Hegemony and Socialist Strategy.*

6. For a compelling critique of the functional distinctions between folklore and popular (or "mass") culture, see Levine ("Folklore").

7. For a reductive reading of the racial politics of *Batman,* see Ross. Given the rigor and subtlety of Ross' previous work, I was surprised and dismayed at the insouciant connections and dismissive tone of this piece. Cultural hierarchies in Western culture, we should not be surprised, are usually laden with racial tropes.

For a most conspicuous example, see Hume's famous essay "Of the Standard of Taste," which has been subjected to a powerful critique in this regard by Barbara Herrnstein Smith (*Contingencies of Value* 55–64). See also Levine *(Highbrow/ Lowbrow* 221–22) for the racial origins of the terms highbrow and lowbrow. But the existence of such master tropes does not mean that they (ever) operate unambiguously and monolithically in specific texts.

8. Elided here, of course, is a *gendered* reading of the Joker's "art." The bodies on which the Joker inscribes his disfiguration-art are female. I would contend that a reading which takes this into account should also factor in the much-debated question of the gendered nature of the modernist avant-grade (see Huyssen 43–62), the sexual politics of the entire film (which may be read as positioning both Batman and the Joker as pubescent boys fighting over a girl and what the Joker calls Batman's "wonderful toys"), and perhaps Burton's work to date. In other words, a gendered reading of the scene will be neither self-evident nor unambiguous.

9. I use the term "rationalism" quite loosely here, including its usual binary empiricism, under the rubric since both share a commitment to working out a formal/procedural theory of credibility. That is, they share a desire to establish certain forms of knowledge as *intrinsically* privileged, rather than culturally (re)produced. For an extended discussion of the principle of symmetrical analysis, see Bloor's *Knowledge and Social Imagery.* Originally published in 1976, this remains the crucial text for understanding the methodology of the various schools of the "sociology of scientific knowledge." The second edition includes a lengthy response to Bloor's critics.

10. For an extended and by now widely known critique of the asymmetrical explanation of the (inherent) credibility of appeals to "correspondence to reality" in Western rationalist philosophy, see Rorty,

11. Rationalists of various sorts argue, in expected dualistic terms, that "validity" must be distinguished from "credibility." But this simply reinscribes their original distinction between formal, objective Reason and "mere" belief. In other words, they argue for a position through the categories and assumptions of the very position that is under question—the classical begging of a question or circularity of argument, which is *necessarily* constitutive of rationalism. As C. S. Pierce noted, "One cannot well demand a reason for reasonableness itself" (332). Barnes and Bloor thus make the pragmatist claim that "validity detached from credibility is nothing" (29).

12. Lest Smith (or I) be misunderstood here, let me address one possible point of contention or source of anxiety. To argue against (or deconstruct) asymmetrical explanations of value is not to give up on the idea of value itself. Smith in fact notes that this would be impossible: "For a responsive creature, to exist is to evaluate. We are always, so to speak, calculating how things 'figure' for us—always pricing them, so to speak, in relation to the total economy of our personal universe" (42). Other poststructuralist value theorists put it even more dramatically: Vincent Leitch

states that "the time of evaluation is always, the place is everywhere" (111); John Frow notes that "there is no escape from the discourse of value" (134).

13. For a particularly scathing review of Smith see Harpham. His attack is primarily fueled by his (relatively) visceral distrust of "theory" and the usual rationalist objection to relativism as self-refuting. Steven Connor also criticizes Smith for the supposed "performative self-contradiction" of "all such attempts to assert the absolute absence of absolutes, the regulation of the field of value by a rule of non-regulation" (*Theory and Cultural Value* 26). Smith responded to Harpham in the next issue of *Raritan* with an equally scathing attack on his argument and tone, but for her longer and quite precise argument against the much-proffered "self-refutation" inherent in relativism, a project she already begins in *Contingencies of Value* (112–14), see "Unloading the Self-Refutation Charge." (For a similar refutation of self-refutation, see Bloor, 17–18.) A much more nuanced and appreciative critique of Smith has been mounted by Guillory (283–303), whose crucial move against Smith has been picked up and succinctly restated by Mary Poovey: according to this account Smith "invokes" a binary opposition between economic theory and aesthetic axiology, but she fails because she "argu[es] philosophically" rather than providing a "properly historical analysis" which would situate Smith's own privileged economic vocabulary as contingent itself (Poovey 79–80). Aside from the issue of whether Smith herself does not realize that her economic metaphors are simply that (in fact she repeatedly and clearly acknowledges the contingency of her own vocabulary) I would point out that Guillory and Poovey invoke their own binary—history and philosophy—and quite uncritically privilege the former. That is, any "properly" (a typical question-begging term which assumes the intrinsic truth of an ontological ground) historical analysis is of course open to philosophical inquiry and critique, as well as vice-versa. But in dismissing philosophy as necessarily trumped by history without acknowledging the chiasmic accountability of history to philosophy, Guillory and Poovey fail to recognize the contingent/historical limits of their own historical vocabulary and methods. They also, of course, demonstrate their own anti-theoretical position and thus their decidedly pre-New Historical historiographic assumptions.

14. Quoted from Baudrillard's *In the Shadow of the Silent Majorities or the End of the Social and Other Essays* in Modleski, 31. Modleski's chapter "Femininity as Mas(s)querade" contains a bemused analysis of Baudrillard's claims about the nature of mass culture. She is drawn to his positive valuations of the "end of the social," because, as scholar and critic of popular culture, she recognizes it as a possible site of resistance and contestation. But she also is repelled by an end to the social when, as a feminist, she insists on access to the social for those to whom it has previously been denied: "Only those who have had privileged access to the social can gleefully announce its decline" (34).

15. The term "entertainment" is as slippery as any other critical term, but again I would insist that an "entertaining" text cannot be defined in advance using

any formal criteria. As Richard Dyer notes, *Oedipus Rex* and *Hamlet* can be viewed or read as "entertaining"; therefore "entertainment is not so much a category of things as an attitude toward things" (12).

16. Frow quotes from Simon Frith's attack on forms of cultural populism: "The Good, the Bad, and the Indifferent: Defending Popular Culture from the Populists," *Diacritics* 21.4 (1991): 104. For a critique of the branch of Cultural Studies associated with the University of Birmingham's Center for Contemporary Cultural Studies, see Leitch, 145–61.

17. I am indebted here to Frow's excellent discussion of the problems of cultural populism in his chapter "Economics of Value" (131–69). Frow is in turn heavily indebted to Smith's book, and to Spivak's discussions of identity politics, which is closely allied to recent forms of cultural populism. Frow quotes Spivak approvingly: "'The position that only the subaltern can know the subaltern, only women can know women, and so on, cannot be held as a theoretical presupposition . . . for it predicates the possibility of knowledge on identity'" (163n).

18. Easthope notes furthermore that different modes of reading/interpretation create different forms of valuation. Thus the "modernist reading" (loosely, various forms of New Critical formalism) not surprisingly finds texts such as *Tarzan* deficient in comparison with *Heart of Darkness*. Easthope's own reading based on the difference between iconic and symbolic modes of representation suggests that "the pleasures of popular culture may exceed those of the high cultural tradition" (93), thus he imperils his own symmetrical account by falling into a reverse axiology.

19. See Honig for a Derridean treatment of this problem in relation to the classical political theories of republicanism, liberalism, and communitarianism.

20. Of course these binaries themselves need interrogating. Commenting on current practices in Cultural Studies, Tony Bennett has warned against the usual division of the cultural field into "two opposing . . . ideological camps . . . locked in a zero-sum game in which one side gains only at the expense of the other." Instead, Bennett argues, we must realize that it is impossible "to locate a source of popular culture or expression which is not . . . profoundly shot through with elements of the dominant culture . . . That is what dominant culture does: it dominates" (quoted in Frow 83n). I would only add that this holds true of *all* cultural expression, popular or otherwise.

21. I refer to Greenblatt's much-discussed claim in *Renaissance Self-Fashioning* that "great art is an extraordinarily sensitive register of the complex struggles and harmonies of culture" (quoted in Newton 150 and in Thomas 158).

22. I would amend Thomas here: literature, like any other social institution, has "social functions," but there is no reason to believe that such functions are reducible to a singular monolithic "function," or that any single function is identical to itself, i.e., without the internal antagonisms of any *socius*.

23. For prominent examples see Certeau, Fiske, Longhurst, and Laclau and Mouffe (163–65). For appreciative critiques of Certeau and Fiske, see Frow. For

my own extended argument against the formalist distinction of subversive "literature" and the merely complicitous "popular," see Sarchett.

24. Vincent Leitch also agrees: "The choice between literary and cultural studies is best conceived as both/and, not either/or" (xv).

Works Cited

Ashley, Bob. *The Study of Popular Fiction: A Source Book.* Philadelphia: U of Pennsylvania P, 1989.

Barnes, Barry, and David Bloor. "Relativism, Rationalism, and the Sociology of Knowledge." *Rationality and Relativism.* Ed. Martin Hollis and Steven Lukes. Cambridge: MIT, 1982. 21–47.

Bennett, Tony. "Marxism and Popular Fiction." *Popular Fictions: Essays in Literature and History.* Ed. Peter Humm, Paul Stigant, and Peter Widdowson. New York: Methuen, 1986. 237–65.

———. *Outside Literature.* New York: Routledge, 1990.

Bloor, David. *Knowledge and Social Imagery.* 2nd ed. Chicago: U of Chicago P, 1991.

Brantlinger, Patrick. *Bread and Circuses: Theories of Mass Culture as Social Decay.* Ithaca: Cornell UP, 1983.

Clayton, Jay. *The Pleasures of Babel: Contemporary American Literature and Theory.* New York: Oxford UP, 1993.

Cohn, Jan, "Redefining Literature." *Journal of Popular Culture* 23.3 (1989): 23–29.

Collins, Jim. "Batman: The Movie, Narrative: The Hyperconscious." *The Many Lives of Batman: Critical Approaches to a Superhero and His Media.* Ed. Roberta E. Pearson and William Uricchio. New York: Routledge, 1991. 164–81.

———. *Uncommon Cultures: Popular Culture and Post-Modernism.* New York: Routledge, 1989.

Connor, Steven. *Postmodernist Culture: An Introduction to Theories of the Contemporary.* Cambridge, MA: Basil Blackwell, 1989.

———. *Theory and Cultural Value.* Cambridge, MA: Basil Blackwell, 1992.

De Certeau, Michel. *The Practice of Everyday Life.* Berkeley: U of California P, 1984.

Dyer, Richard. *Only Entertainment.* New York: Routledge, 1992.

Eagleton, Terry. *Literary Theory: An Introduction.* Minneapolis: U of Minnesota P, 1983.

Easthope, Antony. *Literary into Cultural Studies.* New York: Routledge, 1991.

Fiedler, Leslie. *What Was Literature?* New York: Simon and Schuster, 1982.

Fish, Stanley. *There's No Such Thing as Free Speech and It's a Good Thing, Too.* New York: Oxford UP, 1994.

Fiske, John. *Understanding Popular Culture.* Boston: Unwin Hyman, 1989.

Frow, John. *Cultural Studies and Cultural Value.* New York: Oxford UP, 1995.

Giannetti, Louis. *Masters of the American Cinema.* Englewood Cliffs, NJ: Prentice-Hall, 1981.

Guillory, John. *Cultural Capital: The Problem of Literary Canon Formation.* Chicago: U of Chicago P, 1993.

Harpham, Geoffrey Galt. "Valuemania." *Raritan* 9.1 (1989): 134–49.

Honig, Bonnie. *Political Theory and the Displacement of Politics.* Ithaca: Cornell UP, 1993.

Huyssen, Andreas. *After the Great Divide: Modernism, Mass Culture, Postmodernism.* Bloomington: Indiana UP, 1986.

Laclau, Ernesto, and Chantal Mouffe. *Hegemony and Socialist Strategy: Towards a Radical Democratic Politics.* New York: Verso, 1985.

Leitch, Vincent B. *Cultural Criticism, Literary Theory, Post-Structuralism.* New York: Columbia UP, 1992.

Levine, Lawrence W. "The Folklore of Industrial Society: Popular Culture and Its Audiences." *American Historical Review* 97 (Dec. 1992): 1369–99.

———. *Highbrow/Lowbrow: The Emergence of Cultural Hierachy in America.* Cambridge: Havard UP, 1988.

Longhurst, Derek. Introduction. *Gender, Genre, and Narrative Pleasure.* Ed. Derek Longhurst. London: Unwin Hyman, 1989. 1–9.

Marcuse, Herbert. *Negations: Essays in Critical Theory.* Boston: Beacon, 1968.

Modleski, Tania. *Feminism without Women: Culture and Criticism in a "Postfeminist" Age.* New York: Routledge, 1991.

Newton, K. M. "Aesthetics, Cultural Studies and the Teaching of English." *The State of Theory.* Ed. Richard Bradford. New York: Routledge, 1993. 145–61.

Parrinder, Patrick. "Having Your Assumptions Questioned: A Guide to the 'Theory Guides.'" *The State of Theory.* Ed. Richard Bradford. New York: Routledge, 1993. 127–44.

Pierce, C. S. *Collected Writings.* Ed. Philip Weiner. New York: Dover, 1958.

Poovey, Mary. "Aesthetics and Political Economy in the Eighteenth Century: The Place of Gender in the Social Constitution of Knowledge." *Aesthetics and Ideology.* Ed. George Levine. New Brunswick: Rutgers UP, 1994. 79–105.

Reynolds, Richard. *Super Heroes: A Modern Mythology.* Jackson: UP of Mississippi, 1992.

Rorty, Richard. *Philosophy and the Mirror of Nature.* Princeton, NJ: Princeton UP, 1979.

Ross, Andrew. "Ballots, Bullets, or Batmen: Can Cultural Studies Do the Right Thing?" *Screen* 31.1 (1990): 26–44.

Sarchett, Barry. "Unreading the Spy Thriller: The Example of William F. Buckley, Jr." *Journal of Popular Culture* 26.2 (Fall 1992): 127–39.

Smith, Barbara Herrnstein. *Contingencies of Value: Alternative Perspectives for Critical Theory.* Cambridge: Harvard UP, 1988.

———. "Unloading the Self-Refutation Charge." *Common Knowledge* 2.2 (1993): 81–95.

Spivak, Gayatri Chakravorty. "Can the Subaltern Speak?" *Marxism and the Interpretation of Culture.* Ed. Cary Nelson and Lawrence Grossberg. Urbana: U of Illinois P, 1988. 271–313.

Storey, John. *An Introductory Guide to Cultural Theory and Popular Culture.* Athens, GA: U of Georgia P, 1993.

Thomas, Brook. *The New Historicism and Other Old-fashioned Topics.* Princeton, NJ: Princeton UP, 1991.

Uricchio, William, and Roberta E. Pearson. "'I'm Not Fooled By That Cheap Disguise.'" *The Many Lives of Batman: Critical Approaches to a Superhero and His Media.* Ed. Roberta E. Pearson and William Uricchio. New York: Routledge, 1991. 182–213.

III.
Macro How-to-Do-It
Approaches
to the Study
of Popular Culture

NOTES TOWARD A METHODOLOGY
OF POPULAR CULTURE STUDY

Lawrence E. Mintz

Lawrence Mintz's brief essay poses the questions (at least many of them) necessary for "serious, scholarly and methodologically sophisticated studies of popular culture." Taken together these questions constitute an outline for a comprehensive approach to the study of popular culture. Specifically, Mintz focuses on the production, distribution, consumption, themes, aesthetics, and cultural contexts of popular culture. Mintz, Professor of American Studies at the University of Maryland, is author of several studies on contemporary American performance comedy.

The best contemporary work being done in popular culture studies is radically different from that of the decades of the 1940s through the early 1960s.[1] Compared to the often limited sociological studies and the highly impressionistic arguments for and against popular culture characteristic of the "B.B. era" (before Ray Browne and the founding of the *Journal of Popular Culture* and the Popular Culture Association), these more recent efforts exhibit a "mature" or "third generation" methodology—"third generation" in the sense that they display a marked advance over the merely descriptive, superficially explicatory, or uncritically enthusiastic examinations of popular culture which weakened some programs and publications of the organization's early years.[2] This is not to suggest that no sound and useful work has been done in the field until recently, nor that anemic scholarship in popular culture is no longer being promulgated. The tide has been effectively stemmed if not entirely dammed, however, and largely because increasing numbers of popular culture scholars have been drawing upon the full range of analytical and critical approaches developed by contemporary humanists and social scientists.

Reviewing these latest trends in popular culture theory and methodology is not, however, the purpose of the essay.[3] Rather, it is to offer a series of questions that might serve as starting points for any serious inquiry into

Lawrence E. Mintz, "Notes Toward a Methodology of Popular Culture Study,." Studies in Popular Culture *6 (1983): 26–34.*

a popular culture subject, as directions for a search of the data relevant to the subject, and as suggestions for developing a methodology appropriate to such a subject.

At the outset it must be noted that some of the questions to be asked regarding popular culture texts, artifacts, and experiences cannot always be answered authoritatively. For in some cases the data are not accessible or even obtainable and in others not even the most meticulous and carefully applied methodologies are adequate to the task. Moreover, to ask and attempt to answer every possible question relevant to a given popular culture subject under study would result in a lengthy volume for every analysis. On the other hand, merely describing such a subject, or superficially explicating it, or simplistically evaluating it only serves to belabor the obvious and can seldom advance popular culture studies as a whole. It is serious, scholarly, and methodologically sophisticated studies of popular culture as a human phenomenon that justify the time and efforts of scholars and their audiences alike.[4] The questions cited below are intended to foster and facilitate such inquiries.

i. What facts concerning the production, distribution, and consumption
of the popular culture artifact can we locate and comprehend?

Obviously we want to know who produced the artifact, when, where, and with what acknowledged motives. But we also want to know who was responsible for making it available, to whom, and how (e.g., was it advertised, promoted, marketed in tandem with other products, etc.?). How was it received, critically and popularly, in qualitative and quantitative terms? How was it used?

When we deal with popular books, for example, we must be aware of differences in mass-market, trade, and hardbound book-marketing policies. (If a book is available in grocery and drug stores as well as in book stores, its sales and its audiences will be distinctly different.) And what of the role of book clubs, the factor of promotions (advertising, television talk-show "flogging"), the reputation of the author, the popularity of the genre or the series, the "clout" of the publishing house? (One speaks of a "gothic," a "hard-boiled detective novel," a "Harold Robbins novel," a "Harlequin," as meaningfully or perhaps more meaningfully than one does of a particular title.)

In popular music genre is also an important factor, but so too is subgenre, if one considers country music, say, to be a genre and Nashville, Bakersfield, Outlaw, Progressive, Country-Rock, Tex-Mex and others to be distinct variations of it. Also to be taken into account are: taste-public audiences (e.g., "teeny-boppers," "heads," ethnics, etc.); the economics of promotion (tours, incentives for radio airing); the concert as a theatrical as well as a musical phenomenon, even as a rite or ritual; the historical origins and fusions that have led to the development of the product; the relationships between music and dancing, dating, dope, and other factors of the music's consumption. In sum, how did the music work, for whom, and why?

In the case of comic strips and cartoons we have to consider the role of the syndicates and editors. (For example, in the course of the author's research into Milton Caniff, it was discovered that the basic elements of *Terry and the Pirates* were outlined for Caniff by the syndicate head on the basis of what seemed to be selling in the industry at the time.) Technical factors, such as the size allotted to a given strip or cartoon, must also be investigated.

Competitive trends are of importance in the study of magazines: for example, the success of *People* has led other popular magazines to be more receptive to celebrity biography than they previously were. Also significant may be changes in ownership and personnel, alterations in postal rates, the imperatives of subscription versus newsstand sales—witness *Runner's World's* employment of two different covers, one aimed at hard-core runners, the other at soft-core pornography buffs. Any element which affects what the magazine will ultimately look like merits attention.

When we deal with film, we must somehow sort out the ongoing arguments over who is responsible for the directions such projects take, whether it be the producers, directors, cameramen, actors, screenwriters, or, more recently, the businessmen and bankers who finance the project without ever having set foot in Hollywood. Here too we must inquire about such factors as genre, sub-genre, box-office track records, marketing and promotion, technical limitations or possibilities, critical support, and public reception.

Similarly, a study of television must take into account such extrinsic factors as scheduling, for industry people tend to be as concerned about the slot into which a program is scheduled as they are about its intrinsic features. Other extrinsic factors requiring attention are: audience demographics; the role of advertising; censorship, both internal and external, actual or potential; and industry trends, as well as all of the aspects of product creation and development mentioned thus far.

Many more specific questions could be enumerated. The point remains that issues of production, distribution, and consumption should be raised early, seriously, and carefully in any scholar inquiry into a popular culture subject.

ii. What themes can we identify in the popular culture text or artifact?

Most popular culture has, as its primary motive, commercial success, and as its primary function, entertainment. At the same time, however, every popular culture artifact, like any other cultural artifact, can be seen to make some kind of statement. Such themes may be perceived to be explicit in the work or implicit, consciously incorporated into its form and content, or unconsciously.

Explicit or overt themes are often broadly homiletic—"Love conquers all," "Crime does not pay." Or they are orthodox to a particular society—"The United States is the greatest country in the world." Although popular culture as a rule avoids controversy, its overt themes can sometimes be ideological, even argumentative, as when, in the comic strip *Steve Canyon* the hero's wife directly addressed the readers, asking them to write their congressmen in support of "our boys" in Vietnam. Explicit themes tend to be clear and direct, but popular culture, like other literary and artistic productions, may also be found to feature covert or latent themes. Such themes are articulated or implied by secondary characters (e.g., through stereotypes) or through sub-plots, settings, and other less noticeable elements of the work.

Consideration should also be given to the possible existence in the popular culture work of unconscious themes, conveyed unintentionally through formulas, conventions, structures, imagery, symbols, language, setting, and other intrinsic features. To get at such themes popular culture scholars have begun to employ intellectually advanced methodologies for textual analysis developed in recent years by cultural theorists and critics drawing upon the latest findings of the social scientists.

For example, formalism, structuralism, stylistics, and other linguistically-oriented approaches to texts are being employed to discover meanings encoded in word choice, word order, sentence structure, the organization of images, as well as in the relationships among various elements of a text and between these elements and the work as a whole. Marxist, feminist, and other social, political, and economic theories have proved useful for explicating covert as well as overt "messages" imbedded in popular culture. Psychological criticism, in both its Freudian and Jungian variations, or as informed by research in social psychology or semiology (the study of signs) is increasingly used by popular culture scholars to reveal possible unconscious themes. Subjective criticism, a distinct and growing "movement" within psychological criticism, puts its emphasis upon audience response. Applied to popular culture it explains the extent to which an encounter or "transaction" with the artifact changes with each encounter and with each encounterer, and stresses the need to consider the context—personal, cultural, even environmental—in which the encounter takes place. (For example, the author's investigation of live, "standup comedy" performances has led to the conclusion that the comedian-audience interaction is often quite separate from the jokes and the comic behavior themselves—and generally more important to an understanding of standup comedy as social and cultural mediation.)[5]

Works of popular culture may then be approached as having many possible covert themes. Scholars may never be able to develop tools sufficiently sophisticated and reliable to discern and understand them all, indeed may never even arrive at a common language or an approach that will facilitate consensus as to the motives, natures, functions, and effects of these themes. But again, to approach popular culture without carefully considering what methods might be best for decoding such "messages" is to ignore what might well be the most important aspect of a given popular culture study.

iii. What kinds of aesthetic evaluation might further our understanding and appreciation of the popular culture artifact?

From the early days of Popular Culture Association activities a debate has flourished, if not raged, over the importance of aesthetics to popular culture inquiry and over the possible nature of an appropriate popular culture aesthetic. Since aesthetic investigation is neither apparently nor particularly useful to the kinds of sociocultural approaches outlined and urged above, Roger Rollin's argument "against evaluation"[6] as a method of analyzing popular culture or as an aspect of other methodologies is persuasive. Nonetheless, the question of popular culture aesthetics is an interesting and challenging one which could have some connections with questions of reception and popularity.

The aesthetic quality of a work—or at least the nature of the aesthetic response it evokes—may be relevant to the work's popularity, to its effectiveness as communication, and to its significance. It is in any case unlikely that a single popular culture aesthetic will emerge from the debate over such matters. Nevertheless, students of popular culture should at least consider whether aesthetic analysis might facilitate their understanding of a given work and of its cultural significance and importance.

iv. How can we relate the popular culture artifact to the society in which it is found?

Can we compare and contrast the artifact to others in the same culture? to others in different cultures or societies (both within the larger national society and internationally)? to popular culture of the past?

Does the kind of thematic analysis we have employed seem to be consistent with or disparate from the values, attitudes, and dispositions in other institutions such as the government, the church, the educational system? Are there important trends, changes, ambivalences, or contradictions which might reveal the existence in the culture-at-large of complexities parallel to those of the popular culture object? Or might these same phenomena suggest a role for popular culture in a process of acculturation and/or cultural transition?

Such questions are in a sense centrifugal, suggesting that any inquiry into popular culture must at some time detach itself from the subject itself and swing outward into its "environment." That environment, whether personal (the room housing one's TV set), communal, cultural (one's membership in an "interpretive community"—of political conservatives, teenagers, etc.), national, or even international (e.g., ecology activists), will at least influence and possibly even condition perception of and response to the popular culture artifact.

But inquiry will inevitably be centripetal as well, with questions such as "What does that which we have learned about what a popular culture artifact seems to mean to others now mean to us?" and "How can we relate that artifact to what we ourselves know and feel about culture, about society, even about life itself?" Popular culture then must be seen as existing, not in a vacuum or in the world of Plato's ideal forms, but in space and time. Its creators and consumers exist in space and time as well, though not necessarily in the same space and time. And neither are necessarily the space and time in which the popular culture student exists. Although such matters may seem to border on the metaphysical, in fact they have very practical implications. Literary criticism in the middle third of the twentieth century chose to ignore the fact that literature is made by authentic human beings, living in history, for other authentic human beings living in their own histories. Popular culture studies will be that much more advanced by the extent to which they recognize the limitations of such a methodology.

By way of conclusion, this series of notes and queries has moved from an insistence upon a more careful and comprehensive collection of facts—dates, costs, distributive systems, etc.—to suggestions for deliberately broad, even philosophical kinds of inquiry. Such a range of investigation is called for because if popular culture studies are to be credible as intellectual or scholarly activities, they must be ever more accurate, more systematic, more disciplined, indeed more profound. Models exist for this more mature and sophisticated kind of popular culture study. It is the responsibility of the entire community of popular culture scholars to encourage and perform more substantive and thus more useful work and actively to discourage methodologies that only provide critical ammunition for those who do not understand why we bother with popular culture at all.[7]

Notes

1. See the essay by Dennis R. Hall, "The Study of Popular Culture," *Studies in Popular Culture,* 6 (1983): 16–25.

2. There are numerous anthologies which collect the early investigations of popular culture. Perhaps the best example is the Bernard Rosenberg and David Man-

ning White volume, *Mass Culture: The Popular Arts in America* (New York: Free P, 1956).

3. A review of early issues of the *Journal of Popular Culture* and of PCA conference presentations from the same era suggests the dominance of descriptive and appreciative approaches to popular culture and the lack of much in the way of up-to-date methodology. The enthusiasm and interest with which scholars argued the importance of popular culture's place in curricula and in the list of sources for cultural analysis is indeed important and admirable, and there certainly were many individual studies published that are as sound and useful as anything being produced today. On the other hand, it could be argued that the highly democratic orientation of PCA and its related enterprises, the lack of governing standards in a new field of study, and the fact that many of the early practitioners were aficionados of popular culture whose scholarly training and practice were often in more traditional or unrelated areas—all these factors resulted in the presentation and sometimes the publication of some work of less-than-high merit. A review of PCA-sponsored scholarly activities in recent years should suggest that progress is indeed being made.

4. See Gene Wise's important theory-method essay, "Some Elementary Axioms for American Culture Studies," *Prospects* 4 (1979): 517–47.

5. See Lawrence E. Mintz, "The Standup Comedian as Social and Cultural Mediator," forthcoming in *American Quarterly* (1983).

6. Roger B. Rollin, "Against Evaluation: The Role of the Critic of Popular Culture," *Journal of Popular Culture* 9.2 (Fall 1975): 355–65. Rollin's arguments have been debated in print and both formally and informally at PCA conventions.

7. See Lawrence E. Mintz, "Recent Trends in the Study of Popular Culture: An Update, 1971–1981," forthcoming in the second edition of Robert Walker's anthology, *American Studies* (Greenwood P, 1982). This longer bibliographic essay describes some of the techniques available to popular culture scholars and offers bibliographical suggestions for examples of the application of those techniques.

Selected Bibliography

American Quarterly 32. Bibliography Issue: 1980.

Bigsby, C. W. E., ed. *Approaches to Popular Culture.* Bowling Green, OH: Bowling Green State U Popular P, 1977.

Blum, Eleanor. *Basic Books in the Mass Media.* 2nd ed. Urbana: U of Illinois, 1980.

Browne, Ray B., ed. *Rituals and Ceremonies of Popular Culture.* Bowling Green, OH: Bowling Green State U Popular P, 1980.

Browne, Ray B., Sam Grogg, Jr., and Larry Landrum, eds. Special Issue: Theories & Methodologies in Popular Culture. *Journal of Popular Culture* 9.2 (Fall 1975).

Cawelti, John. *Adventure, Mystery, Romance: Formula Studies as Art and Popular Culture.* Chicago: U of Chicago, 1976.

Cohn, William, and Susan Tamke, eds. "History of Popular Culture." Special Issue. *Journal of Popular Culture* 11.1 (Summer 1977).

Fine, Gary, ed. "Sociology in Depth." Special Issue. *Journal of Popular Culture* 11.2 (Fall 1977).

Gans, Herbert. *Popular Culture and High Culture.* New York: Basic, 1974.

Real, Michael. *Mass-Mediated Culture.* Englewood Cliff, NJ: Prentice-Hall, 1977.

A HOLISTIC APPROACH TO THE STUDY OF POPULAR CULTURE: CONTEXT, TEXT, AUDIENCE, AND RECODING

Harold E. Hinds, Jr.

Inspired by Lawrence Mintz's essay reproduced in this collection, Harold Hinds draws on an extensive literature on popular culture published in the decade following Mintz' "Notes." Like Mintz, Hinds argues for a comprehensive approach to the study of popular culture: one which gives serious attention to placing the subject under scrutiny within its multiple contexts, to the "text" in all its permutations and complexities, to the text's implied and actual audience(s), and to the consumers' readings and uses of the texts and their influence on future texts. Hinds is Professor of History and Director of Latin American Area Studies at University Minnesota-Morris, a founding co-editor with Charles Tatum of Studies in Latin American Popular Culture, *and author of several studies of Mexican popular culture.*

Culture which is widely disseminated and consumed by large numbers of people—that is, popular culture—has attracted ever more study and analysis. In spite of this promising beginning, it remains in many ways inadequately studied, since only one aspect of this culture has received extensive examination. The overwhelming emphasis has been on "texts" or groups of "texts," ranging from Harlequin romances to block-buster movies and even to cereal-box premiums. These texts have been analyzed from a wide range of critical strategies. Yet the emergence of most popular culture from the commercial and industrial revolution; and the more specific economic, technological, social, and cultural factors that account for its production, are given only an occasional nod by popular culture scholars. Likewise, how, and for what purposes, such texts are used or consumed, has only begun to receive attention. Finally, rarely acknowledged, let alone analyzed, is the complexity of the consumers' role. Nearly endless consumer discussion of the consumed texts, and limited consumer feedback to cultural industries, helps fashion new generations of popular culture products

Harold E. Hinds, Jr., "A Holistic Approach to the Study of Popular Culture: Context, Text, Audience, and Recoding," Studies in Latin American Popular Culture *16 (1996): 11–29.*

and assists in creating or reworking society's master narratives and dominant symbols. That is, through consumption consumers are themselves partially responsible for creating the cultural context within which future popular texts are produced.

Given the very uneven progress in the study of popular culture, how might a more holistic study of a popular culture text be done? At a minimum, each of the following topics ought to be acknowledged in a complete study, even if they could not all be examined. Needless to say, article-length studies can only choose a few of the approaches outlined below, but hopefully monograph-length investigations might incorporate many, if not all, of them.

The Context(s)

Having selected a popular text for study, it will be necessary to place it within its broad historical, temporal, economic, technological, and cultural contexts.

Although there is a general tendency historically to see popular culture as one consequence of the Western, capitalist, industrial, and democratic revolutions,[1] this is disputed. Peter Burke, writing about Europe, suggests seven "main periods," all of which witnessed "important modifications" in Europe's popular culture: (1) Middle Ages, c1200–1350, (2) pre-Reformation or late Middle Ages, 1350–1500, (3) Reformation and Counter-Reformation, 1500–1650, (4) the commercial revolution, 1650–1800, (5) the industrial revolution, 1800–1900, (6) the second industrial revolution, 1900–1950, and (7) the age of television, 1950–present.[2] Fred Schroeder offers an even more radical extension of the age of popular culture, locating its origins more than 5000 years ago, and stressing urbanization, centralized political power, and the means to replicate and distribute texts as the keys to popular culture and its periodization.[3]

The history of communications, with which most popular culture analysts will be especially concerned, also has been variously conceptualized. One scenario stresses the rise of an independent "fourth estate," or free press. Another scenario focuses on technological stages, and in particular the transitions from one stage to another, e.g., from print to electronic communications. And, as suggested above, yet another conceptualization sees nineteenth-century industrialization as the critical moment in the history of communications.[4]

There is not even a consensus about the contemporary period: Is it the age of mass culture, because "All culture is mass culture under capitalism";[5] or is it a post-modern age, as conceptualized by Jim Collins, in which mass culture is an impossibility because even if each of us does find a group of texts suited to us, "there are so many 'conflicting modes of representation and divergent ideological positions' that any suggestion that we are all part of the same 'popular culture' is ludicrous"?[6]

A culture's classification of texts as either high or low, elite or popular, should also be taken into consideration when exploring the context of a popular text. Paul DiMaggio and Lawrence Levine's analyses of the nineteenth-century United States discovered that this distinction emerged late in that century,[7] and, quoting DiMaggio, derived from " the efforts of urban elites to build organization forms that first, isolated high culture and second, differentiated it from popular culture."[8] Not only is this distinction probably time bound, it is culturally restricted as well. For example, evidently Japan has a more holistic view of culture and does not so divide cultural texts.[9]

There is also the question of the text's context within the rhythms of daily, monthly, seasonal, and annual schedules. Much of popular culture is not consumed randomly but either on special occasions or on holidays. In addition, widely watched popular culture events such as the Academy Awards become in Elihu Katz's words "high holidays" which add new dates to the traditional round of calendar holidays.[10] Evitar Zerubavel's sociology of time, *Hidden Rhythms,* is particularly useful in considering the temporal context, as it systematically explores and analyzes the "subtle and diverse significance of time in organizing our social relationships and lives."[11]

The economic context is of paramount importance, but only Marxist scholars routinely take it into consideration. Although the idea that capitalism naturally spawns popular culture is frequently an unstated assumption, little attention is given to specifics. What stage of capitalism is the text embedded in? Emergent capitalism, corporate capitalism, or multi-transnational capitalism?[12] Is the text part of a capitalist democracy or a mixed economy? Is it a native-born capitalist product or is it an import, most probably from a United States transnational cultural industry such as Disney? Does it replace local traditions? Is it less popular than indigenous products, but still finding a niche as part of a "second culture," thus helping to create "a certain cultural bilingualism"?[13]

The assumption that popular culture is synonymous with democratic capitalism is itself highly suspect. Capitalism and mass culture can coexist with garrison or totalitarian states. Unfettered markets, democratic elections, and freedom of the press are not preconditions to widespread adoption of cultural texts, as the cultural history of the 1970s and 1980s in Latin America and Eastern Europe so amply demonstrates.[14] The transition, however, to democratic capitalism can make a major difference in the types of texts that are popular. For example, in communist Poland serious original *and* state-supported fiction and poetry sold very well; but under capitalism sales of such works have plummeted, while "trash" literature, e.g., para-psychology and Harlequin romances, have become best sellers.[15]

What type of industry produces and distributes the text is also of importance, but is all too often ignored by popular culture scholars. Market structures and the organizational environments of specific cultural industries do make a difference. If the text is a product of an oligarchical industry where a few giants control nearly 100 percent of market share, e.g., 1980s Brazilian television, David Nord's hypothesis may be born out: "The greater the market power a producer has (the greater the opportunity to control risk), the tighter and more standardized will be the formulas."[16] The range of consumer choices will be limited. Many popular culture texts, on the other hand, are products of industries where a mix of a few large companies coexists with numerous small firms, e.g., the contemporary United States book and record publishing industries, both of which produce a great variety of texts. Paul Hirsch's 1972 essay, "Processing Fads and Fashions," is the classic analysis of this mix. Such cultural industries are often characterized by both a surplus and a wide variety of products, by uncertain demand, by cheap technology, and by autonomous gatekeepers. In order to spot and promote possible successes (the failure rate being quite high) and to more narrowly focus consumer choices, these industries are dependent on a "throughput sector," e.g., reviewers, agents, talk shows, radio station air-play, talent scouts, and acquisitions editors.[17]

Is the text a product of a vertically integrated industry, where huge production companies control the distribution and sales networks, both wholesale and retail; e.g., the 1930s United States movie moguls?[18] Or is production and manufacture largely independent of distribution and sales; e.g., the 1980s United States magazine industry, where sales depended on a mix of subscriptions and sales in multi-product retail outlets?[19]

How significant is advertising? Does the cultural industry heavily advertise all its products, or only a few? For example, compare the lavish use of advertising in the contemporary European automobile industry with that continent's paperback industry, where many, if not most, titles receive only minimal advertising. Is the product heavily dependent on the financial support of advertisers for production costs, as in United States commercial television, and if so, what direct control, if any, does the advertiser have over texts? The content of United States radio soaps in the 1930s was significantly controlled by advertising firms. If advertising is not significant, what role(s) does Hirsch's "throughput sector" play in promoting products and arbitrating the content of texts?[20]

Finally, nearly all the models that have been advanced for the study of popular culture, and in particular for the various mass mediums ranging from the penny press to television, are based on United States and Western

European examples and are articulated by this cultural hearth's scholarly communities. Unfortunately the models are then exported to the rest of the world, where the fit is frequently poor, both for local cultural reasons and because models based on mature cultural industries are applied to industries which are still at earlier stages of development. Conrad Kottak's analysis of Brazil's television industry, *Prime-Time Society,* is a striking example of avoiding this misapplication. For example, Kottak does not just mechanically apply George Gerbner's "cultivation effect": "The more time people spend watching TV, the more they perceive the real world as being similar to that of TV." Gerbner's model describes reasonably well one effect of television programming on 1970s United States television audiences.[21] TV has only recently arrived in some regions, while in others it has been widely assimilated into daily life, the length of home TV exposure (measured in years) predicted the effects of TV better than current viewing levels did. Thus the stage of audience acceptance of TV is critical to understanding TV's uses and effects on audiences.[22]

While an earlier generation tended to focus narrowly on the content of the text under scrutiny, and to ignore context, such a narrow focus is no longer acceptable. The text's relationship to the sweep of history and to particular times and places; the circumstances of the text's production and promotion; its place in the flow of time, seasons, and holidays; and the nature of the societies it is embedded within; *all* are contexts which deserve some attention.

Text(s)

Scholars of popular culture have studied the product, the text(s), more than any other aspect. A vast literature exists both of theoretical critical approaches to the text and of case studies of individual texts or of categories of texts. In analyzing the text one may well want to limit the "close reading" to one critical approach. Fortunately two excellent volumes exist which provide an introduction to the most common and accepted of these approaches and also contain examples of their application: Robert Allen's *Channels of Discourse Reassembled* and Bob Ashley's *The Study of Popular Fiction.* Together these volumes discuss semiotics, structuralism, narrative theory, audience-oriented criticism, genre study, ideological analysis, psychoanalysis, feminist criticism, postmodernism, mass society theory, British cultural studies, British 'literary' theory, continental 'sociological' approaches, post-structuralism, and deconstruction.[23]

The decision on the exact definition of the text to be analyzed, using one or more of the above approaches, deserves careful attention. Not all texts are finite; some are open-ended, such as United States comic strips and television soap operas.[24] One should note, however, that whether or not a particular genre will have finite or open-ended text is a cultural convention. For example, when Robert Allen wrote in his otherwise superb *Speaking of Soap Operas* that "one of the distinctive . . . features of the soap opera is the absence of ultimate narrative closure; it is in fact, one of the few narrative forms predicated upon the impossibility of closure,"[25] he evidently was unaware of Brazilian soaps. In Brazil television soap operas are finite, although length is altered to accommodate a series' level of popularity and audience feedback on plot and characters.[26]

Texts may be unstable. Different editions are not identical. For example, vocals were emphasized, the bass toned down, and rhythms speeded up when Bob Marley's reggae music was released in the United States market.[27] The text may be altered with each performance: as in Shakespeare's *Hamlet* performed by the original company at London's sixteenth-century Globe theater; by a provincial repertory group in mid-nineteenth-century Cincinnati; and by contemporary professional Shakespearean actors at Minneapolis's Guthrie Theater.[28] The degree of alteration may be quite extensive, as when Jamaican "sound men," DJs with large mobile discotheques, improvise or "dub" lyrics over previously recorded music.[29] Texts may also literally be a *bricolage* or montage, i.e., composed of a mixture of not-necessarily-related cultural texts to form a new text.[30] Some *bricolages* are quite purposeful, such as an artist's montage; others are a matter of convention or even accident, e.g., the texts combined to form the books of Deuteronomy and Exodus in the Old Testament.

Texts may also come with a lot of accessory baggage, and thus form what has been termed an "encrusted" text. The "primary" text is encrusted within a sublevel of texts which are produced by the cultural industry to promote it: these consist of such items as ads, criticism and comments, gossip columns, and fan magazines. The original and encrusting text(s) together form a "super" text, the appropriate text for study, according to Nick Browne. In addition, the primary text is further encrusted by anticipatory and after-the-fact gossip.[31] Encrustation, unfortunately, is often ignored in analyses of popular culture.

The text presumably has an author. A traditional part of any analysis would be to discover as much about this author as possible: background, other texts attributed to him or her, and the author's intentions in producing the text. However, this is not always obvious, for many texts in a real sense have collective authors. Indeed, literally hundreds may assist in the creation and production of a Hollywood film or a prime-time television situation comedy. In order to make analysis of such forms somewhat more manageable, some scholars assume that the director of a movie or the producer of a television program is the true author, or *auteur,* of the text. While this approach has its advantages, and certain directors and producers do greatly influence the finished text, its shortcomings are obvious. For example, the cinematographer often receives little notice outside the industry, but his or her technical expertise and style is critical to the text as viewed.[32] Collective authors are not always so obvious, as Michael Foucault points out in "What Is an Author?" Foucault argues that the appearance of an apparent single author, e.g., Ernest Hemingway, author of *The Old Man and the Sea,* is actually deceptive, for all authors are in fact created by the sum of their cultural and literary experiences.[33] There is not one, but many authors. Tom Inge adds that it is always true that even single authors must rely on the assistance of editors, publishers, and the like to produce a text.[34] In some cases, editors are co-authors, even if not so credited, of the published text. Some publishers are well known for promoting only certain literary tastes, and thus, in a sense, help to author a class or category of literature.

Nevertheless, popular culture texts are usually seen as easily understood, simplistic, and formulaic. On a continuum stretching from formula to innovation, popular culture texts most often are closer to the formula than to the innovation pole. So the study of popular culture is especially concerned with genres, stereotypes, conventions, codes, and rules.[35] But formula is overemphasized; for even formulaic texts must have a balance between predictability and suspense, uniformity and variability.[36] Indeed, even if a genre changes only slowly, adhering closely to the "principle of cultural continuity" or incremental changes;[37] and even if a text's initial attraction is the appearance of adherence to the known rules of the game, pleasure, and thus popularity, David Feldman believes, rests on variation.[38] And eventually, many small variations within a group of texts in a genre will add up to the creation/discovery of a new genre.

Finally, and perhaps most conventionally, a popular culture study should include the elements of an aesthetic analysis, but tempered by the understanding that it is popular culture texts which are being analyzed. Such a study should never omit the understanding that we acquire our standards of popular taste, and especially of what is pleasing and successful, through socialization.[39] Taking fiction as an example, Fay Weldon argues that a successful popular novel needs the merits of a popular film: "the accessibility, the excitement of plot, the calculated ability to control, manipulate and surprise an audience, the habit of tying up loose ends, the eye for detail, the ear for dialogue and its not quite naturalistic delivery, a briefness, a pointedness—all things often thought merely vulgar in the literary novel."[40] To these could be added Cawelti's critical standards, which he also argues are peculiar to popular culture: does the text adhere to the conventions of its genre, follow the rules of its formula; does it continue or offer a plausible variation on a serial form; and does it follow the "performance-personal principle," which "involves the recognition of nonverbal aspects of perfor- mance" and "involves the fact that a popular performance is not just a way of presenting a particular work to an audience, but an act by a persona which relates both to a larger social context and to previous acts by the same persona."[41]

The popular text has been the subject of considerable scholarship. Lim- iting a study to one or two particular analytical and critical approach(es) from among the many competing ones will probably be wise. Regardless of the approach(es) selected, some attention needs to be given to exactly what constitutes the text in the given case; to the text's encrustations; to the col- lective of "authors" which, from conception to product, created it; to what extent it conforms to a formula; and to how closely it conforms to aesthetic conventions associated with other successful popular texts.

The Audience

Lawrence Levine, writing on popular culture, observes that "the audi- ence remains the missing link."[42] Levine is only partially correct, for while any type of audience study which involves contact with actual readers re- mains unusual, there has nevertheless been a boom in critical textual analy- ses, or close readings, which infer the "readers'" construction of meanings and pleasures.

Content analysis is an empirical approach which identifies countable units in a text, e.g., the number of women in high status occupations, and then infers meanings and values from the patterns. But some scholars, while finding the revealed patterns and frequencies of interest, argue that they cannot fully reveal meaning. Meaning can only be produced by the in- teraction of a text and its readers. On the other hand, other scholars believe that content analysis can reveal meaning about as well as other forms of analysis, which are not less, but only differently, flawed.[43]

Two competing critical studies' approaches each claim superiority in revealing meaning. The first sees the dominant culture's ideology, although not without some conflicting and competing positions and rationales, as stitched into texts, from which cues literally "interpellate" or hail the reader to respond positively to the powerfully persuasive embedded hegemonic messages. A close reading of the text will reveal the dominant classes' ideology, often disguised as "common sense," which the scholar can then unmask.[44] Variants on this are reception theory and reader-response criti- cism. Both argue that it is the reader who is operational, rather than the text, which cannot act without the reader's agency. But both also respond to the question of what happens when one reads a text by extrapolating answers from the text itself. An "imperial" critic discovers in the text itself structures and content which direct, indeed determine, a reader's response(s). Although more sophisticated analyses discover a number of plausible readings, most analyses strongly suggest the single readings traditionally expected from skilled critics.[45]

In contrast, other critical studies scholars view popular texts as "open." Michael de Certeau's concept of poaching has been very influential. Basing his theory on textual analysis, he asserts that readers "poach" texts, that is, they skillfully make whatever meanings and pleasures they want or need from texts.[46] Most notable is John Fiske's theory that texts are polysemous, open to both dominant and oppositional readings. Fiske, and others who have accepted the notion of polysemy, have identified a large number of structures and inclusions in popular texts which allow for the possibilities of antihegemonic readings and construction of meanings: they especially instruct the scholar to pay close attention to the use of irony, metaphors, jokes, contradictions, and excesses (especially hyperbole and camp).[47] For these critics the very nature of cultural industries produces open texts, e.g., Nico Vink, in a study of Brazilian television, observes that intellectuals, the dominated fraction of the dominant class, at times identify with the dominated class and thus introduce subversive ideas; that the conflict between profit and creativity creates tensions which translate into a source of polysemy; that actors, often from the lower classes, seek to reach the broadest possible audience, and thus seek to appeal to the dominant class ideologically and to the working class with body language; and that some mediums, such as television—incorporating codes for text, image, and sound—can have conflicting codes, thereby providing contradictory information.[48] In Fiske's 1989 *Reading the Popular,* he extends the notion of open texts to conclude that dominated classes erode, subvert, or refashion hegemonic culture to meet their own needs, and the resulting culture is progressive at least at the micro level, even if less than revolutionary at any level in society.[49]

The Colombian communications scholar Jesús Martín-Barbero offers an alternative explanation for textual qualities that attract the allegiance of the popular classes and produce readings which are a fusion of dominant and alternative cultures. The cultural industries, despite their natural preference for the dominant culture, must incorporate some forms and features that are drawn from working-class cultures in order to sell to the widest possible audience. Initially drawn largely from oral cultures, these include: serialization, with short episodes and short sentences and paragraphs; the use of popular language and rhetorical excess; equating physical appearance with moral character; stereotyped characters, sharply divided into good and bad; highly emotional, sensational, and sentimental plots; plot development using 'and then' transitions as opposed to 'in consequence of' ones; and the incorporation of characters and events drawn from contemporary lower-class urban life, and especially its seamier, more violent aspects. The melodrama, in particular, incorporates these features. Thus in the resulting amalgamation, finding "some of the basic forms of their own way of perceiving, experiencing and expressing their world," the popular classes both accommodate to some features of hegemonic culture *and* use these texts "to make communicable their memories and experiences."[50]

All these approaches clearly reach very different conclusions, especially those that see texts as dictatorial as opposed to those that view them as open. Perhaps the problem lies in the fact that both views largely rely on speculation based on close textual readings, and neither are based to any significant extent on empirical studies of actual audience practices, behaviors, and beliefs.[51] It may be acceptable, at a minimum, to extend B. Cohen's observation about newspapers to any text: a text "may not be successful much of the time in telling its readers what to think, but it is stunningly successful in telling its readers what to think *about*."[52] But Thomas Lindlof even more pointedly, and I believe accurately, comments that "It is not clear . . . how one determines what a text means apart from what people say about it."[53] No matter how close the reading, then, one must turn to the actual audience, not to the implied audience, to discover what meanings and pleasures readers derive from encounters with the text. This will also mean overcoming the tendency of some scholars to advance endless reasons why one can never know with certainty what an audience thinks and does.[54]

A few scholars have attempted to discover just what an audience says their encounter with a text means, most notably the British cultural studies scholar David Morley, who studied British television audiences, and Janice Radway, an American English professor who studied a group of romance novel readers. Morley's sample consisted of eighteen television-viewing families. Families were interviewed in depth, in their own homes, using an unstructured, open-ended question format. Radway administered a formal fifty-three-question questionnaire to a small group (forty-two) of romance readers known to a bookstore clerk, a trusted confidant of avid romance readers and a key informant for Radway. Radway also conducted both group and individual interviews with sixteen readers, and had readers summarize plots which then were compared to the text.[55] The sample sizes and techniques used by Morley and Radway are easily within the grasp of most scholars, and are well illustrated in their respective studies.

For a more ambitious audience study, which uses a larger sample and can add more social science research methods to those mentioned above (which are generally drawn from anthropology), Tamar Liebes and Elihu Katz's study of different cultures' reading of the television drama "Dallas" is an ideal model. Their study involved some 400 participants drawn from six quite different cultures. Participants were divided into small culturally homogenous groups to view an episode of "Dallas." They then filled out a background questionnaire, followed by an hour-long participation in a focus-group discussion of the program. Gathered data and taped discussion were subjected to both qualitative and quantitative analyses. Their sophisticated research design is fully described and well demonstrated in *The Export of Meaning.*[56]

Demographic and other background information on the text's readers can be used to show both agreement and differences among different socio-economic, age, ethnic, and cultural audience segments, in their uses of the text, gratifications from it, and construction of meanings. Such differences in responses are well established, even if frequently ignored by popular culture researchers. For example, Hadley Cantril studied Orson Welles's famous 1938 "War of the Worlds" and discovered that the broadcast audience's response ranged from those who quickly determined that the broadcast was fiction to those who panicked, and that these responses could be demographically sorted out. And Herta Herzog, W. Lloyd Warner, and William Henry's classic studies of radio soap opera audiences discerned sharp class differences among listeners' uses and gratifications.[57]

Aside from the techniques mentioned above, there are a number of other useful concepts in the rapidly growing literature on audiences. Stanley Fish developed, and Janice Radway further refined, the idea of "interpretive community": a loosely connected group who share similar values and assumptions, consume similar cultural products, and tend to use and interpret them similarly.[58] Meyer Fortes's concept of "structural domains" is based on the assumption that each of us "participates in several domains simultaneously and fulfills a different role in each."[59] Somewhat similar is Elizabeth Frazer's concept of "discourse registers": each of us has available many different ways of reading and discussing texts, which precludes a singular, ideological reading of them.[60] Also respectful of the audience's intelligence is John Fiske's "'real' fantasy": Actors, to their fans, are simultaneously fantasy figures and real people and fans do not normally confuse the two personas.[61]

The move from an emphasis on passive, textually inscribed audiences to active audiences who show preferences, selecting that which is relevant to them, and constructing meanings and deriving pleasures, has not escaped criticism. Not unexpectedly, it is charged that a text is not an equivalent of an inkblot in a Rorschach test. Ignoring the text's influence, it is argued, simply contradicts empirical evidence. Audience research must not slight the text, but ideally should view reading as a property of both text and audience.[62]

Fortunately such a model, balanced study does exist;[63] and S. Elizabeth Bird very generally describes her research strategy in the following way:

In my own research on supermarket tabloids, I began with immersion in the papers themselves, reading them for two years and interviewing writers and editors before getting to the audience. My research was then in two steps, first soliciting letters from readers. I asked them to write anything about themselves that they cared to share, in addition to information about the tabloids. I received life histories, personal descriptions and discussions of family problems, all of which helped me develop a perception of lives apart from tabloids. Later, when it came to interviewing, I had learned the right words to use, and had some conception of the people I was talking to. During the interviews, I tried to conceive the interaction as a collaborative dialogue, more conversation than interview.[64]

Bird's ethnographical model is indeed a balanced one that most scholars could adapt.

More than any other aspect of popular culture studies, the audience demands serious attention. Equally clearly, scholars are divided. Some believe that attention to textual patterns will reveal meaning or that texts sufficiently position readers so that meaning can be inferred from a scholar's skillful, close reading. Others dispute this and argue that the only way to know the audience's reading of a text is to engage that audience, or a portion of it, directly. Ideally, studies should neither ignore the text's implied audience nor its actual audience.

Recombinant Culture

Analysis of the text should not conclude with an audience study. Stuart Hall's well-known essay on encoding-decoding jump-started British cultural studies to begin giving serious consideration to what audiences did with texts,[65] but overlooked the next stage, recoding or what might be termed (re)creating context.[66] Recent critical audience studies have stressed that reception of popular culture texts takes the form of small groups talking over the text, "gossiping" about it, and in the process creating a folk culture wherein meanings are agreed upon for last night's ballgame, yesterday afternoon's soap, or this month's bestseller.[67] These loose groups of friends, relatives, and acquaintances (or colleagues) are "interpretative communities," the first rung on a long ladder of building master narratives and dominant/key symbols which are part of the glue which holds all societies together, and which themselves are an important part of the cultural context with which this essay began.

The initial, small group discussions, and the end product, master narratives and key symbols, have attracted considerable attention (on the part of speech-communication scholars and intellectual historians and anthropologists respectively), but the intermediate processes remain murky. Particularly interesting for the initial stage is the observation that small "gossip" groups refashion popular culture texts into narratives, into stories. "Facts" and textual bits are embedded in narratives, which are generally moral lessons with accompanying heroes and villains. Communication scholars Walter Fisher ("the narrative paradigm") and Ernest Bormann ("fantasy theme analysis") have studied and theorized about this process.[68] Also insightful is Elizabeth Stone's study of the genesis, composition, evolution, and use of family stories; and particularly their "reducing complex phenomena to single comprehensible causes."[69]

Beyond this "primary exposure context," for a variety of reasons, communication and critical theories essentially have not been probed. For example, although de Certeau's "theory of practice" posits that the popular classes resist hegemonic culture by using it for their own purposes, this appropriation is only for immediate use and is a "silent production" which does not affect the production of culture by the dominant class.[70] But one team (Fry, Alexander, and Fry) argues that talk about texts, and the stories they spawn, continues long after an initial exposure, and they have labeled this more extended stage(s) the "communicative context,"[71] in contrast to the initial "consumption context." An experiment from my grammar school days illustrates this in its earlier stages. One student is briefly shown a picture, who then must relate its contents to another student who has not seen the picture, and so on, down a chain of half-a-dozen students. The resulting story often is considerably different from the original and is considerably simplified, while some surviving elements take on greater symbolic importance.[72] "Symbolic convergence theory," developed by Ernest Bormann, suggests that this chain ends in master narratives, "collective memory," and key symbols. Few studies have attempted to trace such an evolution, and perhaps the best remains Bormann's own study of "the restoration drama," a symbolic purification of America through rebirth and restoration. This "drama" has repeatedly gripped the nation, but Bormann focuses on four instances, stretching from the Great Awakening of 1739–40 to the Lincoln-Douglas debates of 1858.[73] An even more accessible historical study of the evolution of a symbol might be James Shortridge's *Middlewest,* wherein he demonstrates the enduring association of the Midwest with pastoralism. He simultaneously demonstrates that this symbolic region has been quite volatile in the values associated with it and even in its geographical location.[74]

Tracing such a detailed history may well be beyond the scope of a particular study, but one may still be able to determine whether or not the text incorporates key symbols, and/or contributes to their maintenance; or if it is an historical text that appears to have contributed to the fashioning of a dominant narrative. Anthropologists, in particular, have reflected on the nature of symbols, and of special note for popular culture scholars is the work of Sherry Ortner and Victor Turner, for they are especially interested in the characteristics of key symbols. The mechanisms by which these symbols simultaneously are greatly abstracted and simplified and nevertheless are extremely multi-vocal (carrying multiple meanings) is considerably beyond this essay.[75] However, a consideration of the text as a symbol or complex of symbols will increase awareness of its relationship to its broader context and to its location within and contribution to the endless creation of the master narratives and key symbols which bind societies, together, at least momentarily. They are, after all, society's bonding agents and the basic "matter" of a culture's popular culture.

A Final Comment

All this will undoubtedly seem overly ambitious for a single study. Of course, it is. Thus any implementations will need to clearly state their limitations, while acknowledging the work that ideally remains to be done. When we have as many context, audience, and recombinant culture studies as ones devoted to texts, we will know that we are beginning to make true progress on the big picture of popular culture. Then a broad and comprehensive approach to popular culture texts should produce the knowledge and theoretical bases needed to significantly advance popular culture studies.

Notes

1. Russel Nye, *The Unembarrassed Muse: The Popular Arts in America* (New York: Dial P, 1970), 1–9; Ray Browne, "Popular Culture as the New Humanities," *Journal of Popular Culture* 17.4 (Spring 1984): 1–8.

2. Peter Burke, "Popular Culture between History and Ethnology," *Ethnologia Europea* 14 (1984): 5–13.

3. Fred E. H. Schroeder, ed., *5000 Years of Popular Culture: Popular Culture Before Printing* (Bowling Green, OH: Bowling Green State UP, 1980), 4–15.

4. John Nerone, "Theory and History," *Communication History* 3.2 (May 1993): 153–54.

5. Michael Denning, "The End of Mass Culture," *International Labor and Working-Class History* 37 (Spring 1990): 8–9.

6. Simon Frith, "Review Article," *Screen* 31.2 (Summer 1990): 233. Frith is reviewing and quoting from Jim Collin's *Uncommon Cultures* (1989).

7. Paul DiMaggio, "Cultural Entrepreneurship in Nineteenth-Century Boston: The Creation of an Organizational Base for High Culture in America," *Media, Culture and Society* 4 (1982): 33–50; and Lawrence W. Levine, *Highbrow/Lowbrow: The Emergence of Cultural Hierarchy in America* (Cambridge: Harvard UP, 1988).

8. DiMaggio, "Cultural Entrepreneurship," 33.

9. Margaret J. King, "New Definitions and New Approaches," *International Popular Culture* 1.2 (1980): 11–15.

10. Michael R. Real, *Super Media: A Cultural Studies Approach* (Newbury Park, CA: Sage, 1989), 81. Real is discussing Elihu Katz's essay "Media Events."

11. Evitar Zerubavel, *Hidden Rhythms: Schedules and Calendars in Social Life* (Berkeley: U of California P, 1981). Quote is from back cover blurb by Peter M. Blau.

12. John Fiske, *Understanding Popular Culture* (Boston: Unwin Hyman, 1989), 43.

13. Todd Gitlin, "World Leaders: Mickey Mouse, et al.," *New York Times,* 3 May 1992: 1 (Section 2).

14. Personal observations, 1965–1992, in Latin America, and especially Mexico, Cuba, and Nicaragua.

15. Anna Hursarska, "'Mein Kampf' and the Plays of Szekspir: Adventures in the Polish Book Trade," *New York Times* Book Review, 12 July 1992: 14.

16. David Paul Nord, "An Economic Perspective on Formula in Popular Culture," *Journal of American Culture* 3 (1980): 25.

17. Paul M. Hirsch, "Processing Fads and Fashions: An Organization-Set Analysis of Cultural Industry Systems," *American Journal of Sociology,* 77.4 (Jan. 1972): 639–59.

18. See Tino Balio, ed., *The American Film Industry,* rev. ed. (Madison: U of Wisconsin P, 1985).

19. See John Tebbel and Mary Ellen Zuckerman, *The Magazine in America, 1791–1990* (New York: Oxford UP, 1991).

20. See Stephen Fox, *The Mirror Makers: A History of American Advertising and Its Creators* (New York: Morrow, 1984); and Eric Clark, *The Want Makers: Inside the World of Advertising* (New York: Penguin, 1988).

21. Nancy Signorielli and Michael Morgan, eds., *Cultivation Analysis: New Directions in Media Effects Research* (Newbury Park, CA: Sage, 1990). The quote on "cultivation effect" is from Conrad Phillip Kottak *Prime-Time Society: An Anthropological Analysis of Television and Culture* (Belmont, CA: Wadsworth, 1990), 52.

22. Kottak, *Prime-Time Society,* Ch. 12.

23. Bob Ashley, ed., *The Study of Popular Fiction: A Source Book* (Philadelphia: U of Pennsylvania P, 1989); and Robert C. Allen, ed., *Channels of Discourse, Reassembled: Television and Contemporary Criticism,* 2nd ed. (Chapel Hill: U of North Carolina P, 1992).

24. Robert C. Allen, *Speaking of Soaps* (Chapel Hill: U of North Carolina P, 1985), 181.

25. Ibid., 69.

26. Everett M. Rodgers and Livia Antola, *"Telenovelas:* A Latin American Success Story," *Journal of Communication,* 35.4 (Autumn 1985): 24–35.

27. Dick Hebdige, *Cut 'N' Mix: Culture, Identity and Caribbean Music* (London: Comedia, 1987), 82.

28. See Lawrence W. Levine, "William Shakespeare and the American People: A Study in Cultural Transformation," *American Historical Review,* 89.1 (Feb. 1984): 34–66.

29. Hebdige, *Cut 'N' Mix,* 62, 65, 87.

30. Jim Collins, "Television and Postmodernism," *Channels of Discourse, Reassembled,* ed. Allen (1992), 337.

31. Allen, *Speaking of Soaps,* 103, 285–86; and David Morley, "Changing Paradigms in Audience Studies," *Remote Control: Television Audiences, and Cultural Power,* eds. Ellen Seiter, Hans Borchers, Gabriele Kreutzner, and Eva-Maria Warth (London: Routledge, 1989), 22–23.

32. An excellent example of *auteur* criticism is David Marc, *Demographic Vistas: Television in American Culture* (Philadelphia: U of Pennsylvania P, 1984).

33. Michel Foucault, "What Is an Author?" in *Rethinking Popular Culture: Contemporary Perspectives in Cultural Studies,* ed. Chandra Mukerji and Michael Schudson (Berkeley: U of California P, 1991), 446–64.

34. M. Thomas Inge, "The Art of Collaboration in Popular Culture," paper presented at conference on "The Future of Popular Culture Studies in the Twenty-First Century," Bowling Green State University, Bowling Green, OH, 4–6 June 1992.

35. John G. Cawelti, "The Concept of Formula in the Study of Popular Culture," *Journal of Popular Culture,* 3.3 (Winter 1969): 381–90.

36. Ashley, ed., *The Study of Popular Fiction,* 86.

37. Elizabeth D. Lowe, and John W. G. Lowe, "Quantitative Analysis of Women's Dress," *The Psychology of Fashion,* ed. Michael Solomon, (Lexington, MA: Heath, 1985), 193–206.

38. Umberto Eco, "The Narrative Structure in Fleming," *The Study of Popular Fiction,* ed. Ashley (1989), 131; David N. Feldman, "Formalism and Popular Culture," *Journal of Popular Culture,* 9.2 (Fall 1975): 384–402.

39. Roger B. Rollin, "Popular Culture and the Death of Good Taste," *National Forum,* forthcoming.

40. Fay Weldon, review of *Among the Dead,* by Michael Tolkin, in *New York Times Book Review,* 25 Apr. 1993: 4.

41. John G. Cawelti, "With the Benefit of Hindsight: Popular Culture Criticism," *Critical Studies in Mass Communication,* 2.4 (Dec. 1985): 368–71.

42. Lawrence W. Levine, "The Folklore of Industrial Society: Popular Culture and Its Audience," *American Historical Review,* 97.2 (Dec. 1992): 1380.

43. John Fiske, *Introduction to Communication Studies,* 2nd ed. (London: Routledge, 1990), 136–44; and Real, *Super Media,* especially chapters 2 and 3.

44. Fiske, *Introduction,* 175–77; and Mimi White, "Ideological Analysis and Television," *Channels of Discourse, Reassembled,* ed. Allen (1992), 168–69. Roger B. Rollin, personal communication, 24 Dec. 1993.

45. Robert C. Holub, *Reception Theory: A Critical Introduction* (London: Methuen, 1984); and Wolfgang Iser, *The Implied Reader: Patterns in Communication in Prose Fiction from Bunyan to Beckett* (Baltimore: John Hopkins UP, 1974). The term "imperial reader" is used in Dinesh D'Souza, "Illiberal Education," *Atlantic* 267.3 (Mar. 1991): 74.

46. Michel de Certeau, *The Practice of Everyday Life* (Berkeley: U of California P, 1984).

47. John Fiske, *Television Culture* (London: Methuen, 1987), ch. 6.

48. Nico Vink, *The Telenovela and Emancipation: A Study on TV and Social Change in Brazil* (Amsterdam: Royal Tropical Institute, 1988), 128–69.

49. Fiske, *Understanding,* 1–12.

50. Jesús Martín-Barbero, *Communication, Culture and Hegemony: From the Media to Mediations,* trans. Elizabeth Fox and Robert A. White (London: Sage, 1993). The two quotes are from pages 99 and 159.

51. Morley, "Changing Paradigms," *Remote Control,* eds. Seiter et. al. (1989), 39.

52. Quoted in Real, *Super Media,* 98.

53. Thomas R. Lindlof, "The Qualitative Study of Media Audiences," *Journal of Broadcasting and Electronic Media,* 35.1 (Winter 1991): 23–42.

54. S. Elizabeth Bird, "Travels in Nowhere Land: Ethnography and the 'Impossible' Audience," *Critical Studies in Mass Communication,* 9.3 (Sept. 1992): 250–60.

55. David Morley, *Family Television: Cultural Power and Domestic Leisure* (London: Comedia, 1986); Janice Radway, "Interpretive Communities and Variable Literacies: The Functions of Romance Reading," *Daedalus,* 113.3 (Summer 1984): 49–73; Janice Radway, *Reading the Romance: Women, Patriarchy, and Popular Literature* (Chapel Hill: U of North Carolina P, 1984).

56. Tamar Liebes and Elihu Katz, *The Export of Meaning: Cross-Cultural Readings of "Dallas"* (Oxford: Oxford UP, 1990).

57. Hadley Cantril, *The Invasion from Mars: A Study in the Psychology of Panic* (Princeton: Princeton UP, 1940); Herta Herzog, "On Borrowed Experience: An Analysis of Listening to Daytime Sketches," *Studies in Philosophy and Social Science,* 9.1 (1941): 65–95; and W. Lloyd Warner and William E, Henry, "The Radio Day Time Serial: A Symbolic Analysis," *General Psychology Monographs,* 37 (1948): 3–71.

58. Radway, "Interpretive Communities," 53–54, 71.

59. Rodrick P. Hart and John D. H. Downing, "Is There An American Public? An Exchange of Correspondence," *Critical Studies in Mass Communication,* 9.2 (June 1992): 201–15.

60. Elizabeth Frazer, "Teenage Girls Reading *Jackie,*" *The Study of Popular Fiction,* ed. Ashley (1989), 225–27.

61. Fiske, *Reading the Popular* (Boston: Unwin Hyman, 1989), 125.

62. Morley, "Changing Paradigms," *Remote Control,* ed. Seiter et. al. (1989), 39; Real, *Super Media,* 98; Graeme Turner, *British Cultural Studies: An Introduction* (London: Routledge, 1990), 117; and Arnold S. Wolfe, "Who's Gotta Have It?: The Ownership of Meaning and Mass Media Texts," *Critical Studies in Mass Communication,* 9.3 (Sept. 1993): 262.

63. S. Elizabeth Bird, *For Inquiring Minds: A Cultural Study of Supermarket Tabloids* (Knoxville: U of Tennessee P, 1992).

64. Bird, "Travels," 254.

65. Stuart Hall, "Encoding/Decoding," *Culture, Media, Language,* eds. Stuart Hall, Dorothy Hobson, Andrew Lowe, and Paul Willis (London: Hutchinson, 1980), 128–38.

66. John Erni, "Where Is the 'Audience'?: Discerning the (Impossible) Subject," *Journal of Communication Inquiry,* 13.2 (Summer 1989): 33, 35.

67. Fiske, *Television Culture,* 77–80, 105–7; Minu Lee and Chong Heup Cho, "Women Watching Together: An Ethnographic Study of Korean Soap Opera Fans in the U.S.," *Cultural Studies,* 4.1 (Jan. 1990): 30–44.

68. Ernest G. Bormann and Nancy C. Bormann, *Effective Small Group Communication,* 4th ed. (Edina, MN: Burgess, 1988), 79–96; Walter R. Fisher, *Human Communication as Narration: Toward a Philosophy of Reason, Value, and Action* (Columbia, SC: U of South Carolina P, 1987).

69. Elizabeth Stone, *Black Sheep and Kissing Cousins: How Our Family Stories Shape Us* (New York: Penguin, 1988), 98–99.

70. Tony Schirato, "My Space or Yours?: De Certeau, Frow and the Meanings of Popular Culture," *Cultural Studies,* 7.2 (May 1993): 283–86. John Fiske takes a similar position. It is only at the local or the "microlevel," where oral, face-to-face interactions take place, that oppositional or dissenting readings can be produced. See Fiske, *Understanding,* 172, 174, 192, and *Reading,* 186–89.

71. Virginia H. Fry, Alison Alexander, and Donald L. Fry, "Textual Status, the Stigmatized Self, and Media Consumption," *Communication Yearbook,* 13 (1990): 519–29.

72. Barbara Kingsolver, *The Bean Trees* (New York: Harper & Row, 1988). See description of "Gossip" game on 91.

73. Ernest G. Bormann, *The Force of Fantasy: Restoring the American Dream* (Carbondale: Southern Illinois UP, 1985), 1–25.

74. James R. Shortridge, *The Middlewest: Its Meaning in American Culture* (Lawrence KS: UP of Kansas, 1989).

75. Sherry B. Ortner, "On Key Symbols," *American Anthropologist,* 75.5 (Oct. 1973): 1338–47; and Victor Turner, "Symbols and African Ritual," *Science* 179 (1973): 1100–05.

IV.
Formula:
A Pioneering Theory

THE CONCEPT OF FORMULA
IN THE STUDY OF POPULAR LITERATURE

John G. Cawelti

John G. Cawelti believed that the study of popular culture needed its own analytic concepts, but that alone the concepts of cultural themes, myth, and medium were inadequate. Formula, with its combination of patterned conventions and dimensions of ritual, game, and dream, could prove another useful analytic concept. Cawelti, Professor of English at the University of Kentucky, further developed this key idea in two important monographs, The Six-Gun Mystique *(1971), and* Adventure, Mystery, and Romance *(1976).*

The growing interest among humanistic scholars and teachers in popular culture is one of the more exciting academic trends of the present day. This field of study represents a great expansion in the range of human expression and activity subjected to the scrutiny of historians and scholars of the arts. Consequently one of the central problems in giving some shape to our inquiries into popular culture has been the need for analytical concepts which might enable us to find our way through the huge amount of material which is the potential subject-matter of studies in popular culture. Moreover, we badly need some way of relating the various perspectives, historical, psychological, sociological and aesthetic, which are being used in the investigation of such phenomena as the Western, the spy story, pop music, the comic strip, film and TV.

To some extent, students of popular culture have simply applied to a wider range of materials the historical and critical methods of traditional humanistic scholarship. This practice has led to more complex analyses of such popular forms as the detective story and richer, more carefully researched accounts of the development of various popular traditions. Approaching the materials of popular culture with the traditional arsenal of humanistic disciplines is certainly a necessary first step. Nonetheless, the analysis of popular culture is somewhat different from that of the fine arts.

John G. Cawelti, "The Concept of Formula in the Study of Popular Literature," Journal of Popular Culture, *3.3 (Winter 1969): 381–90.*

When we are studying the fine arts, we are essentially interested in the unique achievement of the individual artist, while in the case of popular culture, we are dealing with a product that is in some sense collective. Of course it is possible to study the fine arts as collective products just as it is possible to examine individual works of popular culture as unique artistic creations. In the former case, the present discussion should apply with some qualifications to the fine arts, while in the latter, the traditional methods of humanistic scholarship are obviously the most appropriate, with some allowance for the special aesthetic problems of the popular arts.

Students of popular culture have defined the field in terms of several different concepts. When scholars were first interesting themselves in dime novels, detective stories, etc., they thought of them as sub literature. This concept reflected the traditional qualitative distinction between high culture and mass culture. Unfortunately it was really too vague to be of much analytical use. Even if one could determine where literature left off and sub literature began, a distinction that usually depended on the individual tastes of the inquirer, the term suggested only that the object of study was a debased form of something better. Like many concepts that have been applied to the study of popular culture, the idea of sub literature inextricably confused normative and descriptive problems.

Four additional concepts have come into fairly wide use in recent work: a) The analysis of cultural themes; b) the concept of medium; c) the idea of myth and d) the concept of formula. I would like to deal briefly with the first three, mainly by way of getting to a fuller discussion of what I consider the most promising concept of all.

The analysis of cultural, social, or psychological themes is certainly a tried and true method of dealing with popular culture. In essence, what the analyst does is to determine what themes appear most often or most prominently in the works under analysis and to group different works according to the presence or absence of the themes he is interested in. Unfortunately, there is a certain vagueness about the concept of theme. Such various things as the ideal of progress, the oedipal conflict, racism, and innocence have all been treated as themes. In effect, a theme turns out to be any prominent element or characteristic of a group of works which seems to have some relevance to a social or cultural problem. Though the vagueness of the concept can be cleared up when the investigator defines the particular theme or set of themes he is interested in, the concept of theme still seems inadequate because it depends on the isolation of particular elements from a total structure. This not only tends to over simplify the works under investigation, but to lead to the kind of falsifying reduction that translates one kind of experience into another. Thus, a story of a certain kind becomes a piece of social rhetoric or the revelation of an unconscious urge. No doubt a story is or can be these things and many others, but to treat it as if it were only one or another social or psychological function is too great a reduction. What we need is a concept that will enable us to deal with the total structure of themes and its relationship to the story elements in the complete work.

The concept of medium has become notorious through the fascinating theories of Marshall McLuhan, Walter Ong and others who insist that medium rather than content or form as we have traditionally understood them ought to be the focus of our cultural analyses. This concept seems to have a particular application to studies in popular culture because many of the works we are concerned with are transmitted through the new electric media which McLuhan sees as so different from the Gutenberg galaxy, the media associated with print. The concept of medium is an important one and McLuhan is doubtless correct that it has been insufficiently explored in the past, but I am not persuaded that more sophisticated studies of the nature of media will do away with the need for generalizations about content. I am sure that we will need to revise many of our notions about where medium leaves off and content begins as the new studies in media progress, but for the present, I would like to forget about the idea of medium altogether with the explanation that I'm concerned with a different kind of problem, the exploration of the content of the popular media.

One more distinction along these lines is necessary. In this paper I will be concerned primarily with stories and with understanding the various cultural significances of these stories. While a large proportion of popular culture can be defined as stories of different kinds, this is certainly not an exhaustive way of defining popular culture. Just as there are other arts than fiction, so there are works of popular culture which do not tell stories. With additional qualifications the concepts I am seeking to define are applicable to the analysis of other expressions of popular culture than those embodied in stories, but to keep my task as simple as possible, I have chosen to limit myself to the discussion of stories.

The most important generalizing concept which has been applied to cultural studies in recent years is that of myth. Indeed, it could be argued that the concept of formula which I will develop in the course of this paper is simply another variation on the idea of myth. But if this is the case, I would argue that distinctions between meanings of the concept of myth are worth making and naming, for many different meanings can be ascribed to the term. In fact, the way in which some people use the term myth hardly separates it from the concept of theme, as when we talk about the myth of progress or the myth of success. There is also another common meaning of the term which further obfuscates its use, namely myth as a common belief which is demonstrably false as in the common opposition between myth and reality. Thus, when a critic uses the term myth one must first get clear whether he means to say that the object he is describing is a false belief, or simply a belief, or something still more complicated like an archetypal pattern. Moreover, because of the special connection of the term myth with a group of stories which have survived from ancient cultures, particularly the Greco-Roman, the scholar who uses the concept in the analysis of contemporary popular culture sometimes finds himself drawn into another kind of reductionism which takes the form of statements like the following: "the solution of the paradox of James Bond's popularity may be, not in considering the novels as thrillers, but as something very different, as historic epic and romance, based on the stuff of myth and legend." But if the retelling of myth is what makes something popular why on earth didn't Mr. Fleming simply retell the ancient myths.

Because of this great confusion about the term myth, I propose to develop another concept which I think I can define more clearly and then to differentiate this concept from that of myth, thereby giving us two more clearly defined generalizing concepts to work with. Let me begin with a kind of axiom or assumption which I hope I can persuade you to accept without elaborate argumentation: all cultural products contain a mixture of two kinds of elements: conventions and inventions. Conventions are elements which are known to both the creator and his audience beforehand— they consist of things like favorite plots, stereotyped characters, accepted ideas, commonly known metaphors and other linguistic devices, etc. Inventions, on the other hand, are elements which are uniquely imagined by the creator such as new kinds of characters, ideas, or linguistic forms. Of course it is difficult to distinguish in every case between conventions and inventions because many elements lie somewhere along a continuum between the two poles. Nonetheless, familiarity with a group of literary works will usually soon reveal what the major conventions are and therefore, what in the case of an individual work is unique to that creator.

Convention and invention have quite different cultural functions. Conventions represent familiar shared images and meanings and they assert an ongoing continuity of values; inventions confront us with a new perception or meaning which we have not realized before. Both these functions are important to culture. Conventions help maintain a culture's stability while inventions help it respond to changing circumstances and provide new information about the world. The same thing is true on the individual level. If the individual does not encounter a large number of conventionalized experiences and situations, the strain on his sense of continuity and identity will lead to great tensions and even to neurotic breakdowns. On the other hand, without new information about his world, the individual will be increasingly unable to cope with it and will withdraw behind a barrier of conventions as some people withdraw from life into compulsive reading of detective stories.

Most works of art contain a mixture of convention and invention. Both Homer and Shakespeare show a large proportion of conventional elements mixed with inventions of great genius. Hamlet, for example, depends on a long tradition of stories of revenge, but only Shakespeare could have invented a character who embodies so many complex perceptions of life that every generation is able to find new ways of viewing him. So long as cultures were relatively stable over long periods of time and homogeneous in their structure, the relation between convention and invention in works of literature posed relatively few problems. Since the Renaissance, however, modern cultures have become increasingly heterogeneous and pluralistic in their structure and discontinuous in time. In consequence, while public communications have become increasingly conventional in order to be understood by an extremely broad and diverse audience, the intellectual elites have placed ever higher evaluation on invention out of a sense that rapid cultural changes require continually new perceptions of the world. Thus we have arrived at a situation in which the model great work of literature is Joyce's *Finnegan's Wake,* a creation which is almost as far as possible along the continuum toward total invention as it is possible to go without leaving the possibility of shared meanings behind. At the same time, there has developed a vast amount of literature characterized by the highest degree of conventionalization.

This brings us to an initial definition of formula. A formula is a conventional system for structuring cultural products. It can be distinguished from form which is an invented system of organization. Like the distinction between convention and invention, the distinction between formula and form can be best envisaged as a continuum between two poles; one pole is that of a completely conventional structure of conventions—an episode of the Lone Ranger or one of the Tarzan books come close to this pole; the other end of the continuum is a completely original structure which orders inventions—*Finnegan's Wake* is perhaps the best example of this, though one might also cite such examples as Resnais' film "Last Year at Marienbad," T. S. Eliot's poem "The Waste Land," or Beckett's play "Waiting for Godot." All of these works not only manifest a high degree of invention in their elements but unique organizing principles. "The Waste Land" makes the distinction even sharper for that poem contains a substantial number of conventional elements—even to the point of using quotations from past literary works—but these elements are structured in such a fashion that a new perception of familiar elements is forced upon the reader.

I would like to emphasize that the distinction between form and formula as I am using it here is a descriptive rather than a qualitative one. Though it is likely for a number of reasons that a work possessing more form than formula will be a greater work, we should avoid this easy judgment in our study of popular culture. In distinguishing form from formula we are trying to deal with the relationship between the work and its culture, and not with its artistic quality. Whether or not a different set of aesthetic criteria are necessary in the judgment of formal as opposed to formulaic works is an important and interesting question, but necessarily the subject of another series of reflections.

We can further differentiate the conception of formula by comparing it to genre and myth. Genre, in the sense of tragedy, comedy, romance, etc., seems to be based on a difference between basic attitudes or feelings about life. I find Northrop Frye's suggestion that the genres embody fundamental archetypal patterns, reflecting stages of the human life cycle, a very fruitful idea here. In Frye's sense of the term genre and myth are universal patterns of action which manifest themselves in all human cultures. Following Frye, let me briefly suggest a formulation of this kind—genre can be defined as a structural pattern which embodies a universal life pattern or myth in the materials of language: formula, on the other hand is cultural; it represents the way in which a culture has embodied both mythical archetypes and its own preoccupations in narrative form.

An example will help clarify this distinction. The western and the spy story can both be seen as embodiments of the archetypal pattern of the hero's quest which Frye discusses under the general heading of the mythos of romance. Or if we prefer psychoanalytic archetypes these formulas embody the oedipal myth in fairly explicit fashion, since they deal with the hero's conquest of a dangerous and powerful figure. However, though we can doubtless characterize both western and spy stories in terms of these universal archetypes, they do not account for the basic and important differences in setting, characters, and action between the western and the spy story. These differences are clearly cultural and they reflect the particular preoccupations and needs of the time in which they were created and the group which created them: the western shows its nineteenth century American origin while the spy story reflects the fact that it is largely a twentieth century British creation. Of course, a formula articulated by one culture can be taken over by another. However, we will often find important differences in the formula as it moves from one culture or from one period to another. For example, the gunfighter Western of the 1950s is importantly different from the cowboy romances of Owen Wister and Zane Grey, just as the American spy stories of Donald Hamilton differ from the British secret agent adventures of Eric Ambler and Graham Greene.

The cultural nature of formulas suggests two further points about them.

First, while myths, because of their basic and universal nature, turn up in many different manifestations, formulas, because of their close connection to a particular culture and period of time, tend to have a much more limited repertory of plots, characters, and settings. For example, the pattern of action known generally as the Oedipus myth can be discerned in an enormous range of stories from *Oedipus Rex* to the latest Western. Indeed, the very difficulty with this myth as an analytical tool is that it is so universal that it hardly serves to differentiate one story from another. Formulas, however, are much more specific: Westerns must have a certain kind of setting, a particular cast of characters, and follow a limited number of lines of action. A Western that does not take place in the West, near the frontiers, at a point in history when social order and anarchy are in tension, and that does not involve some form of pursuit, is simply not a Western. A detective story that does not involve the solution of a mysterious crime is not a detective story. This greater specificity of plot, character, and setting reflects a more limited framework of interest, values, and tensions that relate to culture rather than to the generic nature of man.

The second point is a hypothesis about why formulas come into existence and enjoy such wide popular use. Why of all the infinite possible subjects for fictions do a few like the adventures of the detective, the secret agent, and the cowboy so dominate the field.

I suggest that formulas are important because they represent syntheses of several important cultural functions which, in modern cultures, have been taken over by the popular arts. Let me suggest just one or two examples of what I mean. In earlier more homogeneous cultures religious ritual performed the important function of articulating and reaffirming the primary cultural values. Today, with cultures composed of a multiplicity of differing religious groups, the synthesis of values and their reaffirmation has become an increasingly important function of the mass media and the popular arts. Thus, one important dimension of formula is social or cultural ritual. Homogeneous cultures also possessed a large repertory of games and songs which all members of the culture understood and could participate in both for a sense of group solidarity and for personal enjoyment and recreation. Today, the great spectator sports provide one way in which a mass audience can participate in games together. Artistic formulas also fulfill this function in that they constitute entertainments with rules known to everyone. Thus, a very wide audience can follow a Western, appreciate its fine points and vicariously participate in its pattern of suspense and resolution. Indeed one of the more interesting ways of defining a western is as a game: a western is a three-sided game played on a field where the middle line is the frontier and the two main areas of play are the settled town and the savage wilderness. The three sides are the good group of townspeople who stand for law and order, but are handicapped by lack of force; the villains who reject law and order and have force; and the hero who has ties with both sides. The object of the game is to get the hero to lend his force to the good group and to destroy the villain. Various rules determine how this can be done; for example, the hero cannot use force against the villain unless strongly provoked. Also like games, the formula always gets to its goal. Someone must win, and the story must be resolved.

This game dimension of formulas had two aspects. First, there is the patterned experience of excitement, suspense, and release which we associate with the functions of entertainment and recreation. Second, there is the aspect of play as ego-enhancement through the temporary resolution of inescapable frustrations and tensions through fantasy. As Piaget sums up this aspect of play:

Conflicts are foreign to play, or, if they do occur, it is so that the ego may be freed from them by compensation or liquidation, whereas serious activity has to grapple with conflicts which are inescapable. The conflict between obedience and individual liberty is, for example, the affliction of childhood [and we might note a key theme of the Western] and in real life the only solutions to this conflict are submission, revolt, or cooperation which involves some measure of compromise. In play, however, the conflicts are transposed in such a way that the ego is revenged, either by suppression of the problem or by giving it an acceptable solution . . . it is because the ego dominates the whole universe in play that it is freed from conflict.

Thus, the game dimension of formula is a culture's way of simultaneously entertaining itself and of creating an acceptable pattern of temporary escape from the serious restrictions and limitations of human life. In formula stories, the detective always solves the crime, the hero always determines and carries out true justice, and the agent accomplishes his mission or at least preserves himself from the omnipresent threats of the enemy.

Finally, formula stories seem to be one way in which the individuals in a culture act out certain unconscious or repressed needs, or express in an overt and symbolic fashion certain latent motives which they must give expression to, but cannot face openly. This is the most difficult aspect of formula to pin down. Many would argue that one cannot meaningfully discuss latent contents or unconscious motives beyond the individual level or outside of the clinical context. Certainly it is easy to generate a great deal of pseudo-psychoanalytic theories about literary formulas and to make deep symbolic interpretations which it is clearly impossible to substantiate convincingly. However, though it may be difficult to develop a reliable method of analysis of this aspect of formulas, I am convinced that the Freudian insight that recurrent myths and stories embody a kind of collective dreaming process is essentially correct and has an important application on the cultural as well as the universal level, that is, that the idea of a collective dream applies to formula as well as to myth. But there is no doubt that we need to put much more thought into our approach to these additional dimensions of formula and about their relation to the basic dimension of a narrative construction.

My argument, then, is that formula stories like the detective story, the Western, the seduction novel, the biblical epic, and many others are structures of narrative conventions which carry out a variety of cultural functions in a unified way. We can best define these formulas as principles for the selection of certain plots, characters, and settings, which possess in addition to their basic narrative structure the dimensions of collective ritual, game and dream. To analyze these formulas we must first define them as narrative structures of a certain kind and then investigate how the additional dimensions of ritual, game and dream have been synthesized into the particular patterns of plot, character and setting which have become associated with the formula. Once we have understood the way in which particular formulas are structured, we will be able to compare them, and also to relate them to the cultures which use them. By these methods I feel that we will arrive at a new understanding of the phenomena of popular literature and new insights into the patterns of culture.

FORMALISM AND POPULAR CULTURE

David N. Feldman

David N. Feldman critiques Cawelti's concept of formula, then uses some of the basic analytical concepts of Russian Formalism (defamiliarization, story, plot, free and bound motifs, and re-familiarization) to supplement Cawelti's concept. Rather than reject formula entirely, Feldman acknowledges that the conventions that works share in common are important; but thinks that only by focusing on innovations (the transformation of free motifs into bound motives or re-familiarization), that is, by using the concepts of Formalism, can we answer the critically important points of why the public prefers one work to another and why each new formulaic work might be consumed with pleasure rather than boredom. Feldman is a graduate of Bowling Green State University's Masters program in Popular Culture, a soap opera writer, and author of the popular Imponderables series.

I: The Concept of Formula

The publication of "The Concept of Formula in the Study of Popular Literature"[1] was a milestone in Popular Culture Studies. John Cawelti's essay argued that it is possible to ascertain recurrent conventional systems, or "formulas," in popular literature that are peculiar to a given culture, and suggested that these narrative formulas could tell us much about the dreams, values and often otherwise unarticulated needs of that culture.

Popular Culture scholars were grateful for any tool that would assist them in beginning to organize and analyze the plethora of popular stories. The concept of formula was especially well received, perhaps, by the variously trained Popular Culture constituency because Cawelti's theory embraced the social scientists' methodology (usually content analysis) while exploring primarily literary/humanistic concerns (plots, themes, characterizations, etc.). David Soneschein's work with romance magazines[2] and particularly Morton Cronin's essay on Currier and Ives prints[3] are excellent examples of the compatibility of formula and orthodox content analysis techniques.

David N. Feldman, "Formalism and Popular Culture," Journal of Popular Culture 9.2 *(Fall 1975): 384–402.*

Most of the extended applications of the concept of formula, however, have used analytical rather than quantitative methods, including Cawelti's own examination of the western formula, *The Six-Gun Mystique*.[4] Cawelti's influence is evident, and acknowledged, in Horace Newcomb's *TV: The Most Popular Art*.[5] In this first serious attempt at forging a television aesthetic, Newcomb utilizes a formulaic approach.

Formula studies have proven, often, to be cultural analyses in the best sense; they have told us much about American society without ignoring the artistic context of their subject matter. In my study and teaching of popular culture, however, many questions and problems have developed in applying the concept of formula; it will be the attempt to outline three major problems (while ungraciously ignoring the concept's strengths) that will comprise the first section of the paper.

THE WEAKNESSES OF FORMULA

It has not been demonstrated why popular literature should be studies differently than elite literature. Are "formula," "convention," and "invention" empirical terms or descriptions of the audience's perceptions? The rationale for the concept of formula is that:

The analysis of popular culture is somewhat different from that of the fine arts. When we are studying the fine arts, we are essentially interested in the unique achievement of the individual artist, while in the case of popular culture, we are dealing with a product that is in some sense collective.[6]

Surely, most popular art is collective. The dialogue that appears on a television screen, for example, may bear little resemblance to the original teleplay after the director, producer, actor, agent, editor, script consultant, network executive, legal counsel, research department, advertiser and program practices department all "improve" it. The economics of popular art usually preclude the possibility of the audience receiving an "individual effort."

Cawelti's theory does not contend with the fact that the elite artist faces at least three forces that turn his/her effort into a collective work. First, any form which requires a performance is by definition a collective venture. We cannot possibly consider Peter Brooks' *King Lear* or a rendition of "Moonlight Sonata," by Vladimir Horowitz or Vanilla Fudge, as the unique achievement of the individual artist. But do we study "Moonlight Sonata" as popular culture?

Second, the elite artist faces commercial considerations that can modify his work. Any elite artist who had a patron was necessarily involved in a collective process not unlike the commercial pressures put upon the popular artist. Likewise, the "independent" author of today faces editing, censorship and cutting by publishers. (Indeed, we must face the problem of how an author's foreknowledge of editors' tastes and preferences pre-censor the author's work). The *auteur* theory in movies might be applicable to both elite and popular literature. Can one detect the work and vision of one editor's hands in several writers, or the philosophy of one publishing company in its handling of a series of authors?

Third, even if the original content of a work remains intact, the context in which the artists' work is seen is dependent upon others. Perhaps art and sculpture are the forms most conducive to "unique achievement of the individual artist." A Giacometti sculpture, unless it ages or is defaced, will theoretically always appear the way it was conceived. However, the slightest changes in lighting or positioning can greatly alter one's perception of the piece; one would perceive a statue differently if it were juxtaposed with the *Venus de Milo* than if it were displayed next to Oldenburg's *Shoestring Potatoes*. These variables are compounded once Giacometti's work is mass-produced (in postcards, reproductions, etc.)—can the "message" possibly remain the same when the "medium" is so radically different? Similarly, the paperback covers that make *Dr. Zhivago* appear to be an exploitative rip-off of the movie turn the novel into a collective entity. Reproductions of *Mona Lisa* are omnipresent in our society—on postcards, television, posters and advertisements. Is *Mona Lisa* popular culture or elite art? Even when the difficult distinction between individual and collective processes can be drawn, it doesn't clarify why it is important, necessary, or even valuable to study *Dr. Zhivago* in a different context than a Perry Mason novel.

Furthermore, Cawelti avoids a most important problem: despite the historical realities, it is not to be assumed that the *audience* perceives collective works as collective works. How many readers knew that the *Rover Boys* series, always credited to Arthur Winfield, was authored by a collective of writers, or that Charlie Goren's bridge column, which has attained wide syndication on the strength of his name, has been ghosted for decades? How many owners of a Kandinsky lithograph proclaim to their friends, "Look at this fine mechanical reproduction of an original drawing"?

On the other hand, we study the work of Homer as if it were the artistically controlled creation of one man, even though the *Iliad* might well be the product of scores of people. Does this invalidate all elite scholarship on Homer? I think not. We do not have the equipment to study "the making of the *Iliad*" as a collective process, so we study it *as the audience preceives it anyway,* as an individual masterpiece.

In clarification of his position, Cawelti indicated that the word "collective" was a reference not to the literal creation by individuals as opposed to creation by groups but to the popular writer's practice of capitalizing on the popularity of bestsellers by imitating their formats. "If enough readers and writers choose to produce and consume this type of story a formula arises and is a collective creation in that sense."[7]

Except for the patina of economic motivation among popular artists, it is not at all clear how this interpretation of "collective" differentiates the popular and elite arts. Surely, the belief in an elite collective tradition has been the driving force behind such venerable institutions as freshman Humanities courses and *Great Books.* The positive connotation of such words as "classic," "genre," or "literary school" would be impossible without the recognition of the collective nature of elite art. Whether *Tom Jones* was written in order to cash in on the success of *Pamela* is not ascertainable and not relevant. The fact is that both elite and popular artists have a dynamic relationship with their peers, their predecessors and their audience: The denial of the collective nature of elite art is untenable.

The study of the collaborative nature of a popular or elite artifact is immensely important, but why is it not equally important to lend the same dignity to the "collective" Perry Mason novel that we invest in an *Iliad,* by studying it as a "unique artistic creation" rather than lumping all Gardner novels together. The implication that individual pieces of elite art are worthy of individual study, while "collective" popular arts are best looked at collectively is, unacceptably, tantamount to deeming popular fiction subliterature. Despite disclaimers and because of rather noticeable revelations (e.g., "Though it is likely for a number of reasons that a work possessing more form than formula will be a greater work. . . ."[8] and references to elite art as "Works" and popular art as "product"), does not formula become a negatively loaded word?

Is it not likewise a condescending assumption to conclude that what is most important about a popular culture work is necessarily that which it shares with other works within its genre? Although those elements consistently found to be included in a formula can tell us much about a culture, it is a dangerous form of reductionism to ignore not only the anti-formulaic works within a genre, but also those elements within a given formulaic work that are either antipathetic, irrelevant or in addition to the usual formula. If we look only at those elements that all works in a given genre have in common, and then use these elements to extract information about our culture, we would not have a valid formula: rather, we would have the lowest common denominator, only a fraction of our potential findings. If we studied human beings in this manner, perhaps all we could prove is that humans have a respiratory and circulatory system.

Is there a difference between the "recurrent images," "repeated modalities," and "consistent themes" of the elite artists and the "conventions" and "repetitiveness" of the popular artist? The answer is unclear, but we would certainly not stop our comparison of *King Lear* and *Macbeth* with the potentially rewarding but obviously limited question of what the two plays have in common; is it not equally unwise, equally trivializing to the detective genre not to interest ourselves intensely with the question of how *The Case of the Blonde Bonanza* differs from *The Case of the Perjured Parrot*?

The concept of formula does not help us to discriminate between different pieces of fiction within one genre.[9] Would it not be fair to say that the reason we can easily differentiate a Raymond Chandler novel from a Mickey Spillane novel is that each has created his own *inventional* (in Cawelti's sense of the word) system? Is it not because each, to use Cawelti's examples, has created new kinds of characters, ideas and linguistic forms within the genre? To say that the introduction of the Spillane hero as a detective (a type some would associate with characters in non-detective stories pre-dating Mike Hammer) is not inventional is like claiming that Dali's utilization of commonplace objects in his surrealistic paintings is not inventional.

Although Cawelti does separate the ratiocinative detective formula from the hard boiled school of detective fiction, surely we must differentiate Raymond Chandler from Mickey Spillane somehow. Cawelti rightly sees the convention/invention scale as a continuum rather than a dichotomy, but does not tell us what to do with the "left-over" non-conventional elements in a formulaic work[10] which might well constitute the majority of any work that we can easily differentiate from any other work. The auteur theory, again, might be useful in analyzing an author's "personal" formulas— those elements that might be found within one artist's work, even if he/she crosses lines of genre and medium. These patterns of personal idiosyncrasies might outnumber the similarities between two different artists within the same genre.

It is undeniably true that a writer who sets out to create detective stories must accept certain conventions if he/she is to be perceived as a detective writer, but these conventions are so few, so basic, so flexible, that to categorize these conventions as formula is not to find the appeal or even necessarily the outstanding characteristics of the genre, but only its common denominator. If the ultimate aim of formula is the analysis of a culture, why are its conclusions predicated upon historical and aesthetic judgments rather than the audience's conception of the work?

In Cawelti's scheme, Samuel Beckett's players would be said to be inventional; Mickey Spillane's novels would be deemed conventional. Why? Beckett broke many formal conventions in playwriting. *Waiting for Godot* came as a shock to the theatergoers of its time. But was not *Godot* a realistic depiction of its creator's vision? It may be considered absurd or surrealistic in comparison to other plays of its period, but the sentiments expressed in *Godot* were echoed by many existential and absurdist philosophers and artists before Beckett—*Godot* was a shocker because it was inventional within its genre.

Just as the dramatic world should have been prepared for *Godot* (at least if it had been reading philosophy), so the detective world should have been prepared for Spillane. Such "tough guys" as Sam Spade predated Mike Hammer, but Spillane's hero was as starkly tough and violent as Beckett's vision was bleak; more importantly, Spillane's vision of the world was as unsettling to his constituency as Beckett's was to his. Both portrayed visions of the world that have been expressed by many before them (although Beckett's more elite influences might not have had as wide a circulation as Spillane—but then neither have Beckett's plays). Both were forced to create a new formal structure, new characters and new types of dialogue within their chosen genres. Even if one considers Spillane merely a hybrid of pornography, pulp, action and detective fiction, surely it must be conceded that such a synthesis must have been a unique artistic achievement for it to be absorbed by the detective genre. Both Beckett's and Spillane's works seemed novel to their constituencies. How can it be so easy to differentiate which is inventional and which is conventional? Last season on *Gunsmoke,* after nineteen years of unconsummated fidelity to Matt Dillon, Kitty had an affair with another man. A one-hour John Cage recital on *Hee-Haw* could not serve the cultural functions of invention any more than this *Gunsmoke* episode, and yet formally, it perfectly fit the (*Gunsmoke*) western formula. Where does this fit in the invention/convention continuum? *The Wasteland* is one of Cawelti's archetypal inventional works:

The Wasteland . . . contains a substantial number of conventional elements—even to the point of using quotations from past literary works—but these elements are structured *in such a fashion* that a *new perception* of familiar elements is forced upon the reader.[11] (Italics mine)

Although it is probable that this "new perception" is continually achieved by popular artists, most obviously so in the *Gunsmoke* episode, one need not accept this premise to realize that there are at least two inherent dangers in applying the tag "inventional" to *The Wastland* and "conventional" to *Gunsmoke.*

One, how are we to judge whether a work with conventional elements is "structured in such a fashion" as to be inventional? This guideline, although probably purposely vague so as to allow flexibility, eventually becomes an aesthetic prescriptive judgment. Furthermore, do inventional works become conventional when others imitate them? How are we to differentiate *Last Year at Marienbad* from its host of imitators? Does the concept of formula force us to make strictly historical judgments (e.g., the movie was inventional when released but now is conventional because it would be perceived as such by a devoted art film patron who missed it when it was first released)? If so, does the theory of formulas work in application to *Marienbad*? If so, why did it not originally?

Although it might be historically important, the *reductio ad absurdum* of this approach is threatening to any cultural analysis. The ritualized Chinese opera might be formulaic to the Chinese, but totally inventive and startling to an American audience. Conversely, if a nineteenth century antecedent of Picasso's were unearthed, would we relegate Picasso's "imitations" to mere genre studies? There is the real danger that formula can be used unwittingly to cast away artifacts worthy of further study into the oblivion of a work only valuable for a formulaic genre study. Is there not too great a possibility, for example, that a movie subsequent to *Marienbad*, that shares many of its conventional elements, might automatically be branded formulaic, thus depriving it of study as a "unique artistic creation"? The even greater danger, of course, is that we would not be analyzing the cultural impact of any popular culture artifact if we refuse to acknowledge the mass perception of that artifact. Some film buffs might scoff at the sentimentality and melodrama of *A Man and A Woman,* yet there is much evidence to support the supposition that its commercial success hinged on it being sold and perceived as a "heavy art film."

Two, the definition of the convention/invention dichotomy mixes formal matters (e.g., plots, characterization) with non-formal matters (e.g., "ideas") in a confusing fashion. Is every sonnet ever composed conventional because of the repetition of its formal motifs? What we call the "challenge" of the haiku or sonnet structure we call the "cliché" or "hackwork" in a Tarzan story. One seldom hears the complaint: "Shakespeare is so boring and predictable—every damn poem is iambic pentameter." Conversely, must a fictional writer develop new "ideas" in order to be termed "inventional"? Is *A Day in the Life of Ivan Denisovich* formulaic because Solzhenitsyn did not create any new ideas in the book? How can we evaluate the relative importance of the formal and nonformal components of the aforementioned *Gunsmoke* episode unless we measure convention and invention in terms of the audience's perception of the show? The word "convention" implies a sharing and commonality of experience among a group of people—when we base our decisions upon aesthetic, historical and formal analyses alone, we are dodging the most pressing issue in the application of formula: how can we develop a mechanism for gauging the audience's comprehension of conventional/inventional elements so that we may extrapolate valid cultural analyses from popular culture material?

While Cawelti defines formula as "conventional SYSTEM (emphasis mine) for structuring cultural products,"[12] almost all of the work in the field has concentrated on isolating conventional elements without placing the conventions in a systemic context. This lack has served to underemphasize the one thing all popular writers have in common—their "literariness" (as the Russian Formalists phrased it).

Popular fiction probably reflects cultural values (although not necessarily any more than anything else in this society, it is important to remember), but it is a dangerous assumption to believe that changes in writing styles or preoccupations are caused by shifts in cultural values. An artist is as likely to be influenced by other writers as by a shift in popular opinions. In other words, about the only thing all writers have in common is their writing. The attempt to extract cultural values, myths, icons, and formulas from popular works is manifestly worthwhile, but to fail to work with the form and structure of a writer's work is to deny the study of what is often the main concern of the artist. We must not jump to the conclusion that a change of characterization in a Ross Macdonald novel is based on changing American values or even changing Macdonald values. Often, as will be shown in the Perry Mason analysis, the changes may be concessions or realignments in response to the dictates of a story's structural system or because of a desire on the part of the author to experiment with form.

Perhaps the strongest portion of Cawelti's essay is his discussion of how myths (e.g., Oedipus) have been trivialized by reductionism. He effectively argues that the universality of myths, when abused and simplified, can be stretched to extend to virtually any work, thus robbing the "universal myth" of its meaning. Cawelti might have performed a similar disservice to his own theory by focusing only on those elements that each genre has in common and ignoring the multitude of loose ends. Why must we conclude that the conventional elements of a formula are what constitute the success of traditional popular works? The fact that *not every* soap opera, western or detective work evokes a deep response from the American public indicates to me that the components of a formula might only be the *given* rather than the *essence* of a formula's appeal. It is here, perhaps, where the Formalists' notion of *story* and *plot* are most useful. Yes, the plot, characters, ideas, etc., of a work do form a pattern, the story, but the *arrangement* of these elements by the author, the plot, forms a new and more precise pattern.

The concept of formula is the only theoretical handle that has been of value to me in analyzing popular stories. I have listed my gripes, questions and problems with Cawelti's position at the risk of being unfair. The following is an attempt to resolve some of the problems and questions posed by the preceding material, and a tentative stop toward placing conventional material in a systemic context.

II. Formalism and Popular Culture

It was my custom during my senior year at college to watch two consecutive hours of Perry Mason reruns on television every weekday evening. I had always loved the show, but I was an execrable sleuth. Suddenly, after studying Russian Formalism in a literature course, I began guessing the identity of the killers consistently (more than 90%), and it was weeks before I made the connection that the concepts of this highbrow criticism were spoon-feeding me the identity of the murderers in Perry Mason.

This study originated, in part, as an attempt to discover whether Russian Formalism would apply as well to Gardner's novels as it did to television programs. It was evident after reading several novels and studying one, *The Case of the Blonde Bonanza,* intensively, that Russian Formalism could not only solve murder cases, but help to answer some important questions about popular, conventional stories: how are they structured? why do we not get bored with highly conventional stories? why do we like mystery stories? why do we become so involved in a story that we often forget it hours after we finish it?

Russian Formalism, it is necessary to point out, is offered here as one legitimate, potentially fruitful, way of studying popular culture, not necessarily as the only, the best or even the most desirable way. Formalism is not a refutation or substitute for "formula." Although formalism offers concrete help with many of the questions and complaints posed above, it will be contended later that the two may be used as complements. Finally, this is a far from comprehensive look at Russian Formalism. I have merely extracted three concepts that were found to be useful and applicable to popular culture.[13]

THE RUSSIAN FORMALISTS

During the 1920s in Russia, a group of critics, dismayed by the didactic emphasis of their contemporaries, attempted to separate literary from political/social/moral/historical/philological theory. Eschewing any ready-made methodology, the "so-called 'formal' method grew out of a struggle for a science of literature that would be both independent and factual . . . by the examination of specific material in its specific context."[14] In short, the Formalists believed that the only thing that joins all literature together is its "literariness," and they burdened themselves with the chore of defining what elements all literature has in common: " . . . the question for the formalist is not how to study literature, but what the subject matter of literary study actually is."[15]

Even if we in Popular Culture reject their single-mindedness, the Formalists isolated three elements—defamiliarization, story and plot, and motifs—that obviously apply to our studies of popular literature, if not to all conventional artifacts.

Traditionally, "artistic" writers were thought of as men or women with exceptional sensitivity and vision, who could render their images clearly to a reader. The artist could make his/her unique vision intelligible to all, even it "all" meant the intelligentsia of a given society.

The Formalists, considering themselves scientists, decided to make no *a priori* assumptions about such matters, so they investigated what was generally considered to be the greatest literature from all over the world. Their empirical studies led them to refute the notion, then generally held, that technical changes in literature are the results of new images, themes, cultural values and the need to transform the techniques of literature in order to adjust to the new content.[16] On the contrary, the Formalists found that the images of the most brilliant poets were virtually taken unchanged from other poets. Indeed, they found that the images of poetry serve much the same relationship to the poet as conventions do to the popular artist: "Images are given to poets; the ability to remember them is far more important than the ability to create them."[17]

The more poems Victor Shklovsky and his peers studied, the more evident it became that poets were much more concerned with how to arrange given images than with creating them. Shklovsky concluded that not only does imagistic thought not include all aspects of art or even all aspects of verbal art, but that "a change in imagery is not essential to the development of poetry."[18]

When the Formalists eventually extended Shklovsky's determination to prose, images or themes became to them "merely" another *device* in literary language, as important as repetition, diction, or plotting, but not necessarily any more important. The implications of this conclusion, obviously, were staggering. Form no longer was seen as the vessel into which "content" was poured. Because the Formalists empirically demonstrated that art's uniqueness "consists not in the parts which enter into it but in their original *use* . . . the notion of form was changed . . . it is a complete thing, something concrete, dynamic, self-contained and without a correlative of any kind."[19] The Formalists then broke with the Symbolists, since there was no longer any "content" to shine through the "form."

It may be argued that such a theory constitutes the most blatant and irrelevant kind of aestheticism, antipathetic to the spirit and history of Popular Culture Studies, since it seems to undermine the importance of content (the subject of most of our cultural criticism). In actuality, Formalism lends a new dignity and credibility to the study of themes, for Formalists believed strongly in not extracting content, or any other element of form, out of context. Other critics attempt(ed) to isolate elements of form from content, thereby simplifying the content by reductionism and at best, failing to demonstrate why the content of some works are so powerfully received by audiences while other with the same themes are scorned. The Formalists treated "content" as it obviously is—an element in the form of a work, affecting and affected by every other element of the work. Formalists nowithstanding, it is clear that large segments of both popular and elite audiences *do* perceive content as "the message" that the form of a work is constructed to deliver. It is thus a most valuable effort to study the *audience's perception* about content even if, as the Formalists would have it, we are studying a popular misconception.

Armed with a new set of assumptions, the Formalists contended that the primary aesthetic value of art was its roughening of form. Shklovsky, particularly, argued that our *habitual* way of thinking is to render the unfamiliar as easily digestible as possible. Lemon and Reis compare our reading of ordinary prose to driving a car—we demonstrate our proficiency by operating unconsciously. Just as we avoid pedestrians without actually noticing them in detail, so we read most prose automatically, with minimal perception, because efficient functioning in reading or driving is often dependent upon ignoring detail. The purpose of art, according to Shklovsky, is to force us to notice, and the purpose of the study of art is to examine the artist's techniques designed to impede perceptions, or at least designed to call attention to themselves. To Formalists, then, art exists to force us to notice, to

impart the sensation of things as they are perceived and not as they are known. The technique of art is to make objects "unfamiliar," to make forms difficult, to increase the difficulty and length of perception because the perception is an aesthetic end in itself and must be prolonged. *Art is a way of experiencing the artfulness of an object; the object is not important.*[20]

According to Shklovsky, then, the purpose of an image or theme is not to present an exact or even approximate meaning for our understanding, but to create a *special* perception of the object—if it is immediately understandable, then it probably is not art.

It is too simplistic to conclude that because popular fiction is repetitive in images, characters, themes, or techniques, that it is safe to say, as Cawelti does, that these are conventions which serve the cultural purpose of "familiarizing" the reader with him/herself or environment or fellow human beings. Perhaps this conclusion was reached because it seems self-evident that readers do try to move past the "defamiliar" *back* to the familiar. The human mind, faced with the complexity and distortions of a puzzling mystery story, spontaneously, if consciously, tries to make sense out of the quagmire of motifs, and to return to the secure world of the familiar. Proof of the existence of defamiliarization in elite literature is manifested by the number of people who have gained employment by analyzing it—the longevity and popularity of literary interpretations/criticism indicate not only that we have been defamiliarized by the art, but that we have a strong need to reintegrate the motifs, to make sense of the artwork, to apply it to our own lives.

By applying the term "convention" as a historical judgment rather than a description of the audience's perception of the work, we have diverted our efforts in an unfruitful direction. Whether or not Shakespeare's love sonnets are formulaic merely because they are all about love or all in iambic pentameter is irrelevant. The scansion of Shakespeare's sonnets, like the stereotyped characters of Perry Mason novels, may be taken as givens, but as long as our detective fan scrupulously labors over details in order to decipher who killed whom, he is undergoing the same process of aesthetic defamiliarization and refamiliarization as our Shakespeare buff.

STORY, PLOT AND MOTIFS

Conventions do not necessarily breed familiarity. The Formalist notion of story, plot and motifs offers us a possible answer to why, given the many conventions of a Gardner or a Christie, their twentieth novel is as exciting and absorbing to us as the first that we read.

Victor Shklovsky, by differentiating "story" from "plot," developed the methodology to describe how narrative writers achieved the effect of defamiliarization. Shklovsky's translators, Lemon and Reis, succinctly define the two terms, and summarize well their importance to formalistic studies:

Story is essentially the temporal-causal sequence of narrated events. Its formula, capable of infinite extension, is always "because of A, then B." Because Raskolnikov is an impoverished intellectual, he killed . . . ; because Pip fed a convict . . . Such is the pattern of the story, each event coming in the order in which it would occur in real life and the events bound each to each in a cause and effect relationship. This, to return to the notion of defamiliarization, is the familiar way, it is not the artistic way. Artistry, for Shklovsky, requires both defamiliarization and an obvious display of the devices by which the familiar is made strange.[21] [In this last sentence, Shklovsky unknowingly defends popular culture against the charge that it is worthless because it is so obviously "contrived, unrealistic and obvious." Shklovsky did not at all accept the argument good art conceals its technique.]

In these terms, plot becomes the story as distorted or defamiliarized in the process of telling. [Defamiliarization in this context refers to the distortion of the temporal-causal sequence, not the conclusion that all techniques or themes are strange, unique, or even unfamiliar.] Even a novel as superficially simple in construction as Hawthorne's *Scarlet Letter* distorts both temporal and cause-effect relations by, for example, beginning in the middle, after the adultery that properly begins the main action. Or such a seemingly orthodox novel as *Vanity Fair* has plot rather than story partly by virtue of the parallel development of two strands that are causally unrelated—the Becky Sharp strand and the Amelia strand. As Shklovsky shows . . . the ways of making a story into a plot are innumerable, but all involve some kind of disarrangement of what we would call the natural, or real-life, sequence of events. Since plot distinguishes the natural from the artistic method of narration, Shklovsky is interested in plot.[22]

In another brilliant essay, "The Relationship of Devices of Plot Constructions to General Devices of Style," Shklovsky cited scores of examples to prove that special arrangements of plot do exist. Shklovsky "changed the traditional notion of plot as a combination of a group of motifs and made plot a *compositional rather than a thematic concept*[23] [emphasis mine]. Plot construction, now seen as the one specific technique *peculiar to narrative fiction,* became the focus of the Formalist's study. Form not longer was an abstract concept to the Formalists; rather, form was studied as *plotting.*

In order to study plotting, it was obviously necessary to delineate the components of the story:

> After reducing a work to its thematic elements, we come to parts that are irreducible, the smallest particles of thematic material: "evening comes," "Raskilnikov kills the old woman," "the hero dies," "the letter is received," and so on. The theme of an irreducible part of a work is called the *motif.*[24]

There are two kinds of motifs found in most kinds of stories. *Bound motifs* cannot be omitted without disturbing the causal connections between events; *free motifs* are those which may be omitted without upsetting the causal/logical/chronological order of events. Shklovsky found that although only bound motifs are required by the story, free motifs often dominate works. Free motifs, like conventions, tend to be determined by a literary/cultural tradition, whereas bound motifs (like archetypes?) tend to appear unchanged in the works of various schools.

It is important to remember that the plot contains the *identical* motifs as the story. The story arranges motifs in their logical, causal, chronological order; the plot arranges the motifs in the context and order in which they can be found in the artistic work.

A series of real incidents, motifs not fictionalized by an author, can make a story. It has been our practice in Popular Culture Studies to focus on the story, the purely thematic elements, ignoring the fact that it is the plot, not the story, that differentiates the popular or elite artistic creation from a factual account, even if the plot is as familiar as the story.

Cawelti's desire for an "aesthetic of performance" can and should be applied even to the written narrative, for one possible definition of plot is "the performance of a given story." All of the embellishments that the song stylist, for example, lends to his/her material as printed on the sheet music— accented phrasing, repeated or slurred passages, speeding up the prescribed beat—are equivalent to the transformation of the story by techniques of plotting. After all, as Shklovsky reminds us, "The place in the work in which the reader learns of an even, whether the information is given by the author, or by a character, or by a series of indirect hints—all this is irrelevant to the story."[25] So the aesthetic function of the plot, like the function of a great monologist, is precisely to draw attention to technique, to this arrangement of motifs. It is the *arrangement* of motifs, the artistic context of the work, not the story, that explains how audiences can be conditioned psychologically to embrace themes they would ordinarily reject. How else can one explain why "liberal" audiences cheered on the vigilantism of *Walking Tall, Dirty Harry,* and *Death Wish* while "conservative" audiences gleefully condoned the brutality and hostility to authority that *Billy Jack* or *The Longest Yard* exhibited? Certainly these movies are a testimony to the ability of plotting to transform the meanings ordinarily assigned to a story. It is absolutely essential, then, that we study not only the story of narratives, but the techniques, the arrangement of motifs, in order to understand how we are persuaded to accept and even like *plots* whose *stories* we would reject.

III: Formalism and The Case of the Blonde Bonanza

In order to see if Formalism would assist in the analysis of *The Case of the Blonde Bonanza,* I transcribed what I thought was every motif while reading the book for the first time (e.g., "Perry and Della meet at beach." "Perry and Della see blonde eating excessive amounts." "The blonde, Dianne Alder, meets Mason at Aunt Mae's house." "Dianne tells Mason she needed to put on weight for her modeling." "Mason tells Della to talk to Dianne about Dianne's contract." "Mason reads contract.").

In this novel, Mason's client, Dianne Alder, is accused of murdering a blackguard named Boring. There are at least five people, including Dianne, seen by Moose (Paul Drake's operative) entering the deceased man's motel room during the night of his demise. The vast majority of the book delves into Dianne's history, which also establishes that the five visitor to Boring's motel room had equally good murder motives. In reality, however, Moose, the detective, accidentally—without premeditation, in a fit of temper—killed Boring and framed Dianne Alder by altering his eyewitness account.

What better showcase for our formalistic concepts could we possess than this novel? Although the murder was a simple case of a hard-boiled detective letting his temper get away from him, Gardner constructs an elaborate camouflage to make it impossible for us to perceive the simplicity of the murder. If a newspaper reported stories in this fashion, it would be accused of lying, distortion and verbosity; when Gardner deceives us, it is art—a perfect example of defamiliarization.[26]

Even the most cursory reading of *The Case of the Blonde Bonanza* will reveal that ninety percent of the motifs in this book are free motifs. The entire matrix of machinations in this book is irrelevant to the murder. Understanding the backgrounds of the suspects, or even the victim, is totally unnecessary in order to determine how or why Moose killed Boring; Moose could just as well have accidentally knocked off anyone he was following without the story making any more or less sense. Nevertheless, Gardner's plotting forces Mason, and therefore the reader, to be preoccupied with these "irrelevant" motifs for over ninety percent of the book.

There are undoubtedly intellectual questions of greater magnitude than whether formalism can solve *The Case of the Blonde Bonanza,* but few of them can be answered unequivocally, "yes." From a formalistic viewpoint, the solution jumps out at the reader. The first eighty-eight pages of the novel are in strict chronological order; the first major deviation occur when Moose recounts to Mason whom he had seen going in and out of Boring's apartment. Although it is true that such a slight deviation between the story and the plot (only about an hour chronologically) does not upset the reader, it is certainly a clue to the identity of the murderer. From the moment we are introduced to Moose in this fashion, we feel that he may be the murderer for two reasons. First, in previous Mason novels, Drake's operative has gone unnamed. In this novel, Moose is not only named but put in the table of contents (i.e., cast of characters) and given a larger role than a few of the suspects. This, to me, seemed like a suspicious *free motif,* one that was unnecessary to the murder plot.[27] Whereas most of Mason's briefings were a few sentences or a paragraph, Moose recounted his observations for six pages. The length of Moose's descriptions, especially when the visitations could have been as efficiently described by the omniscient narrator, convinced me that not only the material in the descriptions must have been bound motifs, but the fact that *Moose* was doing all of the describing must have been a bound motif. It could only be a bound motif if he was connected with the murder; since Moose was at all times operating by himself, I concluded that he was the murderer. Second, since the plot and story were congruent until the arrival of Moose as a character, I felt that the event that upset this chronological pattern must be a significant one. As it turned out, I was right; this is an example of how isolating a technical formal matter can have a great impact upon understanding the "content."

We in Popular Culture Studies sometimes abstract cultural values from works of literature without taking into consideration the technical or formal reasons for certain conventions and intentions in stories. For example, if George Winlock, the defendant's wealthy estranged father, had committed the murder, we might assume that Gardner was making a "statement" about (against) the *nouveau riche*. Are we to conclude that because a detective committed this murder, that Gardner is making a "statement" about low-grade private detectives? Such a conclusion is true only if we believe that "content" is not just another device, but the very stuff of literature. But upon sampling many Gardner novels, we find that there seems to be no pattern or bias to his selection of murderers. And yet don't we all seem to possess an intuitive barometer that indicates, even if after the fact, whether the author has selected the "right" murderer? What do all Mason novels seem to have in common?

There is a recurrent formal pattern in Gardner's novels. What Mason novels have in common is not so much a formulaic set of conventions as a constant strategy—to create an aesthetic uneasiness in the reader by introducing a few free motifs in the midst of a multitude of bound motifs necessary to the solution of the murder. Because these free, realistically unmotivated motifs are mixed in with other motifs that are vital to the solution of the crime, the very superfluity of the free motifs causes them to stand out in our minds—as Cawelti might put it, they are inventions in a conventional world. Although throughout the book the reader is undergoing the constant process of defamiliarization (for the case could easily be summarized in ten declarative statements), at the very end of the book, when the murderer is revealed, the reader is re-familiarized. These elements that were unclear or seemingly extraneous (i.e., free motifs) are usually explained in the post-trial patter among Mason, Della, and Drake.

The Case of the Blond Bonanza is an exception to the usual Gardner novel; he reverses his usual strategy by flooding the novel with free motifs, disguising them as bound motifs, in an attempt to confuse the reader. Nevertheless, the aesthetic function and process for the reader is the same—it is the easing of the tension caused by the conflicting purposes of bound and free motifs in literature. If the ending does not refamiliarize us to our world, at least in the sense of affording us some ways of applying the defamiliarized perceptions found in the novel to our real world, we feel more *angst* than pleasure from our experience.

There is plenty of room for peaceful co-existence, even mutual support, between the free/bound motif system of the Formalists and the conventional/inventional system of Cawelti's. Free motifs and inventions tends to serve much the same purposes; likewise, bound motifs serve the same cultural functions as conventions. Popular literature, far more than elite literature, tends to dwell on bound, realistically motivated motifs.

Those motifs that recur in each Mason novel could legitimately be deemed conventions. For example, Mason's relationship with Della is not bound motivationally to the plot, yet it does not seem free. Cawelti's term seems useful here, for the Formalists don't cover such situations. On the other hand, Gardner's surprising use of the detective, Moose, is bound to the plot, but only in the sense that *Oliver Twist* had to be about Oliver Twist. Gardner's use of Moose in this story was novel within the author's *oeuvre:* it is intentional, not in the sense that Gardner is the first person ever to write about a guilty detective, but in the context of Gardner's work.[28] Again, the notion of "invention" provides us with a useful handle that Formalism has no answer for.

Nevertheless, it is undoubtedly the concept of bound and free motifs that led to the successful solution by the television Mason and led me to understand how Gardner structures his novels. I had previously failed to ferret out the murderer because I was looking for familiar and realistic motivation in the plots rather than artistic motivation. The Mason novels roughen up my perception about murder detection. Deciphering the murderer in *The Case of the Blonde Bonanza,* as well as every detective novel I have read, demands not the determination of which suspect has the best motive but rather the reader transforming seemingly free motifs into bound motifs.

IV: The Uses of Formalism

The previous two sections represent a tentative step toward supplementing the concept of formula with a concept that hopefully will enable us to better grasp the rich experience which popular arts so often provides its audience. John Cawelti rightly recognizes that the ascertainment of formulaic structures is only the start of a cultural analysis of an artwork:

We can use our concept of formulaic structures as a means of measuring the individual work by its departure from or its unique treatment of the formulaic elements. I am tempted to go a little further and say that each formula presents both limitations and potential for variation so that the imaginative writer can capitalize on both whatever artistic, psychological, and cultural interest there is in the formula and on his own individual inventions and interests.[29]

If other Popular Culturists follow Cawelti's lead and shift their focus from labeling conventional and inventional elements in a story to examine the dynamic interrelationship between four concerns—the artistic traditions of a genre or cultural milieu, the form of the artwork at hand, the expectations of the audience, and the audience's final perception of the work—we will have begun to treat popular art with the dignity it deserves.

Before concluding with a summary of the advantages and insights that formalism affords Popular Culture Studies, it is necessary to acknowledge the several questions and problems raised or left unanswered by the preceding material. Since the infallibility of the concept of formalism cannot be trumpeted until these obstacles are hurdled, these areas for further consideration have been incorporated into the conclusion.

The concept of Formalism forces us to confront even the simplest narrative in its artistic context. The tendency to dwell on "content" in formulaic studies often leads us to ignore what is most important to the creator of the artwork. In order to continue my winning streak in selecting the Mason murderers, it was often necessary to choose the killer on purely technical grounds. Often these considerations were not strictly free motifs, but only because the Formalists did not have to contend with mass media. For example, if a character displayed an annoying habit, diction or posture (especially if I had seen the actor before and knew it wasn't *his* mannerisms), this actor was often selected as murderer, since the television show (and its actors) seldom incorporated free motifs extraneous to the murder plot. If a character seemed totally unrelated to the murder plot (i.e., unrelated to bound motifs), I would select him or her as the murderer, if only because of the presumption that the studio would not want to pay for a character who was irrelevant to the bound motifs. The concept of bound/free motifs, in particular, forces us to contend with the very decisions that the artists themselves must face when creating their work: what motifs are necessary? how should I arrange these motifs? what are the functions of these motifs? etc.

Both the film and novel of *Murder on the Orient Express* (originally titled *Murder on the Calais Coach*) are affectionate and lighthearted tributes to formalism and the importance of artistic, rather than realistic, motivation in the creation of an artwork. Hercules Poirot's two amateur assistants, Dr. Constantine and M. Bouc, are presented as hopelessly inept and gullible sleuths, for they expect every development in the case to be realistically motivated. There are twelve possible suspects in the case—each of them initially lies under questioning by Poirot; each of them admits and partially corrects his/her lie when confronted by Poirot; each has a strong motive for murder and each has an excellent alibi. As with the *The Case of the Blonde Bonanza,* the clues are established so that any of the suspects could have logically been the murderer, but if any one of them were indeed the murderer, we would have felt cheated, because the reader/viewer unconsciously demands that his/her murderer have artistic motivation (i.e., that the character is surrounded by free motifs that turn into bound motifs) as well as a logical context for his/her actions.

The wonder and humor of *Murder on the Orient Express,* as in many other detective works, is that the depressing nature of the story is totally transformed by the plot. Realistic/logical motivation is subordinated to artistic motivation. In this case, the fact that either none or all of the suspects could have been responsible for the murder on the train renders the idea of detective story as logical problem, let alone as a realistic puzzle, less feasible; we are dealing with an artistic problem when attempting to decipher a detective story—the process of defamiliarization. While ostensibly proposing a solution to the murder, Poirot, as if speaking for the Formalists, recognizes the aesthetic rather than the logical or thematic nature of a detective case, and beautifully summarizes the nature, attraction, and idiosyncrasy of the classic detective art:

I saw it as a perfect mosaic, each person playing his or her allotted part . . . Every minute detail of their evidence was worked out beforehand. The whole thing was a very cleverly planned jigsaw puzzle, so arranged that every fresh piece of knowledge that came to light made the solution of the whole *more* difficult. As my friend M. Bouc remarked, the case seemed fantastically impossible! That was *exactly* the impression intended to be conveyed.[30] [emphasis mine]

If the analysis of Poirot's and the Formalists is accurate, we are faced with the problem of reconciling their contention that the purpose of art is to complicate, obstruct, roughen and create difficulties, with the contention of Cawelti that the psychological and cultural significance of formulaic works lies in the security, reinforcement of previously held views, and in the ego esteem it provides for the audience who is familiar with the formula. Although the Formalists did not bend from their rigid stance on this position, one somehow intuitively feels that Perry Mason novels or Gothic romances are not disruptive or threatening to the individuals or the culture that embraces them.

The reconciliation of these conflicting views on the cultural and psychological effects of formulaic stories is essential to the symbiotic relationship between the concepts of formula and formalism. Although this is a complicated problem, a tentative answer is proposed.

It was previously asserted that the final stage of reading involves a refamiliarization. Perhaps there are two kinds of re-familiarization. The first is simply the conversion of free motifs into bound motifs, the aesthetic process wherein the reader is able to integrate material previously comprehended as unrelated, to tie up "loose ends" in the story, and to arrive at a final evaluation of the characters and themes in the story. The psychological effect of the "aesthetic re-familiarization," in the reading of elite or popular stories, may be postulated as one of security and self-esteem regardless of any threatening elements in the work. The act of integrating previously diffuse material seems to be fulfilling in itself; in some cases, re-familiarization might stop here.

The second type of re-familiarization, a "pragmatic" extension of the first, might be the application of the now integrated material in the story to the "real world," the reader's life. Whether or not every reader exercises "pragmatic re-familiarization" whenever finishing a book is a difficult question indeed, but there is little doubt that stories such as *Uncle Tom's Cabin, Jonathan Livingston Seagull,* and *Looking Backward* were seen by many readers as directly relevant to their lives. The recent novel *Fear of Flying* has been marketed almost as if it were a self-help manual rather than a fictional narrative. The cultural psychological effects of the "pragmatic re-familiarization" are clearly infinite in range—from total affirmation to total negation of the values of the reader(s).

Discerning the relationship between a story and its readers' lives seems to overwhelm the importance of "aesthetic re-familiarization," but it would be a serious error to even attempt to determine the social influence without first analyzing the reader's interaction with the construction of the work. We cannot ignore the fact that plots can become as familiar to readers as the story; without first determining how the reader integrated the motifs in the story, we cannot begin to assess what has caused a particular effect on the reader. There are even certain archetypal structural patterns that seem to transcend not only formulas, but genres and media. Indeed, the importance of the conversion of free motifs into bound motifs would be small without a cultural bias for symmetry and balance in art. Neither disaster epics nor morality tales would be understood by someone who did not understand the concepts of retribution and rewards. Someone unacquainted with the conventions might be astonished at the number of narrative works which begin and end with the same thought, setting or action—this technique, so popular in modern stories, might be seen by a hypothetical eighteenth century person as evidence that nothing of worth happened in the story. The recurrence and acceptance of these thematic and structural patterns indicate that the clarification of the process of "aesthetic re-familiarization" will tell us much about our cultural preferences.

Without finding these artistic patterns that often transcend formulaic differentiations, we are left with one of the initial arguments against the concept of formula—that it doesn't help us to discriminate between different works within the same genre. Obviously, not every film that allows vicarious violence and not every formulaic top-40 song attains financial success. The concepts of bound versus free motifs, as well as "aesthetic re-familiarization," finally liberates us from looking upon each formulaic artifact as essentially the same as others within the genre, without ignoring their similarities. Surely, we respond to some familiar works generically. It would be silly to suggest that there are no conventional elements in Mason novels, or that the Gardner buff opens a new book without expectations. But the notion of motifs and "aesthetic re-familiarization" explains why we are not bored with reading one Mason novel after another. We are not bored with successive rounds of golf—we get exercise, we go through the same kind of process, our equipment remains the same, but we encounter new obstacles every time we play. Reading a new Mason novel is like playing a new golf course. The concept of formula can determine what all detective stories have in common, and that is surely important information. But don't we also want to know why our culture prefers one work over another? And we want to know what makes one different from the other. And if we become infatuated with one work, or if it captures the imagination of our culture, we may not even care how the work compares to others in its genre; we may want to study this work as a separate entity, as a special artistic creation. Formalism can help in this endeavor.

Notes

1. John G. Cawelti, "The Concept of Formula in the Study of Popular Literature," *Journal of Popular Culture,* 3.3 (Winter 1969).

2. David Soneschein, "Love and Sex in the Romance Magazines," *Journal of Popular Culture,* 4.2 (Fall 1970).

3. Morton Cronin, "Currier and Ives: A Content Analysis," *Things in the Driver's Seat,* ed. Harry Russel Huebel (Chicago: Rand McNally, 1972).

4. John G. Cawelti, *The Six-Gun Mystique* (Bowling Green, OH: Bowling Green State U Popular P, 1970).

5. Horace Newcomb, *TV: The Most Popular Art* (New York: Doubleday, 1974).

6. Cawelti, "Concept of Formula," 382.

7. Letter from John Cawelti to author, April 11, 1975.

8. Cawelti, "Concept of Formula," 386.

9. Cawelti himself made a brilliant stab at finding a way in his unpublished essay, "Historical and Mythical Consciousness in Popular Culture."

10. Whether or not all non-conventional elements are necessarily inventional is another question that must be confronted.

11. Cawelti, "Concept of Formula," 386.

12. Ibid., 386.

13. Perhaps the best overview of Russian Formalism is Victor Erlich's *Russian Formalism* (The Hague: Mouton, 1965).

14. Boris Eichenbaum, "The Theory of the 'Formal Method,'" *Russian For-*

malist Criticism, edited and translated by Lee Lemon and Marion Reis (Lincoln: U of Nebraska P), 102.

15. Ibid., 102.

16. This notion is probably still held by the majority of scholars; indeed, Cawelti includes new images and themes as major criteria for the classification of an inventional work.

17. Victor Shklovsky, "Art as Technique," *Russian Formalist Criticism,* 13.

18. Ibid., 13.

19. Eichenbaum, 112.

20. Shklovsky, 13.

21. Lee Lemon and Marion Reis, "Introduction to 'Sterne's *Tristam Shandy,*'" *Russian Formalist Criticism,* 25.

22. Ibid., 25–26.

23. Boris Tomashevsky, "Thematics," *Russian Formalist Criticism,* 67.

24. Ibid., 68.

25. Ibid., 68.

26. "Defamiliarization," in this context, does not imply that the reader is left with a feeling of strangeness or disorientation. It refers to the blatant distortion and manipulation of a simple story by the author—in this case, the obvious attempt to impede the reader from solving the case. Such machinations, accepted in fiction, would be considered ridiculous if attempted by a biographer or cookbook writer.

27. Although Moose's prominence is an important formalistic matter, this suspicion is dependent upon a notion of conventions.

28. This example reflects the previously expressed weaknesses of deeming works "conventional" by historical criteria alone. To someone who had previously read only one detective story, in which an operative was the murderer, Gardner's "surprise ending" in *The Case of the Blonde Bonanza* may be seen as conventional.

29. Letter from John Cawelti to author, April 11, 1975.

30. Agatha Christie, *Murder on the Orient Express* (New York: Pocket Books, 1974), 192.

AN ECONOMIC PERSPECTIVE ON FORMULA
IN POPULAR CULTURE

David Paul Nord

The influence of producers on the content of popular culture, David Paul Nord states, has not been adequately taken into account. While he finds John Cawelti's concept of formula useful, he demonstrates that the need for manufacturers to reduce risk, and thus maximize profit, largely explains the adoption of formulas: "The main argument here is that formulas are largely the creation of producers rather than audience . . ." (24). And he advances a specific hypothesis to predict the use of formulas: "The greater the market power a producer has (the greater the opportunity to control risk), the tighter and more standardized will be the formulas" *[italics in original, 25]; and argues that Cawelti's theory would not predict this relationship. David Paul Nord teaches journalism at Indiana University, and is the author of numerous studies on the history of American journalism.*

One of the best recent studies of popular culture in America, John Cawelti's *Adventure, Mystery, and Romance,* also deals seriously with the problems of linking popular art and society. In his first chapter, Cawelti asks the key question: "Can we infer from the popularity of a work that it reflects public attitudes and motives, or is it impossible to go beyond the circular observation that a story is successful with the public because the public finds it a good story?"[19] The answer is not a simple one. As Cawelti explains, at least three different approaches have been applied to this rather impenetrable problem: (1) impact or effect theories; (2) deterministic theories; and (3) symbolic or reflective theories.[20] Cawelti finds serious fault with all three. Effect theories, as I have noted already, have been largely abandoned by communication researchers as too simple-minded. Deterministic theories, usually Marxist or Freudian, are also too simplistic in that they depend on *a priori* assumptions about human behavior. They also tend to equate literary experience with other experience, an equation which may be quite invalid psychologically. The symbolic approach has never been able to dem-

David Paul Nord, "An Economic Perspective on Formula in Popular Culture," Journal of American Culture 3 (1980): 20–29.

onstrate convincingly that there is a direct connection between literary symbols and other forms of behavior.[21]

Despite these problems, Cawelti does assume that the popular arts reflect the culture in certain ways. And the key to understanding this link is the concept "formula," which he develops in detail in the book. According to Cawelti, "formulas are ways in which specific cultural themes and stereotypes become embodied in more universal story archetypes."[22] A particular literary formula is successful, not because it creates or captures the collective mentality, but because it maximizes a great number of psychological, social, and artistic dynamics. He begins with the phenomenon of enjoyment:

While the psychology of literary response is certainly not without its mysteries, it seems safe to assume that people choose to read certain stories because they enjoy them. This at least gives us a straightforward if not simple psychological connection between literature and the rest of life . . . The basic assumption of this theory is that conventional story patterns work because they bring into an effective conventional order a large variety of existing cultural and artistic interests and concerns.[23]

The bulk of the book is concerned with the definition of specific formulas, especially the detective story and the western. But underlying the descriptive chapters are several hypotheses about the relationship between formulaic literature and the culture that produces it.[24] The evidence that Cawelti marshals in support of these hypotheses is derived from a study of the formulas themselves. He hypothesizes, for example, that readers of formulaic detective stories "share a need for a temporary release from doubt and guilt, generated at least in part by the decline of traditional moral and spiritual authorities."[25] The strength of this inference rests upon the assumption that people have a need or desire for this particular kind of story, or they would not buy it. This is an economic assumption that may not be warranted.

IV

Cawelti's formula approach to the study of popular culture is clearly a useful method for the classification of popular story forms. He nicely defines and organizes concepts that other popular culture scholars have used haphazardly. He also makes a strong case (as does Nye) that enjoyment, escape, and fantasy are the central features of popular literature and art. But the argument that *specific* formulas, such as the detective story and the western, reflect the specific needs and interests of the audience is perhaps going a bit too far. Perhaps the assumption that people "get what they want" is unwarranted. Of course, the assumption is at least partly true at least in

America and Western Europe. But it may not be true enough to make the inferences that Cawelti and others make.

The task of the remainder of this paper will be to develop an alternative theory to explain the role of formula in popular magazines, books, movies, and the like. This theory will be based on the assumption that consumers may not always get what they want, that producers of popular culture sometimes exert strong control over the market and use this control to their own advantage. I will offer a general hypothesis which, if true, would be more consistent with this theory than with Cawelti's. And I will offer some impressionistic evidence that this hypothesis is true.

A good case study of the limitations of the assumption that people get what they want is Theodore Greene's book, *America's Heroes: The Changing Models of Success in American Magazines.* Greene believes "that a more complex, more precise sense of changing values in our past can be gained from a sustained analysis of general magazines."[26] He assumes that the larger a magazine's circulation in a period, the more closely it reflected the attitudes and values of the nation in that period. The study is a content analysis of the four most popular magazines in four periods, 1787–1820, 1894–1903, 1904–1913, and 1914–1918. By focusing on the kinds of people treated in biographies in these magazines, Greene hopes to infer something about the characteristics of "America's heroes." Briefly, he finds a decline in the importance of individualism in the American hero by 1918.[27] In the period 1787–1820, the typical hero of magazine biographies was something of a patriot, a gentleman, and a scholar. From 1894–1903, the hero was a Napoleonic individualist, the master of his environment. From 1904–1913, the individualistic hero was more socially conscious and was likely to have been a politician or social reformer. In the period 1914–1918, the hero was no longer an individualist at all but was now an organization man.

Greene infers from all this that these were America's heroes and that these heroes reflected popular values and ideals. Even if Greene's assumption that popular magazines reflected popular values is accepted, his conclusions remain unsupported. First, he never offers any reason for believing that the *biographies* were part of what made these magazines popular. Biographies were a small and decreasing part of the content of these magazines over the years. They may have been highly unrepresentative of popular content, and we would never know it. Second, Greene's last period of study, 1914–1918, was a time of war. At best all he has found in the end is that individualism decreased and group solidarity increased in wartime. This is a well-known phenomenon, and Greene's rediscovery of it adds little to our understanding of the general trend in individualism in popular thinking over time—which is what he set out to study.

But suppose that Greene's assumption that general magazines reflected popular values is not valid. Suppose we assume instead that magazines did provide their readers light, bright entertainment, but that the specific values conveyed were those of the publishers and not necessarily of the audience. The evidence collected by Greene himself seems much more consistent with this view than with his view. Greene never seems to ponder the significance of the fact that the publishers of the magazines in each period looked remarkably like the heroes of the biographies. In summarizing changes in the business of publishing over time, Greene writes:

The economics of magazine publishing passed from a stage of virtual patronage to one of independent entrepreneurship and finally to that of large corporate organizations catering to mass audiences for the benefit of other large corporate advertisers. The editors of magazines changed from independent professional men to independent businessmen and finally to managers employed to keep the constituent parts of vast publishing empires running profitably.[28]

This might just as well be a summary of the changing characteristics of the heroes. In the period 1787–1820, Greene finds "magazines by gentlemen, for gentlemen, and containing biographies of gentlemen." In the 1890s, he finds " energetic entrepreneurs ambitiously carving out successful careers in the promising new field of popular magazines." In the early 1900s, he finds magazines dominated by independent publishers and socially-conscious writers, such as Steffens, Tarbell, and Sullivan. After 1914, he notes that magazines were becoming large-scale organizations dominated by advertisers, managers, and other organization men.[29] These changes in magazine management correspond almost exactly to changes in magazine biographies. Yet Greene never seems to get the point: The biographies are of the *publishers'* heroes.

Evidence abounds of the increasing market power of large magazines in the early twentieth century. This market power meant that supply need not have responded directly to demand, that magazines need not have closely reflected popular values. Greene himself notes that the rise of the popular mass magazines in the 1890s was first associated closely with price competition, not with competition in content.[30] By World War I, the concentration of national advertising in a handful of general magazines assured their success. They could offer a good product and more of it at a lower cost.[31] They had only to offer what the people would accept, not necessarily what the people wanted. Interestingly, Greene is aware that the content of large magazines came to be more and more in tune with advertisers' values.[32] Yet he resists the implication. The data that he himself collects are much more consistent with an assumption of market control by mass magazine publishers than with the assumption that the values in popular magazines responded in a free market to the values of the American people.

Greene's book, as well as the work of Cawelti, Nye, and others, is marred by a faulty understanding of the economics of popular culture. The producers of popular literature and art will, almost invariably, attempt to maximize their profits. But this does not mean they will necessarily "give the people what they want." In broadcasting, and to a lesser extent in publishing, much of the expense of production goes into the making of the first "unit." Each additional copy of a book, magazine, record, or picture-print sold costs comparatively little to make.[33] In broadcasting, the cost of delivering a program to an additional listener is zero.[34] Furthermore, for media that depend on advertising and that can increase their ad rates with increased circulation, marginal revenues actually increase as marginal costs decrease. In such situations, economies of scale are very large and very important. The incentive is to produce a lot of the same thing—to circulate each book, magazine, or television show as widely as possible. Each new sale at the margin is largely profit. It was the publishers of the new mass-circulation magazines of the 1890s—S. S. McClure, Frank Munsey, Cyrus Curtis—who first learned this simple lesson in the economics of publishing and advertising.[35] It was the builders of the three broadcasting networks in the twentieth century who refined the techniques to a precise and exceedingly lucrative science.

Of course, publishing is not a classic monopoly industry for several reasons. First, people prefer and will, within limits, pay for deviations from a standardized product. Second, most advertisers have an incentive to concentrate their efforts on specialized segments of the general public. Third, and perhaps most important, paper, ink, postage, and diesel fuel are not free and have boosted costs greatly in recent years. Nevertheless, the decreasing-cost character of publishing (especially ad-based publishing) has fostered at least a measure of oligopoly in most sectors of the industry today, and was even more important in the past, when mass magazines carried the national advertising now carried by television. It can safely be said that in most cases the aim of a profit maximizer has always been to standardize the product, to control risk and thus control initial costs, and to expand to the limit sales of each type of product. In the area of popular culture, what would best serve these interests? The answer is clear: formula production.

What I am proposing might be called a "risk theory" of formula in popular literature and art.[36] At one extreme, each consumer in the country would probably like to have his own individual style of popular art. At the other extreme, each producer would like to sell the exact same product to everyone. The compromise is the formula. A formula is something the audience will accept. The producer will avoid risk by staying with the "acceptable," though this may only approximate what the people "really want." In sticking with tested formulas (or imposing them), the producer lowers costs by standardizing production, and he avoids risk. Revenue will also be steady or increasing because the market has already been established (or "softened" as they sometimes, revealingly, say). The writer of formula stories has the same advantages. Writing formula stories is low cost (in time especially) and low risk since a market already exists. All the most prolific writers of fiction have written to formula. For both publisher and writer, formula stories may not be run-away bestsellers, but they usually will not be complete flops either. Minimum risk means steady profits. Consumers have their own risk calculus. They may not get exactly what they want in a particular formula, but at least they know what to expect. They won't be completely disappointed.

This concern with producer control of the content of popular culture is not new, of course, though it has been neglected by some of the historians of popular culture working today.[37] Gilbert Seldes makes the point in a critique of television content. It is misleading to argue, he says, that television gives the people what they want:

> The average man does not know the specific way in which his wants may be satisfied. He shops around among the entertainment offered to him. The desire for "escape" may be satisfied by a western movie or a slapstick farce or a polite comedy. . . . By offering their wares, the mass media create audiences. When the wares are withdrawn, the audiences cease to exist; they become only potential audiences. When the wares which could satisfy a particular want are not offered and others are offered in profusion, the latent desire for the unoffered kind may dwindle or disappear.[38]

In other words, all we really know is that people want to be entertained. They may choose the specific formulas they do partly because they have little choice and partly because they don't want to risk something new.

The main argument here is that formulas are largely the creation of producers rather than audiences, that producers frequently are not under strong market pressures from audiences, and hence formulas are, if anything, more likely to reflect producers' rather than audiences' values. A key hypothesis can be posed that will allow a test of this theory against the theory that formulas reflect audience needs and desires, as stated by Cawelti, Nye, and others. The hypothesis is this: *The greater the market power a producer has (the greater the opportunity to control risk), the tighter and more standardized will be the formulas.*[39]

Neither Nye's nor Cawelti's theories would predict the relationship posed by this hypothesis. If formula is the product of audience tastes and needs, it should have nothing to do with producer market control. If producers are engaged in giving the people what they want, the organization of production should have little impact. The evidence, however, is otherwise. The business history of book and magazine publishing, film making, song selling, comic stripping, and radio and television broadcasting provides evidence in support of this hypothesis.

As book publishing became more consolidated and "rationalized" in the twentieth century, the market power of the producers increased in some lines of popular book publishing and the formulas became more predictable and rationalized. The popular formulas of the nineteenth century—family romance, historical romance, and the like—seem to have been broader, looser categories than the tight twentieth-century formulas such as the classic western, the detective story, and the "hardboiled" detective story. At the same time, through massive advertising campaigns, book clubs, saturation paperback distribution, phony bestseller lists, and the like, publishers were able increasingly to control the market and to create demand. Even James Hart admits that demand has sometimes followed supply in twentieth-century publishing.[40] A particularly good example of market power in action is the career of Edward Stratemeyer. As Stratemeyer's syndicate came to dominate the juvenile field in the early twentieth century, the juvenile formulas became tighter than ever. Stratemeyer used assembly-line techniques to turn out hundreds of volumes of the Rover Boys, Tom Swift, the Hardy Boys, and other famous series.[41] It was a publisher's dream come true: low cost, low risk, high volume, steady profit. The key was tight, easily duplicated formulas.

The history of the rise and fall of the mass magazine in the twentieth century also offers evidence to suggest the connection between market power and formula. In the pre-World War II era, when giants like *Life, Look, Colliers,* and the *Saturday Evening Post* dominated the magazine market through their control of national advertising, the formulas were quite standardized: light fiction, news and people features, news and feature photography, and bland editorials. The aim of the mass magazines was to offend as few people as possible, to serve the status quo, to stick with the tried and the true. All the mass magazines were highly imitative in the manner that the television networks are today.[42] The national magazines not only adhered to tested formulas in their stories and features, they also frequently reflected directly the interests and values of the publishers and large advertisers. Theodore White, for example, tells about his days on *Collier's* in the mid-1950s when he did two kinds of stories, political and advertising. The political stories were those he wanted to do; the advertising stories were those he had to do from time to time to keep some big advertiser happy. If travel and airline advertising were falling off a bit, he was assigned to do an aviation story, and the aviation industry was duly notified of *Collier's* continued interest and devotion.[43]

Television destroyed the market power of the large national magazines in the 1950s and '60s. As general national advertising moved out of the magazine field into television, the publication of mass-circulation national magazines become uneconomical.[44] The market power of the large magazine producers declined, and the magazine industry became increasingly fragmented. The industry itself did not die, however; in some ways it was revitalized. There had always been specialized magazines. But with the death of the giants, the market for these smaller magazines with specialized content for specialized audiences boomed in the 1960s and '70s. Some observers of the magazine industry, such as Roland Wolseley, talk about the impact on the magazine market of the changing tastes of the American reader, as if audiences themselves grew less standardized after the 1950s.[45] This may have an element of truth to it. But surely the more important change was in the magazine industry, not in the magazine audience. Readers accepted the standardized formulas of the mass magazines as a compromise between preference and price. A formula from the heyday of *Life, Look,* and *Post* did not necessarily reflect the specific values or interests of what was really a heterogeneous mass audience; it merely did not offend.

The history of film making in America also tends to support the hypothesis that market power breeds standardization and formula. Movie making is expensive, and as the great studios began to monopolize production and distribution in the 1920s, they sought ways to avoid risk. As Russel Nye puts it: "With millions riding on each major picture, studios could afford few mistakes; like other industries they had to standardize the product to minimize risks and maximize profits."[46] The main techniques of standardization were the "star" system and formula stories.[47] The years of the greatest market power of the studios, the 1930s and '40s, were also the years of the tightest formulas. With the rise of independent production in the late 1950s and '60s, and the outlawing of distribution controls such as block-booking, the formulas loosened considerably. Today the old studios have less market power, and films are much more diverse and non-formulaic than in the 1930s and '40s.

It also seems likely that during the height of studio power in the 1930s, the movies more clearly than ever reflected the values of the producers. Andrew Bergman argues persuasively that in the '30s "the movies made a central contribution toward *educating* [my italics] Americans in the fact that wrongs could be set right within their existing institutions."[48] Even the gangster films portrayed something like a traditional American success model. In an era of fairly popular radicalism, the movies continued to reflect the conservative values of the monopolistic, capitalistic studios.[49]

Even the usually forgotten history of popular songs lends some support to the hypothesis that increased market control leads to tighter formulas. Song writing and selling has never been tightly controlled by an oligopoly like the movie studios. And as a result there has been much more diversity and less formula. But when a sector of the music industry has been able to organize and rationalize its production and distribution techniques to gain some market control, the tendency has been for formula to tighten. A good example is the control Tin Pan Alley had over popular song writing and sheet music sales in the 1890s and early 1900s.[50] In recent decades, the large recording companies have wielded greater market power at some times than at other times, and pop music and rock 'n' roll has been more formulaic during the periods of greater control. Like other popular culture producers, the contemporary pop music industry has tried its best to restrict the market and to conventionalize its output, but with only moderate success.[51]

The business history of the comic strip is similar to that of movies. Again, the tightness of the formula corresponds to the market power of the producers. Comic strips are contemporaries of movies, beginning in American newspapers in the late 1890s. For comic strips the great age of diversity was 1900–1910. One history calls it

a great age, filled with astonishing innovations, exciting experiments, and daring attempts. This period of 1900–1910 is considered by some to be the golden age of the comic strip. In any event it was the golden age of the cartoonists, who were not yet laboring under the difficulties nowadays imposed upon them and who were able to give free rein to their originality, talent, and imagination.[52]

Then came the syndicates. As in any decreasing cost industry, the tendency is towards consolidation, standardization, and expansion of sales. Most of the strips had been created by local newspaper artists. Now they were taken up by big business and marketed nationwide. And as a result American comics became increasingly formulaic. The aim, as usual, was not to give the people what they wanted, but to give them what they would accept— and to displease no one. Comics even took up movie formulas.[53] As the power of the great syndicates has declined somewhat in the last twenty years or so, several very different, very innovative strips have emerged and have proven quite popular.

The history of radio and television broadcasting may provide the best evidence that market power is associated with tight formula. Much of the critical writing about television today deals with the lack of diversity in its programming, the unrelenting sameness of its formulas. The very same charges were made against radio forty years ago. In both cases the same villains are pointed out: the networks. As radio and television programming came to be dominated by the three great networks, program content became more stereotyped and predictable and formulas became more rigid. Despite an explicit FCC policy goal favoring diversity in programming, the networks have long persisted in the production of the most standardized and formulaic of all popular arts. Why? To some observers, network behavior smacks of a sinister conspiracy. Bryce Rucker writes:

> The networks have stifled competition, used their tools to propagandize for and against causes, formed large holding corporations which supply their own needs, built industrial empires whose tentacles penetrate every sphere of commerce; they wield tremendous political influence, wheedle from the government rights and concessions private citizens could not hope to win, pressure public opinion to do their bidding—the charges are endless.[54]

Though all these charges are probably as true today as they were ten years ago when Rucker made them, conspiracy theories are not needed to explain network behavior in programming. Since television broadcasting is what economists call a "public good" (i.e., it costs nothing, or almost nothing, to add another consumer because consumption does not "use up" the product), there are enormous economies of scale. Audience-maximizing equals profit-maximizing. The struggle for the One Big Audience coupled with the drive to avoid risk has led the networks, logically and inexorably, into program duplication and dependence on formulas.[55] As formulas evolve gradually on one network, they are seized quickly by the other two. More than in any other popular medium, the need is not necessarily to please but to avoid giving offense.

It seems likely that a relaxation of network control would mean a relaxation of formula programming. At least this is the consensus of most advocates of expanding channels through cable television.[56] This would be the other side of the coin. If market power breeds standardization and formula, competition should breed diversity.

V

The argument presented in this paper does not hold that people do not enjoy popular magazines, books, and television shows. Nor does it hold that audience preferences have no influence over what is produced. In most areas of popular culture, there is a spectrum of choice, and the consumer can indeed vote with his dollars. The choices available are greater in some fields (such as books and modern magazines) than in others (such as movies and television). What this argument does hold, however, is that the economic characteristics of popular culture give the producers a great incentive to standardize and formula-ize the product. And the business history of popular culture seems to indicate that this incentive has had its effect. Oligopoly and market power seem to have been associated with more standardization and more rigid story formulas.[57] Systematic empirical research is needed, however, to give this hypothesis a genuine test.

The implication of this argument for the study of literary formulas is obvious. Formulas, of course, are shaped by the culture that produces them, and they nicely serve what is probably the necessary purpose of balancing novelty with familiarity.[58] Cawelti's explication of the psychological role of conventional forms in general is persuasive. But specific formulas are not shaped directly by audience preferences. They emerge in the contention between consumers and producers, whose interests and whose preferences are not the same. The use of standardized formulas will evolve differently in a competitive market compared with a tightly controlled market like television or pre-television national magazine publishing.

What we require is a more sophisticated understanding of the interaction between consumers and producers in the creation of popular literature and art. This creation is a complex process of communication that is only partly economic. But economic factors cannot be ignored. Cawelti, Nye, and others concentrate their efforts on explaining *what* popular culture is, rather than on explaining *how* it is created. They assume it is somehow created in response to audience needs and desires. But producers, like audiences, also have needs and desires, and in the real world of business the customer is not always right.

Notes

19. John G. Cawelti, *Adventure, Mystery, and Romance: Formula Stories as Art and Popular Culture* (Chicago: U of Chicago P, 1976), 21. See also Cawelti, "Notes Toward a Topology of Literary Formula," *Indiana Social Studies Quarterly,* XXVI (Winter 1973–74); and Cawelti, *The Six-Gun Mystique* (Bowling Green, OH: Bowling Green State U Popular P, 1971).

20. Cawelti, *Adventure, Mystery, and Romance,* 21–22.

21. Ibid., 22–29

22. Ibid., 6.

23. Ibid., 30.

24. Ibid., 35–36.

25. Ibid., 104.

26. Theodore P. Greene, *America's Heroes: The Changing Models of Success in American Magazines* (New York: Oxford UP, 1970), 8.

27. Ibid., 335.

28. Ibid., 7.

29. Ibid., 33, 59, 171, 290–91.

30. Ibid., 65.

31. Ibid., 289.

32. Ibid., 287.

33. Broadcasting and some kinds of publishing have some, though not all, characteristics of a "public good"—a good where the cost of production is independent of the number of consumers. See, for example, Bruce M. Owen, Jack H. Beebe, and Willard G. Manning, Jr., *Televison Economics* (Lexington MA: D. C. Heath, 1974), 15–16; Bruce M. Owen, *Economics and Freedom of Expression* (Cambridge: Ballinger, 1975), 16–20; and Roger G. Noll, Merton J. Peck, and John J. McGowen, *Economic Aspects of Television Regulation* (Washington: Brookings, 1973), 10–11.

The theory of "public goods" has been worked out by economists over the past two decades, led by Paul Samuelson. See Paul Samuelson, "The Pure Theory of Public Expenditure," *Review of Economics and Statistics,* XXXVI (Nov. 1954); Samuelson, "Aspects of Public Expenditure Theories," *Review of Economics and Statistics,* XL (Nov. 1958); James Buchanan, *The Demand and Supply of Public Goods* (New York: Rand McNally, 1968), Jora R. Minasian, "Television Pricing and the Theory of Public Goods," *Journal of Law and Economics,* VII (Oct. 1967); and Harold Demsetz, "The Private Production of Public Goods," *Journal of Law and Economics,* XIII (Oct. 1970).

Very little attention has been paid in popular culture studies to the role of economic markets. One of the few studies is Paul DiMaggio, "Market Structure, the Creative Process, and Popular Culture: Toward an Organizational Reinterpretation of Mass Culture Theory," *Journal of Popular Culture,* XI (Fall 1977): 436–52.

34. Actually, even in broadcasting, where the public goods model is most appropriate, it does cost more to *attract* more viewers, but the assumption of no addtional cost for an additional viewer is not far from reality. See Noll, Peck, and McGowen, *Economic Aspects,* 10–11, 11n.

35. The best account of the rise of the national magazine in America is still Theodore Peterson, *Magazines in the Twentieth Century* (Urbana: U of Illinois P, 1964), chapters 1–4.

36. A similar economic analysis is developed by DiMaggio, "Market Structure," 438.

37. Cawelti is quite aware of the economics of formula production. (See *Adventure, Mystery, and Romance,* 9.) He does, however, neglect the implications of this economic factor. Some writers who do give more attention to the economics of audience-building are Tudor, *Image and Influence: Studies in the Sociology of Film* (New York: St. Martin's, 1975), 70; Dunlop, "Popular Culture and Methodology," *Journal of Popular Culture,* 9.2 (Fall 1975): 378; and Herbert J. Gans, "The

Creator-Audience Relationship in the Mass Media: An Analysis of Movie Making," in *Mass Culture: The Popular Arts in America,* 315–16. See also Gans, *Popular Culture and High Culture* (New York: Basic, 1974).

38. Gilbert Seldes, "Media Managers, Critics, and Audiences," in *Sight, Sound, and Society: Motion Pictures and Television in America,* ed. David Manning White and Richard Averson (Boston: Beacon, 1968), 33. Former FCC Commisioner Nicholas Johnson states this position even more bluntly: "To say that current programming is what the audience 'wants' in any meaningful sense is either pure doubletalk or unbelieveable naivete." *How to Talk Back to Your Television Set* (New York: Bantam, 1970), 19. See also Jeffery Schrank, *Snap, Crackle, and Popular Taste: The Illusion of Free Choice in America* (New York: Dell, 1977).

39. DiMaggio, "Market Structure," 438.

40. Hart, *The Popular Book: A History of America's Literary Taste* (Berkeley: U of California P, 1961), 286. On the mass market paperback book industry in recent years, see Clarence Petersen, *The Bantam Story: Thirty Years of Paperback Publishing* (revised ed.; New York: Bantam, 1975).

41. Russel Nye, *The Unembarrassed Muse: The Popular Arts in America* (New York: Dial, 1970), 76–87.

42. Peterson, *Magazines in the Twentieth Century,* 445–46; Ronald E. Wolseley, *The Changing Magazine: Trends in Readership and Management* (New York: Hastings, 1973). 34.

43. Theodore H. White, *In Search of History: A Personal Adventure* (New York: Harper and Row, 1978), 410–15. See also Wolseley, *The Changing Magazine,* 68–69.

44. The decline of national magazines, described in most texts on American mass media, is nicely summarized by White, *In Search of History,* 419–36. See also Otto Friedrich, *Decline and Fall* (New York: Harper and Row, 1970).

45. Wolseley, *The Changing Magazine,* chapter 1.

46. Nye, *The Unembarrassed Muse,* 374.

47. Ibid., 366. See also Robert Stanley, *The Celluloid Empire: A History of the American Motion Picture Industry* (New York: Hastings, 1978).

48. Andrew Bergman, *We're in the Money: Depression America and Its Films* (New York: New York UP, 1971), 167.

49. Ibid., 167–73; Robert Sklar, *Movie-Made America, A Social History of American Movies* (New York: Random House, 1975),196–97.

50. Nye, *The Unembarrassed Muse,* 314–16. See also David Ewen, *All the Years of American Popular Music* (New York: Prentice-Hall, 1977).

51. Nye, *The Unembarrassed Muse,* 358–59; Richard A. Peterson and David Berger, "Cycles in Symbol Production: The Case of Popular Music," *American Sociological Review,* 40 (1975): 158–73. See also Steve Chapple and Reebee Garofalo, *Rock'n'Roll Is Here to Pay: The History and Politics of the Music Industry* (Chicago: Nelson-Hall, 1977).

52. Pierre Couperie, Maurice C. Horn, et al., *A History of the Comic Strip* (New York: Crown, 1968), 29.

53. Ibid., 45 and 61.

54. Bryce W. Rucker, *The First Freedom* (Carbondale, IL: Southern Illinios UP, 1968), 140. See also Ben H. Bagdikian, *The Information Machines* (New York: Harper and Row, 1971), chapter 8.

55. For good discussions of the economics of oligopolistic competiton in television network programming, see Owen, Beebe and Manning, *Television Economics,* chapter 3; and Christopher H. Sterling and John M. Kittross, *Stay Tuned: A Concise History of American Broadcasting* (Belmont, CA: Wads-worth, 1978), 453–63. See also Owen, *Economics and Freedom of Expression,* chapter 3; Peter Steiner, "Program Patterns and Preferences, and the Workability of Competiton in Radio Broadcasting," *Quarterly Journal of Economics,* LXVI (May 1952); Jerome Rothenberg, "Consumer Sovereignty and the Economics of TV Programming," *Studies in Public Communication,* IV (Fall 1962); John J. McGowen, "Competition, Regulation and Performance in Television Programming," *Washington University Law Quarterly* (Fall 1967); and Harvey J. Levin, "Program Duplication, Diversity and Effective Viewer Choices: Some Empirical Findings," *American Economic Review,* LXI (May 1971). The classic work on oliogopolistic competiton is Harold Hotelling, "Stability in Competition," *Economic Journal,* XXXIV (March 1929).

A differing view that streses the influence that audiences do have on producers can be found in Martin H. Seiden, *Who Controls the Mass Media: Popular Myths and Economic Realities* (New York: Basic, 1974).

56. See Owen, Beebe, and Manning, *Television Economics,* chapter 5; and Noll, Peck, and McGowen, *Economic Aspects,* chapter 7.

57. Paul DiMaggio makes a similar argument. See DiMaggio, "Market Structure," 437.

58. Cawelti, *Adventure, Mystery, and Romance,* 1.

V.
Popular Culture,
A Unique Aesthetics?

AGAINST EVALUATION:
THE ROLE OF THE CRITIC OF POPULAR CULTURE

Roger B. Rollin

It is impossible, Roger B. Rollin argues, to devise an aesthetics of popular culture based upon a "self-consistent, viable set of aesthetic values." There is no basis upon which to judge a work beautiful, good, aesthetically pleasing or bad, other than the vote of the market, of the people who elect to consume it—the rule, Rollin states, is "one person-one vote," and this represents the triumph of a "democratic aesthetic." However, through consumption of popular culture we can enhance our selves or our society. Roger B. Rollin, now retired, taught literature and popular culture at Clemson University, and is a past-President of Popular Culture Association of the South, and President of the American Culture Association.

To evaluate is human, to explicate, divine.

The epigraph is *ersatz,* of course, but it will serve to introduce the argument of this essay: that some of Popular Culture's leading authorities, among them John Cawelti, Leslie Fiedler, and David Madden, have inadvertently proposed what is in effect an impossible mission—to devise an aesthetics of Popular Culture which will incorporate a value-theory. Furthermore, they have suggested that not to accept this "mission" must result in the impeding of the growth and development of Popular Culture study.

The most recent to go on record with this view has been David Madden. In "The Necessity for an Aesthetics of Popular Culture,"[1] he makes it clear that serious students of the Popular Arts have a duty to engage, not only in formulation, but in evaluation as well. He refers approvingly (9) to the English philosopher Bosanquet, who is concerned with the "beauty" and "excellence" of aesthetic objects. Madden also refers to Professor Cawelti (6–7), whose "Notes toward an Aesthetic of Popular Culture" asserts the necessity of developing "a basic core of assumptions about the *nature and value* of artistic work."[2] Admittedly, neither Cawelti nor Madden

Roger B. Rollin, "Against Evaluation: The Role of the Critic of Popular Culture," Journal of Popular Culture *9.2 (Fall 1975): 355–64.*

centers his discussion upon the question of evaluation: their primary concerns are the obviously essential ones of categorizing the intrinsic and extrinsic qualities of Popular Art and suggesting how these are to be explicated by the critic. Yet Madden also claims that we "*must* decide whether Popular Culture works can be termed *beautiful*" (7, italics added). And from both his essay and Cawelti's it can be inferred that their shared conception of the duties and functions of the critic of Popular Art is not so very different from that conception of the duties and functions of the critic of Elite Art that has dominated Western aesthetics for over two thousand years. Yvor Winters has characterized this traditional view with admirable bluntness: "The primary function for criticism is evaluation, and . . . unless criticism succeeds in providing a useful system of evaluation it is worth very little."[3]

No less respected a figure of Elite Art's critical establishment, David Daiches, is similarly direct:

Although literary criticism has acquired many functions in the course of its long history, the function most often demanded of it . . . is judgment, discrimination, the placing of a given work in a scale of values.[4]

And Daiches, of course, believes it to be proper for critics to accede to such demands.

Criticism, like politics, can make for strange bedfellows. Two more radically different scholarly types than David Daiches and Leslie Fiedler are not to be imagined, yet in his remarks at the Popular Culture Association's 1973 meeting (the panel on "Aesthetics and Popular Culture"), Fiedler, like Daiches, seemed to commit himself to the necessity of evaluation, and later defended his stand with the somewhat cryptic observation that evaluation was necessary because it is such a "human" process. At the risk of misconstruing Professor Fiedler, let us consider what might lie behind his assertion.

Evaluation is indeed human, as this essay's epigraph has suggested. Indeed, few encounters in this life, whether they be with other persons or with objects, do not involve evaluation in some form. Certainly encounters with aesthetic objects, Elite or Popular, are no exceptions to this rule. It needs no B. F. Skinner to tell us that stimulus evokes response and that aesthetic objects are *created* to be stimuli. Nor is there any novelty in the notion that a necessary component of the aesthetic response is emotional, or that emotion, however vaguely, will be positive, negative, or mixed.

In truth, it is *impossible* to have *no* emotive reaction to an aesthetic stimulus. Directions on an aspirin bottle can perhaps evoke a neutral or emotion-free response, but a mere television commercial about aspirin, complete with doctor-like actor urging that "Bayer is better," cannot leave the viewer unaffected: even indifference is the next thing to a clearly negative response, for it entails a rejection of the work's basic intentions.

The evaluation of aesthetic objects then is inevitable. *And because it is inevitable it is unnecessary*—unnecessary at least for the serious critic of Popular Culture, and unnecessary to the construction of a critical theory for Popular Culture. *I Love Lucy* will enchant one viewer, merely pass the time for another, and cause a third to experience acute discomfort in his alimentary system, and no theory is likely to alter these patterns of effect significantly.

One qualification, however. I make a distinction here between the scholar-critic of Popular Culture and the commissioned reviewer. *The New York Times*'s "Cyclops," Pauline Kael, and the local newspaper's critic of popular fiction undoubtedly have an obligation to accede to the public's reasonable demand that they, the fraternity of channel-switchers, purchasers of movie tickets, and bookbuyers, receive some guidance so as to minimize the wastage of their time, money, and energy. But no serious student of Popular Culture can lose time, money, or energy by tuning in on *Rhoda,* paying to see *Jaws,* or skimming through Harold Robbins's latest opus. Because for such students these activities are called "research," and whether they entail pleasure or pain is immaterial. Nor is the *argumentum ad academium* relevant here—the argument that since many of these scholar-critics are teachers or would-be teachers of Popular Culture, they need some standard of Popular Culture values in order to be able to design courses or structure curricula. Questions of aesthetic value are irrelevant to such practical matters. (For a defense of this stand, see Appendix.)

The only possible functions of the teacher and serious student of Popular Culture are *description* and *interpretation*—"illumination," in short. Description, because the field of Popular Culture is so vast and so varied that even its most assiduous students are bound to have *lacunae*. Interpretation, because explaining the dynamics of a work of Popular Culture and of audience-response to that work can reveal that which is lost upon the casual viewer: what happens at the interface between a work's aesthetic form and the desires and anxieties of its audience, and also what extrapolations can be made from that interaction with regard to the society of which the audience is a part.

In rendering this important service to scholarship (and possibly to society), the scholar-critic's evaluation of the work has no necessary part. The only evaluation which counts is the strictly quantitative one: how large a proportion of the work's potential audience responded to it positively. Did it receive a respectable Nielsen rating? Did *Variety* rate it a box-office success? Did it appear on the best-seller list?

For the only real authority concerning the "beauty" or "excellence" of a work of Popular Culture is the people. "Taste," formal training, teaching experience, publications—all factors which might be construed as validating the "authority" of a critic of Elite Culture—stand for naught when it comes to his or anyone else's evaluation of the "quality" of a Popular Culture work. For, in Popular Culture, the rule is "one person—one vote." However regrettable this may appear to professional students, it is a fact of the discipline. Unless Mr. Nielson polls me, whether I adore *All in the Family* or detest it is irrelevant. As David Madden has pointed out, works of Popular Art are not primarily produced for the readers of *The Journal of Popular Culture*. For better or worse (and I am not all that certain it is for worse), Popular Art represents the triumph of a democratic aesthetic—or what is probably the nearest approximation of a democratic aesthetic that is possible within the present capitalistic system.

But there is an equally compelling reason for putting aside the question of "artistic merit" when we set about formulating a unified field theory of Popular Culture aesthetics. Simply stated, it is the truth—which is increasingly, if reluctantly, becoming recognized as a truth—that it is *impossible* to erect a self-consistent, viable set of aesthetic values. Even among scholars of Elite Literature there is a growing awareness that the house of literary criticism, insofar as it is grounded upon evaluation, is a house built upon sand. Those who may doubt that the situation is so desperate should consult an essay entitled "Evaluation and English Studies," by John Fraser.[5] Professor Fraser appears nervous, and his nervousness is understandable. Beginning with his admission that "the idea not only of evaluative criticism but of evaluation itself is under something of a professional cloud" (2), and with the recognition that this cloud has cast its gloomy pall over English scholarship and teaching, Fraser sets for himself the task of renewing the profession's confidence that it is "eminently reasonable *to be paid for specializing in what interests us* and communicating our findings to others . . ." (3, italics added). Yet for all his essay's stout defense of the study of literature as an academic discipline, it does nothing to *demonstrate* the existence of a coherent set of standards of literary value. Indeed, that essay becomes (by omission) an inadvertant argument *against* evaluation. More direct, if no more successful defenses of evaluation are to be found in a book of which Professor Fraser seems to have been unaware, *Problems of Literary Evaluation*.[6]

The traditionalist view of literary evaluation is best represented in this collection by David Daiches' essay (cited above). Rejecting both evaluative absolutism and evaluative relativism, Daiches expends eighteen torturous pages begging the question. Try as he might, he cannot avoid merely asserting what he is attempting to prove, that a hierarchy of literary values exists—except that no one, including Daiches himself, can say where it exists, what it consists of, or how it is to be applied.

Lest it be imagined that professional philosophers are further along in this inquiry, Matthew Lipman offers a corrective:

We seem poised on the threshold of an infinite regress, and it is not surprising that skeptics, relativists, positivists and others have joined forces to cast doubt upon both the possibility and the necessity for the evaluation of works of art.[7]

Professor Daiches' problem, and the problem of all who quest for the one true hierarchy of literary values, can be seen in the broadest historical sense as arising our of the thinking of individuals like Darwin, Freud, Einstein, and A. J. Ayer. Relativism, whether it be among cultures or among psychological, physical, or semantic phenomena, is the main issue. Of primary concern to this paper are psychological and semantic relativism. The problem of semantic relativism is so well summarized by Stephen C. Pepper that it merits quoting at some length:

Recently, due largely to the influence in English-speaking countries of the emotive judgment theory of value supported by the linguistic analytical school of Philosophy, a skeptical view of standards has been in the ascendency. It stemmed originally from G. E. Moore's presentation of the "naturalistic fallacy" in ethics which applied to values generally including the aesthetic. Briefly it stated the "good" could not be identified with pleasure or any other "natural character," for the reason that it always made sense to ask after any such identification whether pleasure was "good." Consequently, Moore argued that "good" could not mean just pleasure or any other substituted character. He argued further that "good" must mean an abstract (sort of Platonic) entity known by an "intellectual intuition." A. J. Ayer, coming after Moore, rejected this last conclusion. He questioned the existence of any such abstract entity or of any peculiar intellectual faculty to intuit it. But he was still impressed with Moore's linguistic argument for the "naturalistic fallacy" and suggested that the reason "good" could not be identified with any natural character was that it did not refer to anything knowable at all. It was simply a term referring to emotional attitudes of approval. And "bad" was reciprocally a term for expressing disapproval. It followed that sentences including "good" and "bad" and their equivalents as grammatical predicates . . . are not declarative statements of fact . . . but are expressions of emotive attitudes which are neither true nor false nor probable . . . From this approach it follows that there can be no cognitively justifiable moral or aesthetic standards . . . This is the most skeptical theory of value ever propounded. For the gist of the argument is that, basically, values are not open to cognitive control in terms of evidence for the truth or falsity of statements expressing them.[8]

A similar skepticism pervades an essay by Northrop Frye, "Contexts of Literary Evaluation,"[9] except that the thrust of his argument is sociological and psychological. "Taste," Frye explains, is the result of acculturation:

The sense of value develops out of the struggle with one's cultural environment, and consists largely of acquiring an instinct for the different conventions of verbal expression. All verbal expression is conventionalized, but we quickly realize that some conventions are more acceptable to our social group than are others. In some societies . . . the different conventions were limited to different social classes, and high and low speech were at least symbolic of the conventions of lord and peasant respectively. Today we still have, despite the linguists, distinctions between standard and substandard speech, and a corresponding distinction, though one quite different in its application, between standard and substandard writing. The critic who fights his way through to some kind of intuitive feeling for what literary conventions are accepted in his society becomes a representative of the good taste of his age. Thus value judgments carry with them, as part of their penumbra, so to speak, a sense of social acceptance.[10]

In the covertly Freudian language that is so characteristic of him, Frye has defined "Taste" as the product of id-ego-superego-external reality interaction, a definition which common experience and Popular Culture history must both validate.

A hypothetical example: an imaginative, aesthetically-oriented child seeks gratification in fictions—any fictions, for initially at least he is indiscriminant. But he finds that superhero comics, which give him so much pleasure, do not win the approval of those whose approval he naturally seeks, such as his parents and teachers. But the tales of Beatrix Potter do. If the child's ego is sufficiently adaptive, he will enjoy his superhero comics in secret, thus gratifying his id and giving him pleasure (if also some guilt) in the process. And he will read (and possibly enjoy) Beatrix Potter in public, thus meeting the demands of his super-ego. Eventually, grown up to become a well-adjusted colllege professor (if that is not oxymoronic), that same individual will voice his admiration for Bergman's *Cries and Whispers* at the Dean's cocktail party, but will conceal—perhaps even from himself—the delectation he derived from his out-of-town viewing of *Deep Throat*. Or he will acknowledge his enjoyment of *Deep Throat* or *All in the Family* or Ross MacDonald's latest Lew Archer—whatever current popular works the intellectual establishment has come to allow its members to enjoy without guilt. For our professor's likes and dislikes are not so much an index of the "intrinsic" merits of the works in question as they are a Rorschach of his psycho-social self. As Frye has noted: "When a critic interprets, he is talking about [the artist]; when he evaluates he is talking about himself, or, at most, about himself as a representative of his age" (16). By traditional aesthetic standards, *Cries and Whispers* is an "art" movie— not only "good" but "important." But by The Test of Time, that flanking movement of the defenders of hierarchical standards, *Deep Throat* (conceivably) might prove to be *more* "important" than *Cries and Whispers* in film history, and possibly even a "better" film in some future aesthetics of the cinema. Mindful of Shakespeare and Dickens, Frye has said:

Every age, left to itself, is incredibly narrow in its cultural range, and the critic, unless he is a greater genius than the world has yet seen, shares that narrowness in proportion to his confidence in his taste. (16)

The constant defensiveness of Popular Culture scholarship is not only its most tedious characteristic, but also proof of the correctness of Frye's observations. Trained almost to a man in the conventional aesthetics of the twentieth century, Popular Culturists defend their rebellion against authority by calling for a "new" hierarchy of values to be integrated into the projected Popular Culture aesthetic, even though they have little notion of what shape that aesthetic might assume. That it will be some version of the *auteur* theory—*pace* Professor Cawelti—seems unlikely at best.[11] How practical is it, after all, to try to judge creators of Popular Art by comparing them with themselves? Who could possibly care whether *I, the Jury* is "better" or "worse" than *My Gun Is Quick?* Certainly not Spillane fans, who read both novels anyway and who care not a whit whether the Popular Culture Association believes they should prefer one to the other. And what validates the *auteur* theory as a method of evaluation of Popular Culture works when most of them have been created by committees—and committees whose memberships are constantly changing, at that?

Neither an *auteur* aesthetic nor any other aesthetic incorporating a system of values will automatically endow Popular Culture study with "legitimacy," with the dignity and respectability so fervently desired by some scholars. Indeed, to attempt to formalize a Popular Culture Standard of Taste will result in entrapment in the same philosophical error that has bedeviled traditional literary scholarship and criticism. Elite Literature has always been to an extent beleaguered and will continue to be so as long as some of its makers (but more of its critics) still insist that it be evaluated and even ranked—but only by that "fit audience though few" who possess Good Taste. And those millions of readers and would-be readers who have in one way or another gotten the message that they lack such taste become resentful and suspicious—and justifiably so. If Popular Culture must make a case for itself that case has to be made—not on the supposed intrinsic aesthetic merits of its subject matter—but upon that subject matter's demonstrable interest and importance. After all, any aesthetic object of the past or present, "good" or "bad," can become what Frye calls "a source of imaginative illumination" (17). How any one individual *feels* about that object is *another* source of *another* kind of illumination. As Professor Frye puts it,

the experience of literature is not criticism, just as religious experience is not theology. . . . In the experience of literature a great many things are felt and can be said, which have no functional role to play in criticism. [Thus,] the attempt to make criticism either begin or end in value judgments turns the subject wrong side out. . . . The value sense is, as the phenomenological people say, pre-predictive. (18)

Norman N. Holland seems to have been the first to demonstrate as much. His clinical-type experiments at the Center for the Psychological Study of the Arts (the State University of New York at Buffalo) have confirmed what every student of the arts' experience is likely to suggest—that whether or not an aesthetic object will please cannot be accurately predicted, even though an individual's "tastes" are known, even if (as in the case of Holland's subjects) the individual's psychological "profile" or "identity theme" is known.[12] (I refer here only to an individual's private, "sincere" response, which can of course be different from his public response—in class, in print, etc.—for that public response can, as Frye has indicated, be to varying degrees conditioned without the individual being aware of it.)

How do we evaluate aesthetic objects? All of Holland's investigations lead him to this conclusion: *"we will enjoy and value those literary works from which we can achieve an exciting balance of fantasy and management of fantasy"* (298). Thus my own evaluation of *The Sting,* for example, is based, not primarily upon my conscious, rational, objective, trained analysis of such elements as its script, direction, acting, camerawork, etc., for I will likely be able to find merits in such elements if I enjoyed the movie, defects in them if I did not. Rather, my evaluation will mainly depend upon: (1) the extent to which *The Sting* offered aesthetic materials out of which my mind was able to "shape" a largely unconscious fantasy, thereby "involving" me in the movie; (2) the extent to which my ego was able to cope with, "manage" that fantasy, preventing me from feeling either so threatened or so uninvolved that I walked out of the theatre.

Holland's theoretical model of the complex psychological process which results in such effects is itself complex, but can be generally described as follows:

A reader responds to a literary work by assimilating it to his own psychological processes, that is, to his search for successful solutions within his identity theme to the multiple demands, both inner and outer, on his ego. (128)

If I enjoyed *The Sting* and evaluated it as "good"—which is usually, but not always, the same thing, for the ego of the trained critic, especially, can "split" itself—according to Holland at least four processes have been simultaneously involved. 1. I have been able to put the elements of the movie together so that they act out at any given moment my hopes with regard to the work as a whole (114)—for example, my desire to have the heroes get away with their scheme. 2. The movie provides me with materials to create a wish-fulfillment fantasy that is characteristic of my personality (117–21), for example, my tendency to imagine myself to be a handsome, debonair, rogue-hero. 3. I have been able to synthesize from the movie my characteristic strategies of psychological defense or adaptation (115–17); for example, the movie afforded me sufficient materials to enable me to "defend against" the anxiety I feel (will Robert Redford escape the assassin?) in the ways that I customarily handle anxiety (ranging from outright repression to my scholar's expectation that *The Sting* is a comic romance). 4. I have been able to "make sense" of the movie, have been able to render the fantasy I have synthesized into some intellectual content that is characteristic of—and pleasing to—me (121–22), for example, that the very powerful can be brought low by the less powerful.

Thus what my statement that "*The Sting* is a good movie" really means is (to paraphrase Holland, 125) this: "My ego was able to use the movie to build from my own unconscious drives through my own patterns of adaptation and defense toward a conscious significance and unity that mattered to me." The fact that this mental process has been replicated by millions of movie goers now improves the odds on predicting whether Jane Doe will evaluate *The Sting* as a "good" movie, but at the time of its release the odds would have been much longer, even were we in possession of Jane's identity theme and had tried to match it up with a psychoanalytical analysis of the depth structure of the Newman-Redford film. Movies *are* in a sense ink blots, but some repressed trauma concerning the era in which *The Sting* is set—or even an over-heated theatre—could alter the response she makes. Thus, even the highly formulaic nature of most Popular Culture works cannot be of much help in predicting how any one individual or even a mass audience will evaluate a movie, television program, or popular novel. What is more important, however, is that by recognizing how aesthetic evaluations arise—out of idiosyncratic unconscious processes at one extreme, out of cultural conditioning at the other extreme—theorists will be given pause when they contemplate attempting to construct standards of aesthetic value for Popular Culture. Not only does the best evidence suggest that such an attempt is philosophically unsound and scientifically ill-founded, but of all people students of Popular Culture should be aware of the ways in which standards of aesthetic value can be transformed into moral imperatives which are then employed to celebrate some human beings and oppress others.

"The attempt of genuine criticism," in Professor Frye's words, "is to bring literature to 'life' by annihilating stock responses, which of course are always value judgments, and which regularly confuse literature with life" (20). Frye's concern here is with Elite Literature but the goal he sets is no less valid for Popular Culture criticism. Serious students of Popular Culture, those who write for other serious students, fulfill their high-minded and useful purpose when they penetrate the stock response to *The Waltons,* for example—as Anne Rolphe has done so well[13]—and describe that series accurately, analyze the psychological, mythic, religious, social, political, economic, and ethical components of its structure and texture, and interpret what the fact that America "likes" *The Waltons* tells us about the character of our society in the 1970s. Such information and insights cannot help but be valuable. Dr. Johnson said that "All truth is valuable . . .,"[14] but although aestheticians may be loath to admit it, the quantifiable aspect of a truth does count for something. This is so whether it be the number of critics who have pronounced *Lycidas* to be a "great" poem versus the number of those who, like Dr. Johnson, regard Milton's pastoral elegy as a "bad" poem, or whether it is the millions of viewers who turned for solace to that American pastoral, *Bonanza,* every week for fourteen years, versus those comparatively few who watched whatever was being offered on competing networks.

It will be argued, as David Madden implicitly has argued, that social, political, psychological and other aspects of the mass audience's response to works of Popular Art are not the proper concern of aesthetics, are not to be "considered part of the aesthetic experience."[15] But if the aesthetic experience is not deeply involved with the experiencer's id, ego, superego, and external reality, what is it involved with? As has been said above, the aesthetic experience will entail evaluation, but how is the *ranking* of aesthetic objects to be squared with a thorough understanding of the limitations of criticism as an intellectual activity? As Frye astutely observes, "the more consistently one conceives of criticism as the pursuit of values, the more firmly one becomes attached to that great sect of anti-intellectualism" (20). Or as Professor Lipman has put it, "an eagerness to portray the population of works of art as made up of 'good works of art versus bad works of art' is rather akin to the infantile moralism that reduces the human population to a contrast between 'good guys' and 'bad guys.'"[16]

While my personal approval of *Paradise Lost* is not only "sincere" but public evidence of my "good taste," I have no way of knowing whether the students to whom I teach Milton or the Milton scholars for whom I write are equally well endowed. —Or even whether they can somehow acquire the faculty through exposure to my own "superior" taste. And if they do not or cannot, what does it matter? I can no more read *Paradise Lost* for them than I can force them to like it: all I can do is to try to illuminate Milton's poem for them.

Likewise, my positive response, for example, to *Deep Throat* and my negative response to *The Godfather* finally must say more about me than they do about the aesthetic merits of those two cinema landmarks. That, of the two, *Deep Throat* has more historical importance and *The Godfather* is more obscene, can, I think, be reasonably argued, although the place to do so is not here. Such issues an aesthetic of Popular Culture can confront, but such a confrontation will only result in confusion if the question of "intrinsic" aesthetic merit be introduced. For such questions constitute a trap in which the experience of literature becomes largely divorced from the experience of life. While we may grant that the experience of literature is not infrequently superior to that of life, the two are inextricably linked through the central nervous system, a physiological fact that the practice of criticism ignores at its peril.

Let there be no more judges then—at least among the scholar-critics of Popular Culture. To describe, analyze, and interpret a mass audience's judgment of a work can be a way of knowing one's society; to judge a work of Popular Art can only be a way of knowing oneself, which unlike true criticism is a personal rather than a public *desideratum*. As one of the most ancient communicators to a mass audience has put it: "Judge not lest ye be judged."[17]

Notes

1. *Journal of Popular Culture,* 7.1 (Summer 1973), 2.

2. *Journal of Popular Culture,* 5.2 (Fall 1971), 255 (italics added).

3. *The Function of Criticism* (Denver: Alan Swallow, 1957), 17.

4. "Literary Evaluation," *Problems of Literary Evaluation,* ed. Joseph Strelka (University Park, PA: Pennsylvania State UP, 1969), 163.

5. *College English,* 35 (Oct. 1973): 1–16.

6. See fn. 4, above.

7. *Contemporary Aesthetics,* ed. Matthew Lipman (Boston: Allyn and Bacon, 1973), 429.

8. "The Justification of Aesthetic Judgments," *Problems of Literary Evaluation,* 140–41. It should be noted that Professor Pepper rejects the skeptical view and in his essay goes to great lengths to attempt to refute it.

9. *Problems of Literary Evaluation,* 14–21.

10. *Ibid.,* 15.

11. "Notes toward an Aesthetic of Popular Culture," *Journal of Popular Culture,* 5.2 (Fall 1971): 255–68.

12. *Five Readers Reading* (New Haven: Yale UP, 1975). This work incorporates (with important modifications) ideas advanced by Professor Holland in his seminal study, *The Dynamics of Literary Response* (New York: Oxford UP, 1968). See also his *Poems in Persons: An Introduction to the Psychoanalysis of Literature* (New York: W. W. Norton & Co., 1973).

13. "The Waltons," *New York Times Magazine* (18 Nov. 1973): 40ff.

14. *The Critical Opinions of Samuel Jackson,* ed., Joseph Epes Brown (Princeton: UP, 1926), 253.

15. "The Necessity for an Aesthetics of Popular Culture," *Journal of Popular Culture,* 7.1 (Summer 1973): 4.

16. *Contemporary Aesthetics* (Boston: Allyn & Bacon, 1973), 429.

17. The original version of this paper was presented at the 1973 meeting of the Popular Culture Association (Milwaukee, Wisconsin).

Appendix
Popular Culture in the Schools

If, as academicians, we can convince insecure colleagues and supicious deans that it is important to study a phenomenon which engages millions of our fellow citizens—including not only most of our students but most of those same colleagues and deans—then it should be easy enough to satisfy their queries as to the methodology for such a study with the simple answer, "historical." After all, the field of English study, for example, was for much of its little more than a century of existence primarily historical in its methodology. (In certain bastions of academic purity, of course, it still is.) Although Russel Nye and others have made a beginning, the historical study of Popular Culture remains a vast *terra incognita,* whose charting could occupy us permanently, given the expansion rate of contemporary Popular Culture.

But while there can be no easy separation between the critic and the historian of Popular Culture, it could be argued that to study the subject only from the historical point-of-view is in one sense an abdication of responsibility, an avoidance of the problem of Popular Culture aesthetics and the question of evaluation. And I would agree. My only point is that the heavy artillery of history can be employed to defend the study of Popular Culture against tradition-bound academic hostiles. For what it is worth, in my personal opinion any aspect of Popular Culture, like any aspect of history, of elite literature, of physics, can be worth serious study, though what will be worth studying may well be something different for the specialist and for the generalist. But only different, not more or less important. The evolution of the English form of government versus the character of the Rump Parliament, the nature of the Romantic Sensibility versus Keats' conception of the ode, the development of detective fiction versus the style of

Ross MacDonald—the places of all these in curricula can be determined only by such extrinsic criteria as faculty expertise and availability, student interests, and technical resources.

To summarize: not all academics are aware that "the Humanities" need no longer be restricted to the study of "the best that has been thought and said," and some of those academicians who are aware of this development continue, in spite of common sense, logic, and hard data, to resist it. But students of Popular Culture should resist being put in the position of justifying their interests and activities on grounds of aesthetic merit. Not only are those grounds now discovered to be a wonderland—they always have been. And even if it is presumed possible to make meaningful statements about aesthetic values, generic and other aesthetic considerations make plain the bankruptcy of drawing qualitative comparisons between, say, *Crime and Punishment* and *I, the Jury.* "Excellence" and "importance" have never been synonymous.

A CRITICAL ANALYSIS
OF ROGER B. ROLLIN'S "AGAINST EVALUATION"

John Shelton Lawrence

John Shelton Lawrence labels Roger B. Rollin's statement that it is "imperative to describe and explicate, but never to evaluate" as "escapism." Aesthetic experience is not solely a private matter, but is one of public policy as well, and properly so since creators do attempt to affect our moral beliefs. We can, Lawrence argues, evaluate the evaluators. To evaluate is intrinsically human, and thus even if evaluational subjectivity is inevitable, we should make our values explicit and then proceed to evaluate in as objective and scholarly a manner as possible. Lawrence in essence counsels us not to throw the baby out with the bathwater. However, he does not in this essay advance his own or a particular value theory. John Shelton Lawrence, now retired, was Professor of Philosophy at Morningside College. He co-authored with Robert Jewett a key study of United States popular culture, The American Monomyth *(1977).*

> Let there be no more judges then—at least among the scholar-critics of Popular Culture. To describe, analyze, and interpret a mass audience's judgment is a way of knowing one's society; to judge a work of Popular Art can only be a way of knowing oneself, which unlike true criticism is a personal rather than a public *desideraturm*. As one of the most ancient communicators to a mass audience has put it: "Judge not lest ye be judged."

> —Roger B. Rollin

In his article, "Against Evaluation: The Role of the Critic of Popular Culture" (*JPC* 9.2 [1975]). Roger B. Rollin has forcefully articulated a position that is doubtless shared by other scholars who experience intellectual discomfort with evaluative aesthetics. His arguments therefore merit careful consideration by anyone inclined to pass public value judgments on works of popular culture.

John Shelton Lawrence, "A Critical Analysis of Roger B. Rollin's 'Against Evaluation,'"
Journal of Popular Culture *12.1 (Summer 1978): 99–112.*

Although Rollin does not cite any thinkers between Jesus and the contemporary period, it is clear that he writes within a tradition of debate that stretches back at least to the Renaissance. Since the fateful moment when Galileo invited the Professor of Philosophy at Padua to look through his telescope,[1] humanistic disciplines have experienced anxiety about their methods and autonomy. Galileo, with his intellectually fearsome "optical reed," wanted his colleagues to see the craters and peaks of the moon, the satellites of Jupiter. Unfortunately, such phenomena were incompatible with the orthodox Christian cosmology of seven perfectly crystalline spheres (planets) moving in perfect circles—each standing for a cardinal virtue of which God wished to remind us on each cloudless evening. The Professor's commitment to the values associated with the older cosmology prevented him from gazing through the telescope, for he was certain that Galileo's "facts" were impossible—or, at best, a devilish confusion.

By the eighteenth century, philosopher David Hume—impressed by Newton's extensions of the modern physics launched by Galileo—conceded defeat for the older humanistic claims about reality, knowledge and beauty because of the deficient interpretive methods through which they had been reached. Having stated his empiricist program for purifying all beliefs, including those regarding the arts, Hume concluded his *Inquiry Concerning Human Understanding* with these words: "Morals and criticism are not so properly objects of the understanding as of taste and sentiment. Beauty, whether moral or natural, is felt more properly than perceived. . . . When we run over our libraries persuaded of these principles, what havoc must we make? If we take in our hand any volume . . . let us ask, *Does it contain any abstract reasoning concerning quantity and number?* No. *Does it contain any experimental reasoning concerning matter of fact and existence?* No. Commit it then to the flames, for it can contain nothing but sophistry and illusion."[2]

While Rollin doesn't zealously invite us to burn the offending authors of our libraries (including friends Cawelti, Fiedler and Madden —the targets of his anti-evaluative polemics), his message is identical to Hume's: abandon evaluation (the expression of "taste and sentiment") as an activity with any pretense to public wisdom, since the values of art are not "properly the objects of understanding."

In the essay that follows, an alternative interpretation of evaluative aesthetics is developed: it assigns to them a public character of legitimacy and urgency. Moreover, it suggests that academic purity—defined by the imperative to describe and to explicate, but never to evaluate—is a form of academic escapism that insulates the resources of scholarship from questions of social interest posed by contemporary pop marterials.

I

The central contention of Rollin's argument is that it is "an impossible mission—to devise an aesthetics of Popular Culture which will incorporate a value theory" (355). He rejects David Madden's proposal to develop "a basic core of assumptions about the nature and value of artistic work" (*ibid.*). Rollin distrusts generalized value judgments because he accepts a privatistic model of aesthetic experience and its concomitant value standards. To judge a movie as good merely means, in his adaptation of a psychoanalytic model, "My ego was able to use the movie to build from my unconscious drives through my own patterns of adaptation toward a conscious significance and unity that mattered to me" (362). Considering the more private egos in aggregate, Rollin recommends a kind of cultural populism: "the only real authority concerning the 'beauty' or 'excellence' of a work of Popular Culture is the people" (357). And this is claimed to be a "fact of the discipline" (*ibid.*). To think that one, as individual scholar, might pass a public value judgment—one that varies from Vox Populi—is to flirt with the repressive role of a Savonarola, since "standards of aesthetic value can be transformed into moral imperatives which are then employed to celebrate some human beings and to oppress others" (362). But even if a critic could restrain the impulse to thwart other egos in their legitimate, private enjoyments, Rollin would see their evaluation as a kind of "infantile moralism that reduces the human population to a contrast between 'good guys' and 'bad guys'" (363). Furthermore, the act of evaluation, which Rollin tends to equate with ranking, is seen as an unworthy use of intellect: "Who could possibly care whether *I, The Jury* is 'better' or 'worse' than *My Gun Is Quick?*" (360). The tasks of evaluation, framed in this way, do seem unquestionably frivolous.

What then is the critical program for Rollin? "To evaluate is human, to explicate, divine," he states humorously in his epigraph. More soberly, "The only possible functions of the teacher and serious student of Popular Culture are *description and interpretation*—'illumination,' in short" (363). The sole permissible exceptions are those granted to the "commissioned reviewer" who works in the interest of cultural consumers "to minimize the wastage of their time, money and energy" (363). Consumer considerations therefore define the only public *desideratum* for aesthetic evaluation.

With his emphasis upon the privately emotional character of aesthetic experience, Rollin is in good company. His words clearly echo those of Susan Sontag's *Against Evaluation:* "What is needed is a vocabulary—a descriptive rather than a prescriptive vocabulary—for forms."[3] In a similar vein, Herbert Gans has argued in *Popular Culture and High Culture* that popular art "should not be harmful"—a possibility that he discounts—"but beyond that, it should serve its users and creators . . . ," a function which

Gans locates in the experience of diversion. He suggests a proliferation of cultural channels to better serve the divergent, private taste cultures—as opposed to discriminating relative degrees of public desirability for the sake of fostering commonly desirable aesthetic experiences.

The evaluative critic of popular culture faces therefore a formidable series of reproaches from Rollin and his like-minded colleagues: evaluation is either frivolous or potentially repressive. In either case, it is antidemocratic, because it fails to respect the integrity of private experience. Evaluation thus becomes not merely an alternative task or method within the field of popular culture study but an activity so reprehensible that any scholar understanding the limits of knowledge and the implications of democratic social values will scrupulously repress the temptation to make value judgments.

In response to such a sweeping denunciation of evaluation, it is necessary to seek a wider perspective by looking at a few details from the history of the "value-free science" debate.

II

The impetus for value-free disciplines of study was provided in part by momentous occasions when the intrusion of particular value considerations, usually rooted in traditional wisdom, threatened to retard the growth of knowledge. Galileo's struggle with the church was only the most notable instance; we know of similarly motivated attacks against other pioneers like Darwin and Freud. To its credit, the tradition of value-free scholarship has sought to liberate itself from provincialism and intolerance. The suspension of moralizing impulses and the willingness to contemplate without passing judgment often allowed scholars to transcend their limiting tribal mores and to accept formerly alien insights.

However, it is one thing to notice the interference of individual values in particular situations and another to suggest that understanding can be achieved only through the exclusion of value judgments. This recommendation, which itself so clearly embodies a value judgment, has always been afflicted by serious oversights and paradoxes, most of which have been revealed in the long tradition of debate associated with the issues.

Probably the most instructive of such discussions for the disciplines of popular culture has taken place in the social sciences, where the 'value-free' terminology originated and has so often provided a rallying point. It was Max Weber who gave the value-free ideal an early and balanced formulation. He developed the doctrine at the turn of the century during crises in the German universities occasioned by nationalist and war-related fervor. Weber believed that his colleagues often acted as propagandists in the lecture hall, while disguising their royalist and chauvinist value judgments as the results of "scientific deliberation." Weber declared in opposition, "The professor should not demand the right as a professor to carry the marshall's baton of the statesman or reformer in his knapsack. This is just what he does when he uses the unassailability of the academic chair for the expression of political . . . evaluations."[5] Weber also argued for some separation of the scientific and public role as regards the scholar's authority, because "an empirical science" cannot "tell anyone what he *should* do—but rather what he *can* do—and under certain circumstances—what he wished to do."[6] Scholarship, in other words, cannot be a prescriptive science of values or conduct.

However, Weber by no means wished to eliminate the expression of value concerns from scholarship, nor did he equate them with merely private feelings. "An *attitude of moral indifference* has no connection with *scientific* 'objectivity.'"[7] He insisted that the personal integrity of the scholar, the vitality of the disciplines through responsiveness to the issues of the day demanded the incorporation of personal value judgment within the mainstreams of scholarly investigation. He stated emphatically, "In the press, in public meetings, in associations, in essays, in every avenue which is open to every other citizen, he can and should do what his God or daemon demands."[8] But he should avoid such personal value affirmations, so far as possible, in the classroom; the authority of the professor could be too easily construed as a license to impose personal value judgments upon others. Weber's concern then, insofar as he called for restrictions upon evaluation, was primarily to limit their expression to those situations where they could be counter-balanced through opinions by others possessing comparable expertise and authority. Evaluation, though lacking the credentials for authoritative prescription, was otherwise to remain important for the processes of topic selection, hypothesis formation and policy recommendations.

Weber's complex position on "value-free science" (actually something of a misnomer) was, of course, incompatible with the nationalistic and revolutionary fervor that increasingly dominated the German universities during the 1920s and 1930s. Some of those who sought to remain detached from extreme positions seemed to develop an amnesia, rather characteristic for the history of debate, regarding the several elements that Weber had attempted to reconcile. The awareness of his position became characterized by the "value-free" slogan—interpreted in such a way as to suggest the elimination of evaluation entirely.

The most conspicuous manifestation of this forgetful tendency was provided by the Vienna Circle of logical positivists, who worked in the lengthening shadow of German and Austrian fascism—yet gave the idea of neutral scholarship a powerful impetus in the Anglo-American world. Leading members of the group like Rudolf Carnap philosophically reduced all value judgments to pure expressions of feeling: "the value statement 'Killing is evil' . . . is merely an expression of a certain wish. . . .'"[9] A. J.

Ayer, who during the mid 1930s began to popularize the doctrines of the logical positivists for the English-speaking world, gave the so-called "emotivist doctrine" formulations of classical elegance and simplicity that still resonate in the words of Rollin. Like Carnap, he asserted that value judgments have "no objective validity whatsoever" and that "the only information which we can legitimately derive from the study of our aesthetic and moral experiences is information about our mental and physical makeup."[10] Using this interpretation of value as the basis for purging philosophy—just as Hume had earlier proposed—Ayer promised to place it on a scientific footing, the rational equal of the hard sciences. The price, of course, was a radical pruning of the traditional philosophical subject matters, which were to be doled out to the empirical disciplines. There the intractable issues, to the extent that they represented genuine questions at all, would find their resolution through neutral description.

Such formulations soon began to appear as methodological ideals for both humanistic and social science disciplines.[11] So prevalent became the ideal of purely descriptive social science, whose stance was defined by slogans such as "impersonal objectivity" and "aloofness from the strife of rival values," that Robert Lynd felt compelled to write his classic rebuttal, *Knowledge for What?* in 1939. The book contained a critical analysis of the purely descriptive ideal of social science and an alternative interpretation suggesting that the social sciences had come into being and were justified by their affinity for socially troublesome issues.

There would be no social sciences if there were not perplexities in . . . culture that call for solution. And it is precisely the role of the social sciences to be troublesome, to disconcert the habitual arrangements by which we manage to get along, and to demonstrate the possibility of change in more adequate directions.[12]

Lynd suggested that the social scientist, in addition to facing socially problematic subject matters, could never himself be wholly neutral, since "culture is not neutral, because culture is interested personalities in action." He also feared that those adopting the stance of neutrality are rather likely to become captives of what they refuse to examine critically from the standpoint of values. Morris Cohen had suggested as early as 1931 that "Those who boast that they are not, as social scientists, in what ought to be, generally assume (tacitly) that the prevailing order is the proper ideal of what ought to be."[14] He added, "But the questions of human value are inescapable, and those who banish them at the front door admit them unavowedly and uncritically at the back."[15] Thinkers like Cohen and Lynd understood silence to be consent, especially in an America besieged by intense social and economic agonies.

Weber, Lynd, Cohen and others who have taken similar attitudes in the social sciences debate about values seem to converge on the following points. The study of culture is inescapably evaluative, a circumstance not to be regretted, since a major task of social science is to suggest policy alternatives. Because the scholar cannot avoid making some judgments of value in the presence of his subject matter, the problem is—rather than attempting to banish—that of making them serve the purposes of the discipline and of the larger society which supports its work. There is no rejection of the ideal of objectivity in description, but rather an acknowledgment that objectivity must co-exist with the problems of the day and with the subjectivities that propel the individual scholar and his discipline.

III

Now the question naturally arises whether these ideas from the social sciences discussion have any relevance for the issue of evaluation in popular culture. If popular art provides nothing more than purely private aesthetic experiences, shouldn't it be exempted from public evaluation as Rollin contends? In contrast, I would suggest that aesthetic experience does not benignly compartmentalize itself in a private region; it is fused, often deliberately, with stances and activities that obviously call for evaluative response. To exclude these from critical consideration will doubtless protect scholarship from strife—but at the expense of preventing any contribution to the practical decisions of national importance that are made regarding the values of popular culture. This becomes apparent when one examines issue and evidence regarding the effects of popular art, the morally persuasive aims associated with it, and the persistent censorship controversies.

Some of the oldest questions about popular aesthetic experience, dating in their modern form at least to the eighteenth century, concern social results. Goethe, Pope, Lamb, Schiller, Wordsworth and a host of others began raising serious issues about the effects of mass, commercial entertainments upon the imagination, perception and behavior of modern audiences.[17] America, with its Puritan heritage, has periodically lent careful and hostile attention to the search for innocent amusement. The appearance of the Nickelodeon aroused immediate fears, particularly after "Dolorita in the Passion Dance" was shown at an Atlantic City boardwalk in 1894.[18] In more recent times, there has been a proliferation of studies dealing with the effects of popular material upon its audience. A scattered sampling of critical scholarly analysis would include themes like the following:

• George Gerbner and Larry Gross have analyzed links between fantasy experience in television and the resultant beliefs and behavior. They have plausibly argued that the repeated experience of serial crime shows and movies distort the viewer's self-image as citizen and his estimate of the likelihood that he will be the victim of a crime.[19]

- Richard M. Merlman's excellent *JPC* article, "Power and Community in Television," raised important issues about the vision of power and institutions that are characteristic for television.[20] Distortions of vision in presenting life, society and heroism can be plausibly traced to serialization, the dominant dramatic convention under the commercial television system.[21]
- Stephen Arons and Ethan Katsh have discussed the relationship between constitutional ideals of criminal procedure and the "heroic" behavior of police on the crime shows; they have asked what impact these regular programs might be having upon public expectations for law enforcement agencies.[22]
- Behavioral scientists have been working experimentally for at least two decades on the effect that visual fantasies of violence exert upon attitudes toward real violence;[23] the stylized, slow-motion violence of programs like *Kung Fu* and *Six Million Dollar Man,* for example, is very appealing. Does it desensitize us through its abstraction of the normal concomitants of violence?

When we consider a wide range of such popular experiences and the issues they pose for us, it is impossible to separate neatly the private, aesthetic component, which repels evaluation as an illegitimate intrusion, and the public component (non-aesthetic), which invites, if not demands, evaluation. To define aesthetic experience as the essentially private experience of "beauty," as Rollin does, is to preclude the possibility of dealing with issues like those enumerated above.

Moralism is rampant throughout popular culture. Sometimes this moralism reflects a producer's fear of displeasing a popular audience; in other instances, it reflects an affirmative understanding of popular art as a means of socialization and moral persuasion. To take an institutional example, the Television Code of the National Association of Broadcasters describes its purpose as educational and states that "Education via television may be taken to mean that process by which the individual is brought toward informed adjustment to his society."[24] This code and others like it contain numerous moral restrictions on aesthetic possibility: ". . . violence and illicit sex shall not be presented in an attractive manner, not to an extent such as will lead a child to believe that they play a greater part in life than they do. They should not be presented without indications of the resultant retribution and punishment."[25] Such statements are hardly a call to provide purely private entertainment, but rather to uphold particular visions of social order and morality. Even after a generous discount of such statements in recognition of commerical hypocrisy, the media must still be seen as moralistic agencies.

It is equally apparent that individual producers often intend their programs to have a morally persuasive impact on viewers. Robert S. Alley, in his *Television: Ethics for Hire?* presents several interviews with producers who voice the particular viewpoints they wish to disseminate through their dramatic art. Allen Alda of M*A*S*H, for example, intended the series to be critical of America's Vietnam involvement. He did not want the program to be "a commerial for the army . . . didn't want to take a position that was neutral to the war."[26] Much of the enjoyment that viewers derived from the program was related to their feeling that a humane judgment on the institutions of war was being dramatized and that a counterforce to American militarism had emerged on the screen.

Norman Lear stated to Alley, in explaining the purpose of his programs, "The more interesting lives are led with great and wonderful conflict. It is not possible to exist without it. I like the people who get mad enough to cry and fierce enough to throw things. . . . There is room in the tube for lots of passion."[27] The vicarious enjoyment of these passions, particularly as they relate to prominent moral and social issues, has been one of the persistent appeals of the Lear experience. Such affirmations of morally persuasive intent are routine in the world of popular culture and stand as a constant invitation for the audience either to confirm values already held or to accept a challenge to their values. It may be convenient for analytic purposes to distinguish between the aesthetics of form, structure and surface, on the one hand, and moral persuasion, on the other. But the total experience in popular art possesses a unity that calls for evaluative response.

That popular culture is frequently understood as an important channel for value influence can be seen in the controversies surrounding it. The debate about sex in films during the 1920s produced the Code of Production for movies; controversies of the 1940s and 1950s centered upon comic books and led to the Comics Code Authority, a scheme of self-censorship similar to those of television and film.[28] The 1950s also brought McCarthyism and blacklisting of performers and writers, eventually discouraging television from presenting dramatic works produced by individual authors; at that time, the serial format, so suitable for commercial advertising functions and assembly line production techniques, became the dominant dramatic form of television.[29] The 1960s, shaken by repeated assassinations and attempts on national leaders, brought several national commissions into being, a substantial part of whose purpose was to study the effects of popular aesthetic experience upon its audiences. These issues are persisting in the 1970s and will probably continue into the 1980s. The formation of groups like TOT (Turn Off Television), the prolonged attention to televisions by the national PTA and other broad based movements of concern about the quality of popular culture all indicate that we continue to live during a period of debate which is highly judgmental. Citizens will debate the meaning of popular culture and attempt to give its content a direction consistent with their own ideals. It is difficult to understand why scholars of popular culture should not, as a matter of principle, participate in these evaluative debates. If those who have studied the popular aesthetic experience the most carefully are not qualified to make evaluative suggestions about it, should we conclude that the matters must be resolved through a wide-scale war of private subjectivities, undisciplined by systematic and rigorous viewpoints?

IV

In spite of Rollin's firm rejection of evaluation as a program of scholarship, he does not concede that emotive-evaluative reactions are a normal and inevitable component of our experience of art: "In truth, it is *impossible* to have *no* emotive reaction to an aesthetic stimulus" (356). Rollin excludes such reactions because of their alleged inevitable and apparently uncontrollable character. "The evaluation of aesthetic objects then is inevitable. And because it is inevitable, it is unnecessary—unnecessary at least for the serious critic of Popular Culture, and unnecessary to the construction of a critical theory for Popular Culture" (356). The implausibility of such an argument from inevitability to dispensability can be seen by attempting to apply its principle to other universal impulses or responses. We all have sexual impulses, for example. Should we therefore ignore the differences of expression in a Marquis de Sade as opposed to a Tolstoi? Religious experience of some sort is universal and inevitable. Should we therefore ignore the differences between Saint Francis and Cotton Mather? Does the universal instinct to eat erase all distinctions between the behavior of the cannibal and the ethical vegetarian? Rather than excluding an activity from consideration because of its universality, it is imperative to ask what purpose or form we might seek to impose. When we examine the work of evaluative thinkers in the field of popular studies, we find radically different models and practices. Just as in other areas of the "inevitable," there are important choices to be made.

One can see this clearly by examining a pair of contrasting evaluative opinions expressed by William Gass and John Cawelti. Gass's "Even if by all the Oxen in the World" is well known as a severe appraisal of popular culture from an elitist stance. He focuses upon the economic and institutional interests lying behind pop entertainments and suggests something comparable to a fascist conspiracy:

... if a great portion of any population is spending many hours every day driving all life from the mind, in worship of low cost divinities like the goddess of the golden udder, there's been another plague of the spirit, and there are deaths to show for it, and endless deformities. . . . One senses an effort to Hitlerize the culture of the Folk. . . . Popular culture is the product of an industrial machine that makes baubles to amuse the savages while missionaries steal their souls and merchants steal their money.[31]

The power and evil of popular culture are here ascribed with a lyrical eloquence that will seldom be surpassed.

Cawelti, in his equally well known "Beatles, Batman and the New Aesthetic," addresses the popular art of the "put on" and attempts to draw conclusions from it about shifting insights and stances toward personal responsibility:

... acting without deep emotional involvement or implication prevents our commitments from being complete and satisfying. In desperation we turn to pure sensation or some form of mysticism, hoping to escape the sense of imposture. Much of the new art is a strategy of escape. . . . It is better to use these strategies than to commit ourselves to the destruction of man, but it is more important to recognize our predicament. The best of the new art tries to use these strategies of evasion to explore and represent the experience of our ambiguous relation to culture. In this, the new art is the most authentic response to the desperation of the times.[32]

Comparing the two, one can see that Gass's statement is strongly subjective, absolutistic and indiscriminate; in his entire essay, there is not a single analysis of a popular artifact. Cawelti, on the other hand, is sympathetic and tentative; he discriminates within his essay an ample number of details that support his final judgment. Their respective styles of evaluation are obviously related to the impulse toward rejection in Gass and to the spirit of reforming acceptance in Cawelti. Gass would like to spread his sense of revulsion and indignation while Cawelti finds a new understanding of contemporary dilemmas in popular art—though he is troubled by its ambivalence toward personal commitment.

From this simple example, briefly analyzed, we may confirm the notion that the "inevitability" of evaluation tells us nothing about the purpose, style and content of individual evaluations. Taking them all into consideration, we can evaluate evaluations, so to speak, asking how they serve the aims of the popular culture disciplines, whether they are properly appreciative of positive values in popular culture, or whether they serve the purpose of serious reform (if such is held to be desirable).

V

To recognize that there are different purposes and styles in evaluation indicates possibilities for choice rather than compulsion, but does not deal with the kernel of truth that lies behind the positions of Hume, the logical positivists, and Rollin. Such thinkers have identified something intellectually troublesome in evaluation as contrasted with description. For there is an inescapable subjectivity in it; the issues that spring from popular aesthetic experience, social though they be, do not guarentee a method for treating its associated value issues in a rational framework.

Historical perspective is again useful here. The descriptive-evaluative contrast embodies a polarity that has often puzzled Western culture and scholarly thought. It is the most recent manifestation of long standing conflicts between faith and reason, heart and head, subjectivity and objectivity. Some of the previous ad hoc resolutions that have allowed scholars to co-exist with their cultures in prudent comfort remind one of the value-free stances that have been adopted so conspicuously in the social sciences and are now recommended for the field of popular culture.

As an earlier instance of the conflict and its unsatisfactory resolution, Alvin Gouldner has called attention to the strategy of the Averroists during the Middle Ages. They coped with the tension between Greek rationalism and Christian dogmatism by declaredly ignoring it.[33] Faced with contradictions between Aristotle and the Bible, scholars like John of Jandun would conclude their learned discourses with statements like, "It must be noted that, although the dicta are . . . according to the principle of Aristotle and the Commentator [Averroes], it must be replied firmly according to faith and truth that the world is not eternal."[34] The Averroist strategem, in addition to preserving the contradictions, ruled out the development of any adequate method for moving beyond them. It amounted to a tacit prohibition against inquiries of a type that could have placed their philosophy and theology on a firmer footing.

Rollin's suggestion that we cope with evaluational subjectivity by banning it represents a similarly barren response to a perennial problem. Understanding is rarely advanced by a mere prohibition. Given the circumstances that value controversies have surrounded popular aesthetic experience during every decade of the twentieth century, it is far preferable to overcome whatever deficiences are characteristic of evaluative practice, rather than imagining it to be somehow more responsible to withdraw totally from the subject. Unless there is some connection between widely perceived social concerns and the content of scholarly disciplines, the latter will lose any claim to assist society in comprehending its needs and experiences. Description, history and interpretation—indispensable as a foundation for scholarship—are not enough in a time that clamors for a more comprehensive and critical understanding of its value-laden experiences.

Fortunately there are some procedures for coping with values and their associated subjectivity that promise to move beyond the perplexing discovery of fierce and apparently intractable divergences. Weber suggested, for example, that the scholar, driven by his daemons, should expose his value judgments for the attention of others who possess critical capability.

Gunnar Myrdal, another social scientist, wrote a path-breaking study of the American racial problem, *The American Dilemma,* as a result of his commitment to the ideals of the Constitution—even though he was a foreigner. Having often reflected on the interplay between value and description in scholarship, Myrdal made these suggestions:

Efforts to run away from valuations are misdirected and foredoomed to be fruitless and damaging. The valuations are with us, even when they are driven underground, and they guide our work. When kept implicit and unconscious, they allow biases to enter. They only way we can strive for objectivity . . . is to lift up the valuations into the full light, make them conscious and explicit, and permit them to determine the viewpoints, the approaches and the concepts used.[35]

Myrdal cautions that "we must not naively expect our ideas, even in scientific research, to be unconditioned by anything other than the desire for truth."[36] The task of clarifying valuations and their subjective components is more than an individual process; as Weber suggests, the context of scholarship is required, where other scholars are free to criticize and to provide a better understanding of our ideals and their consequences than we can attain by working alone. This is true even after we have resolved to follow a path of exposing and following our valuations openly.

It is in the play of free discussion about values in popular culture, rather than the refusal to evaluate for fear of tyranny, that democratic ideals of scholarship receive a more sensible embodiment. It is also a fulfillment of democratic ideals for scholars to feel a sense of shared responsibility with their fellow citizens for the content of their culture and to use whatever special insights they derive from their discipline to assist in its shaping. Popular art deserves no immunity from criticism, least of all in a democracy. Like any other activity, it must be judged on the basis of its influence on the life of the community and its relationship to the ideals that the community strives to realize.

Concerning the question of cultural responsibility, there is in Rollin's article a belated and half-hearted acknowledgment of the evasive drift of his argument. In an Appendix, he concedes, "it could be argued that to study the subject only from the historical point-of-view is in one sense an abdication of responsibility, an avoidance of the problem of Popular Culture aesthetics and the question of evaluation. And I would agree" (364). To this somewhat puzzling confession, whose implications are not developed, he adds that the primary reason for his denunciation of evaluation is to help defend the study of popular culture against attacks from "tradition-bound academic hostiles." His recommended strategy is to avoid the study of popular culture "on the grounds of aesthetic merit" (365). So in the end Rollin has constructed an ad hominem apologetic, tailored for those academic opponents who might suspect popular culture scholars of believing that there is something aesthetically valuable in popdom. Their barbs are to be repelled by refusing to evaluate anything at all!

Rather than cloaking our studies in arguments that are so embarrassingly contradictory, it seems more forthright and convincing simply to give the obvious reasons for their importance. Popular culture has become a central arena in the twentieth century for the experience of meaning. Humanistic disciplines above all, which often vaguely claim to "deal with values" when pressed against the academic wall, should follow the logic of this commitment wherever it leads them. Humanists cannot tap the vital impulses of the contemporary world by functioning merely as custodians for the classics or by helping students to become more expert in the description of their private feelings.

There is a tempestuous world of value conflict and vital feeling associated with popular culture that awaits disciplined 'illumination'—not the kind that is limited to mere description and interpretation, but the sort that springs from the conscious articulation of value standards accompanied by a careful description of the domains in which they are applied. There is an important place, in a discipline that claims a sense of responsibility to society, for drawing inferences about cultural sickness and health as well as the tastes and policies that sustain them. Popular culture at its best has achieved these aims and will doubtless continue to do so—unless it takes the vow of academic chastity proposed by Rollin.

Notes

1. For an account, see Girgio Santillana, *The Crime of Galileo* (Chicago: U of Chicago P, 1955), 10ff.

2. David Hume, *An Inquiry Concerning Human Understanding,* ed. Charles W. Hendel (Indianapolis: Bobbs-Merrill, 1955), 173.

3. Susan Sontag, *Against Interpretation* (New York: Strauss & Giroux, 1966), 12.

4. Herbert Gans, *Popular Culture and High Culture: An Analysis and Evaluation of Taste* (New York: Basic Books, 1974), 123.

5. Max Weber, "On the Meaning of 'Ethical Neutrality,'" *The Methodology of the Social Sciences,* trans. and ed. Edward A. Shils and Henry A. Finch (Glencoe: Free Press, 1949), 5.

6. "'Objectivity' in Social Science," ibid., 54.

7. Ibid., 60.

8. Ibid., 5.

9. Rudolph Carnap, "Logical Positivism," *The Age of Analysis,* ed. Morton White (New York: Mentor, 1955), 217.

10. Alfred J. Ayer, *Language, Truth and Logic* (New York: Dover, 1946), 108, 107. These views have been subjected to severe critique repeatedly. W. T. Jones, *The Sciences and the Humanities: Conflict and Reconciliation* (Berkeley: U of California P, 1965), provides an excellent treatment that plausibly erases firm distinctions between objectivity and subjectivity.

11. Floyd W. Matson, *The Broken Image: Man, Science and Society* (New York: Doubleday, 1964) provides a brief history of positivism in American social science. Cf. esp. "The Values of Neutralism," 76–85.

12. Robert Lynd, *Knowledge for What?* (Princeton: Princeton UP, 1939), 181.

13. Ibid., 181.

14. Morris R. Cohen, *Reason and Nature* (New York: Harcourt-Brace, 1931), 343; cited by Lynd.

15. Cohen, ibid., 349; cited by Lynd.

16. My account of their positions is sympathetic and simplified. For more complex statements of the opposing positions, see Arnold Brecht, *Political Theory* (Princeton: Princeton UP, 1959); and Duncan McRae, *The Social Function of Social Science* (New Haven: Yale UP, 1976), esp. Ch. 3, "Positivism and the Devaluation of Ethics," ed. Gresham Riley, *Values, Objectivity, and the Social Sciences* (Reading, MA: Addison-Wesley, 1974), brings together clear, conflicting statements on a number of related issues.

17. Cf. Leo Lowenthal, *Literature, Popular Culture and Society* (Englewood Cliffs: Prentice-Hall, 1961), reprinted by Pacific Books of Palo Alto, CA, in 1968).

18. Cf. Terry Ramsaye, "The Rise and Place of the Motion Picture," *Mass Communications,* ed. Wilbur Schramm (Urbana: U of Illinois P, 1972).

19. George Gerbner and Larry Gross, *Trends in Network Drama and Viewer Conception of Social Reality, 1969–1973 (Violence Profile* No. 6, University of Pennsylvania, 1974). A condensed account is found in their "The Scary World of TV's Heavy Viewer," *Psychology Today,* 9.11 (April 1976). An analysis of responsibility that relates it to the dominant myth system in popular culture is in Robert Jewett and John Shelton Lawrence, *The American Monomyth* (New York: Doubleday, 1977).

20. Richard M. Merlman, "Power and Community in Television," *JPC,* 2.1 (1968), reprinted in Horace Newcomb, *TV: The Critical View* (New York: Oxford UP, 1976).

21. On some of the limits of the serial aesthetic, see Fred Schroeder, "The Aesthetics of the Serial," Horace Newcomb, ibid.

22. Stephen Arons and Ethan Katsh, "How TV Cops Flout the Law," *Saturday Review,* 19 Mar. 1977.

23. For a brief overview, see Marie Winn, *The Plug-In Drug: Television, Children, and the Family* (New York: Viking, 1977), esp. "Television and Violence," 65ff.

24. Cited in Wilbur Schramm, *op.cit.,* 637.

25. Schramm, *op. cit.,* 640.

26. Robert S. Alley, *Television: Ethics for Hire?* (Nashville: Abingdon, 1977), 143.

27. Alley, ibid., 137.

28. Cf. Murrary Schumach, *The Face on the Cutting Room Floor* (New York: DaCapo P, 1974), for a history of movie censorship. On comics, see Les Daniels, *Comix* (New York: Bonanza, 1971), ch. 5, "The Comics Code Controversy."

29. See Erik Barnouw, *The Tube of Plenty: The Evolution of American Television* (New York: Oxford UP, 1975), 118–30.

30. Cf. *To Establish Justice, To Insure Domestic Tranquility: The Final Report of the National Commission on the Causes and Prevention of Violence* (New York: Bantam, 1970), Ch. VIII, "Violence in Television Entertainment Programs."

31. William Gass, "Even if By All the Oxen in the World," *Frontiers of American Culture,* ed. Ray B. Browne, et. al. (Lafayette, IN: Purdue UP, 1968), 198.

32. John Cawelti, "Beatles, Batman and the New Aesthetic," *Midway,* Autumn 1970: 70. More extensive reflections on the theme of responsibility are found in Cawelti's *Adventure, Mystery and Romance* (Chicago: U of Chicago P, 1976), esp. in his analysis of the "Godfather" crime genre.

33. Alvin Gouldner, "Anti-Minotaur: The Myth of Value-Free Sociology," *Social Problems,* 9.199 (Winter 1962).

34. Cited in Stuart McClintock, "John of Jandun," *Encyclopedia of Philosophy,* Vol. IV., ed. Paul Edwards (New York: Macmillan, 1967), 281.

35. Gunnar Myrdal, *Asian Drama* (New York: Pantheon, 1968), "A Methodological Note," 33. Cf. also *An American Dilemma: The Negro Problem and American Democracy* (New York: Harper, 1944), esp. "A Methodological Note on Valuation and Beliefs" and "A Methodological Note on Facts and Valuation in Social Sciences."

36. Idem.

The author acknowledges support from the National Endowment of Humanities Summer Stipend program. Colleagues B. Gist, R. Jewett and F. Terry provided valuable criticism and suggestions.

SON OF "AGAINST EVALUATION":
A REPLY TO JOHN SHELTON LAWRENCE

Roger B. Rollin

Rollin critiques Lawrence's critique of him with special attention to the distinction between aesthetic and moral evaluation.

As every author knows, to be read at all is gratifying, to evoke a bona fide response, nothing less than exhilarating. John Shelton Lawrence has not only read "Against Evaluation," my probe into Popular Culture theory, thoughtfully—for which I respect him—but he has taken my ideas seriously—for which I am grateful. So the dialogue goes on, and in my view nothing is more vital to the health and progress of Popular Culture studies than continuing the attempt to develop a viable theoretical base, one that can transform our "field" (as Michael Real characterizes it) into a "discipline."

Professor Lawrence, moreover, has tried to be accurate and fair in his critique, even to recognizing that while my essay is always serious, it is not always solemn. Finally, his work complements mine by providing some background in the history-of-ideas to my discussion, background for which I lacked space and which he, as a philosopher, is better qualified than I am to supply. Nonetheless, he does on occasion appear to misconstrue my argument. In response it will be best to begin with those occasions.

Evaluation: Inevitable and Unnecessary. Professor Lawrence has some trouble in handling paradox. "Against Evaluation" argues (356/4–357/5) that while aesthetic evaluation is an inevitable aspect of the *aesthetic* experience of Popular Culture (you do or do not "like" *Star Wars* as you watch it), aesthetic evaluation need not and should not play a major role in the *critical* experience of Popular Culture (the writing of your essay on *Star Wars*). Whether you "liked" *Star Wars* or not may well become evident to the scholars who read your essay, but this manifestation of your "taste" is or should be immaterial to them, for their main concern must be that you expand their *understanding* of the movie. Anyone who has suffered through the presentation of a "scholarly" paper whose sole critical strategy has been

Roger B. Rollin, "Son of 'Against Evaluation': A Reply to John Shelton Lawrence," Journal of Popular Culture *12.1 (Summer 1978): 113–17.*

to celebrate a TV series the author adores or to excoriate a movie he or she detests will recognize the intellectual bankruptcy of criticism whose main function is to parade the author's taste—and, as so often happens, to extrapolate that expression of taste into an implied "universal" judgment.

To support his view that my arguing "from inevitability to dispensability" is "implausible," Lawrence offers a series of analogies, including one which invites us to compare the withholding of aesthetic judgment to the condoning of cannibalism. Not taken into account here are the significant and material differences between the experiencing of culture and "real-life" experience. If we're at all normal, at some level of our minds we know "it's only a movie"; thus, evaluating that movie and its implications cannot be as consequential as evaluating an act like making a missionary into an entree. Lawrence's critique generally fails to maintain this distinction between Art and Life, between our perceptions of Fantasy and of Reality, which—as Freud affirmed and Piaget and other have confirmed—not only normal adults but even very young children are readily capable of.

Evaluation and the Justification of Popular Culture to the Academy. Curiously, to give the *coup de grâce* to my essay, Lawrence focuses upon an issue so peripheral to the main argument of "Against Evaluation" that I relegated it to an appendix (and even invited the *JPC* editor to omit it if he was pressed for space). Simply stated, the purpose of that appendix was to observe to my fellow teachers that, given the main thrust of my essay, they would be well advised to choose other than aesthetic grounds for justifying the inclusion of Popular Culture in curricula, for concerning matters of taste there can be little rational discussion, even with academics. On the other hand, concerning the historical (or, I would add, the formal, psychological, and sociological) study of Popular Culture, rational discussion is at least possible. If this be "evasion," as Lawrence charges, it constitutes an evasion of pointless squabbles about "good taste" vs. "bad taste" and the advancement of the case for Popular Culture study to the high ground of intellectual debate.

Nowhere in that appendix do I "confess" that my "primary reason" for writing "Against Evaluation" is to provide my fellows with ammunition for meetings of the Curriculum Committee: readers can determine as much for themselves by re-examining the first three pages of the main body of my essay and then its Appendix. It is only in the latter, in a passage which (I do confess) may not be a model of clarity, that I suggest that, unlike Popular Culture *analysis,* the *historical* approach to Popular Culture, despite its limitations, is one which traditionalist academics may understand and perhaps sanction.

The Red Herring of "Value-Free" Science and Scholarship. The third section of Lawrence's critique is devoted mainly to an exposition of the

checkered history of the movement for "value-free" science. Though interesting, this discussion is beside the point at issue, for I never claimed that
Popular Culture study could be totally "value-free" or that understanding
Popular Culture "can be achieved *only* through the exclusion of value judgments" (emphasis added). What "Against Evaluation" *does* argue is that our
intellectual cause is not well served when private passions or group tastes
are permitted to become central to the very foundations of our scholarship.
If to assert as much is itself "clearly" a value judgment, as Lawrence says,
it is one which the history of criticism, the history of aesthetic taste, and the
history of cultural fads and fashions amply and embarrassingly document.
The insistence upon the "objective" reality of "good taste" (possessed by a
happy few) and "bad taste" (harbored by the benighted many), of Sublime
Culture and Non- or Quasi- or Pseudo-Culture, has for centuries mainly
served to set class against class and to discourage much of society from full
and unfettered participation in culture's total range of experiences.

*The Case for—and against—the Moral Evaluation of Popular Cul-
ture.* The main weakness of Lawrence's critique is that it obfuscates the
important distinction between *aesthetic* evaluation—upon which "Against
Evaluation" centered—and *moral* evaluation—quite another matter, and
one to which my essay did not address itself. Readers may be forgiven if
they do not immediately realize that Lawrence begins "For Evaluation" by
discussing *taste* and ends up discussing *morality.*

This shift nears completion in the transition between the second and
third sections of Lawrence's critique. There he states, "The study of culture
is inescapably evaluative," and, "The scholar cannot avoid making some
judgments of value in the presence of his subject matter." My reply is: Of
course!—as "Against Evaluation" makes plain. Readers, however, should
keep in mind that, as I have claimed (and Lawrence even confirms), aesthetic evaluations ("Great movie!"/"Lousy movie!") are highly subjective,
highly personal, in nature. Consequently, both logic and intellectual rigor
indicate that the better part of wisdom is to put such evaluations in their
proper perspective by minimizing their role in scholarship.

From establishing the inevitability of evaluation (sound familiar?),
Lawrence concludes his second section with the following, curiously detached and rather abstractly stated, opinion: "There is no rejection of the
ideal of objectivity . . . but rather an acknowledgment that objectivity must
co-exist with *the problems of the day* and with the subjectivities that propel
the individual scholar and his discipline" (emphasis added). What this will
come to mean as Lawrence proceeds with his argument is that for him Popular Culture scholars should make their criticism vehicles for advocating
their personal stands on "the problems of the day."

The chain of reasoning by which Lawrence arrives at this viewpoint can be briefly summarized: (1) Popular Culture affects attitudes and behaviors; (2) since Popular Culture embodies and expresses moral values, it may affect moral standards and human actions adversely; (3) as experts on the mass media, we have the obligation to perform moral evaluations of Popular Culture so as to prevent the moral collapse of the less enlightened citizenry.

To take these point by point:

- *The effects of the mass media:* as every reputable researcher admits, this is an extremely complex media problem, one with which the techniques and the technology of the social sciences are as yet poorly equipped to deal. (Even the investigations Lawrence cites are severely limited, admittedly conditional, as a close reading of his careful descriptions of them reveals.)
- *The moral structure and content of Popular Culture:* a commonplace of Popular Culture study. It would be hard to find a *JPC* article in applied criticism that did not at least allude to the moral patternings of its subject.
- *Students of Popular Culture as moral critics:* Lawrence asks: If those who have studied the popular aesthetic experience the most carefully are not qualified to make evaluative suggestions about it, should we conclude that the matters must be resolved through a wide-scale war of private subjectivities, undisciplined by systematic and rigorous viewpoints?"

While I would be the last to suggest that, as *citizens,* students of Popular Culture should not write irate or glowing letters to the editor or join any pressure group they please (I've done my share of both), I would argue that they do not necessarily have any more *moral authority* than any other citizen, even the "undisciplined." One of the axioms with which my own profession, English, has always buttressed its claim to importance is that the study of "good" literature improves character. If this were so, departments of English should be comprised, in the main, of saints. I invite my readers to test that hypothesis against their own experience. And though some of my best friends are philosophers, I must confess that, for all their study, their behavior has impressed me as no *more* moral than anyone else's.

The critical position Lawrence advocates—the moral evaluation of culture—is not, of course, a new one: it was the position taken by Plato (the Plato who banished poets from his republic), of Christian critics of the middle ages (as Chaucer was well aware), of Dr. Johnson, and, in our own century, of T. S. Eliot. It has also, knowingly or not, been the position of every censor since time immemorial. And today it is the position, advanced with varying degrees of passion, by most Marxists, many minority critics, some feminist critics, and by organizations such as the national P. T. A. and the Committee for Decent Literature.

If nothing else, moral critics do take culture seriously, and if they sometimes tend to oversimplify or exaggerate its effects on individual and group attitudes and behaviors (affective research is still in its infancy), they do manifest great concern for the quality of human life. However, when such critics gain access to the centers of power—the ecclesiastical, educational, social, or political establishments—time and time again that concern has figured forth in control. The results of their attempts to make culture conform to whatever their ideological vision happens to be have been amply recorded in legal and social history.

Happy Ending: There can be little question that today Popular Culture is produced and disseminated under conditions that are far from free; that the capitalistic system and the media conglomerates to a far from desirable extent control what is presented to the mass audience so as to reinforce the status quo; that there has to be a better way. What that way is, however, I am not at all sure. What I am sure of is that the way to clean up the present messy situation, in which the producers of Popular Culture and its consumers co-exist in an uneasy, shifting symbiotic relationship—with the producers' vast technological and financial empires rising and falling each week with Nielsen's and *Variety's* consumer head-count—is not by the clean sweep of an ideological broom—anybody's broom, including Lawrence's and mine. What he and I and all students of Popular Culture *can* do, though, is to make more of an effort to take our specialization to the public.

For example, as a group we have done little to advocate and assist the development of academically sound Popular Culture courses in the primary and secondary schools, the very places where the need is greatest. And we have yet as evolved no formal means for disseminating Popular Culture scholarship to the general public or for offering our services as "resource persons"—for example, in the role of *amicus curiae* to the legal and political systems. Students of the mass media, we have developed no coherent plan for approaching the media with our concerns or for utilizing the media to further the Popular Culture education of the public.

It is in this last regard that Professor Lawrence and I might find some common ground. Although I see no more merit in trying to convert other Popular Culture scholars to our personal ideologies by making moral evaluations than I see in trying to impose our personal tastes on our peers by making aesthetic evaluations, this much we can do: we can continue to advance each other's moral and cultural *educations* by continuing to *explicate* the ideological thrusts of Popular Culture. Even more importantly, we can make a greater effort to do so for the mass audience itself. Most of us are, after all, educators, not priests. To reveal the moral assumptions, arguments and implications of Popular Culture to the Popular Audience itself—and thus enhance its ability to make informed choices of its own, would not only be work consonant with our profession, it would be important and useful work. And it would, indeed, be the work of ages.

WITH THE BENEFIT OF HINDSIGHT:
POPULAR CULTURE CRITICISM

John G. Cawelti

John Cawelti believes that the study of popular culture has been associated with two conceptual approaches to its study: aesthetics and formula or genre. The following excerpt summarizes his case for a distinctive aesthetic of popular culture. As noted in a previous selection, Cawelti is a distinguished scholar of popular culture.

. . . In essence, the idea of a popular aesthetic assumes that different modes of evaluation are appropriate for different kinds of artistry. Instead of a single set of aesthetic standards, popular aestheticians hold the view that those creations most typical of popular culture—for example, detective stories and westerns, rock and country music, horror films and science-fiction, circuses and sports—cannot be meaningfully analyzed and evaluated by the same standards, and, in comparison with, for example, the novels of Henry James, the paintings of Picasso, the poetry of Wordsworth, or the music of Beethoven.

Perhaps the most important distinction developed so far by the popular aestheticians is that between the essentially conventional nature of the popular arts and the ideals of originality and unique genius so characteristic of the fine arts, at least since the Renaissance (Hall & Whannel, 1965; Deer & Deer, 1967; Thorburn, 1976; Cawelti, 1976). Though the media are frequently criticized for the formulaic character of most of their productions, popular aestheticians have accepted the idea that conventionality is a necessary, perhaps even a desirable characteristic of a truly popular art form. In support of this proposition, they cite the dominantly formulaic character of many creations of the past now accepted as great art, such as ancient bardic narrative, Medieval liturgical drama, Elizabethan theater and the Victorian novel (Thorburn, 1976; Fiske and Hartley, 1978). Once one accepts the validity of conventional forms like the detective story, the ro-

John G. Cawelti, "With the Benefit of Hindsight: Popular Culture Criticism," Critical Studies in Mass Communication 2.4 *(December 1985): 369–71. Used by permission of the National Communication Association.*

mance, the popular ballad or the situation comedy, it becomes possible to recognize many different kinds of creativity and artistry within the limits of these conventions. Detective stories, for example, range all the way from the artistry of Raymond Chandler and Ross Macdonald to the humdrum whodunits of hordes of detecticians, even though no detective story ever written has explored the nature of crime with anything like the depth and complexity of Shakespeare's *Macbeth* (1969), Dostoyevsky's *Crime and Punishment* (1914/1960) or Camus' *The Stranger* (1942/1965).

While conventional forms may be limited from some aesthetic perspectives, they do constitute a complex of widely recognized and understood patterns. Broad accessibility is another aesthetic principle valued by popular aestheticians. While Joyce's *Finnegan's Wake* (1958) is undoubtedly a great literary masterpiece, its understanding requires a kind of preparation and effort which few people will ever be able to give. The forms of popular culture, however, perform something like what Fiske and Hartley (1978) call a "bardic" function: they communicate to nearly everyone in the culture by depending on an established repertory of basic stories and other artistic patterns in a fashion analogous to the traditional bard's use of epic formulas and a well-known mythology. These conventional patterns guarantee a high degree of accessibility. Of course mere accessibility is no guarantee of artistic interest. However, there is a sense in which the best popular art is not only fairly easy to interpret, but compels audiences to want to understand it, because it deals in an interesting way with stories and themes that seem important.

Some popular aestheticians would go farther and say that conventional patterns which have survived over a period of time contain basic cultural meanings which can only be expressed by invoking these established formulas. The extent to which the narrative formulas of popular culture constitute a true mythology is still a matter of controversy. However, it is interesting that many major writers and filmmakers of the second half of the twentieth century have used popular forms like the western and the detective story as mythical materials (Holquist, 1971–1972; Spanos, 1972; Cawelti, 1984).

Another important concept of popular aesthetics is the centrality of serial form (Radway, 1984; Fiske and Hartley, 1978). The programming imperatives of mass communications and mass publishing makes serial form, either as a continuing narrative or as sets of variations on a single basic pattern (e.g., television soap opera or a series with the same basic form in each episode like *Magnum, P.I.*), a dominant type of creation and production. Though serial productions such as dime novels, most comic books, or movie adventure serials have marginal artistic pretensions, popular aestheticians insist that both types of serial are legitimate artistic approaches with special

powers possible only in this form. Though we are only beginning to understand and explore the aesthetics of serial form, many important twentieth-
century artists like Arnold Schonberg or Alain Robbe-Grillet have been fascinated by the serial principle (Meyer, 1967).

Finally, popular aestheticians have developed the idea of what might
be called the performance-persona principle of much popular art. This principle has two major aspects. First it involves the recognition of nonverbal
aspects of performance. We are all familiar with the way in which a great
performer can take quite commonplace or even banal material and turn it
into a moving and complex experience. However, until the advent of modern visual and aural recording techniques, these aspects of performance
were largely ephemeral. Consequently, an adequate critical vocabulary for
the analysis and interpretation of performance had never developed. Now,
however, performances can be recorded, filmed or taped. Thus, modern
communications technology has given the nonverbal aspects of performance an even greater importance. Indeed, popular culture has been in the
avant-garde in new developments of performance techniques and forms.
Our critical vocabulary for describing and analyzing these developments is
sadly in arrears.

The other important aspect of the performance-persona principle involves the fact that a popular performance is not just a way of presenting a
particular work to an audience, but an act by a persona which relates both
to a larger social context and to previous acts by the same persona. A good
example of this larger social context is the rock concert which has developed into a social ritual that can assume awesome proportions. In the case
of such creations as Woodstock in the sixties or the Michael Jackson Victory Tour of the eighties, individual works and performances are caught up
in a larger and more complex artistic construction which includes such
components as showmanship, promotion, media coverage, etc. From this
point of view, what has come to be known as "hype" is an important part of
the artistic work as a whole.

Examples of the influence on a particular performance of previous acts
by the same persona are the phenomena of stardom and celebrity. Creating
stars and celebrities has become a major twentieth century art form which
has developed its own patterns, forms of production, and media uses. While
these patterns were pioneered by nineteenth century showmen like P. T.
Barnum and "Buffalo Bill" Cody, they have become even more complex in
the twentieth century (Harris, 1973; Russell, 1960). When a star like John
Wayne portrayed a character in a film, he brought to that individual performance a whole aura derived from his existing star persona. When Elvis
Presley sang a song, it was not just another popular ballad, but a major cul-

tural statement. Here, too, we need to create a new critical vocabulary to describe and analyze such examples of the performance-persona principle.

These popular aesthetic principles lead us toward a pluralistic aesthetics rather than a single set of artistic standards. However, we have yet to deal fully with the problem of how these different sets of standards relate to each other. Some popular aestheticians assume that the popular aesthetic principles can still be subsumed in some fashion under traditional aesthetic ideals, while others insist on the aesthetic independence of popular principles. I will attempt to deal in part with this problem in the final section of this essay, though it is still too early in the exploration of popular aesthetics to make a definitive resolution of this issue. Nonetheless it remains important and should be continually on our minds as we explore these newer approaches to the analysis and evaluation of popular culture.

The second major conception of popular culture studies is that of popular genres, an idea which grows out of the basically conventional character of popular culture. Popular genres are those types of story, song, game, dance, sport, etc. which have become recognizable as such by writers, directors, publishers, producers and their audiences. In terms of stories, which will be our chief example here, popular genres are immediately recognizable by certain key features such as a certain type of protagonist, a particular kind of plot pattern and setting and a distinctive iconography. A story that begins with a crime suggests one genre, while one that ends in a shoot-out implies another. In many cases, these characteristics are so clear that a glance at a book cover or movie poster is sufficient to indicate the generic type: a cowboy on horseback means a western; a bottle of poison, a detective story; and a young woman with wind-tossed hair, a romance. . . .

References

Cawelti, J. G. (1976). *Adventure, Mystery and Romance: Formula Stories as Art and Popular Culture.* Chicago: U of Chicago P.

———. (1984). *The Six-Gun Mystique* (2nd ed.). Bowling Green, OH: Bowling Green State U Popular P.

Deer, I., and H. Deer, eds. (1967). *The Popular Arts.* New York: Scribner's.

Fiske, J., and J. Hartley. (1978). *Reading Television.* London: Methuen.

Hall, S., and P. Whannel. (1965). *The Popular Arts.* New York: Pantheon.

Harris, N. (1973). *Humbug: The Art of P. T. Barnum.* Boston: Little, Brown.

Holquist, M. (1971–72). "Whodunit and Other Questions: Metaphysical Detective Stories in Post-War Fiction." *New Literary History* 3: 135–56.

Meyer, L. B. (1967). *Music, the Arts, and Ideas.* Chicago: U of Chicago P.

Radway, J. (1984). *Reading the Romance: Reading, Patriarchy, and Popular Literature.* Chapel Hill: U of North Carolina P.

Russell, D. (1960). *The Life and Legends of Buffalo Bill.* Norman: U of of Oklahoma P.

Spanos, W. V. (1972). "The Detective and the Boundary: Some Notes on the Postmodern Literary Imagination." *Boundary* 2.1: 147–68.

Thorburn, D. (1976). "Television Melodrama." *Television as a Cultural Force.* Ed. R. Adler and D. Cater. (77–94). New York: Praeger.

NEW EXPERIMENTAL AESTHETICS AND POPULAR CULTURE

Dan Ash

Dan Ash, in an essay not previously published and written especially for this collection, proposes a taxonomy of popular culture and also the adaptation of D. E. Berlyne's "new experimental aesthetics" to the study of popular culture. Then, Ash provides us with one model for applying these ideas and constructs to one particular subject, the study of popular music. Ash is an experimental psychologist who also is a professional musician. Currently, he is Executive Director of Metropolitan College in Louisville, KY.

I was browsing through the used CDs in the music store just before Christmas when I overheard a couple of teens, discussing music. Both were male, white, about fifteen, standing in the section labeled "Alternative/ Hardcore." I paid little attention to their exchange of superlatives extolling the virtues of Phish and Dave Matthews, until I heard a familiar but long-forgotten name.

"Have you ever heard of the Bee Gees, man?" one youth asked the other. "Who?"

"The Bee Gees! They're the ones on TV the other night [more description, in a speedy avalanche of words too blurred for my ancient ears to make out]."

"Oh yeah!" the second teen blurted out, followed by a weak rendition. "Ah-ah-ah-ah, stayin' alive, stayin' alive. Ah-ah-ah-ah, stayin' aliiiiiiii-iiiive. Yeah, cool!"

It was obvious the boys were delighted with their new discovery. I fantasized for a moment about their lunchroom conversations with classmates, easily blending the Bee Gees and Blind Melons. I shuddered.

What did these new ears hear that I was so inured to? How was it that their ready embrace of the latest MTV trend could so ably accommodate the commercial, corporate pop icons of the Seventies? It was more than mere lack of knowledge on the part of the teens. The TV special they referred to had portrayed a cornucopia of Seventies pop artists, in a wild celebration of the Disco-beat and leisure suits. In the program the enthusiastic young studio audience had reacted to something in the Bee Gees music that resonated in these young listeners who were not saddled with my "superior" listening skills.

In many ways this incident is anecdotal evidence of the issues vigorously debated by Rollin (1978a, 1978b) and Lawrence (1978) regarding the role of the popular culture scholar as an evaluator of the popular culture. As an experimental psychologist I may appreciate only a portion of the implications contained in the arguments of these eloquent spokesmen. I nevertheless venture to say that their contentions seek to solve a thorny dilemma that has confronted the scholar of aesthetics for centuries. On the one extreme is the claim that the aesthetic experience is a purely individualistic one, such that the phenomenon enjoying my designation of "good" could receive a "bad" by others. This is tantamount to the claim that all popular culture has equal merit (and demerit), and is an untenable position for some. Conversely, to regard the learned scholar as the final repository of evaluative reliability is not only elitist, but practically unattainable in the view of other students of popular culture.

The music store encounter amply illustrates this argument. The teens' view of the value of the Bee Gees' music was incompatible with mine. Their assignment of "cool" as an all-purpose critique of the music could be countered on an equal level by my disdain. On the other hand, although it is certainly arrogant to proclaim that my viewpoint is superior, the uncritical manner in which the adolescents accepted the Bee Gees betrayed a lack of that musical depth and breadth which I value in what I consider a more learned perspective. I should add that this condescension stems in part from my personal experience over the last fifteen years as a professional popular music musician performing across the country.

The trouble is, either extreme exclusive of the other is discomforting. Instead, I would argue that neither theoretical approach is correct in and of itself, but that both perspectives taken together can produce a more fruitful viewpoint. Neither extreme alone captures the totality of experiencing popular culture. Each must truncate some aspect of that experience if they are to avoid internal contradiction. In this light, each theory is *necessary* to rightly characterize popular culture, but neither is *sufficient* to fully capture the truth.

As many disciplines have discovered since World War II, truth may be more ably served when multiple perspectives are integrated. The emergence, for example, of cognitive science in the Fifties received enormous impetus from the amalgamation of psychology, computer science, engineering, and linguistics (Solso, 1988). The collective experience gained from the debates and developments in this and other areas benefiting from assimilation of various perspectives have left us with at least three foundational insights which may be applied to address an important question: just how have we become so polarized in our views of the legitimacy of evaluation in popular culture study?

First, extreme perspectives often gain a lucidity of view at the expense of disregarding disconfirming evidence. Research on human cognitive processes amply documents that we are prone to seek out evidence which confirms our view while simultaneously disregarding evidence which contradicts our position (Benjafield, 1992). In fact, encountering disconfirming evidence can easily result in renewed effort to find further *confirming* evidence rather than considering the different perspective. Thus arguments over time may tend to produce an accumulation of reliable observations at each pole of an argument. As in the evaluation versus no-evaluation debate, the tendency is to establish a false dichotomy of choices when in fact there may not be any single unitary "correct" stance.

Second, the "truth" of a perspective is often dependent on the level of complexity and amount of information being considered at any given time. In the behavioral sciences this is expressed in the realization that explanations can inhabit differing "levels of analysis." The individual consumer's view of popular culture can be thought of as existing on a "molar" level, using information and influences that are meaningful only to the individual. In contrast, the popular culture scholar, necessarily incorporating a view informed by multiple sources, provides a more "macro"-level perspective of popular culture. These differences in influence and amount of information used to evaluate a given popular culture phenomenon may serve some explanatory function in resolving the current debate.

Finally, evaluation processes are viewed as most legitimate and persuasive when the source of the evaluation is viewed by the listener as competent, trustworthy, attractive, and similar to the listener (Brehm & Kassin, 1990). This is another way of saying that, among other things, listeners invest legitimacy in an evaluator when they are convinced the evaluator has gathered and masterfully presented sufficient information before making the evaluation. Additionally, evaluators gain further endorsement when they are liked by and perceived as similar to the listener. This dynamic helps explain why movies such as *There's Something about Mary* and *Teenage Mutant Ninja Turtles,* panned by professional critics, are embraced by large contingencies of the general population. Of course, professional critics may counter that they are not attempting to predict the number of people who will like the movies, but rather addressing the issue of *whether* people *should* like these particular movies. This is a red herring. The point remains that differing evaluations do emerge, along with the concomitant debate with which we are now involved.

What is called for when considering the evaluation of popular culture phenomena is not the abandonment of Rollin's or Lawrence's views. Indeed, the variety of approaches to the study of popular culture produces a rich environment of views complementary, supplementary, in agreement with, and in opposition to some other view. This tension is not only tolerable, but desirable for a healthy exchange of ideas. However, it is instructive that the resolution of the Rollin-Lawrence debate has made little headway in the past fifteen years. Again, from my imperfect outsider's perspective, it appears that the sheer breadth of scholarly effort in the study of popular culture has created something of a logjam in the advancement of the area.

It is my contention that the study of popular culture is sufficiently accommodative to allow a new approach, a new methodology peacefully co-existing with and complimenting existing ones, which may provide a resolution and synthesis of differing contentions. If the reader accepts the proposal that the three characteristics described above—confirmation bias, varying levels of analysis, and differing perspectives on legitimate evaluation—help perpetuate the debate, then it may be logical that an approach which accounts for these qualities may be instrumental in helping to resolve the debate. The models proposed in the remainder of this paper seek to move toward achieving this resolution.

A Taxonomy of Popular Culture

In his renowned work *The Discoverers,* Daniel Boorstein (1983) recounts the difficulties encountered by European commercial ventures during the early Medieval period of European history. A central problem of this time period concerned the inability to rectify the growing body of geographic and navigational information with the religious authorities' insistence that geographic reality be viewed through the glasses of scriptural interpretation. The biblical understanding of geographic reality dictated that Jerusalem, having been identified in God's word as being located at the center of the earth, must be centered on all official maps used for navigation and travel. As trading territory expanded, this requirement grew so cumbersome and impossible to abide by, that official maps accumulated errors over the years which cost money, time and lives. To counter this danger, illegal maps were drawn and surreptitiously passed around. Eventually the official version, although enjoying the approval of government and church authorities, contained little correspondence with reality and was inevitably abandoned.

This example is a graphic instance of how extreme humans can be in avoiding the realities that contradict their cherished opinions. At the risk of offering an imperfect analogy, could it be possible that the prodigious growth of popular culture scholarship has created a similar environment without the authority of church or scripture to serve as a guiding force? It appears that we have an abundance of maps being drawn with no agreement as to what constitutes reality. The Twenty-Fourth Annual Meeting of the Popular Culture Association (1994), for example, contained 494 separate sessions in which approximately 1,860 papers were presented in four days. Any environment this rich in information would provide generous opportunity to find support for personally favored contentions, ranging from facile to profound.

This is not to berate the existence of popular culture scholarship. I fully support the diversity of ideas and directions represented in the area. Further, there should be no constraint on the marketplace of ideas beyond the ethical and professional considerations afforded to all ideas. However, with no impetus to establish some synthesis of ideas, advancement of the field as a whole is easily impeded. With so many ideas flowing in so many directions, the net result could easily lead to intense activity with little progress.

We can observe the beneficial impact of synthetic efforts when we review the history of science. Even a cursory overview of the manner in which astrology was transformed into astronomy, or of the metamorphosis of alchemy into chemistry, reveals that advances on a large scale were often contingent on the establishment of some taxonomic organizational scheme. These organizational structures were based on agreed-upon principles, and on a systematic effort to comprehend the subject matter, predicated on the cumulative goal paths of description, prediction, explanation and control.

Such a taxonomy and direction would be helpful to the study of popular culture. In fact, establishing a taxonomy is an instrumental step in achieving the first goal of description. But does such a taxonomy even potentially exist for the study of popular culture, which is more ethereal and more fraught with the need to account for variability than the natural sciences?

Other disciplines, facing similar challenges, have addressed the issue by initiating their own taxonomic system upon which to build knowledge of the discipline. The Diagnostic and Statistical Manual has been created for psychology, for instance, which is used in the categorization and diagnosis of mental disorders. Although the system is certainly incomplete, it provides a common focus for research in diagnosis, treatment and theoretical understanding of behavioral disorders in the ongoing effort of revising and building on existing information.

Without calling for the abandonment of existing popular culture scholarship, I propose a similar effort for the study of popular culture. John E. Kaemmer (1980) proposed one such system, which may offer a rudimentary starting point for popular culture, in ethnomusicology. His organizational scheme was originally intended to be applied to the study of music, but reasonable adaptation and expansion of his ideas can potentially be used by popular culture scholars.

Although I consider this approach to be a reasonable starting point, it is in no way intended to be the sole one. Equally valid proposals can be forwarded from several fronts. Similarly, this system is not intended to be comprehensive. Mutually exclusive and exhaustive categorization requires considerably greater detail and considerably more time to build upon the existing knowledge base than I have been able to invest as yet. It is, nevertheless, a starting point, one whose merit or lack thereof can best be assessed through the test of challenges and modifications over time.

Kaemmer posits that music and society interact in specific ways, which he categorizes into music complexes. His classification system is organized on the basis of the roles involved in the realization of a musical event. These roles he identifies as the performer/composer, the audience, and the agent who makes provision for the occurrence of the event. Combining these roles in various permutations within and across people produces predictable ways in which musical events vary. Five musical complexes emerge from this strategy.

The *individualistic music complex* is composed of musical events that occur strictly through the desires of the performer. An audience may or may not be present in this complex. Music is performed for its inherent intrinsic reward or for personal nonmusical goals, such as singing a child to sleep.

In the *communal complex* more than one person is actively involved in the musical event. Participants move freely between the roles of performer and audience with minimal distinction between the two. The motivation for the occurrence of this complex is musical sharing or the use of music in a secondary or support capacity, such as providing auditory cues for group dancing. The role of the agent, as in the previous complex, is either nonexistent or played by the performer and/or audience.

The *contractual complex* is comprised of musical events in which an agent, usually a member of the audience, makes arrangements for the performer to appear before the audience. The performer in this case is motivated by contractual obligations based upon some reward other than or in addition to the inherent pleasure of performance. The agent does not usually receive monetary compensation, but as an active audience participant s/he is motivated by the effect of the performance on the success of the event.

A *sponsored complex* is similar to the contractual one, except that the agent makes an arrangement for musical events over an extended period of time. An example of this complex is the patronage system responsible for the music of courts in Europe.

Finally, the *commercial complex* occurs when there is a highly developed separation between performer, audience, and agent. In this instance, the motivation for the event's occurrence is external or monetary, both for the performer and for the agent who acts as an intermediary between the performer and the audience.

To expand on Kaemmer's model, consider the multiple roles played by the performer in the individualistic complex. Minimally the performer must also be the audience. How does one accomplish these simultaneous roles? John Sloboda (1985) proposes such a model based on research findings on the cognitive processes occurring during the composition-performance creative activity. A full description of this model is beyond the scope of this paper, but Sloboda identifies four processes, some occurring in sequence, others occurring simultaneously, which are important to our considerations.

The first process involves the generation of the musical idea, which emerges from non-conscious influences based on general tonal and stylistic knowledge. This is similar to the composition-performer role described by Kaemmer.

Sloboda further suggests that an interpretive step follows the initial generative process. Interpretation, akin to the audience component in Kaemmer's model, is conducted through additional non-conscious processes representing cultural and "superordinate" constraints and influences.

There are two more elements to Sloboda's model which exist on a conscious level. One relates to Kaemmer's role of agent. The agent, as mediator between the occurrence of the event and the audience, serves as an entity whose skills lie in the ability to read audience desires in an anticipative predictive manner. In the commercial complex, for example, the agent is an expert observer and predictor of anticipated audience response. The agent searches for and/or modifies those who generate the type of event the agent anticipates will be the most successful, that is, will most likely fulfill the desires and preferences of the audience. In essence, the agent represents what Sloboda might consider the conscious active component of the interpretive process. On the individualistic complex level, then, the person involved in the generation of the musical idea, influenced by non-conscious elements, also functions on the conscious level as an agent who observes the generated product and anticipates the effect of the product on the anticipated audience. The generator of the product then modifies and develops the product in anticipation of creating the desired effect on the audience.

Sloboda also accounts for a fourth element. In a process which is converse to the role of the agent, a conscious process is undertaken in which the generated product, rather than the anticipated audience response, is focused on. This observation is then used to hypothesize the listener's anticipated interpretive response. It is my contention that this element represents much the same role that the critic plays for many popular culture events. The critic "reads" the generated product and anticipates the interpretation of that product.

Thus, a reciprocal cyclical internal process occurs wherein a person generates a product based on non-conscious sources, primarily general stylistic knowledge. An interpretation of this product is next based on non-conscious sources stemming from cultural influences. A process fulfilling the agent role operates on a conscious level to read the interpretation and modify the generated product to be more consistent with desired interpretive response. The critic role is carried out by a process in which the individual consciously observes the generated product and hypothesizes the anticipated interpretive response. If the anticipated interpretation does not fit the desired response, further modification of the generated product takes place. A graphical depiction of this process is shown in Figure 1. The arrows represent flow of information. Each of the roles represented (G = generator, I = interpreter, A = agent, C = critic) is contained within a single circle to indicate that these are internal processes which can be carried out by one person. Thus information flows from the generator to the interpreter and vice versa. Information also flows from the generator to the critic and from the critic to the interpreter. Similarly, the agent receives information from the interpreter and provides information to the generator.

Of course, the scope of Kaemmer's and Sloboda's interests are restricted to musical expression, but if we can discover non-musical elements which may be common to a variety of popular culture expressions, then we may be able to develop a more general model. Such an adaptation may be possible if we examine the roles described above as we move from one complex to another. What non-musical dimensions of these roles are responsible for differentiation among complexes?

One fundamental dimension involves the degree to which any one person actively engaged in a complex is playing the role under question. For example, the individualistic complex can exist when a single person interchangeably plays the various roles described above. The commercial complex, in contrast, is characterized by these roles being played by separate individuals. Although there may be some individuals playing more than one role at any given juncture in the event, the commercial complex by definition requires that there be different individuals who play the individual roles.

The point at which roles can be transferred to individuals other than the generator is instrumental to the establishment of taxonomic categories. Specifically, in the individualistic complex the person is able to piece together the event based totally on internal processes. In this case the interpreter (audience) is totally in control of the performer. But once an interpreter other than the performer is present, the performer's ability to control all aspects of the event is greatly reduced. Now the generator must also rely on the *reality* of the interpreter response rather than the mere anticipation of the response. A degree of freedom thus is lost to the person generating the event as we move across complexes.

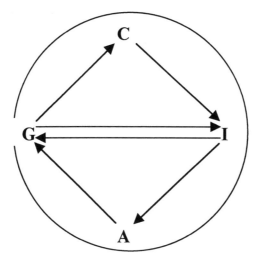

Fig. 1.

The importance of this transfer of control can be more fully appreciated when we consider how onerous it is for humans to surrender control
voluntarily. In fact, as we learn more of the internal psychological processes
common to all humans, it becomes increasingly clear that our perception
of our ability to control consequences appears to be a central component of
our psychological makeup. This perception is a fundamental coping mechanism of all humans for dealing with anxiety and uncertainty.

In order for the performer to surrender this control willingly, a highly
desirable outcome must be sufficiently powerful to overcome the added uncertainty brought on by this abdication. The question we must ask is, what
does the performer potentially gain to offset this loss? There appear to be at
least three factors that provide the impetus for this relinquishment of perceived control.

Separation of roles. The first can be seen in the source of the motivation for the occurrence of an event. At one extreme, the individualistic complex, the person is motivated in large measure by intrinsic factors, those
characteristics inherent in the performance of the musical material. External reward may be forthcoming, but it can be considered to be redundant
when added to this intrinsic factor. The performer would perform whether
she were paid or not. At the other extreme, a commercial complex's occurrence could be predicated strictly on extrinsic rewards without any intrinsic
factors entering into the motivation for the performer. The performer may
be totally unmotivated by intrinsic characteristics of the material, but may
perform nonetheless to get paid, monetarily or otherwise. Thus, as the performer's motivation by external reward becomes more prominent, the need

for others to play the various roles formerly relegated to internal role-playing becomes more important. Foundationally, no external reward is possible without the audience to provide it. Thus the performer makes the step toward externalizing the roles: the music is performed for or with someone who serves as the interpreter separate from the generator.

Figure 2 shows this relationship using the same legend as that described for Figure 1. The overlapping circles indicate that different individuals may play the generator and interpreter roles, but there may also be individuals serving both roles, indicated by the intersection of the circles. Additionally, note the location of the critic and agent roles. The figure indicates that the agent role tends to remain within the generator while the critic is more likely to be an interpreter also rather than the generator. This is not to suggest that the critic and agent roles cannot be played by any or all individuals involved in the event; but the objectification of the interpreter does influence the development of different individuals playing different roles. For example, the reality of response rather than the anticipated response drives the complex at this point and the critic-interpreter and generator-agent as separate persons logically offer greater ability to verify this reality. The critic's role can also be made more veridical by externalizing it so that it can now be more readily observed. Moreover, critical acclaim of the generated product by other interpreters (recall similarity as a key influence on persuasiveness) increases the probability that interpreters will be present for the event. The agent role, however, is most able to alter the generated product if the generator still maintains that element of control. With the added objectivity of observing the actual interpreter response, the generator as agent can more accurately gauge interpreter response and subsequently modify the generated product to correspond more closely with interpreter preferences. Some sense of the control which was sacrificed in the objectification of the interpreter is then regained by the generator.

Specialization of roles. If this level of reward is sufficient for the individuals involved, there is no reason to project further complexes. But a series of factors may develop which produce the need for a qualitative change. First, the generator may begin to produce an event that is sufficiently pleasurable such that the interpreter may abandon further effort to play the dual roles of generator and interpreter. When this happens the motivation to be actively involved in the performance may be replaced by other motivations, especially the desire to affiliate with others, a central social need of humans. As interpreters seek to affiliate with other interpreters, some may take it upon themselves to process the generated product and communicate their critique to other potential interpreters. Other individuals, focusing on the interpretive process, may seek to expand the scope of potential interpreters by serving as agents, modifying and exploiting the generated product to

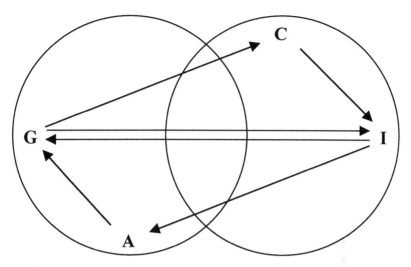

Fig. 2.

more consistently fit the preferences of the potential interpreter. The notion that persons other than the generator may take on the roles of critic and agent does not preclude the generator from doing the same. On the contrary, the person generating the product may intensify efforts to maintain control over the agent and critic roles. Popular music anecdotes are replete with stories of performers rejecting critical comments and insisting on artistic control of their product. But the important change from the previous complex is that now *specialization* of all role functions begins to occur outside and independent of the person who originally generated the product. Whether the original generator desires it or not, others may pursue critic and agent roles which may or may not be legitimized by the generator.

Figure 3 graphically portrays this relationship. Note that the generator may now rely totally on external sources for the critic, agent, and interpreter roles to be realized. Note also that the interpreter and generator roles overlap with those of the critic and agent, although specialization can and often does take place.

Exclusivity of roles. Once specialization of the agent and critic roles begins, the control of the popular culture event has largely been given over to external sources. The person generating the original product may indeed be responsible for the genesis of the event, but the agent and critic roles, now added to the interpreter role, emerge as instrumental in the establishment of the ultimate popularity of the event. This final surrender of control on the part of the generator produces some interesting dynamics.

The first of these can be seen in the roles of agent and critic as the popularity of the generator and the product grows. As more and more interpreters

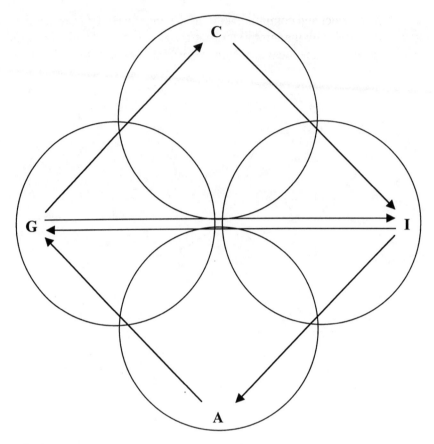

Fig. 3.

become interested, often on a broader geographical basis, each of the critic and agent roles becomes more complex. The agent must eventually not only arrange the mediation of generator and interpreter but must also deal with sometimes elaborate logistic concerns. As an army of support personnel emerges to ensure successful delivery of the product, the agent must attend to ever-greater detail. As specialization of this role increases, the investment of time and energy in the role grows commensurately.

Moreover, the increase in the potential number of interpreters alters the consequences of the event. On a smaller scale, not only is mediation between generator and interpreter more straightforward; but the success or failure of the event, in terms of material reward, is mitigated. As the scale increases, the potential consequences grow more influential. Success of a product may yield enormous economic and/or cultural gain while failure can result in equally momentous disaster.

The critic experiences similar influences. On a smaller scale, the reading of the product and communication of the anticipated interpretation can be verified easily by the interpreter. If a friend provides a critical description of an artist at the local alternative music nightspot, I am just as likely as he to have attended the same or another performance by the artist. Consequently, I can evaluate the friend's critique based on my interpretation of the event. A critique that is consistent with mine is likely to encourage me to talk with my friend on other occasions about this or even other artists. Because our interpretations are similar, he can now function as my surrogate interpreter.

But increase in numbers and expansion of geographic range changes this relationship. Professional critics often are harbingers of new popular culture expressions which potential interpreters have not yet had the opportunity to be exposed to. The process of verification is still possible, that is, I can still attend an event and determine if a critic's anticipated interpretation is consistent with mine; but the consequences of the presence or absence of a consistent interpretation between the critic and myself have changed. On the smaller scale, even if my friend and I had different interpretations of the same product, there are other bases for our relationship. But when the professional critic and I do not have consistent interpretations of the same product or event, our sole common basis for a relationship is eroded.

Similar to the situation of the agent then, growth of the numbers and geographic locations of potential interpreters elevates the consequences of the effects of the other roles. When the complexity of the roles, the economic consequences, and critical legitimacy are sufficiently important to become central to the maintenance of these roles, then the agent and critic must move beyond mere specialization. Those who are successful in these roles on a larger scale must take on the functions of their roles *exclusive* of other roles. The agent must now operate in an expert capacity independent of the generator and the casual interpreter. Attention to reading broad-based interpreter response and modifying the generated product to fit these readings becomes crucial. The ability to process, not just experience, the generated product and to anticipate the broad-based interpretive response becomes essential to the legitimacy and very existence of the critic, who must now devote sufficient time and effort to developing the expertise which will allow for a more legitimate critique in the eyes of the interpreter.

Figure 4 illustrates this role relationship. The exclusivity of roles is indicated by the lack of intersection of any circle in the model. The generator still provides the product directly to the interpreter, and the interpreter still provides direct information back to the generator (applause, purchase of material), but now the roles of agent and critic have grown complex and important enough to be independent of the generator and interpreter. Keep in mind that considerable flexibility of role-playing still exists. Audiences at

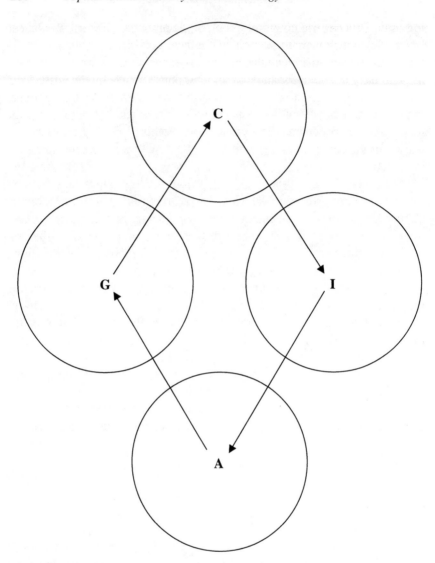

Fig. 4.

live performances can still involve themselves to the point where the roles of generator and interpreter are blurred. Nevertheless, on this level, unlike the previous ones, each role may now function fully separated, specialized and exclusive from all others.

Popular Culture Taxonomy

After considering these concepts, I propose that the Kaemmer and Sloboda models be adapted and generalized to a variety of popular culture expressions. This general taxonomy should be comprised of four complexes, each distinguished from the others by the factors described above.

The *inclusive-role complex* (Figure 1) occurs when a single individual plays all roles of the production processes: generator, interpreter, critic, and agent. The initial generation and interpretation of the product are based on nonconscious processes described earlier. Active processing of the product occurs as the individual interchangeably adopts the roles of agent, to attend to anticipated interpreter response and modify the generated product, and critic, to evaluate the generated product and to create anticipated interpreter response.

The *separated-role complex* (Figure 2) exists when external rewards become prominent to the generator and the need for external interpreters emerges and is realized. The agent role remains largely in the purview of the generator while the critic role becomes more likely under the control of the interpreter.

The *specialized-role complex* (Figure 3) comes into being when the pool of potential interpreters not involved in generation of the product grows and mediation between the generator and potential interpreters becomes necessary. As some interpreters seek further reward (affiliation with other like-minded interpreters and/or material gain) and as the generator further abandons roles previously under personal control, some interpreters emerge to more fully take on the roles of critic and/or agent.

Finally the *exclusive-roles complex* (Figure 4) is realized when the potential pool of interpreters grows sufficiently in numbers and geographic diversity to require the designation of fully separate, specialized, and mutually exclusive roles of generator, interpreter, critic, and agent. In this case the consequences and importance of the critic and agent roles become so integral to the maintenance of all the roles that individuals may take them on fully to the exclusion of other roles.

Before further discussion several points need to be made. First, this taxonomy is merely a proposal based in part on deductive reasoning, speculation, and empirical research. It is not intended to be comprehensive of all popular culture, nor complete in detail. Rather, these are potential classifications that may provide, with further development, a hierarchical structure for a more comprehensive system that explicates the commonalities and differences within and across popular culture phenomena. Recall that the purpose of this paper is to seek more objective study of popular culture by providing a descriptive framework upon which to build.

It may also be worthwhile to speculate on the developmental or longitudinal nature this taxonomy suggests. Many popular culture phenomena start as an internal process within one person and eventually expand to include individuals involved in the roles posited above. Early in his career,

Steven Spielberg played multiple roles as he wrote, directed, and marketed his films. Today he neither writes reviews of his movies, which appear in national syndication, nor does he personally arrange for his films to be shown in the various theaters across the world. Additionally, his role as interpreter, although important to him personally, is trivial in establishing the popularity of his material compared to the millions of people who attend his movies but do not write critical reviews or arrange for the film to be booked in the local movie house. Equally important at this level, the gain or loss of millions of dollars may be contingent on the agent getting the Spielberg movie to the right locations at the right times with the proper modifications of the generated product (e.g., audience testing). And the critic's readership is not dependent on whether she personally likes or dislikes the movie, but upon the degree to which her anticipated interpretation of the movie matches that of the person reading the critical review.

If these complexes do indeed reflect realistic qualitative and developmental differentiations, then popular culture study may be able to initiate advances in its ability to categorize and understand what music, visual arts and other forms of popular culture have in common and what truly discriminates one from another.

Methodology and Focus

If we can accept that these complexes are reasonable and potentially fruitful organizational tools, then we must explore the details of this taxonomy further. One aspect that is instrumental to this exploration concerns the mechanism by which differentiation occurs. Is there some common causal factor that determines when a given cultural event is transformed?

If we consider what occurs at each juncture of differentiation in the proposed complexes, at least one common causal factor is apparent: an increase in the number of interpreters. This increase may be the result of the generator's pursuit of a purposeful goal of expanding the number of interpreters or it may be a serendipitous event which no one can explain. Regardless, the increase in the number of interpreters is a necessary and often sufficient cause for a transition to another taxonomic category. Something happens within the potential or actual interpreter which makes the generated product more sought after, more valued.

Thus, the interpreter role is a key focus for the proposed taxonomy. In fact, the central position of the interpreter may have a recursive feature. In every case a central activity of the persona carrying out the role in that category concerns the function of interpretation. The generator, for instance, can be considered an interpreter of chosen aspects of the popular culture. The complex permutations which translate these interpretations into a newly generated product are so poorly understood at this point that the bulk of our comprehension is made up of speculation and anecdote (Sloboda, 1985). Nevertheless, it is logical to assert that for popular culture to be generative, that is, for events which occur within popular culture to beget further popular culture events, this interpretive process carried out by the generator is a necessary component of the popular culture creation experience. The interpreter is processing and interpreting primarily the information contained within and pertaining to the generated product. Sources of this information include minimally the generator and the critic.

Keep in mind that the agent and critic, by definition, exist at least in part for external reward which modifies their interpretive process and imparts a distinct characteristic in contrast to the interpretive process of the other personae in the model. More specifically, interpreter response attended to by the agent becomes the "generated product" for the agent. In a similar manner the critic seeks to become a "preter-interpreter" in hopes of legitimately anticipating the response of the intended interpreter.

Note that in each case, personae involved in carrying out the roles of the model are attending to information. The term "information" is used in the tradition developed by proponents of Information Theory, especially the work of Daniel Berlyne, a pioneer in the empirical study of the psychology of the aesthetic experience. Berlyne (1974) asserts that information is composed of those elements of knowledge which are passed as messages from one individual to another. Adaptation of Berlyne's ideas to our model suggests that the message contains three elements. *Expressive information* is made up of the psychological processes occurring within the person generating the product. These processes can be transmitted to the interpreter in an impressively accurate and reliable manner (Senju & Ohgushi, 1987; Thompson & Robitaille, 1992). *Cultural information* is composed of the social and cultural norms applicable to the generated product and the environment in which the product is generated and/or reproduced. The importance of this type of information was demonstrated in the early 1960s in a study by Etzkorn (1963) which showed that popular music is more characterized by the structure and format of previously successful works and by the cultural and social values of the time than by any sense of artistic innovation. Finally, *syntactic information* is comprised of the characteristics of other elements of the generated product being attended to. Thus, a song in a music video performed by Madonna has multiple elements competing for the interpreter's attention such as choreographed dance and visual dramatic components. If information is a key characteristic for the interpretive process, is there something in the nature of information for a given generated product which gives rise to an increase in the number of interpreters?

According to Berlyne (1971, 1974) there are certain variables contained in the transmitted information of the message which produce optimal neurophysiological arousal, which then produce an increase in preference in the interpreter, which Berlyne terms the positive hedonic value of the event under consideration. This is a crucially important concept. In the proposed model, it represents a central focus for the study of popular culture. Recall that the argument was made earlier that in the evaluation versus no-evaluation debate, the resolution may lie in arriving at an agreed upon evaluation methodology which goes beyond the notion of taking sides. Recall further that it was proposed that such a methodology should be able to co-exist peacefully with other approaches to the study of popular culture without claims of superiority over these existing scholarly modes of study. The concepts and techniques espoused and developed by Berlyne and his supporters, known as new experimental aesthetics, adapted to and in conjunction with the taxonomic model discussed here, offer an avenue toward a potentially successful resolution of the debate.

We should consider the idea of interpreter preference in greater detail if it is to be the theoretical cornerstone and focus of our methodology. Interpreter preference has a long and esteemed tradition of being recognized as a critical aspect of the aesthetic perception of a work in a variety of settings, including movies (Cohen, 1990), theater (Levy, 1988), and music (Lewis, 1975; Smith, 1987). In addition, using interpreters' preferences as the focus of study has important implications outside the purely theoretical or scholarly arena. Regardless of one's opinions about the worth of any particular work, popular culture phenomena have received enormous scrutiny over the last fifty years, recently escalating as increases in claims are made about the influence of movies, music, etc. in criminal behavior. Popular culture events have been imputed as the causes of social change (Welch, 1990), harm to minors (Kennedy, 1990), bigotry (DeCurtis, 1989), suicide (Tannenbaum, 1990) and desensitization toward sexual violence (Donnerstein & Linz, 1986). Who is better equipped than the popular culture scholar to address these issues in a more informed manner? An objective methodology built around sound theoretical principles may provide society with some much needed voices of reason in determining just what effect popular culture has on the general public. New experimental aesthetics adopts such an approach by relying on techniques which seek to employ empirical and objective data collection and reasoned conclusions rather than asserting untested—and untestable—opinions.

Equally important, new experimental aesthetics occupies a distinguishable niche in the academic study of aesthetics which is independent of and complementary to the type of study of aesthetics which current popular culture scholars so ably conduct. Berlyne (1974) points out that the study of aesthetics since Baumgarten's early works in the mid 1700s has branched into several disciplines. Speculative aesthetics depend largely on deduction "from definitions of concepts, from self-evident principles, from generally accepted propositions, [and] from . . . [self contained] beliefs, intuitions and experiences" (2). There are two branches of this discipline, comprised of philosophical aesthetics, which makes "general statements about . . . concepts, terms, and values connected with art, beauty, etc." (3), and art theory, distinguished from the philosophical branch, according to Berlyne, in its greater concentration on individual "works, artists, and styles." A second group of disciplines focuses on the behaviors that are centered on aesthetic works. This branch of study is composed of disciplines separated mainly by their definitive levels of analyses, including psychology, sociology, anthropology and linguistics. Berlyne asserts that an important portion of this discipline is experimental aesthetics, the study of aesthetic behavior under experimental and quasi-experimental conditions.

To summarize, such a focus as the one proposed here then contains the advantage of obviating arguments over who does or does not have the right to judge the worth of a popular culture phenomenon by providing an identifiable, distinctive strand of the study of aesthetics, drawn together by a taxonomic model applicable to a variety of settings. Further, this focus is based on objective, empirical examination of the aesthetic experiences and perceptions of the interpreter of popular culture. We now consider in greater detail how such a methodology can be operationalized and realized.

The New Experimental Aesthetics of Popular Culture

Berlyne (1971) terms his approach new experimental aesthetics, new in the sense that it uses techniques and insights into behavior gained since the early studies in aesthetics were made in the late 1800s. Since the inception of this discipline, an enormous amount of research has been generated studying nearly all genres of artistic expression (Crozier, 1980); and although specific details have been challenged and found in need of development (e.g., Martindale & Moon, 1989), Berlyne's influence and foundational legacy has grown over the years (Cupchick, 1988).

Rather than present Berlyne's techniques in all their complexity and technical detail, it is probably more fruitful to describe the application of these methods on a more basic level. Advanced methods, although more powerful in their sensitivity and ability to detect and identify statistically significant relationships, have enormous potential for misuse and inappropriate application. As Crozier (1980) points out, there seem to be two schools of thought regarding these advanced techniques: "those who, because they have no personal experience with these routines, think they do not have an adequate grasp of what is going on, and those who, because they do have personal experience with these routines, know they do not have an adequate grasp of what is going on" (147). In addition, the disciplinary training in empirical methodology among popular culture scholars is so diverse that advanced methods are best left to that future when an agreed upon research methodology is included in graduate training programs. For now we must begin with a language and method which can readily be communicated, appreciated and applied by anyone with a relative basic foundation in research methods. This is not to say that the more erudite aspects of empirical research are beyond the grasp of the popular culture scholar. But we are embarking on new territory. Until that time when our footing is more certain, basic techniques provide the least ambiguous and most reliable means of pursuing our goals.

Consequently, the bulk of the methods proposed here can be initiated using naturalistic observation, longitudinal case studies, and correlational survey techniques. In like manner, the statistical tests called for here can probably be successfully conducted by those who have mastered basic descriptive statistics and the more fundamental aspects of inferential tests and metrics, such as basic hypothesis testing, linear correlation coefficients, t-tests, multiple regression analysis, and, in a few cases, multivariate tests.

Theoretical Foundations and Operational Definitions

Recall that Berlyne (1971, 1974) implicates the degree of neurophysiological arousal evoked by the information contained in a stimulus as a key element in understanding the aesthetic experience. More specifically, if a person is processing information that produces optimal arousal, then aesthetic preference takes place. Stimuli that do not sufficiently arouse the person, or stimuli that over-arouse the individual, are aversive and not usually preferred by the interpreter of the information. As mentioned earlier, although this concept of arousal as a foundational mechanism has been challenged, there is more than ample evidence supporting its role in understanding the aesthetic experience (see Biaggio & Supplee, 1983).

Berlyne claims that the preference for a given stimulus can be ascertained, and to some degree measured, by considering the detailed components which comprise the multidimensional experience of aesthetic perception. For our purposes we can adopt Berlyne's theory to distinguish two separate but interdependent dimensions: (1) processes which are experienced within and/or expressed overtly by the interpreter, which we shall term *hedonic response* and (2) characteristics inherent in the generated product, the environment, or the interpreter's background and personal characteristics, which we shall call *hedonic modifiers*.

HEDONIC RESPONSE

The pleasure experienced by the interpreter and preference for a given generated product is a multifaceted cluster of internal processes and external manifestations. Adapted from Berlyne, these include the following:

Reward. The interpreter experiences reward whenever s/he experiences any or all of the following conditions:

a) The generated product being attended to elicits increased likelihood of attending to the same or a similar stimulus in the future.
b) Informational elements (expressive, cultural, and syntactic, as described above) are perceived as pleasurable.
c) The onset of the generated product removes or attenuates a source of discomfort in the interpreter.

Attentional/Behavioral Focus. If a generated product is sufficiently pleasurable, the interpreter will make efforts to more fully attend to the product. This may take several forms.

d) Abandonment or reduction of other activities in favor of greater attention directed toward the generated product under consideration.
e) Persistence in attending to or remaining in the presence of the generated product when other sources influence or even compel the interpreter to do otherwise.
f) Intensification of attending to the generated product through increased effort of sensory focus or increases in the intensity or frequency of exposure to the generated product.
g) Reduction of competing sources of attention, through verbal or nonverbal communication intended to indicate that the interpreter does not wish to pursue the other sources of information.

Incentive Value. Whenever the interpreter anticipates/expects aesthetic preference for the generated product, then the interpreter is said to be experiencing positive incentive value. This can be expressed in multiple ways.

h) The interpreter's expected degree of pleasure toward the prospect of future exposure to the generated product.
i) The expected degree to which the interpreter finds similar or related generated products to be pleasurable.
j) The degree to which the interpreter chooses future exposure to the generated product to the exclusion of other stimuli.

HEDONIC MODIFIERS

Berlyne posited that specific recognizable components of a stimulus, the environment in which the stimulus is manifested, and the personal background characteristics of the interpreter can be identified. These components increase or decrease what we have termed hedonic response. He separated these components into three classes of variables based upon their potential for affecting the arousal level of the interpreter and consequently affecting hedonic response.

Psychophysical Variables. These are physical properties or changes in physical properties of a generated product, which result in sensory processing eliciting hedonic response. Extremes (as defined by the interpreter) in these variables tend to produce less positive hedonic response. Intensity effects based on sensory modality could include the following examples.

k)   Visual: presentation or modification of amount of light, saturation of color, amount of and movement in the visual field.
l)   Auditory: presentation or modification of sound pressure level, musical pitch, melodic, harmonic, and rhythmic aspects.
m)   Tactile: alterations of pressure at various body locations, changes in ambient temperature.
n)   Chemical: changes in taste or olfaction in terms of more saturated taste and/or smell environment, increases or decreases in food temperature.
o)   Kinesthetic: changes in speed or direction of movement, scope of movement, orientation in three dimensional space.

Ecological Variables. These are components of the stimulus that have biological, psychological, social, or cultural importance for the interpreter. As Berlyne points out, the significance of ecological variables is based largely on the meaningfulness of the content of a generated product for the interpreter. Meaningfulness, however, is exceedingly difficult to determine for groups of people because it is a variable that is extremely sensitive to individual differences. The professional concert musician possesses an impressively complex store of musical knowledge from which to derive meaning compared to the typical fourteen-year-old aspiring rock guitarist. This difficulty dictates that we initially deal with ecological variables on the most salient level possible for the greatest possible number of interpreters. Even though this will produce at best a gross measure and understanding of ecological variables, it is a reasonable departure point for more sensible detailed study in the future. It might be useful at the outset then to locate individual interpreters along the following dimensions:

p) *Gender.* Regardless of whether one is a proponent of nature or nurture in explaining gender differences, differences undoubtedly exist, although the degree of difference is debatable if not miniscule in some instances (Wade & Tavris, 1993). Nevertheless, studies of response to popular music, for example, have shown that males and females attend to different aspects of popular culture experience and respond differently to the same aspect of the experience (Zillman & Mundorf, 1987).

q) *Age.* It is self-evident that age affects the experience of popular culture, but beyond this tautology, systematic study of the nature and etiology of these effects is sparse. There is room for speculation, however, based on research on the effects of aging on information processing ability. It has been well documented that advanced age is associated with increased generation of random neurological activity (Holding, 1981) which would suggest that increases in age might produce an increased preference for reduced rate and intensity of information in order to avoid overload. If this is the case the increase in neurological arousal may explain why some older individuals prefer music which they characterize as less "noisy." This preference can be contrasted with the adolescent who possesses presumably more efficient and less noise ridden neurological structures and processes. At any rate, age is certainly an important factor in the aesthetic experience of popular culture and is deserving of more detailed study.

r) *Experience.* Independent of age and ability, experience is an important influence on the meaningfulness of a generated product and the subsequent hedonic response (Biaggio & Supplee, 1983). This is demonstrated in a very transient manner if one follows the track of popularity of any charted song. Initial exposure may produce negative or at best neutral response to the song. Repeated listening then produces increased liking, as the initially aversive over-arousal gives way to some level of predictability. (See the discussion of predictability below.) For a time the song is highly preferred until over-exposure produces too much predictability and under-arousal which then lowers preference.

s) *Socioeconomic Status.* The social and economic status of the interpreter has been found to produce markedly different responses to popular culture experiences (Frost & Stauffer, 1987). This variable is also influential in determining working and leisure conditions, friendship and relationship patterns, education, and myriad other factors which affect the experience of popular culture.

t) *Race.* Similar to SES, race also appears to be a significant determinant in the meaningfulness of a given popular culture experience (Brown and Schulze, 1990). Persuasiveness is clearly a function of similarity between the communicator and the recipient, which would partially explain the popularity of ethnic or racially identifiable music with persons of like nationality and ethnic origin, but the popularity of cultural experiences which are not consistent with the interpreter's characteristics (middle-class white adolescents enamored with gangsta' rap) is more difficult to understand. Future study on the effect of race/ethnic origin on the popular culture experience should be undertaken to grasp more fully its significance.

u) *Expertise.* Expertise is different from experience in that expertise refers to ability and mastery in a given area while experience can denote mere frequency of exposure with no concomitant changes in abilities. Smith (1987) has confirmed that meaningfulness for experts comprises different considerations than those of novice or naive individuals.

v) *Socio-cultural Factors.* This cluster of influences is less definitive than the previous variables, in part because it is often a self-defined variable. A middle-class white interpreter may decide that Buddhist religious chants produce heightened hedonic response without ever being exposed to Buddhist religion or culture. In addition, the heterogeneity of cultures and ethnic backgrounds existing in any single industrialized country or region have blurred the meaning of popular culture experiences for large numbers of people. For the purposes of studying popular culture we can only note at this stage that this influence is prevalent, but more pilot work must be done in this area to accurately define and identify how these factors can be incorporated in our model.

w) *Personality.* In addition to the above "grouping" variables, individual differences among interpreters exercise considerable influence on the meaningfulness of popular culture material. Many personality psychologists recognize five traits which affect a person's behavioral repertoire: extraversion, emotionally stability, agreeableness, conscientiousness, and cultural sensitivity (Gleitman, 1992). The variable which may have the most important implications for our model is the dimension of extraversion-introversion as proposed by personality researcher H. J. Eysenck (1967). This characteristic is determined by the normal basal arousal level of a person's neurological and biological systems. People who have overactive or oversensitive systems seek to lower their arousal level through engaging in behaviors and exposing themselves to stimuli which we characterize as introverted. Those who have systems which are lower than the optimally preferred level conversely seek to increase arousal through behaviors we call extraverted. In order to more fully understand the variation of meaningfulness across individuals of popular culture, these factors, especially introversion-extraversion, must be taken into account.

Collative Variables. The final group of variables to consider comprises what Berlyne calls collative variables. These factors "involve comparison, and thus response to degree and nature of similarity or difference, between stimulus elements that may be present together or at different times" (Berlyne, 1971, 141). From Berlyne's perspective, these comparisons vary along four dimensions in terms of their arousal modifying properties. For each of these dimensions, excessive amounts can produce over-arousal which produces lowered positive hedonic response. On the other hand, too little of the dimension under consideration can be under-arousing, again resulting in reduced positive hedonic response. It should be kept in mind that the experience of optimal arousal from external sources is not likely to be a fixed point for any one individual but rather a dynamic range which shifts with the internally generated level of arousal. In other words, if the interpreter is experiencing low arousal internally s/he may experience a particularly intense and relatively novel piece of music with a positive hedonic response. Under different circumstances the same person, possibly having been through previously stressful experiences, may find the same piece to be over-arousing and thus lower in positive hedonic response.

x) *Novelty.* Berlyne notes that novelty is relative rather than absolute. That is, novelty is a function of a comparative process in which we constantly monitor existing manifestations of a generated product against previous or other related manifestations. There are two classifications of novelty. *Short-term novelty* involves the degree of similarity or difference in the elements of a stimulus during the "moment" of experience. *Long-term novelty* occurs when this comparison is conducted between what is being experienced now and the same or related experiences in the past, more than 24 hours previous.

y) *Predictability.* The expectations generated by inherent characteristics of a stimulus have a profound effect on the interpreter's hedonic response. The degree to which an interpreter can predict what is going to happen is so effective, entire genres of cultural expression, such as mysteries or suspense novels, have been constructed around it. Berlyne identifies three distinguishable forms of predictability. When a characteristic of a generated product does not agree with what the interpreter predicts then the interpreter is said to be experiencing *surprise.* This is often manipulated across time, for instance when a composer of a musical piece creates expectation through the use of normal musical structure and repetition which is then violated. Or the composer may place musical elements together that do not normally coexist. *Uncertainty* is the same as the everyday understanding of suspense. Uncertainty occurs when the anticipation of several alternative outcomes with approximately equal plausibility is present. Positive hedonic response is evoked by maintaining the interpreter in a suspended but pleasurable level of arousal. *Absence of clear expectations* is the obverse of uncertainty. Interpreters' positive hedonic response is elicited by creating "situations in which no plausible outcome at all can be readily recognized" (Berlyne, 1971, 148).

z) *Complexity.* The greater the number of dissimilar elements a stimulus contains, the more complex it is. According to Berlyne, complexity is manipulated by either creating surprise through embellishment of a central theme or by creating deviations in expected outcomes which the interpreter must maintain in active consciousness for the stimulus to be fully processed or understood.

aa) *Conflict.* Berlyne believes that some form or level of conflict is inherent in all the collative variables. When the term conflict is used separately, however, it denotes the occasion when a stimulus simultaneously produces incompatible responses. This duality is similar to the aesthetic theory proposed by Konrad Lange (cited in Berlyne, 1971) which contends that the aesthetic experience is brought about by the simultaneous similarities and differences between an art object and the reality it relates to. This paradoxical relationship is readily apparent in the use of literary devices, such as simile and metaphor in music lyrics and poetry. Orientation toward the art object produces disorientation toward the reality it represents. But reorienting to the reality produces disorientation toward the art object. Successfully maintaining the optimal level of this alternation is experienced by the interpreter as desirable.

Before the application of these concepts is described, it would be a good idea for the reader to keep several points in mind. First, the taxonomic model and methodology described here are fully recognized as models rather than reality. It is simplistic and arrogant to claim that they contain comprehensive truth. However, as many examples in science and engineering have illustrated, the concept of a model is a useful construct even though it is not reality itself. Models of aircraft are merely simulacra of the real thing. But the insights gained by exposing models to wind tunnel simulations have proved invaluable in understanding the reality. In a similar manner it is hoped that the models and methods proposed here can serve such a worthwhile function.

It should also be recognized that the proposed model is one still under development. Some people may openly disagree even with the notion that popular culture could be subjected to such techniques; and I applaud their integrity. For those who wish to challenge the merit of the ideas contained here, however, I ask only that they test this merit based on empirical and objective argument, rather than on eloquence of opinion. I believe that progress based on this principle is a useful addition to the quantum of scholarly activity in popular culture study.

Sample Research and Implications for the Future

Basing our study upon the proposed taxonomic system and adaptation of Berlyne's new experimental aesthetics, we can now consider how to apply these constructs in a research setting. To embark on this effort is somewhat akin to being placed in the middle of the North American continent and asked how to get to the coast—any coast. There are as many ways to apply these concepts as there are researchers interested and willing to pursue the ideas discussed here. To provide some initial heading, some foundation for application, it might be useful to give an example of how such a study might be undertaken. The example used here will be that of a proposed study of popular music. The level of analysis is the artist's corpus of work, so participants in this study should be asked to focus on the general generated product of the artist rather than on any particular song or performance. Further, let us assume that the generated product has been determined to belong to the exclusive-roles category according to the process described below.

Taxonomic analysis. We first must address the issue of taxonomic categorization. Until greater understanding is gained, initial categorization methods should be gross, flexible and tentative, but as reliable as is practical. A useful metric to determine agreement about whether a given generated product belongs in a given category is to derive a measure of inter-rater reliability, obtained by first identifying a number of judges, then having them complete a standardized instrument which allows for unequivocal categorization of the product.

An instrument such as the Taxonomic Categorization Flowchart (see Figure 5) could be used for such a purpose. This approach has the advantage of being brief, accessible in concept even to nonprofessional popular culture scholars, and requiring straightforward yes or no responses that are the least ambiguous in interpretation.

A minimum of 75 percent agreement (e.g., 3 out of 4 judges should agree on the categorization of the generated product under consideration) should be a reasonable threshold for the categorization process to be reliable. This simple percentage method for determining reliability under these conditions is a well-established practice among behavioral researchers (Leary, 1991).

Interpreter analysis. Earlier it was mentioned that, at least theoretically, each of the role personae in the taxonomic model actively pursued the interpretive process. Theoretically then, analysis of interpretation should be

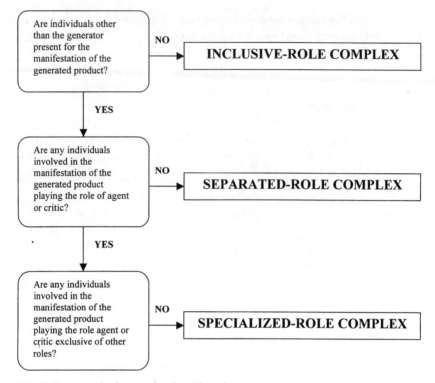

Fig. 5. Taxonomic Categorization Flowchart

achievable for all roles. However, to maintain clarity of focus at the outset and to avoid undue complexity, it may be most instructive to consider only the interpreter's role as described earlier which focuses primarily on the generated product. With further research and verification of the model, similar analyses can be conducted on the other roles. Moreover, the activities and influences involved in the interpreter role may be definitive for the other roles, which suggests that it is the natural beginning point for our research efforts. This allows for more fruitful expansion in the future.

The Interpretation Analysis Survey (IAS) contained in the Appendix is an instrument which can be used to study the hedonic response of the interpreter and the hedonic modifiers which the interpreter attends to. There are several methods for administering the IAS. The most obvious would be a paper and pencil format given individually or in groups to randomly selected interpreters (assuming the researcher wants to generalize to the population at large which the sample represents). The researcher may also choose to use the items on the survey in an interview process. This would ensure clearer interpretation of responses (e.g., the subject could ask for clarification when confused) and the problems encountered by the interviewer could be used to modify and revise the instrument. On the other hand, the potential always exists in an interview that the subject may be less than honest in his responses to avoid embarrassment or to attempt to beneficially impress the interviewer.

Another possibility for administration would be a computer-based instrument that is completed at a computer terminal by the subject. This technique has the advantages of maximizing honesty (there's no one to be embarrassed before or to try to impress), of giving more control of survey completion through visual prompts when responses are missing or inappropriate, and of efficient real-time data analysis.

Elements of hedonic response and hedonic modifiers are in parentheses after each survey item on the IAS in order to show how that item relates to the theoretical construct it addresses. Actual instruments would not include this information. The numbering/lettering system of these elements is identical to that used in the text of the paper. Measures of introversion-extraversion can easily be obtained by using any of the well-developed personality tests that assess this variable. Psychophysical variables are beyond the scope of this survey, requiring more technical instruments, which usually must be used in a controlled lab setting and are probably incompatible with naturalistic studies. As nonintrusive devices are developed in the future, they may be more readily employed.

In conclusion, what specific questions could be appropriately addressed using these instruments? We must come full circle to the concepts originally discussed. Recall that the position of this paper is that the study of popular culture could benefit from an empirical effort that seeks to identify objectively and *describe* the important characteristics of popular culture. There at least four research questions which need to be asked and studied to pursue this goal.

1. Is the taxonomic model valid? Can it be used reliably in a systematic manner which allows for exhaustive categorization within a given popular culture genre? This question will best be answered over time in multiple applications. It is a critical one to be asked and successfully resolved if this model is to have any utility and longevity.
2. What are the important characteristics of hedonic response and hedonic modifiers within taxonomic categories?
3. What reliable differences and commonalities in hedonic response and hedonic modifiers exist across taxonomic categories, especially when considering a specific popular culture genre?

4.   Which popular culture genres can be successfully studied using the model and the instruments proposed here? An obvious area to be addressed first would be popular music, which lends itself naturally to the ideas discussed here, but how applicable are these ideas to other expressions? If they can be applied to different popular culture genres, are the same variables identified in the previous questions relevant?

These questions do not exhaust the possibilities. One mark of a useful model is the generative quality it possesses which allows others to produce testable hypotheses. But these questions represent a reasonable starting point. More issues will surely arise with continued research and interest in the fertile field which is plowed and traversed by the popular culture scholar. It is my hope these ideas may provide some seeds from which new fruit may come forth.

Appendix

INTERPRETER ANALYSIS SURVEY

Directions. As you answer each of the questions below, please think about the musical material of {*identify artist here*} . Do not think about any particular musical piece or performance event but rather your general opinion of the artist's work. Please be as honest as possible. DO NOT put your name on this survey or identify yourself in any other way. All your responses will be kept confidential.

Please answer the questions in this space to provide us with some information about you. We encourage you to answer all questions as honestly as possible. Remember that all responses are confidential. For each question, the information pertains to you; or, in the case of income, to your family if you live with relatives.

1. Age _____ (ecological.b)   2. Gender: Male ❏   Female ❏ (ecological.a)

3. Your (or your family's) yearly net income. Please check one only. Estimate if you are not certain.(ecological.d)
   - ❏ less than $20,000
   - ❏ $20,000 - $30,000
   - ❏ $30,000 - $40,000
   - ❏ $40,000 - $50,000
   - ❏ $50,000 - $60,000
   - ❏ $60,000 - $70,000
   - ❏ $70,000 - $80,000
   - ❏ $80,000 - $90,000
   - ❏ $90,000 - $100,000
   - ❏ greater than $100,000

4. Race (ecological.e)
   - ❏ African-American
   - ❏ Hispanic
   - ❏ Native American
   - ❏ Asian-American
   - ❏ White
   - ❏ Other (_____)

5. How familiar are you with this artist's work? Place a check beside the most appropriate category. (ecological.c)
   - ❏ not familiar at all
   - ❏ slightly familiar
   - ❏ moderately familiar
   - ❏ very familiar

6. What type(s) of music do you like to listen to? Check as many items as are appropriate.(ecological.c)
   - ❏ Adult contemporary
   - ❏ Alternative
   - ❏ Classical
   - ❏ Country
   - ❏ Folk
   - ❏ Heavy metal
   - ❏ Other: _____
   - ❏ Jazz
   - ❏ New age
   - ❏ Pop
   - ❏ Urban Hip Hop
   - ❏ Religious
   - ❏ World music

7. Indicate your general musical abilities, regardless of instrument, by circling the appropriate number. Please circle only one item. (ecological.f)

No musical ability	Slight musical ability	Moderate musical ability	High musical ability	Virtuoso musical ability
1	2	3	4	5

8. How likely are you to do the following in the future? Circle one appropriate number for each item. (reward.a)

	Not likely at all	Slightly likely	Moderately likely	Very likely	Certain
a. Listen to the artist's material	1	2	3	4	5
b. Watch videos of the artist's material	1	2	3	4	5
c. Purchase the artist's recorded material	1	2	3	4	5
d. Purchase other products relating to the artist	1	2	3	4	5
e. Attend the artist's live performances	1	2	3	4	5

9. Below are some aspects of your experience of the artist's material. Please indicate how pleasurable each of these aspects is to you by circling the appropriate number beside that item. Circle only one number for each item. If you are unfamiliar with any item, place a check beside that item in the left hand column and go on to the next item. (reward.b)

Not familiar		Not pleasurable at all	Slightly unpleasurable	Neutral	Slightly pleasurable	Very pleasurable
❑	a. The artist's personality	1	2	3	4	5
❑	b. The emotions you perceive in the artist when you attend to the artist's material	1	2	3	4	5
❑	c. Others' perceptions and reactions to the artist and/or the artist's material	1	2	3	4	5
❑	d. The behavior of the artist during live performances.	1	2	3	4	5
❑	e. The environment and circumstances in which you usually experience the artist's material.	1	2	3	4	5

10. Below are some emotional states we sometimes experience. For each state indicate how likely you are to expose yourself to the artist's material when you feel that emotion by circling the appropriate number to the right of that item. Circle only one number for each item. (reward.c)

	Not likely at all	Slightly likely	Moderately likely	Very likely	Certain
f. Sad	1	2	3	4	5
g. Bored	1	2	3	4	5
h. Stressful	1	2	3	4	5
i. Relaxed	1	2	3	4	5
j. Happy	1	2	3	4	5
k. Uncomfortable	1	2	3	4	5
l. Excited	1	2	3	4	5

11. When you are involved in an activity unrelated to the artist and unexpectedly have the opportunity to be exposed to the artist's material, how likely are you to stop what you are doing, if you have the ability to do so, and attend to the artist's material? Circle the single most appropriate number. (attentional/behavioral.a)

Not likely at all	Slightly likely	Moderately likely	Very likely	Certain
1	2	3	4	5

12. When you are listening to, watching or otherwise attending to the artist, how important must an interruption be to cause you to stop attending to the artist and attend to the interruption? Circle the single most appropriate number. (attentional/behavioral.b)

Not important at all	Slightly important	Moderately important	Very important	Critically Important
1	2	3	4	5

13. If you were not involved in any other required activities and were attending to the artist's material, how much of your attention would you typically focus on the material? Circle the one number (percentage) which is most appropriate. (attentional/behavioral.c)

0%	10%	20%	30%	40%	50%	60%	70%	80%	90%	100%

14. If you were listening to, watching, or otherwise attending to the artist, and other people attempted to talk with you or otherwise get your attention, which of the following would you most likely do? Place a check beside the single item that is most correct. (attentional/behavioral.d)

☐ Interact fully with the person(s) wanting my attention.
☐ Mostly interact with the person(s) wanting my attention, but indicate the desire to attend to the artist's material.
☐ Partially interact with the person(s) wanting my attention, and partially attend to the artist's material showing no preference either way.
☐ Indicate verbally or otherwise the desire to attend to the artist's material rather than interact with the person(s).
☐ Totally ignore the other person(s) wanting my attention.

15. When you think about listening to, watching, or otherwise attending to the artist's material in the future, how much pleasure do you anticipate? Circle the one number most appropriate. (incentive value.a)

High displeasure	Slight/moderate displeasure	Neutral	Slight/moderate pleasure	High Pleasure
1	2	3	4	5

16. How pleasurable in your opinion are other artists who seem similar to the artist under consideration? Circle the one number most appropriate. (incentive value.b)

High displeasure	Slight/moderate displeasure	Neutral	Slight/moderate pleasure	High pleasure
1	2	3	4	5

17. How likely would you be to listen to, watch, or otherwise attend to the artist under consideration if you had the opportunity to listen to, watch, or otherwise attend to the following? Circle the most appropriate number for each item. (incentive value.c)

	Not likely at all	Slightly likely	Moderately likely	Very likely	Certain
a. Another artist with similar material	1	2	3	4	5
b. Another artist with different material	1	2	3	4	5
c. Some activity not related to the artist	1	2	3	4	5

18. Think of the typical material by this artist you listen to, watch, or otherwise attend to. Within a typical piece, how similar or different are the parts within that piece? Place a check beside the single most appropriate category. If you are not familiar with the artist, place a check beside that category. (collative.novelty)

☐ Not familiar with the artist.
☐ Very similar throughout the piece with almost no changes.
☐ Mostly similar with some changes in the piece.
☐ Equally similar and changing within the piece.
☐ Mostly changing with some similarities in the piece.
☐ Changes greatly throughout the piece with almost no similarities

19. As you have been exposed to the artist's material over time, how similar or changing does the material typically seem to you? Place a check beside the single most appropriate category. If you are not familiar with the artist, place a check beside that category. (collative.novelty)

☐ Not familiar with the artist.
☐ Very similar over time with almost no changes.
☐ Mostly similar with some changes over time.
☐ Equally similar and changing over time.
☐ Mostly changing with some similarities over time.
☐ Changes greatly over time with almost no similarities

20. When you listen to, watch, or otherwise attend to material by the artist which you have not previously been exposed to, typically how predictable are the various parts of the piece? Place a check beside the single most appropriate category. If you are not familiar with the artist, place a check beside that category. (collative.predictability)

☐ Not familiar with the artist.
☐ Highly predictable with almost no surprises.
☐ Mostly predictable with some surprising elements.
☐ Equally predictable and surprising.
☐ Mostly surprising with some predictable elements.

☐ Very surprising with almost no predictability.

21. When you listen to, watch, or otherwise attend to typical material by this artist, how complex is the material in your opinion? Place a check beside the single most appropriate category. If you are not familiar with the artist, place a check beside that category. (collative.complexity)

☐ Not familiar with the artist.

☐ Very complex, not simple at all.

☐ Mostly complex with some simple elements.

☐ Equally complex and simple.

☐ Mostly simple with some complex elements.

☐ Very simple, not complex at all.

22. When you listen to, watch, or otherwise attend to typical material by this artist, how much conflict versus peacefulness do you perceive? Place a check beside the single most appropriate category. If you are not familiar with the artist, place a check beside that category. (collative.conflict)

☐ Not familiar with the artist.

☐ Almost total calm, no sense of conflict at all.

☐ Mostly calm with some conflict.

☐ Equal senses of calm and conflict.

☐ Mostly conflict with some sense of calm.

☐ Almost total conflict, no sense of calm at all.

References

Aron, A., and E. N. Aron. (1994). *Statistics for Psychology.* Englewood Cliffs, NJ: Prentice Hall.

Benjafield, J. G. (1992). *Cognition.* Englewood Cliffs, NJ: Prentice Hall.

Berlyne, D. E. (1971). *Aesthetics and Psychobiology.* New York: Appleton- Century-Crofts.

———. (1974). "The New Experimental Aesthetics." *Studies in the New Experimental Aesthetics: Steps Toward an Objective Psychology of Aesthetic Appreciation.* Ed. D. E. Berlyne. Washington, DC: Hemisphere.

Biaggio, M. K., and K. A. Supplee. (1983). "Dimensions of Aesthetic Perception." *Journal of Psychology* 114: 29–35.

Boorstein, D. (1983). *The Discoverers.* New York: Vintage.

Brehm, S. S., and S. M. Kassin. (1990). *Social Psychology.* Boston: Houghton Mifflin.

Brown, J. D., and L. Schulze. (1990). "The Effects of Race, Gender, and Fandom on Audience Interpretation of Madonna's Music Videos." *Journal of Communication* 40.2: 88–102.

Cohen, A. J. (1990). "Understanding Musical Soundtracks." *Empirical Studies of the Arts* 8.2: 111–24.

Crozier, J. B. (1980). "The New Experimental Aesthetics—The Beginning or the End?" *Motivation and Emotion* 4.2: 143–48.

Cupchik, G. C. (1988). "The Legacy of Daniel E. Berlyne." *Empirical Studies of the Arts* 6.2: 171–86.

DeCurtis, A. (1989). "Music's Mean Season." *Rolling Stone* 567 (Dec.): 14, 15–16.

Donnerstein, E., and D. Lenz. (1986). "Mass Media Sexual Violence and Male Viewers." *American Behavioral Scientist* 29.5: 601–18.

Etzkorn, K. P. (1963). "Social Context of Songwriting in the United States." *Ethnomusicology* 7: 96–106.

Eysenck, H. J. (1967). *The Biological Basis of Personality.* Springfield, IL: Thomas.

Frost, R., and J. Stauffer. (1987). "The Effects of Social Class, Gender, and Personality on Physiological Responses to Filmed Violence." *Journal of Communication* 37: 29–44.

Gleitman, H. (1992). *Basic psychology.* New York: Norton.

Holding, D. H. (1981). "Final Survey." *Human Skills.* Ed. D. H. Holding. Chichester: Wiley & Son. 257–68.

Kaemmer, J. E. (1980). "Between the Event and the Tradition: A New Look at Music in Sociocultural Systems." *Ethnomusicology* 24.1: 61–74.

Kennedy, D. (1990). "Frankenchrist versus the State: The New Right, Rock Music, and the Case of Jello Biafra." *Journal of Popular Culture* 24: 131–48.

Lawrence, J. S. (1978). "A Critical Analysis of Roger B. Rollin's "Against Evaluation." *Journal of Popular Culture* 12.1: 99–112.

Leary, M. R. (1991). *Introduction to Behavioral Research Methods.* Belmont, CA: Wadsworth.

Levy, E. (1988). "Art Critics and Art Publics: A Study in the Sociology and Politics of Taste." *Empirical Studies of the Arts* 6.2: 127–48.

Lewis, G. H. (1975). "Cultural Socialization and the Development of Taste Cultures and Culture Classes in American Popular Music: Existing Evidence and Proposed Research Directions." *Popular Music and Society* 4: 226–41.

Martindale, C., and K. Moon. (1989). "Relationship of Musical Preference to Collative, Ecological, and Psychophysical Variables." *Music Perception* 6.4: 431–46.

Rollin, R. B. (1975). "Against Evaluation: The Role of the Critic of Popular Culture." *Journal of Popular Culture* 9.2: 355–65.

———. (1978). "Son of 'Against Evaluation': A Reply to John Shelton Lawrence." *Journal of Popular Culture* 12.1: 113–17.

Senjee, M., and K. Ohgushi. (1987). "How Are Players' Ideas Conveyed to the Audience?" *Music Perception* 4.4: 311–23.

Sloboda, J. L. (1985). *The Musical Mind: The Cognitive Psychology of Music.* Oxford: Oxford UP.

Smith, J. D. (1987). "Conflicting Aesthetic Ideals in a Musical Culture." *Music Perception* 4.4: 373–92.

Solso, R. L. (1988). *Cognitive Psychology.* Boston: Allyn and Bacon.

Tannenbaum, R. (1990). "Church Assails Heavy Metal." *Rolling Stone* 19 Apr.: 32.

Thompson, W. F., and B. Robitaille. (1992). "Can Composers Express Emotions through Music?" *Empirical Studies of the Arts* 10.1: 78–89.

Wade, C., and C. Tavris. (1993). *Psychology.* New York: Harper Collins.

Welch, R. (1990). "Rock'N'Roll and Social Change." *History Today* 40: 32–39.

Zillman, D., and N. Mundorf. (1987). "Image Effects in the Appreciation of Video Rock." *Communication Research* 14.3: 316–34.

VI.
Popular Culture
and Folk Culture

THE FOLKLORE-POPULAR CULTURE CONTINUUM

Peter Narváez and Martin Laba

Peter Narváez and Martin Laba distinguish popular culture from folklore in terms of how it is transmitted, the "spatial and social distance between performers and audiences," the size of the audience, and the social uses that are made of it; but not by how it is produced, the type of consumer, or its content. Furthermore, pop and folk are two ends of a continuum, along which are found examples/cases that mix elements of both. Narváez teaches folklore at the Memorial University of Newfoundland, and Laba teaches communication courses at Simon Fraser University. Both are not only publishing scholars on popular culture, but creators of mass media programs on popular music. Their edited collection, Media Sense, *contains a number of excellent case studies demonstrating that folk culture can become popular culture and vice versa, or that a given "cultural element" can simultaneously be both folk and popular culture.*

This volume of essays arises out of a growing concern with establishing a folkloristic perspective on contemporary popular culture.[1] As the expression is used here, popular culture refers, in a restrictive interpretation, to cultural events which are transmitted by technological media and communicated in mass societal contexts.[2] Accordingly, the performance contexts of popular culture are usually characterized by significant spatial and social distances between performers and audiences. In contrast to popular culture, folklore performance is artistic performance which is transmitted and communicated by the sensory media of living, small group encounters.[3] The spatial and social distances between performers and audiences in folklore events is slight or nonexistent and there tends to be a high degree of performer-audience interaction. These conceptions of folklore and popular culture focus upon media of transmission and group size rather than on socio-economic class or matters of content. . . .

In keeping with Russel Nye's view "to consider all levels of artistic

Peter Narváez and Martin Laba, "Introduction: The Folklore-Popular Culture Continuum," in Peter Narváez and Martin Laba (eds.), Media Sense: The Folklore-Popular Culture Continuum *(Bowling Green, OH: Bowling Green State University Popular Press, 1986), 1.*

accomplishment as related rather than disparate," artistic communication within small groups (folklore) and mass societies (popular culture) may be understood as polar types spanned by a complex continuum of different sized groups in which communications are transmitted via various configurations of sensory and technological media. . . .[4]

Notes

1. The articles by Martin Laba, Robert McCarl, James Hornby, Neil V. Rosenberg and Martin Lovelace have developed from papers initially delivered at the session on "Folklore and Popular Culture" at the annual meeting of the Folklore Studies Association of Canada, London, Ontario, June 1978. The second essay by Peter Narváez is a revised version of a paper read on the "Popularization" panel at the annual meeting of the Folklore Studies Association of Canada, Ottawa, Ontario, June 3, 1982. Three other approaches to folklore and popular culture are Joseph J. Arpad, "Between Folklore and Literature: Popular Culture as Anomaly," *Journal of Popular Culture,* 9 (1975): 403–22; Donald Allport Bird, "A Theory of Folklore in Mass Media: Traditional Patterns in the Mass Media," *Southern Folklore Quarterly,* 40 (1976): 285–305; Tom Burns, "Folklore in the Mass Media: Television," *Folklore Forum,* 2 (1969): 90–106. For a descriptive classification of regional folklore derived from popular culture, see Philip Hiscock, "The Mass Media in the Folk Culture of Newfoundland: A Survey of Materials in the MUN Folklore and Language Archive," *Culture and Tradition,* 8 (1984): 20–38.

2. The association of contemporary popular culture with the expressive culture of the mass media is common. For example, see Paul M. Hirsch, "Social Science Approaches to Popular Culture: A Review and Critique," *Journal of Popular Culture,* 11.2 (1977): 401–13; Michael R. Real, *Mass-Mediated Culture* (Englewood Cliffs, NJ: Prentice-Hall, 1977), 14.

3. This definition of folklore coincides with that of Dan Ben-Amos, "Toward a Definition of Folklore in Context," *Journal of American Folklore,* 84 (1971): 3–15.

4. Russel B. Nye, *The Unembarrassed Muse: The Popular Arts in America* (New York: Dial, 1970), 420. Another inclusive image of the arts is Ray B. Browne's "flattened ellipsis, or lens" in "Popular Culture: Notes Toward a Definition," *Popular Culture and Curriculum,* Ray B. Browne and Ronald J. Ambrosetti, eds. (Bowling Green, OH: Bowling Green State U Popular P, 1970), 3–11.

THE BOSOM SERPENT

Harold Schechter

Harold Schechter's basic thesis is "that in our high-tech time and consumerist culture, the traditional folk narratives that have provided pleasure to human beings since storytelling began are transmitted to us largely through the popular media." Following Chapter 1, from which the following excerpt is drawn, and where Schechter spells out his thesis, he offers a number of convincing chapter-length studies of modern popular culture that illustrate that thesis. For Schechter, popular culture does not significantly differ from folk culture, except in its manner of transmission. Schechter is Professor of English at Queens College, the City University of New York, and the author of several books on popular culture and cinema.

. . . Popular fiction (a category which includes comic books as well as such "post-Gutenberg"[1] forms as TV soap operas and most Hollywood movies) may therefore be defined as mass-produced art whose primary goal (whatever else it may achieve, intentionally or not, in terms of style or theme) is to reach out to (and into) the widest possible audience by telling a story that triggers a very basic and powerful emotional response: wonder or terror, laughter or tears, suspense or erotic arousal.

This definition, it seems to me, clears up some of the basic confusion that has always surrounded popular culture studies, particularly the problem I began by discussing: the general inability of critics to find cogent ways of distinguishing pop art from high. Efforts to define the former according to standards of popularity, for example (which might, on the face of it, seem logical), are inevitably frustrated by the awkward existence of legions of mass-market paperbacks and Grade-Z exploitation movies that are complete commercial failures—in short that aren't popular at all. The issue, however, isn't the size of the audience that a particular work attracts but the nature of the material: that is, the extent to which it relies on pure story appeal to sell the product to the consumer.

Harold Schechter, The Bosom Serpent: Folklore and Popular Art *(Iowa City: University of Iowa Press, 1988), 7–11, 18–19.*

More importantly, this definition makes it clear that any piece of criticism that evaluates a popular narrative—a Robert Ludlum thriller, say, or a movie like *Porky's* or *Flashdance*—according to criteria appropriated from traditional literary scholarship is inevitably going to make both the work and the critic look unnecessarily bad. The critic, by insisting so emphatically on the seriousness of his subject matter, is bound to come across as someone who protests a bit too much, while the work can only end up looking like decidedly second- (or third- or tenth-) rate art: skillfully constructed, perhaps, but completely devoid of "higher" value. ("Staggeringly inept on any human level," is the way Morris Dickstein puts it in an attack on *The Road Warrior*,[2] as though a stunning feat of storytelling were not in itself a significant human achievement.) By the same token, high art is apt to seem seriously deficient when measured against the standards by which the general public gauges the success of a movie or book. While a film by Eric Rohmer may offer pleasures that cannot be matched by *Rocky IV*, an exciting, action-packed plot isn't likely to be one of them—and the fan of Sly Stallone who finds himself sitting (no doubt against his will) through *My Night at Maud's* has some justification for feeling that he's watching a movie in which, as far as he's concerned, "nothing happens."

What all this suggests is that it may be time to start looking at pop art in a different light—not as a primitive, rudimentary form of "real art" (as though Harold Robbins, say, were a kind of literary Neanderthal on a ladder of aesthetic evolution whose highest rung is represented by the late novels of Henry James) but as part of an age-old tradition of popular or communal storytelling, a form of fiction which, in spite of superficial similarities to serious art (both *The Carpetbaggers* and *Wings of the Dove* have characters and plots and can be purchased in either clothbound or paperback editions), actually bears a much closer resemblance to folklore.

The relationship between folklore and popular art has been noted by a number of critics and scholars. In his classic 1934 essay "Style and Medium in the Motion Pictures," for example, Erwin Panofsky examines the "folkloristic" background of the movies and shows how, by appealing to the mass audience's taste for "sentiment, sensation, pornography, and crude humor," pop films continue to reflect a "folk-art mentality."[3] Leslie Fiedler, too, though he reserves the term "folk literature" for the story and song "of pre-literate society,"[4] clearly perceives an affinity between the two types of narrative, popular and folk. One of the defining characteristics of the former, he points out, is a certain anonymous quality that is also characteristic of folklore. Like fairy tales and legends, popular fiction is distinguished by a special kind of immortality: what remains alive is not the language of the original text or even the name of the creator but simply the story itself:

As a matter of fact, one of the distinctions between popular and high literature can be made on the basis of this, as Edgar Allan Poe, in a review of James Fenimore Cooper, pointed out. There is a certain kind of book, he wrote, which is forgotten though its author is remembered (High Literature); and there is a certain kind of book whose author is forgotten though the work is remembered. And it is indeed true, isn't it, that at the present moment there are far more people who can identify Hemingway than can identify Lt. Henry or Jake Barnes; while Sherlock Holmes is a familiar name to many people who have never heard of Conan Doyle. And the name of Tarzan is known to everyone in the world, including those who never heard of the name Edgar Rice Burroughs.[5]

Interestingly, Burroughs himself seems to have understood the anonymous nature of his art, proclaiming at the very start of *The Land That Time Forgot,* "Read page one and I will be forgotten," a striking confirmation of Poe's idea that, in the realm of pop literature, it is only the story that matters.[6]

On the whole, specialists in folklore have been somewhat more alert than pop culture critics to the connections between the two fields. Though certain folklorists, such as MacEdward Leach, condemn modern "mass culture" as completely destructive of "folk song and story,"[7] others recognize a more complex and vital interplay between traditional, oral legendary and the media. Writing in 1968, for example, German scholar Hermann Bausinger argued that industrialization has not meant "the end of . . . folk culture" but rather its "mutation and modification,"[8] a point of view shared by American folklorist Linda Dégh, who, in an influential 1971 essay, called on her colleagues to "expand their field of exploration . . . beyond the 'folk' level to identify their material as it blends into mass culture."[9]

Perhaps the most clear-sighted effort to pursue Dégh's suggestion is a 1976 study by Ronald L. Baker, "The Influence of Mass Culture on Modern Legends," which examines the reciprocal relationship of pop culture and folklore.[10] "On the one hand," Baker writes, "the products, institutions, and heroes of mass culture have had an enormous impact on the subject matter of contemporary legends," a phenomenon that can be seen in a wide range of "belief tales" from the so-called "Paul McCartney Death Rumor"[11] to such consumerist horror stories as the widely circulated report that Bubble Yum chewing gum is manufactured from spider's eggs or that a child actor in a popular TV commercial died by internal explosion after consuming a pack of Pop Rocks candy then washing it down with a Coke.

On the other hand, Baker continues, pop fiction and music, motion pictures, television, radio, "and other mass media have engulfed and spread a number of legendary themes."[12] Although Baker himself provides only a few examples of this process (a radio version of "The Vanishing Hitchhiker" legend and a scene in a Doris Day movie based on the tale of the "Weekend Camper"), his point is supported by W. M. S. Russell, whose 1981 presidential address to the Folklore Society of London examines the "folktale background" of scores of science fiction novels, from H. G. Wells' *When the Sleeper Wakes* (a version of the "venerable motif of Magic Sleep Extending over Many Years") to Isaac Asimov's *Foundation* trilogy (a scientific elaboration of the Golem legend).[13]

Seeing popular art as a kind of mass-produced folklore—as the form of storytelling that has taken the place of traditional folk narrative in the technological world. . . .

This is not to say, of course, that it is only popular art which has close ties to folk belief. On the contrary, folklore has served as an inexhaustible source of inspiration (and material) for serious artists throughout the ages, and scholarly journals are filled with articles examining the folklore borrowings of writers from Chaucer to Thomas Pynchon, from the *Beowulf* poet to Joyce Carol Oates. The difference between the serious and the popular artist in relation to folklore is that, almost invariably, the former will utilize a folk motif as a way of achieving some larger (frequently thematic) end. As H. R. Ellis Davidson says in an essay on "Folklore and Literature," the "method of the creative writer . . . who makes use of folk beliefs is not to declare his position either for or against them but to use them to suggest various meanings."[14] What we tend to get in popular works, on the other hand, is pure folklore cast, to be sure, in contemporary terms and communicated through sophisticated, technological means, but essentially unmodified. In short, whereas serious art transforms the raw material of folk literature, popular art simply transmits it. For the most part, popular narratives are nothing more (or less) than folk stories: the same spooky or amusing or salacious or cautionary tales that people have always wanted, or needed, to hear.

Notes

1. Fiedler, "Giving the Devil His Due," 199.

2. Dickstein, "Peter Panavision," 21.

3. Panofsky, "Style and Medium," 33.

4. Fiedler, "Giving the Devil His Due," 197.

5. Ibid., 200.

6. Stephen King, who describes it as his favorite statement of the pop writer's overriding commitment to sheer "story value," quotes Burrough's line in his foreword to *Night Shift,* xxi.

7. Leach, "Folklore in American Regional Literature," 395.

8. Bausinger, "Folklore Research," 127.

9. Dégh, "The Belief Legend in Modern Society," 59. In a later essay, Dégh is

even more emphatic, asserting that "it is not enough to acknowledge that mass media has a 'role' in modern legend-transmission. It is closer to the truth to state that the mass media are *part* of folklore." See Dégh and Vázsonyi, "The Dialectics of the Legend," 37.

10. Baker, "The Influence of Mass Culture," 367–76.

11. In his essay "A Theory for Folklore in Mass Media," Bird discusses the "Paul McCartney Death Rumor" as a "multimedia event . . . fusing with folklore processes." See 290.

12. Baker, "The Influence of Mass Culture," 368. Cf. Brunvand's observation that "today's legends are also disseminated by the mass media" in *The Vanishing Hitchhiker,* 3. As early as 1943, a contributor to the *Journal of American Folklore* noted that contemporary folklore "may be viewed as functioning through literature and drama—both of which are recognizable today by their mechanical accompaniments, printed matter and radio." See Smith, "Musings on Folklore, 1943," 72.

13. Russell, "Folktales and Science Fiction," 3–30.

14. H. R. Ellis Davidson, "Folklore and Literature," *Folklore* 86 (1975): 87.

Works Consulted

Baker, Ronald L. "The Influence of Mass Culture on Modern Legends." *Southern Folklore Quarterly* 40 (1976): 367–76.

Bird, Donald Allport. "A Theory for Folklore in Mass Media." *Southern Folklore Quarterly* 40 (1976): 285–305.

Brunvand, Jan Harold. *The Vanishing Hitchhiker: American Urban Legends and Their Meanings.* New York: Norton, 1981.

Dégh, Linda. "The 'Belief Legend' in Modern Society: Form, Function, and Relationship to Other Genres." *American Folk Legend.* Ed. Wayland D. Hand. Berkeley: U of California P, 1971. 55–68.

Dégh, Linda, and Andrew Vázsonyi. "The Dialectics of the Legend." *Folklore Reprint Series* 1.6 (Dec. 1973).

Dickson, Paul, and Joseph C. Goulden. *There Are Alligators in Our Sewers and Other American Credos.* New York: Delacorte, 1983.

Fiedler, Leslie. "Giving the Devil His Due." *Journal of Popular Culture* 12 (1979): 197–207.

King, Stephen. *Night Shift.* New York: New American Library/Signet, 1979.

Leach, MacEdward. "Folklore in American Regional Literature." *Journal of the Folklore Institute* 3 (1966): 376–97.

Panofsky, Erwin. "Style and Medium in the Motion Pictures." *Awake in the Dark.* Ed. David Denby. New York: Vintage, 1977. 30–48.

Russell, W. M. S. "Folktales and Science Fiction." *Folklore* 93 (1982): 3–30.

Smith, Marion W. "Musings on Folklore, 1943." *Journal of American Folklore* 57 (1946): 70–72.

CONTEMPORARY LEGENDS AND POPULAR CULTURE: "IT'S THE REAL THING"

Paul Smith

Paul Smith provides a model for examining "the nature of the relationships between contemporary legends, related beliefs, and the popular, and even elite, cultural aspects" of a popular culture product. Given Coke's vast popularity, surprising range of uses, and complex relationships with a variety of beliefs, it is the perfect vehicle for Smith to illustrate just how varied, frequent, and complex exchanges between folklore and popular culture can be. Smith teaches folklore at the Memorial University of Newfoundland.

That a relationship between folklore and popular culture exists is not in doubt (Arpad 1975: 403–33; Denby 1971: 113–25; Glassie 1970: 103–22; Lewis 1978: 32–64; Narváez 1986a: 1–8; Sonnichsen 1976: 88–95; Truzzi 1978: 279–89). Similarly, the fact that contemporary legends are incorporated into popular culture (Bird 1976: 285–305; Smith 1989: 96–99), and vice versa (Narváez 1986b: 125–43), has been clearly demonstrated. However, the qualitative and quantitative nature of this relationship appears to have caused many problems for researchers over the years. Perhaps this situation is not surprising when we see that folklorists cannot agree on what folklore is all about (Leach 1949: 398–403), or for that matter, how to define contemporary legends (Bennett and Smith 1989: 17–22). Similarly, researchers working in the area of popular culture define their subject matter in many different ways.

For the purpose of this discussion, it is not my intention to propose yet more definitions of folklore, contemporary legend and/or popular culture. Instead, I intend to explore the nature of these complex interactions—with special reference to contemporary legends and related belief systems.

As an initial observation, we need to remember that case studies of specific relationships between contemporary legends and items of popular culture have demonstrated that a highly complex set of direct and indirect

Paul Smith, "Contemporary Legends and Popular Culture: 'It's the Real Thing,'" Contemporary Legend *1 (1991): 123–52.*

interactions, transformations and simulations are in constant and simultaneous operation. By *interactions* I mean the *act* of exchange of information; *transformations* and *simulations,* on the other hand, are the *types of change* which take place during any given interaction.

Although within the corpus of contemporary legends collected to date, we can see and document many examples of complex interactions and changes taking place, the questions must be, how can we unlock such a mass of material, make sense of it, and give it some shape. In order to demonstrate some of the possibilities which exist, I intend to explore here the traditional narratives and beliefs which surround one of the classic popular culture products of the twentieth century—namely Coca-Cola (The Coca-Cola Company 1974; Dietz 1973; Hall 1977: 32–41; Kahn 1950; Louis and Harvey 1980; Oliver 1986; Riley 1946).

In a recent issue of *FLS News,* Steve Roud discussed a range of traditional beliefs about, and applications of, the soft drink Coca-Cola (Roud 1988: 10–11). Roud's brief article and subsequent follow ups (Roud 1989: 11; Bowman, 1989: 2; Robson 1990: 5) built on previous essays on "Coke-Lore" by Michael Bell (Bell 1976: 59–65) and Gary Alan Fine (Fine 1979: 477–82). The pieces taken together demonstrate that Coca-Cola is well entrenched in not only popular culture, but also folk culture.

Having said that, the label "Coke-Lore" in this instance actually stands as a folk-generic term for the lore associated with a whole range of soft drinks. As Steve Roud suggests, "The genre should perhaps be termed 'Fizz-Lore'" (Roud 1988: 10). Regardless, these studies show that Coke-Lore beliefs and narratives fall into many diverse categories covering such issues as health systems (Roud 1988: 10–11); food contamination (Domowitz 1979: 91); corporate dominance (Fine 1985: 63–84); and sex (Bell 1976: 61; Roud 1988: 10)—issues which are also reflected in currently circulating Photocopy-Lore cartoons (see Fig. 1 [Smith Collection 1989: Item 1]) and oral Coke-Jokes.

—What do you get when you cross a frog and a Coke? A Croak-a Cola (MUN 1989)

—What happened to the boy who drank eight Cokes? He burped 7-Up. (Lederer 1988: 6)

—I tried snorting Coke one time, but the can got stuck in the straw. (MUN 1989)

In order to unravel this mass of Coke-Lore, I intend to use a simple model which will highlight the nature of the relationships between contemporary legends, related beliefs, and the popular, and even elite, cultural

Fig. 1. Example of a "fizz-lore" photocopy-lore cartoon.

aspects of Coca-Cola. I have opted to include both contemporary legends *and* related beliefs in this case study for two reasons. Firstly, if I just focused on the relationship amongst contemporary legend and popular culture, I would be presenting a naive view of a complex interaction. In a recent essay I made the observation that narratives of this type do not appear out of the blue. We may call them contemporary legends, but this does not, and cannot, dissociate them from other manifestations of traditional culture. Contemporary Legends are, in part, the product of evolving belief systems which directly influence the narrative content of the tales (Smith 1990: 122). Secondly, I consider that beliefs play a crucial and overlooked part in such networks of relationships. In fact, I would go so far as to suggest that many items we label as beliefs are *mini-encapsulations,* or *digests,* of narratives or potential narratives. As such, they can express ideas about what *did* happen, what *may* have happened, or what *could* happen. In these cases, it would not be all that difficult to present an extended narrative based on any one of these *belief digests.*

Consequently, I feel that when we are examining contemporary legends, we need to consider them as parts of a *cultural complex* which includes both synchronic and diachronic perspectives, and related narratives and beliefs—traditional and otherwise. All these forms are subject to the same types of transformations and simulations as contemporary legends. Likewise, both related narratives and beliefs can provide pathways for interactions and reinforcements for exchanges, amongst contemporary legends and other forms of traditional, popular and elite culture.

To begin this process of exploration, we can set out a simple sequential model of the events which take place during the creation of an item of popular culture (see Fig. 2).

A. *Creation.* Drawing upon some source, be it embedded in traditional culture, popular culture, elite culture, or some unique "invention," the creator devises a prototype.
B. *Duplication.* Identical, multiple copies of the prototype are mass-produced, thereby providing a marketable product.
C. *Marketing*
D. *Sales*
E. *Application.* The product is *used* as per the creator's intentions. However, we also know that popular culture products are *unofficially* used in the areas of folk and elite culture. Similarly, folklore has developed about such products and their *official* and *unofficial* applications. Likewise, elite culture draws upon popular culture products for ideas. Consequently, we need to take these factors into account in our model.

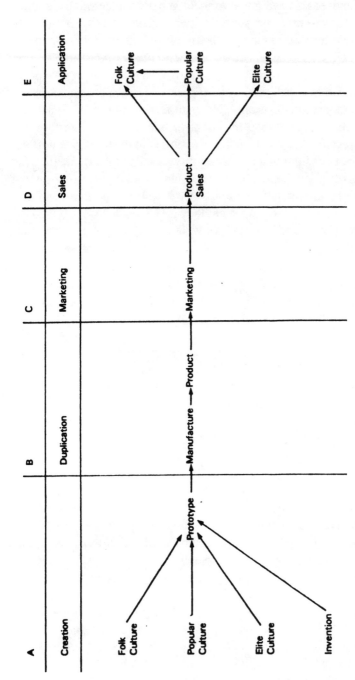

Fig. 2. Sequential model of the creation of an item of popular culture.

Having devised this preliminary model, the next stage was to examine the corpus of "Coke-Lore," and identify specific interactions. Summarized below, these have been added to the initial model using a series of numbered arrows (see Fig. 3).

1. Popular culture draws on traditional health systems to develop commercial health cures. All during the nineteenth century American students and physicians went to Edinburgh, Dublin, or London, to Paris, Vienna, and Berlin for a sound medical education. Benjamin Rush gave this bit of advice to his students: When you go abroad always take a memorandum book and whenever you hear an old woman say such and such herbs are good, or such a compound makes a good medicine or ointment, put it down, for, gentlemen, you may need it (Gebhard 1976: 90).

2A/2B. Traditional health systems and existing commercial cures provide the basis for the prototype of Coca-Cola. Once upon a time, in the days when a snake-oil salesman could still make a respectable living and when every druggist concocted his own syrups for the soda fountain in his store, there lived in Atlanta a druggist named Pemberton. Pemberton sold such patent medicines as Triplex Liver Pills, Globe of Flower Cough Syrup, and 'French Wine Coca-Ideal Nerve Tonic Stimulant.' In 1886 he went into his kitchen and devised a " 'new" proprietary elixir,' a syrup containing extracts from the Andean coca leaf and the African kola nut. By chance, the elixir got mixed with soda water and was discovered to be not just a medicine but a beverage as well (*Consumers' Reports* 1984: 66).

3. The marketing policy of Coca-Cola frequently makes use of traditional images and stereotypes. Mieder has pointed out that for several decades the Coca-Cola Company has made use of proverbial expressions in its advertising. In 1932 the company used "Thirst Come—Thirst Served," in 1948 "Where There's Coca-Cola, There's Hospitality," and in 1963 there appeared "A Chore's Best Friend" (Mieder and Mieder 1977: 311).

That this practice is not at all new is best illustrated by two older proverbial slogans of the Coca-Cola Company: 'All roads lead by Coca-Cola signs' (1925) and 'All trails lead to ice-cold Coca-Cola' (1935). (Mieder 1978: 49)

However, Coca-Cola's use of traditional images doesn't stop at slogans. We are just as regularly bombarded with ethnic and regional stereotypes (Coca-Cola 1944) and images of calendar customs and festivals (Coca-Cola 1954). Likewise, some of Coca-Cola's advertising has even been based on the "Value of Tradition" (Coca-Cola 1988).

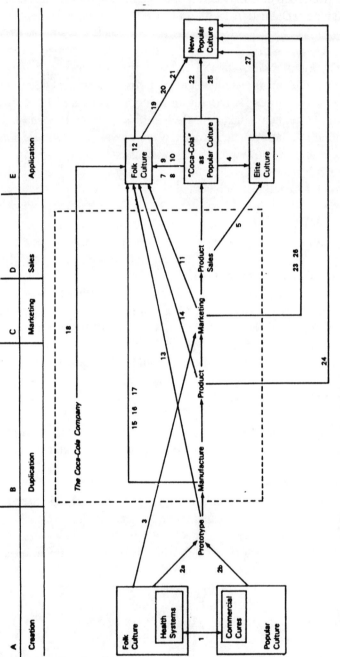

Fig. 3. Interactive model of coke-lore beliefs and narratives.

Such advertising appears to have developed with a change in marketing—moving from focusing on Coca-Cola as a "medicinal" drink, to Coca-Cola as a "pastime" (Dietz 1973: 23–24).

4. Within Elite Culture artists have incorporated Coca-Cola artifacts into their works.

America's pop artists, flamboyant recorders of the commonplace, singled out the Coke bottle as one of their earliest subjects. The first "pop" depiction of the bottle was Robert Rauschenberg's "Coca-Cola Plan," a sculptural construction of 1958 incorporating three bottles. (Gilborn 1970: 23)

This "landmark" in Coca-Cola's history was to be followed by a series of sculptures produced by H. C. Westermann which also incorporated Coca-Cola bottles (Stich 1987: 94–97).

5. Within Elite Culture artists have incorporated advertising images presented by Coca-Cola into their works.

Among other early treatments was Andy Warhol's large canvas of 1962 illustrating 210 Coke bottles. The bottle's unparalleled success as a commercial and cultural symbol (Raymond Loewy called it the 'most perfectly designed package today') is suggested by an egg and a Coke bottle in a still-life painting done for the author by Jonathan Fairbanks. (Gilborn 1970: 23)

In a different vein, Robert Hollander in 1968 published the poem "You Too? Me Too—Why Not? Soda Pop," the text of which was type set in the shape of a Coca-Cola bottle (Hollander 1981: 712).

6. Within Elite Culture artists have incorporated folk narratives and beliefs about Coca-Cola into their works. For example, Thomas Wolfe in his novel, *Look Homeward Angel,* uses such stories and beliefs.

The window on the corner was filled with rubber syringes and thermos bottles. Drink Coca-Cola. They say he stole the formula from old mountain woman [sic]. $50,000,000 now. Rats in the vats. Dope at Wood's better. Too weak here. He had recently acquired a taste for the beverage and drank four or five glasses a day. (Wolfe 1929: 225)

7. Within Folk Culture there have developed alternative uses for Coca-Cola, the beverage. Coke is regularly used as a solvent to remove rust from nuts and bolts, remove rust from chrome work, clean coins, unblock drains and remove old oil from car engines (Bell 1976: 60–61). It has also been used to remove stains from clothing and clean windows, jewelry, and brass (MUN 1989).

It has been suggested that Coca-Cola has other practical properties in that it can be used to remove fingernail polish, revitalize old car batteries, or used instead of battery acid (Bell 1976: 60–61). Similarly, it is said that it can act as a substitute for brake fluid, and when shaken, can be used to inflate balloons (MUN 1989).

Coca-Cola is also seen as having somewhat peculiar medicinal qualities. For instance, it has been reported that Coke and aspirin has been tried as an aphrodisiac (Dickson and Goulden 1983: 34). Likewise, people drink Coke to relieve flatulence, ease a stomachache (MUN 1989), relieve nausea and cure hangovers (Bowman 1989: 2; Kahn 1950: 96).

By far the largest number of beliefs and narratives about the medicinal properties of Coke focus on its supposed contraceptive applications (Fish 1982: 33).

I went to a family planning conference once where all morning we listened to enthusiastic obstetricians talking about the relative contraceptive merits of the Loop, the Pill, the Cap, the Coil and the Headache, but it was over tea and the whole meal digestives that an elderly Dublin GP told me that in pill-prohibited Eire the most popular and effective form of contraception was the Coca-Cola douche. 'Good Heavens,' I said, 'Before or after?' 'Both, to be on the safe side,' she replied. (Arnold 1987: 10)

However, the use of other brands of soft drinks for this purpose is not always recommended.

In one upstate New York village, when a schoolgirl got into trouble and her boyfriend was questioned, he burst into tears and cried, 'It was all the fault of that damned Pepsi-Cola!' It seemed they had been relying on Coke for months in a precautionary way, had none around one romantic night and had switched brands, and were now about to pay the sordid consequences. (Kahn 1950: 158–59)

The contraceptive properties of Coca-Cola have recently been tested. In the experiment the effects of Coke on sperm mobility was compared for "Classic Coke," "New Coke," "New Coke-Caffeine Free," and "Diet Coke." Overall, "Diet Coke" came out as the most effective spermicidal agent (Umpierre *et al.* 1985: 1351).

It is also believed that douching with Coke can be used to terminate a pregnancy.

Many of the abortion methods reported were similar to those used for contraceptive purposes. Girls who fear they are pregnant often douche with soapsuds or detergent, alcohol, Pepsi-Cola or Coca-Cola. (Fish 1972: 34)

8. Within Folk Culture there have developed alternative uses for Coca-Cola containers

The Coke bottle's *raison d'être,* of course, is to serve as a package for a particular liquid, but, with so many of the slim-waisted beauties in circulation, auxiliary uses have inevitably cropped up. During the war, the irrepressible Seabees also converted empties into insulators, and the natives of one of two South Sea islands fancy them as drumsticks. American housewives fancy them as hammers. In many a tempestuous part of the world, Coke bottles have been pressed into service as weapons—a use that Coca-Cola officials do not espouse, or even condone. During Vice-President Nixon's turbulent visit to Venezuela in 1958, the local Coke bottler ordered his trucks to stay off the streets. One company executive has said, 'Coke bottles can be pretty bad in riots. They're such handy, wonderful things to throw.' (Kahn 1950: 158)

A number of accounts identify Coke bottles as an "artifact" in folk beliefs.

In Indiana, you always check the bottom of your empty Coke bottle . . . according to local superstition, if it's stamped from a plant outside the state, you'll soon have an important call, letter, or date . . . (Good Housekeeping 1959: 20)

If a person could peel the label of a Coke bottle without tearing it, it was said that person was not a virgin. If the person tears the label, then it's assumed that they are a virgin. (Morgan and Tucker 1984: 45)

Coca-Cola bottles have also become a functional part of some folk games (Grider 1970: 139–46).

A generation ago [1940s] nearly all Coke bottles had a place name stamped on their base, so that every bottler could send his wares to market in a more or less personalized container. Coca-Cola buffs used to play a game, in fact, called Far Away; the winner was the individual who fished from a cooler or vending machine a bottle with the most remote geographical identification on its bottom. (Kahn 1950: 157)

On an entirely different front, Coke bottles have been recorded as being used as substitute penises by both heterosexuals and homosexuals (Aman 1986–87: 300).

The insertion of foreign objects into the vagina is one of the three most common traditional ways to attempt to induce an abortion (Chamberlain 1976: 113), and, in this respect, the potential of the Coca-Cola bottle has not been overlooked.

I have the impression that most of the girls know of the cruder methods used by the people who perform illegal abortions (many said they had heard of using a long pin or wire), but did not themselves think of using them. The only 'home remedy' I heard involving insertion of an object into the vagina was the use of a Coca-Cola or heated wine bottle to 'create a vacuum and pull out the fetus.' (Fish 1972: 35)

However, it is not just the Coca-Cola bottles *per se* for which alternative uses have been found. The pull-tabs from Coke cans have also been put to new uses, including making clothing, hats, lampshades, and even planters (Patton 1975).

9. *Within Folk Culture there have developed beliefs and narratives about Coca-Cola, the beverage.* For example, it is considered that if certain items are left in Coca-Cola for a period of time, they will dissolve. The list of suggested items which will dissolve is wide ranging and includes: rats, mice, bats, flies, nails, bolts, spoons, wood, hotdogs, steak, bacon and bones (Bell 1976: 60).

While the marketed image of Coca-Cola has always presented the product as "clean-cut, up-right, the family, Sunday, the girl next door, *wholesomeness*" (Hall 1977: 33), this is not always a view which has been reflected in our folk beliefs. While, on the one hand, it is said that to drink Coca-Cola in large quantities will double your energy (MUN 1989), it is also believed that drinking excessive Coca-Cola will make your throat transparent, and your tongue may split down the middle. (Bell 1976: 61). It is also a "known fact" that Coca-Cola can stunt your growth, give you pimples and acne, burn your stomach lining and cause high blood pressure (MUN 1989). It also has been charged that Coke is "a cause of ulcers, cancer, heart disease, sterility and impotence" (Kahn 1950: 98).

It is also believed that Coke mixed with certain other items, if ingested, can have unfortunate side effects. For example, Pop Rocks candy and Coke taken together are seen as a lethal combination which makes your stomach explode (Morgan and Tucker 1984: 68–69), while mixing Coke with spirits of ammonia will make you intoxicated (Kahn 1950: 159)—as will mixing it with aspirin (Bowman 1989: 2). It has even been suggested that the combination of Coca-Cola and aspirin is such a powerful intoxicant, it can kill you (Dickson and Goulden 1983: 34).

Another widespread belief is that Coca-Cola is an addictive drug. The probable source for this belief is simply people equating "Coca-Cola" with "cocaine" (Mencken 1966: 346). This mistake has become further compounded because people also use the terms *Coke* and *Dope* for cocaine (Morgan and Tucker 1984: 65–66), both *Coke* and *Dope* as generic names for soda pop (Davis et al. 1969: 48–49), and *Coke* as a nickname (Campbell 1964: 64), and subsequently a trade name for Coca-Cola (Gilborn 1970: 23).

The original product possibly did have a mild stimulating effect, probably more because of the caffeine it contained than the cocaine (Morgan and Tucker 1984: 66). However, this lingering misconception, that Coca-Cola contains cocaine, also has possibly been fueled by the cloak of secrecy which surrounds the actual ingredients of the drink [see Section 14] (Dietz 1973: 25; Morgan and Tucker 1984: 66).

Possibly one of the most bizarre beliefs to surface about Coca-Cola "the beverage" was reported by Kate Roud.

[Kate] (aged 13) was told by her teacher in a sex-education class (July 1988) that boys might try to tell you that if you *drink* Coke after sex you won't get pregnant, but you mustn't believe them! (Roud 1989: 11)

Here we have Coca-Cola identified as an "oral contraceptive." This belief has probably developed from an erroneous interpretation of the many reports of Coke being used as a contraceptive douche (see Section 7), mixed with the popular beliefs that the oral administration of certain everyday drinks and potions can supposedly induce an abortion (Chamberlain 1976: 112–14; Frankel 1977: 63–65; Gordon 1977: 35–39).

Coca-Cola is also believed to be bad for your teeth—to the extent that it has even been suggested it will dissolve them.

Now I can categorically state that this is not true—I have tried it twice with my daughter's shed teeth. On the second occasion we kept detailed notes. The tooth was placed in the Coke at 9:56 pm on 18th August 1987, within minutes of being shed. At 11:42 am next day, the tooth was still perfectly hard, but a bit brown and sticky. Ten days later, at 6:43 pm, the tooth was still hard but somewhat blacker, and so on until the 31st October 11:17 am when the experiment was terminated—the tooth was completely black, but still hard. The Coke, however, was flat and had developed a hard green moldy crust. We can therefore report that whilst Coke isn't too bad for human teeth (beyond discoloration), human teeth are actually bad for Coke as they turn it green! (Roud 1988: 10–11)

Perhaps the ultimate "Guess what will dissolve in Coca-Cola" story was heard in 1946 in the Philippines. There "a man had fallen into a vat . . .

and had rapidly dissolved" (Kahn 1950: 36). More recently, Fredrick Koenig has researched the same story.

The company spokesman wrote that the rumor about a worker falling into a production vat and contaminating the product is at least 30 years old, and that it recurs periodically in the Far East. (Koenig 1985: 86)

10. Within Folk Culture there have developed beliefs and narratives about the alternative uses of Coca-Cola containers. Alongside the recorded alternative uses for Coca-Cola containers (see Section 8), there exists a set of parallel stories and beliefs.

There are thousands of anecdotes about the role that Coke played in the war—from the bomb runs made over Japanese airstrips using empty Coke bottles as projectiles (Coke runs, they were called); to the auctioning off for charity of a single bottle of Coke for $4000; to planes sent from the combat zone, thousands of miles away, to Australia, where they would fill up with Coke; to Ike specifically ordering that ten bottling plants follow his troops into North Africa. (Dietz 1973: 161)

In addition, there are numerous traditional stories in circulation in which a bottle is used as a substitute penis for female masturbation. Vance Randolph gives one such typical example with the story of "Cora and the Bottle" (Randolph 1976: 191–92). However, stories about the bottle's being used in this way frequently contain warnings that this is an unsafe practice "because the suction thus produced would likely do her physical damage" (Smith Collection 1989: Item 2).

Perhaps the most famous contemporary legend to use the substitute penis theme circulated back in 1921 when Roscoe "Fatty" Arbuckle was accused of the manslaughter of Virginia Rappe. Amongst other things, it was popularly believed that Fatty had ruptured Virginia's bladder by thrusting a Coke bottle into her vagina (Anger 1975: 27–45; [Marr 1987: 4–7]; Yallop 1976). This "sensational" fact was soon on everyone's lips, and although a verdict of innocent was returned, Fatty's career was ruined.

He was banned from films by the newly formed Hays office. Even though the ban was lifted shortly after, outcry from the ministers and women's clubs prevented his screen return. His nightclub act was banned in most cities . . . Even as late as 1973, his films were still officially banned in England. ([Marr 1987]: 7)

Folk beliefs and legends have also grown up about the potential uses of the pull-tabs on beverage cans. These narratives often focus on the erroneous belief that the tabs can somehow be redeemed, and aid can be provided for some ill or needy person (Fine 1986: 208–22). Here we have a situation where a *belief,* be it erroneous, provides the motivation for action.

11. Within Folk Culture artists have incorporated advertising images presented by Coca-Cola into their works. One of the classic examples of this application has to be the gravestone incorporating a picture of a Coca-Cola bottle, discovered by Marcia Gaudet in Maringouin, Louisiana [see Fig. 4 and Section 12] (Gaudet 1989: 3).

12. Within Folk Culture there have developed beliefs and narratives about folk artists' portrayals of Coca-Cola. When researching the gravestone in Maringouin, Louisiana, which had the engraving of a Coke bottle on it [see Fig. 4], Marcia Gaudet was told by the graveyard caretaker that Bertha Arbuckle and her husband (neither of whom was related to "Fatty" Arbuckle) kept the local store. When Bertha died, her husband could not face all the arrangements and the local Coca-Cola representative who supplied their store offered to take care of things. Supposedly the selection of design for the stone was his doing—a "fact" the local Coca-Cola Company appears to know nothing about. This "explanation" for the origin of the design on the gravestone must be contrasted with that given by the deceased's mother-in-law who explained to Marcia that her son had selected this design because

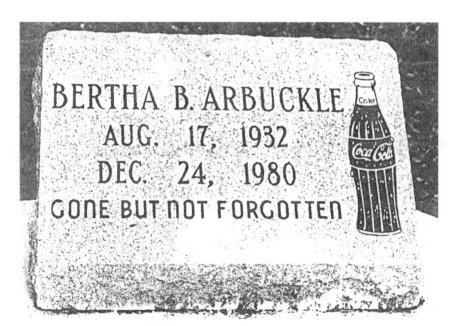

Fig. 4. The gravestone of Bertha Arbuckle, Maringouin, Louisiana. Photographed by Marcia Gaudet.

Coca-Cola was his wife's "most favourite thing in the world" (Smith Collection 1989: Item 3).

13. Within Folk Culture there have developed beliefs and narratives about how the secret recipe for Coca-Cola was first acquired

Some myth-makers ever argue that it was invented by, and stolen from, a Negro slave . . . (Kahn 1950: 56)

14. Within Folk Culture there have developed beliefs and narratives about the ingredients of Coca-Cola. Coca-Cola, not surprisingly, closely guards its list of ingredients, and consequently, a mystique has grown up as to just what goes into the product. As I have already discussed, it has been erroneously believed for many years that Coca-Cola contained cocaine. However, while it is possible to test for the presence of such a substance, the absence of that substance tells us nothing about what it actually does contain. Consequently many alternative suggestions have developed.

For instance, whole tank cars of grape brandy from California vineyards wend their mysterious way to Coca-Cola syrup-making plants. Still another rumor has it that because Woodruff [the President of Coca-Cola] grows peanuts on his plantation, there must be peanuts in Coke. (Kahn 1950: 106)

Unfortunately, not all the suggested ingredients of Coca-Cola are quite so innocuous.

Both Coca-Cola and Pepsi-Cola suffered severely in Egypt eight years ago [ca 1942], when it was alleged that a principal ingredient of all cola drinks was a distillation of the intestines of pigs—animals that are anathema to Moslems. Before the rumor could be scotched, sales of Coke and Pepsi fell off drastically, and when the story was wafted over to Morocco, the reaction was identical. There, for some reason, the libel was directed mainly at Coca-Cola, and a Pepsi bottler took gleeful advantage of this by observing in advertisements that there was no pig's blood in *his* drink. (Kahn 1950: 37)

15. Within Folk Culture there have developed beliefs and narratives about how Coca-Cola became a carbonated drink. In the form originally conceived by Pemberton, Coca-Cola was distributed to soda fountains as a concentrate to which *still* water was added. However, this was soon to change.

On a morning late in 1886, one such victim of the night before dragged himself into an Atlanta drugstore and asked for a dollop of Coca-Cola. Druggists customarily stirred a teaspoonful of syrup into a glass of water, but in this instance the factotum on duty was too lazy to walk to the fresh-water tap, a couple of feet off. Instead, he mixed the syrup with some charged water, which was closer at hand. The suffering customer perked up almost at once, and word quickly spread that the best Coca-Cola was a fizzy one. (Kahn 1950: 56)

16. Within Folk Culture there have developed beliefs and narratives about how Coca-Cola came to be bottled. The most common legendary explanation as to how Coca-Cola came to be bottled (Burnham 1975: 48; Kahn 1950: 69) cloaks this change in marketing policy in humorous intrigue.

There is a terrific legend about Coca-Cola in which some character approaches Candler and demands a sum of money—$50,000 is the amount usually mentioned—for a 'secret' which will make Candler rich. The money is forked over (this is the part that makes it a terrific story) and the man gives Candler the stunning secret: 'Bottle it.' (Dietz 1978: 27)

17. Within Folk Culture there have developed beliefs and narratives about the manufacturing and bottling of Coca-Cola. Probably the classic examples in this case are the alleged contamination stories (Fine 1979). Just on a percentage basis, it is likely that occasionally some foreign object will find its way into a soft drink bottle, and that the manufacturer will be taken to court. For example, in his study "Cokelore and Coke Law," Gary Alan Fine identified that between 1916 and 1976, some 45 cases had been brought before courts in the USA, in which parts of a mouse had been allegedly been found in a soft drink bottle (Fine 1979: 481). Therefore, it is fair to say that some Coke contamination legends may possibly be narratives based on *fact* as opposed to *fiction*.

Having said that, there appears to be an increasing number of fraudulent claims that mice, insects and other foreign objects were allegedly found in drink bottles (Kahn 1950: 91–95).

The [Coke-Bottlers] Association was founded after two bottlers, comparing notes, learned that they had shelled out substantial parcels of hush money to the same woman—a lady who had hit upon the profitable notion of traveling around the country affecting to find frogs in Coke bottles. Since 1937, the Association, with the cooperation of bottlers of other soft drinks, has maintained a roster of people who have been, or purport to have been, egregiously affronted by unwanted objects in their pop bottles. This list, which now harbors a couple of hundred thousand names, indicates that there are a lot of repeaters, and indeed, that whole families exist with no other apparent ambition than to fleece soft drink purveyors by feigning revulsion at their wares. (Kahn 1950: 92)

18. Within Folk Culture there have developed beliefs and narratives about the financial dealings of the Coca-Cola company. As with many companies which have had phenomenal growth and are now well established as market leaders, stories frequently develop about "How I nearly acquired stock in that company for next-to-nothing" (Kahn 1950: 59–60).

Likewise, stories are always surfacing about potential takeover bids.

Lee Iacocca is trying to introduce a new soft drink, to be called Iacocca-Cola, but the Coca-Cola Company has taken legal action to stop him. . . . Lee Iacocca has no plans to enter the soft drink business with Iacocca-Cola or any other beverage, and the Coca-Cola Company has taken no legal action against him. The rumor has become popular among the young set, who presumably like the silly sound of the name, Iacocca-Cola. (Morgan and Tucker 1984: 72)

In a different vein, one persistent belief is that "most foreign Coca-Cola operatives are American spies" (Kahn 1950: 38). This belief is not just confined to Coca-Cola, but is also related about the staffs of many well-known major multinational companies.

19. Within Popular Culture producers have drawn upon folk beliefs and narratives about the alternative uses of Coca-Cola the beverage. In the film *Grease* (1978) the aphrodisiac of Coke and aspirin are alluded to when Rizzo finds that she is pregnant and is telling Marty how it happened:

RIZZO: It wasn't my fault. The guy was usin' a thin, but it broke.
MARTY: Holy cow!
RIZZO: Yeah. He got it in a machine at a gas station. Y'know, one of those four for a quarter jobs.
MARTY: Jeez, what a cheapskate! Hey, it's not Kenickie, is it?
RIZZO: Nah! You don't know the guy.
MARTY: Aahh, they're all the same! Ya remember that disc jockey I met at the dance. I caught him puttin' aspirin in my Coke. (Jacobs and Casey 1972: 52)

20. Within Popular Culture producers have drawn upon folk beliefs and narratives about the alternative uses of Coca-Cola containers. For instance, Coke bottles used as penis substitutes are often found in pornographic films. In the "Teenage Orgy" segment of the composite of short films, *Lolita* (ca 1980), while in a *ménage à trois* (one boy and two girls), one girl uses a coke bottle in her vagina—the other uses it in her rectum.

Echoing the traditional story of "Cora and the Bottle," cited above, in an untitled German feature length film by Ribu Productions, a young woman is masturbating with a Coke bottle when it becomes stuck in her vagina. The female servant who has been watching through the half-opened door calls for a doctor. The doctor proceeds to free the bottle, seduce the young woman with a vibrator, and then both are joined by the male and female servants in an orgy (Ribu ca 1980).

21. Within Popular Culture producers have drawn upon folk beliefs and narratives about the manufacturing and bottling of Coca-Cola. The "I've just found a mouse in my bottle" scenario was central to the plot of the film *Strange Brew* (1983). Here the McKenzie brothers attempted to obtain several free cases of El Sinore beer in return for their silence. Interestingly, an individual who actually attempted a similar hoax has just ended up in prison (Preston 1989: 1–3).

22. Within Popular Culture producers have incorporated Coca-Cola, the beverage, into their products. One obvious area where this occurs is in recipes. *The More Favorite Brand Name Recipes Book,* for instance, gives some nine recipes in which Coca-Cola is an ingredient. These range from "Hungarian Goulash" to exotic "Colombian Fresh Banana Cake with Sea Foam Frosting" (*Consumer Guide* 1984: 105, 251).

23. Within Popular Culture producers have drawn upon the images generated by the marketing policy of Coca-Cola. In the film *The Coca-Cola Kid* (1985), Eric Roberts stars as a young trouble shooter sent into the Australian outback to sort out the Coca-Cola operation. He discovers an isolated valley ruled by a "Soda-Czar" who allows no Coke in his area. Similarly, in *One, Two, Three* (1961) the action is set in West Berlin, where an executive of the company is trying to sell Coca-Cola to the Russians while trying to prevent his boss's daughter from marrying a communist (Grider 1970: 142; Halliwell 1983: 612).

24. Within Popular Culture producers have drawn upon the mystique surrounding the secret ingredients of Coca-Cola. One classic example of this appeared as a double-page illustrated spread in *The National Lampoon Encyclopedia of Humor* under the title "The Secret of Coca-Cola Revealed."

Coca-Cola, originally a medicinal elixir, was once reserved solely for the enjoyment of the holy brethren, but word of mouth spread its fame to the outside world where it quickly caught the popular fancy. . . . To taste it is to return in memory to that tiny French village with its ancient, crumbling monastery clinging to a vine-covered hillside, where all of the world's supply is produced. (O'Donoghue and Betts 1973: 103–5)

While we may smile and think that such a parody is somewhat far-fetched, the following is from an "actual" advertisement for *Norfolk Punch,* a product launched onto the market post-1960.

ORIGINAL OLDE NORFOLK PUNCH is made to a medieval monastic Fenland recipe and includes over eighteen potent herbs and spices pounded by hand in a pestle and mortar and steeped in the natural underground waters of Welle Manor Hall. . . . The ancient formula is kept to as far as possible, even to picking certain herbs at the right phase of the moon and making decoctions, infusions and distillations after soaking in sea water. (*Norfolk Punch* 1987)

25. Within Popular Culture producers have drawn upon the popular image of the universal availability of Coca-Cola. In 1950 *Time* magazine reinforced the popular view as to the ubiquitous distribution of Coca-Cola (Grider 1970: 145) when it featured the product on the front cover with the caption "World and Friend." Inside they carried a story entitled, "The Sun Never Sets on Coca-Cola" (*Time* 1950: 28–32).

This theme of universal availability is also echoed in the science fiction film *Enemy Mine* (1985), "On a distant planet, two beings from warring worlds find themselves stranded. Their only hope for survival is each other . . . if their hatred will give them that chance." (*Movies Unlimited* 1989: 493). Within this scenario, they discover that they are not alone on the planet. The clue? A trail of cola cans wending its way across the rugged landscape.

26. Within Popular Culture producers have drawn upon the advertising images presented by the Coca-Cola Company. By far the most popular image which has been seized upon is the Coke bottle. Currently there is a whole range of products on the market which exploit that image. These include everything from telephones to flashlights, and the Dunhill Confectionery company in Pontefract, Yorkshire, England even produces "Cola Bottles: Cola Flavoured Gums."

Another popular image is the company logo—often packaged as part of some nostalgia item—such as a Coca-Cola Cooler Radio/Cassette Player.

Patterned after the original radio offered to Coca-Cola bottlers in 1949, this Coke brand cooler radio is authentic in every way! Has soft glowing nostalgic dial scale, solid state circuitry, powerful speaker, hidden cassette player and storage for 3 tapes. A recreation with the look of the 50's that everyone loves! By Randix . . . $99.95. (Delta 1989: 16)

By way of a complete contrast, in the cult pornographic film *Deep Throat* (1972) Linda Lovelace, after she discovers that she can only obtain sexual satisfaction by "deep throating" men, goes to work for the doctor who "cured" her. As a "sex therapist," she finds herself on her back on a table, while the patient fills her vagina up from a can of Coke and drinks it via a plastic tube. The segment is introduced with the words, "Things go better with Coke," and into the background comes a voice singing:

> I'd like to try a little trick;
> Please don't think less of me.
> I'd like to drink a little Coke,
> Where you used to be.
> Now, it's the real thing;
> Now lick my straw.
> It's the real thing;
> Now, baby, come and ask for more.

27. Within Popular Culture producers have copied Elite Culture items based on Coca-Cola images. A good example of this would be the many reproductions of Andy Warhol's Coca-Cola paintings which have been reproduced in books and as posters and post cards (Stitch 1987: 92–93).

In working through the model presented in Fig. 2, and inserting the various documented examples of Coca-Cola beliefs and narratives (see Fig. 3), twenty-eight different interactive situations where transformations and simulations have taken place have been identified. In terms of the actual directions of the interactions, these are summarized in Table 1. On closer examination, of these twenty-eight scenarios, in fact only seven distinct types of interactions are apparent (see Table 2).

Having said that, we need to consider just what is the "potential" range and magnitude of possible interactions which could take place. In theory, Folk, Popular and Elite Culture can each act as both "parent" (source) and/or "child" (destination) in any given interaction. Given that, we can tabulate these "potential" exchanges and enter the numbers for each type of interaction already identified in Table 2 (see Table 3).

However, at this stage we need also to consider other values which may be hidden in Table 3. For instance, we need to insert a hypothetical value [X] for the situation when Folk Culture as "source," equates with Folk Culture as "destination." Although we have recorded one such interaction in this dimension (see section twelve), the value [X] must be inserted to reflect that there exists a certain unknown, and often impossible to identify, quantity of folklore material in this corpus which is derived from folklore *per se,* and not from Popular or Elite Culture.

Likewise, we also need to insert a hypothetical value [X] for the situation when Elite Culture, as "source," equates with Elite Culture as "destination."

Table 1
A summary of the directions of the interactions

1:	Folk Culture to Popular Culture
2A:	Folk Culture to Popular Culture
2B:	Popular Culture to Popular Culture
3:	Folk Culture to Popular Culture
4:	Popular Culture to Elite Culture
5:	Popular Culture to Elite Culture
6:	Folk Culture to Elite Culture
7:	Popular Culture to Folk Culture
8:	Popular Culture to Folk Culture
9:	Popular Culture to Folk Culture
10:	Popular Culture to Folk Culture
11:	Popular Culture to Folk Culture
12:	Folk Culture to Folk Culture
13:	Popular Culture to Folk Culture
14:	Popular Culture to Folk Culture
15:	Popular Culture to Folk Culture
16:	Popular Culture to Folk Culture
17:	Popular Culture to Folk Culture
18:	Popular Culture to Folk Culture
19:	Folk Culture to Popular Culture
20:	Folk Culture to Popular Culture
21:	Folk Culture to Popular Culture
22:	Popular Culture to Popular Culture
23:	Popular Culture to Popular Culture
24:	Popular Culture to Popular Culture
25:	Popular Culture to Popular Culture
26:	Popular Culture to Popular Culture
27:	Elite Culture to Popular Culture

Again, this is because there probably exist situations where one artist's work has influenced another—as opposed to two individuals independently looking at Coca-Cola products and advertising, and then going off to create their own unique paintings and sculptures.

It is also apparent from Table 3 that we appear to have no documentations of Elite Culture's providing a basis for Folk Culture material. This "fact" can be interpreted at least two ways. Firstly, there may actually be no interaction in this dimension. Secondly, this situation may be a function of the collection/documentation process (Smith 1985: 45).

Table 2
A classified summary of the types of interactions

1: Folk Culture to Folk Culture	(1)	12
2: Folk Culture to Popular Culture	(6)	1, 2A, 3, 19, 20, 21
3: Folk Culture to Elite Culture	(1)	6
4: Popular Culture to Folk Culture	(11)	7, 8, 9, 10, 11, 13, 14, 15, 16, 17, 18
5: Popular Culture to Popular Culture	(6)	2B, 22, 23, 24, 25, 26
6: Popular Culture to Elite Culture	(2)	4, 5
7: Elite Culture to Popular Culture	(1)	27

Table 3
"Potential" interactions and "actual" interactions

	Destination		
Source	*Folk Culture*	*Popular Culture*	*Elite Culture*
Folk Culture	[X]	6	1
Popular Culture	11	6	2
Elite Culture	0	1	[X]

At this point, the complexity of the relationships amongst Coca-Cola, as a product of Popular Culture, and the various manifestations of "Coke-Lore" is plain. Here, not just "texts" are being exchanged, but instead there are numerous direct and indirect interactions occurring simultaneously. Likewise, a wide variety of transformations and simulations are taking place within each type of interaction.

Similarly, the value of using simple models, such as that presented in Fig. 2, to unlock complex situations is apparent. By exploring the "Coke-Lore complex" in this manner, we have been able to identify where specific interactions, transformations and simulations have taken place. Here, at last, we can see a pattern where previously we had an unstructured mass of narratives and beliefs. Having identified the pattern of interactions, it is a straightforward task to compare the "expected" interactions with the "observed."

In unraveling this corpus of "Coke-Lore," we can see that by far the largest group of interactions occur when Folk Culture draws on Popular Culture—a not altogether unexpected result. However, the overall analysis also shows that in one way or another, the contemporary legends and beliefs recorded to date make comment on *every* aspect of Coca-Cola from its *creation* to its *use*. No part of the process has escaped comment. Likewise, the variety of types of "Coke-Lore" commentary—ranging from the innocuous "It will remove rust," to tales of sex escapades—allows all of us, if we so choose, regardless of our age, sex or social standing, to *become involved* in "Coke-Lore" at a level with which we feel comfortable. And this very aspect of "Coke-Lore" mirrors the ideals and ambitions of the Coca-Cola company itself, in that it hopes to persuade everyone, world-wide, regardless of our age, sex or social standing, to become involved and drink Coca-Cola. As such, *folklore* mirrors *reality* and *reality* mirrors *folklore*. To borrow that well-known phrase—"It's the real thing."

References

Aman, Reinhold. 1986–87. "Kakologia: A Chronicle of Nasty Riddles and Naughty Word Plays." *Maledicta* 9: 269–317.

Anger, Kenneth. 1975. *Hollywood Babylon*. New York: Dell.

Arnold, Sue. 1987. "Sticking Together." *The Observer* 6 Dec.: 10.

Arpad, Joseph J. 1975. "Between Folklore and Literature: Popular Culture as Anomaly." *Journal of Popular Culture* 9.2: 403–22.

Bell, Mike. 1976. "Cokelore." *Western Folklore* 36: 59–65.

Bennett, Gillian, and Paul Smith, eds. 1989. "Introduction: The Birth of Contemporary Legend." *The Questing Beast: Perspectives on Contemporary Legend IV*. Ed. Gillian Bennett and Paul Smith. Sheffield Academic P. 13–26.

———. 1990. *A Nest of Vipers: Perspectives on Contemporary Legend V*. Sheffield: Sheffield Academic P.

Bird, Donald Allport. 1976. "A Theory for Folklore in Mass Media: Traditional Patterns in Mass Media." *Southern Folklore Quarterly* 40: 285–305.

Bowman, Marion. 1989. "Coke-Lore (It's *Not* the Real Thing)." *FLS News* 9 (July): 2.

Burnham, Tom. 1975. *The Dictionary of Misinformation*. New York: Thomas Crowell.

Campbell, Hannah. 1964. *Why Did They Name It . . . ?* New York: Fleet.

Chamberlain, Audrey. 1976. "Gin and Hot Baths." *New Society* 37: 719 (15 July): 112–14.

The Coca-Cola Kid. 1985. Australia: Grand Bay Films International.

Coca-Cola. 1944. Magazine Advertisement.

———. ca 1954. Magazine Advertisement.

———. 1988. Magazine Advertisement.

Coca-Cola Company. 1974. *The Coca-Cola Company: An Illustrated Profile of a Worldwide Company*. Atlanta: Coca-Cola.

Consumer Guide. 1984. *More Favorite Brand Name Recipes Cookbook*. New York: Beekman House.

Consumers' Reports. 1984. The CV Cola Challenge. 49 (Feb.): 66–70.

Davis, Alva L. *et al.* 1969. *A Compilation of the Work Sheets of the Linguistic Atlas of the United States and Canada and Associated Projects.* 2d ed. Chicago: U of Chicago P.

Deep Throat. 1972. USA: Vanguard Films.

Delta Airlines. [1989]. *Delta Flightline Catalog.* Milwaukee: Giftmaster.

Denby, Priscilla. 1971. "Folklore in the Mass Media." *Folklore Forum* 4: 113–25.

Dickson, Paul, and Joseph C. Goulden. 1983. *There Are Alligators in Our Sewers and Other American Credos.* New York: Delacorte.

Dietz, Lawrence. 1973. *Soda Pop: The History, Advertising, Art and Memorabilia of Soft Drinks in America.* New York: Simon and Schuster.

Domowitz, Susan. 1979. "Foreign Matter in Food: A Legend Type." *Indiana Folklore* 12.1: 86–95.

Enemy Mine. 1985. USA: Kings Road Entertainment.

Fine, Gary Alan. 1979. "Cokelore and Coke-Law: Urban Belief Tales and the Problem of Multiple Origins." *Journal of American Folklore* 92: 477–82.

———. 1985. "The Goliath Effect: Corporate Dominance and Mercantile Legends." *Journal of American Folklore* 98: 63–84.

———. 1986. "Redemption Rumors: Mercantile Legends and Corporate Beneficence." *Journal of American Folklore* 99: 208–22.

Fish, Lydia. 1972. "The Old Wife in the Dormitory: Sexual Folklore and Magical Practices from State University College." *New York Folklore Quarterly* 28: 30–36.

Fishwick, Marshall, and Ray B. Browne. 1970. *Icons of Popular Culture.* Bowling Green, OH: Bowling Green State U Popular P.

Frankel, Barbara. 1977. *Childbirth in the Ghetto: Folk Beliefs of Negro Women in a North Philadelphia Hospital Ward.* San Francisco: R and E Research.

Gaudet, Marcia. 1989. "Camera Ready." *American Folklore Society Newsletter* 18.3 (June): 3.

Gebhard, Bruno. 1976. "The Interrelationship of Scientific and Folk Medicine in the United States of America Since 1850." *American Folk Medicine: A Symposium.* Ed. Wayland Hand. Berkley: U of California P. 87–98.

Gilborn, Craig. 1970. "Pop Iconology: Looking at the Coke Bottle." Fishwick and Browne. 13–28.

Glassie, Henry. 1970. "Artifacts: Folk, Popular, Imaginary and Real." Fishwick and Browne. 103–22.

Good Housekeeping. 1959. "The Date Line: Facts and Fancies for the Girl in School." Feb.: 20.

Gordon, Linda. 1977. *Woman's Body, Woman's Right: A Social History of Birth Control in America.* Harmondsworth: Penguin.

Grease. 1978. USA: Paramount.

Grider, Sylvia. 1970. "Bottoms Up: Place Names on Coke Bottles." Fishwick and Browne. 139–46.

Hall, Bob. 1977. "Journey to the White House: The Story of Coca-Cola." *Southern Exposure* 5.1: 32–42.

Halliwell, Leslie. 1983. *Halliwell's Film Guide.* 4th ed. New York: Scribner.

Hollander, Robert. 1981. "You Too? Me Too—Why Not? Soda Pop." *The Norton Introduction to Literature.* 3rd ed. Ed. Carl E. Bain et al. New York: Norton.

Jacobs, Jim, and Warren Casey. 1972. *Grease: A New '50s Rock 'n' Roll Musical.* French's Musical Library. New York: Samuel French.

Kahn, E. J. 1950. *The Big Drink: The Story of Coca-Cola.* New York: Random House.

Koenig, Fredrick. 1985. *Rumor in the Marketplace: The Social Psychology of Commercial Hearsay.* Dover, MA: Auburn House.

Leach, Maria, ed. 1949. *Standard Dictionary of Folklore, Mythology and Legend.* New York: Funk and Wagnall.

Lederer, Richard. 1988. *Get Thee to a Punnery.* Charleston, SC: Wyrick.

Lewis, George. 1978. "The Sociology of Popular Culture." *Current Sociology* 26.3: 32–64.

Lolita. [ca 1980]. Germany: Climax De-Luxe Films.

Louis, J. C., and Harvey Z. Yazijian. 1980. *The Cola Wars.* New York: Everest House.

Marr, Johnny. [1987]. "The Boy and the Bottle." *Murder Can Be Fun* 5: 4–7.

Memorial University of Newfoundland (MUN). 1988. Unpublished Survey of Coke-Lore gathered by Paul Smith from students in Folklore 1000, *Introduction to Folklore course* (Fall).

Memorial University of Newfoundland (MUN). 1988. Unpublished Survey of Coke-Lore gathered by Paul Smith from students in Folklore 1000, *Introduction to Folklore course* (Winter).

Mencken, H. L. 1966. *The American Language: Supplement I.* New York: Knopf.

Mieder, Barbara, and Wolfgang Mieder. 1977. "Tradition and Innovation: Proverbs in Advertising." *Journal of Popular Culture* 11.2: 308–19.

Mieder, Wolfgang. 1978. "Proverbial Slogans Are the Name of the Game." *Kentucky Folklore Record* 24.2: 49–53.

Morgan, Hal, and Kerry Tucker. 1984. *Rumor!* New York: Penguin.

Movies Unlimited. 1989. *Video Catalogue.* Philadelphia: Movies Unlimited.

Narváez, Peter. 1986. "The Folklore of 'Old Foolishness': Newfoundland Media Legends." *Canadian Literature* 108: 125–43.

Narváez, Peter, and Martin Laba, eds. 1986. Introduction. *Media Sense: The Folklore-Popular Culture Continuum.* Bowling Green, OH: Bowling Green State U Popular P. 1–8.

Norfolk Punch. 1987. Advertising Flyer.

O'Donoghue, Michael, and Anne Beatts. 1973. "The Secret of Coca-Cola Revealed!" *The National Lampoon Encyclopedia of Humor.* Ed. Michael O'Donoghue. New York: The National Lampoon. 103–5.

Oliver, Thomas. 1986. *The Real Coke, The Real Story.* New York: Random House.

One, Two, Three. 1961. USA: United Artists.

Patton, Kenneth. 1975. *Pop-Topping.* Radnor, PA: Chilton.

Preston, Mike. 1989. "The Mouse in the Coors Beer Can: Goliath Strikes Back." *Foaftale News* 14 (June): 1–3.

Randolph, Vance. 1976. *Pissing in the Snow and Other Ozark Folktales.* New York: Avon.

Ribu. [ca 1980]. [Untitled Pornographic Film]. Germany: Ribu Film Productions.

Riley, John J. 1946. *Organization in the Soft Drink Industry.* Washington: American Bottlers of Carbonated Beverages.

Robson, Peter. 1990. "Coke-Lore." *FLS News* 10 (Jan.): 15.

Roud, Steve. 1988. "Coke-Lore." *FLS News* 7 (July): 10–11.

———. 1989. "Coke-Lore." *FLS News* 8 (Jan.): 11.

Smith, Paul. 1985. "The Problems of Analysis of Traditional Play Texts: A Taxonomic Approach." *Traditional Drama Studies* 1: 43–65.

———. 1989. "Contemporary Legend: A Legendary Genre?" Bennett and Smith. 91–101.

———. Collection. 1989. Item 1, left anonymously in my internal mailbox. Department of Folklore, Memorial University of Newfoundland (1 March 1989). Item 2, communicated by a female graduate student, Memorial University of Newfoundland (23 March 1989). Item 3, communicated by Marcia Gaudet, Arkansas State University (20 Oct. 1989).

———. 1990. "AIDS—Don't Die of Ignorance: Exploring the Cultural Complex of a Pandemic." Bennett and Smith. 113–41.

Sonnichsen, C. L. 1976. "The Poor Wayfaring Scholar." *Journal of Popular Culture* 10.1: 88–95.

Stich, Sidra. 1987. *Made in U.S.A.: An Americanization in Modern Art, the '50s and '60s.* Berkeley: U of California Art Museum/U of California P.

Strange Brew. 1983. USA: MGM/UG Entertainment.

Time: The Weekly News Magazine. 1950. "The Sun Never Sets on Coca-Cola." 15 May: Front Cover, 28–32.

Truzzi, Marcello. 1978. "Toward a General Sociology of the Folk, Popular, and Elite Arts." *Research in Sociology of Knowledge, Sciences and Art* 1: 279–89.

Umpierre, Sharee *et al.* 1985. "The Effects of 'Coke' on Sperm Mobility." *New England Journal of Medicine* 313:21 (21 Nov.): 1351.

Wolfe, Thomas. 1929. *Look Homeward Angel: A Story of a Buried Life.* New York: Scribner.

Yallop, David A. 1976. *The Day the Laughter Stopped: The True Story of Fatty Arbuckle.* London: Hodder and Stoughton.

CULTURAL STUDIES AS CONFLUENCE:
THE CONVERGENCE OF FOLKLORE AND MEDIA STUDIES

S. Elizabeth Bird

In an essay composed for this collection, S. Elizabeth Bird makes a case that, if folklore and media culture are not identical, cultural studies nevertheless demonstrate that the two are far more "intertwined" than previously believed. Popular narratives often have folk roots, and there are striking parallels in terms of the audience's readings and uses of both cultural forms. Indeed she locates the convergence of folklore and media studies especially in "a new interrogation of the role of the popular culture audience." Bird concludes that "the traditional separation between folklore and popular culture is finally being resolved, via cultural studies, toward a common concern with how audiences and producers negotiate meanings through narratives." Bird is Professor of Anthropology at the University of South Florida and author of several key works on popular culture, among them the study of supermarket tabloids, For Enquiring Minds *(1992).*

Traditional popular culture and communications scholarship, coming from a sociological model, long accepted a fundamental difference between folk culture and "mass" culture. Sociological thinkers like Ferdinand Tonnies had contrasted the notion of *gemeinschaft,* the community in which people were bound together by ties of "organic solidarity," with *gesellschaft,* or society, in which people were tied only by circumstance.[1] The former, of course, produced "folk culture," while the latter had "mass culture" thrust upon it. According to Dwight Mac-Donald, folk art "was a spontaneous, autochthonous expression of the people, shaped by themselves, pretty much without the benefit of High Culture, to suit their own needs. Mass culture is imposed from above. It is fabricated by technicians hired by businessmen; its audiences are passive consumers, their participation limited to the choice between buying and not buying . . ." Mass culture is thus "an instrument of political domination."[2]

Guided by this notion of culture, the idea of any consonance between folk and mass culture seems far-fetched indeed. The mass culture thesis also rests on the traditional view of communication as a linear process, "who says what, in which channel, to whom, and with what effect."[3] From that perspective, mass media can only work one way, with the producer foisting whatever is most profitable upon a passive, gullible public. From this perspective, mass media scholars rarely considered oral or folk culture—it simply was not relevant, since folk culture was by definition participatory and responsive to a culture's needs, while mass culture was simply the manipulation of cheap formulae in order to maximize profit.

Folklorists have long found the relationship between folklore and popular culture to be rather more problematic. They noticed that rumors, legends, and so on were disseminated by newspapers as well as by oral tradition. Study of such phenomena, however, tended to focus primarily on oral genres, while trying to distinguish between "genuine folk tradition" and the media contribution to it.[4] Researchers showed how newspapers sometimes pass on urban legends, taking the approach that although newspapers are primarily concerned with "facts," sometimes they get duped.[5] Even today, some folklorists, while keenly aware of the dominant role of media in culture, still tend to argue that folk culture and media culture are quite clearly distinguishable. Thus Linda Degh, writing on media and folklore, argues for more "reference to the diversity of mass media participation in the transmission of folklore,"[6] rather than for an examination of the way folklore and mediated culture may actually be more closely intertwined. Peter Narváez and Martin Laba, while calling for closer study of the connections between folklore and media, separate the two by describing a "continuum," from one to the other, suggesting that there is a kind of "pure folklore" at one end, and a "pure popular culture" at the other.[7]

Later, however, the relationship between folk and popular culture began to be reappraised by scholars in a range of disciplines — although often these scholars were unaware of each other's work. In the 1970s, folklorists began to study the way media narratives were often actually structured like folk narratives, especially in terms of formulaic composition.[8] At the same time, media scholarship began to move away from sociological approaches, and to question some of the basic assumptions that guided them. For example, popular media tend to be stereotyped and formulaic. "Mass culture" approaches would attribute this to economic considerations—formulaic popular genres are a product of economic forces that make formulaic potboilers easy and profitable to turn out.[9] There can be little question that this is true. However, a purely economic view begs the question that many popular culture scholars began exploring—where did these formulae come from in the first place, and why are they popular? Are "the masses" really so gullible that they will consume whatever is passed off on them? As researchers like John Fiske point out, the success of the popular culture industry is far from predictable; many more offerings fail than succeed.[10]

The relationship, then, between the text and its audience is not as clear and simple as first assumed.

When we start to ask these kind of questions, we start to look for understanding in scholarship outside traditional communications theory, particularly in work guided by an anthropological notion of culture. Once we see culture as more akin to a web or network rather than a series of discrete communication channels, we start to perceive folklore and popular culture more as being interconnected strands in that web.[11] And it has been the eclectic field of cultural studies that has really advanced the idea that folk culture and mass culture, if not identical, are far more intertwined than was ever considered before. For once we except the simple, anthropological notion that culture is "a whole way of life," we find it hard to separate the strands of that culture into distinct channels.

Thus we see a new awareness that contemporary "folk" are surrounded by messages from countless sources, both mediated and face-to-face, and that contemporary media draw, consciously and unconsciously on a range of long-established narrative conventions. David Chaney points to the "necessity of shared representational conventions, a frame, in staging of fictional performances."[12] John Fiske argues that popular television programming draws on oral traditions and in turn feeds those traditions, indeed that it *must* do this in order to be truly popular.[13] Robins and Cohen argued that the popularity of *kung fu* movies among British working class youths in the late 1970s was at least in part due to the correspondence of narrative conventions in the movies with existing oral traditions.[14]

Indeed, there is a growing body of literature that analyzes all kinds of media in terms of their relationship to ritual, storytelling, and myth.[15] If narrative is a central way that we organize experience, as scholars in many disciplines now agree, it makes little sense to argue for mutually exclusive types of narratives, such as "folk" or "popular."[16] For as Richard Johnson writes, in describing cultural studies, a full understanding of any text must take into account the complexity of the relationship between the three components of producer, text, and audience. He argues that this relationship should be seen as circular rather than linear, in that producers incorporate readers in their production of texts, texts in turn may have an impact on readers, whose response then feeds back into the text.[17]

So we need to forget about whether or not popular culture "transmits" folklore. Rather, we begin to consider that certain popular cultural forms succeed because they act like folklore. To some extent they may have replaced folk narratives, but not with something completely new. Thus popular culture is popular because of its resonance, its appeal to an audience's existing set of story conventions. As Harold Schechter writes, successful popular art needs "people with a talent for dreaming up the very fantasies that the mass audience (with or without being aware of it) craves, at a given moment, to hear or read or see. But these fantasies . . . turn out to be precisely those stories which have always amazed, amused, titillated, or terrified listeners . . . stories, in short, with both the function and essential form of traditional folk tales."[18] Thus media and oral tradition are comparable, though not identical, communication processes, during which narratives are constructed from familiar themes that repeat themselves over time. People do not necessarily transmit folklore and attend to media in different ways and for different purposes. Both are part of the complex way in which cultural "reality" is constructed.

Clearly, the development of this perspective has been guided by a new interrogation of the role of the popular culture audience.[19] If audience members are seen as active in helping to shape the way popular culture is created, they become much more comparable with folk "audiences." After all, even in an oral culture, not every individual is a storyteller or an active, performing bearer of all traditions. Rather, the role of people in many contexts is to respond to the storyteller, helping her or him shape future versions of the tale. Cultural studies scholars argue that the popular media audience can play an analogous role.

Jesus Martin-Barbero points out that media texts have long been incorporated into oral culture in Latin America, where many people's experience of print media was gained through listening in groups to someone read the text: "It is a listening marked with applause and whistles, sighs and laughter, a reading whose rhythm is not established by the text but by the group. What was read was not an end in itself but the beginning of a mutual acknowledgment of meaning and an awakening of collective memories that might set in motion a conversation. Thus, reading might end up redoing the text in function of the context, in a sense, *rewriting* the text in order to talk about what the group is living."[20] This description of the role of print in an essentially oral culture is strikingly similar to some recent descriptions of the highly developed fan cultures associated with television shows like soap operas or *Star Trek,* where fans have essentially created folk cultures, complete with languages, oral and written literatures and narrative cycles, all focused around a particular media creation.[21] Even apart from such fan cultures, ethnographic audience studies, whose methodologies are often strikingly similar to studies of folklore in action, have shown the way readers and viewers incorporate the narratives of popular culture into their daily lives, through gossip and fantasy.[22]

Of course, not all audience interaction with popular culture is as social as this. Much TV watching, for example, is done alone or in small groups, and is relatively passive. Yet people choose only certain programs to come back to again and again, and at least one reason is the way these texts succeed in their retellings of established narratives. In certain media genres, the kinship with folk traditions is absolutely clear. The most sensational of the supermarket tabloids, for example, draw deliberately on folklore, and the beliefs and concerns they know their readers already have. According to a tabloid reporter, "When looking for ideas for stories, it's good to look at fears, and it's good to look at real desires. That's why a lot of people win lotteries in the stories, and why people get buried alive all the time . . ."[23] The *Weekly World News, Sun,* and *National Examiner* are full of mythical figures and phenomena that have fascinated people for generations—ancient Egyptian curses, Atlantis, Bigfoot and other monsters, mermaids, reincarnation, fortune-telling and psychic powers generally, and the more modern folk beliefs about UFOs and alien invaders. In addition, the three tabloids often develop stories directly from folk ideas in medicine, such as the use of garlic and vinegar as remedies for everything from colds to AIDS. Tabloid writers rely quite heavily on tips from their readers in developing stories, some of which can grow into long-running narratives fed by reader interest and participation, such as the "Elvis is Alive" saga.[24]

If we look at the more "respectable" tabloids, which prefer to focus on celebrity gossip and self-help, we see less of the direct borrowing of folk beliefs, and more of the incorporation of standard narratives and motifs, such that the specific stories change, but the overarching narratives recur. Editors frequently develop celebrity stories in pre-determined directions— the star who desperately wants a baby, the search of all celebrities for a perfect marriage. The lives of individual stars become molded to the established repertoire of celebrity sagas. Thus, for example, a story in the *Star* cast comedian Roseanne in the time-honored role of the "TV queen" whose life is coming apart because of her success. The "money quote," also paraphrased in a photo cutline, is attributed to a "friend": "Roseanne believes she's destroyed her three children. Her rocket to stardom has brought divorce and tragedy and the kids can no longer bear it. Roseanne wants to quit TV and take the children and return to their simple life in a trailer park."[25] In this one story, we clearly see a retelling of the many folk tales that preach the dangers of hubris and the lesson that money and power cannot buy happiness. As I show elsewhere, much of the pleasure audiences derive from "scandalous" news stories stems from their ability to use the stories as catalysts for the generation of narratives that are relevant to their own lives.[26]

If we move from print to other media, we can again see popular culture doing for audiences what folklore did and still does. Again, some genres have very clear affinities with folk themes, as Schechter thoroughly discusses in his analyses of horror and fantasy movies.[27] Other genres are less clear, such as popular television shows. Yet the key to the popularity of many shows is often their affinities with existing narrative conventions. As George Lipsitz writes, "Television is both an advertising mechanism and the primary discursive medium of our culture . . ."[28] In other words, television may exist to sell products effectively, but it has also become the focus for much of our social interaction. People *like* television, and one of the reasons they do is that its stories are so often familiar, recurring narratives, just as tabloid tales are, and just as folklore is. As Lipsitz continues, "Unlike 'high culture' where a dogmatic formalism privileges abstraction over experience, the effectiveness of popular culture depends on its ability to engage audiences in active and familiar processes."[29] This is clearly a long way from the passive dupes of "mass culture" theory.

Lipsitz argues rightly that popular culture scholarship has tended to play down the importance of the past, and the impact that the resonant narratives have on the present. This is true of all genres from popular television to rock music, where he argues that early rock and roll was so successful precisely because it was a new twist on old ideas: "These folk retentions survived because of their appeal as narratives, but also because they marshaled the resources of the past as part of defining identity in the present."[30] In the context of Latin America, Martin-Barbero also argues that we must understand the persistence of old themes if we are to understand the nature of contemporary popularity. He describes the development of popular street literature similar to tabloids, which, like tabloids, grew out of ballads, folk narratives and traditional beliefs, arguing that the stereotypical style of *literatura de cordel* was "not simply the product of commercialization and demands for certain generic formats, but reflected the repetition and popular styles of narration."[31]

In particular, he discusses the importance of understanding the folk roots of the tradition of melodrama. "The stubborn persistence of the melodrama genre long after the conditions of its genesis have disappeared and its capacity to adapt to different technological formats cannot be explained simply in terms of commercial or ideological manipulations."[32] Like Lipsitz, he sees the conventions of melodrama as crucial to the success of popular media, with its emphasis on morality and excess: "Everything must be extravagantly stated, from the staging which exaggerates the audio and visual contrasts to the dramatic structure which openly exploits the bathos of quick and sentimental emotional reactions. . . . Cultured people might consider all this degrading, but it nevertheless represents a victory over repression, a form of resistance against a particular 'economy' of order, saving and polite restraint."[33]

Thus the media offerings that often prove most popular are also often those that are despised by critics and "high culture," because they tend to be formularized, predictable, and sentimental, with positions on good and evil clearly defined—very much like folk narratives. As characterized by Walter Ong, such popular fare is high on "residual orality, "which inevitably produces and values the familiar and the standardized.[34]

A recent popular television show is a case in point. *Dr. Quinn, Medicine Woman* premiered in Fall 1992, to overwhelming derision from the critics, who described it in terms ranging from "treacle" to "drivel . . . its every nuance calculated out of lowest-common-denominator concerns."[35] The clear message of such criticism is that only an idiot could enjoy the show. Yet the program became the most successful new drama series of the year, and developed a huge fan following. Internet web sites, and an e-mail discussion list, DQMW-L, encouraged fans to share discussion, fan fiction, and endless other creative activities. In fact, the DQMW-L list is arguably a "community," with its own rules, expectations, traditions, metaphors, and values, in much the same way as other "folk communities."[36] These fans spearheaded a campaign to reverse CBS's sudden cancellation of the show in 1998, after a strong six-year run.

Dr. Quinn's stories were indeed conventional. Every week, the title character of the show, played with great conviction by Jane Seymour, does battle with a new form of evil, whether this be sexism, racism, gambling, alcoholism, spouse abuse and so on. Evil was usually personified in the form of a particular individual who was routed by the end of each episode. The doctor had a close and sentimental relationship with her adopted children, and she enjoyed the support of a handsome mountain man with whom she had an on-off love affair before marrying him about half way through the show's run. If one looks at the superficial plot details of *Dr. Quinn,* one might argue that it does not resemble older narratives; the issues that surface each week are straight from the 1990s, such as its feminist slant, and attempts to portray Native Americans in an extremely positive light.[37] Yet a closer look tells us that the show is old-fashioned folk-shaped melodrama *par excellence.* Each story is a morality play about good and evil, the acting of both villains and heros often rather heavy-handed. The show taps into a plethora of American cultural icons that have become part of the folk and popular cultural fabric, from the pristine frontier to the noble savage, from the power of progress to the American melting pot.

Stuart Hall makes the important point that popular culture does not remain static, but that it is constantly "transformed," reworking what came before. He describes the process of transformation as "the active work on existing traditions and activities, their active reworking so that they come out a different way: they appear to 'persist'—yet, from one period to another, they come to stand in a different relation to the ways working people live and the ways they define their relations to each other, to 'the others' and to the conditions of life."[38] Thus a show like *Dr. Quinn* is similar but not identical to other shows that came before, like *Little House on the Prairie.* The audience has indeed changed "the way they define their relations to each other," and that is reflected in changed attitudes to different races, women's role and so on. But the basic simplicity of the melodramatic narrative still persists, as it has done for centuries.

In exploring the relationship between folklore and media culture, I do not wish to argue that the two are identical. There are still areas of culture that are largely oral and owe little to media, and there are mediated narratives that owe more to a highly literate tradition than to folk culture.[39] The relationship between TV producers and audiences is not the same as that between traditional storytellers and their audiences, who interact face to face. In solely oral cultures everyone potentially is a storyteller, even though many in practice are not, while the media writer or producer inscribes the text, no matter how much input readers have. While the role of the reader can be active and creative, it tends to be interpretive, working with the texts offered. Anna-Maria Siikala notes that mediated narratives have replaced folk narratives in most people's lives. Nevertheless, "Even though tales are produced commercially, people are still left with scope for interpretation. Nowadays, instead of the narrator, we increasingly come across the commentator expressing opinions on the narratives transmitted by the media."[40]

Furthermore, this kind of commentary and interpretation is probably quite close to what "audiences" have done with oral narratives for years. Folk culture can be romanticized as a time when everyone was a storyteller, when more accurately, most people were more likely to be "active audiences" of the kind that cultural studies have been describing. Like the audience for popular media, they commented, responded, fantasized, and let the narrator know what worked and what did not. Clearly we can overstate the comparison—people in a post-modern, mediated world are surrounded by far more narrative possibilities than those in an oral culture. Watching a TV show is not the same as listening to a folk tale; a TV show, for instance, comes encrusted with narratives about the stars, other shows, news stories about TV and so on. The popularity of *Dr. Quinn* is connected not only to the show's stories, but also to the recognizability of and audience affection for its stars.

But a re-evaluation of the relationship between media and folklore has produced insight into contemporary culture. We have learned that the power of media's "ideological effect" as discussed by Stuart Hall derives not from coercion and forcing audiences to consume a product they dislike, but from using familiar narrative structures to frame stories in ways that reinforce a shared hegemony.[41] Media scholars, then, have learned from folklorists and anthropologists that culture is participatory, rather than coercive.

In a classic article, William Bascom argued that folklore serves to educate audiences in the values of a culture, validate norms, and also allow an outlet for fantasy and wish fulfillment.[42] Contemporary cultural studies in part argues that media do the same things, and by drawing comparisons with folk narratives, we can see that they achieve this by retelling many of the same stories.

And while media scholars are rediscovering the participatory nature of media culture through audience studies, they are also arguing that audience engagement with media can be resistive, as audiences reinterpret and subvert the intended message and create new meanings for themselves. Meanwhile, as Jay Mechling points out, folklorists are responding to criticisms that their work has so long overlooked the ideological, concentrating too much on the notion of shared meanings and mutual participation.[43] Bascom, in his functions of folklore, overlooked the potentially subversive properties of traditional narratives. In his zeal for demonstrating shared values, he, and many folklorists after him, neglected the way folklore can be an avenue of resistance for the oppressed or disadvantaged.[44] Today, folklorists are finding cultural studies' re-emphasis on the audience useful in thinking through audience participation in oral performances. Cultural studies of audiences have focused on what Fiske calls "moments of semiosis," trying to understand what individuals actively do in their interactions with popular culture.[45] According to Mechling, this is what folklorists are beginning to do too: "Both fields want to throw out the reified notions of 'text' and 'context' in favor of conceptions of a 'moment of semiosis' wherein numbers of discourses come together and intertextual relations flourish in the spaces between the discourses. Both call into question old notions of 'sharing' meanings and look for a process that generates oppositional 'readings.' "[46]

So perhaps the traditional separation between folklore and popular culture is finally being resolved, as scholars in both fields converge, via cultural studies, toward a common concern with how audiences and producers negotiate meanings through narratives. We know now that culture is not something that can be chopped into easily definable, unrelated pieces. Popular media did not spring fully formed from some new state of existence. Rather, they drew on traditional narratives and attitudes, while also transforming those narratives. And culture is not static, but rather is constantly being renegotiated through the everyday conversation and oral discourse of the audience, much of which revolves around media itself. The perspective of cultural studies has enlivened both folklore and media scholarship, allowing us to see both oral and mediated narratives as intertextual strands in a web that constantly reshapes itself.

Notes

1. Ferdinand Tonnies, *Community and Society* (Gemeinschaft and Gessellschaft, 1887, translated and edited by C. P. Loomis, East Lansing: Michigan State UP, 1957).

2. Dwight MacDonald, "A Theory of Mass Culture," *Mass Culture: The Popular Arts in America,* eds. Bernard Rosenberg and David Manning White (Glencoe: Free, 1957), 60.

3. Harold Lasswell, "The Structure and Function of Communication in Society," *The Communication of Ideas,* ed. Lyman Bryson (New York: Harper, 1948).

4. See, for example, Linda Degh and Andrew Vazsonyi, *The Dialectics of Legend* (Bloomington: Indiana UP, 1973).

5. See Jan Harold Brunvand, *The Vanishing Hitchhiker* (New York: Norton, 1981), and Sandy Hobbs, "The Folktale as News," *Oral History,* 6.2 (1978): 74–86.

6. Linda Degh, *American Folklore and the Mass Media* (Bloomington: Indiana UP, 1994), 33.

7. Peter Narváez and Martin Laba, eds. *Media Sense: The Folklore-Popular Culture Continuum* (Bowling Green, OH: Bowling Green State U Popular P, 1986).

8. Early examples of this kind of scholarship include Donald A. Bird, "A Theory of Folklore in Mass Media: Traditional Patterns in the Mass Media," *Southern Folklore Quarterly,* 40 (1976): 285–305; and Anne B. Cohen, *Poor Pearl, Poor Girl: The Murdered Girl Stereotype in Ballad and Newspaper* (Austin, TX: Publications of American Folklore Society Memoir Series, 1973).

9. See, for example, David Paul Nord, "An Economic Perspective on Formula in Popular Culture," *Journal of American Culture,* 3 (1980): 17–31.

10. John Fiske, *Television Culture* (New York: Methuen, 1987); *Understanding Popular Culture* (Boston: Unwin Hyman, 1989).

11. The anthropological notion of culture as a "web of significance" was introduced to a wider audience through the work of Clifford Geertz, in the influential *The Interpretation of Cultures* (New York: Basic, 1973).

12. David Chaney, "Fictions in Mass Entertainment," in John Curran, Michael Gurevitch, and Janet Woolacott, eds. *Mass Communication and Society* (London: Edward Arnold, 1977), 440–51.

13. Fiske, 1987.

14. David Robins and Philip Cohen, *Knuckle Sandwich: Growing Up in the Working Class City* (Harmondsworth: Penguin, 1978).

15. See, for example, essays in James W. Carey, ed., *Media, Myths and Narratives: Television and the Press* (Beverly Hills: Sage, 1988).

16. See, for example, Walter R. Fisher, "The Narrative Paradigm: In the Beginning," *Journal of Communication,* 35 (1985): 74–89; Jay Mechling, "Homo Narrans across the Disciplines," *Western Folklore,* 50 (1991): 41–52; W. J. T. Mitchell, ed., *On Narrative* (Chicago: U of Chicago P, 1981).

17. Richard Johnson, "What Is Cultural Studies Anyway?" in *What Is Cultural Studies: A Reader,* ed. John Storey (London: Edward Arnold, 1996).

18. Harold Schechter, *The Bosom Serpent: Folklore and Popular Art* (Iowa City: U of Iowa P, 1988), 86.

19. See, for example, Martin Allor, "Relocating the Site of the Audience," *Critical Studies in Mass Communication,* 5 (1988): 217–33; S. Elizabeth Bird, "Travels in Nowhere Land: Ethnography and the 'Impossible' Audience," *Critical Studies in Mass Communication,* 9 (1992): 250–60; Shaun Moores, *Interpreting Audiences: The Ethnography of Media Consumption* (Thousand Oaks, CA: Sage, 1993).

20. Jesus Martin-Barbero, *Communication, Culture, and Hegemony: From the Media to Mediations,* translated by Elizabeth Fox and Robert A. White (Newbury Park: Sage, 1993), 120.

21. Significantly, the fan culture of *Star Trek* has been separately studied both by a folklorist and a popular culture scholar. See Camille Bacon-Smith, *Enterprising Women: Television Fandom and the Creation of Popular Myth* (Philadelphia: U of Pennsylvania P, 1992); Henry Jenkins, *Textual Poachers: Television Fans and Participatory Culture* (New York: Routledge, 1992). The folkloric quality of Internet soap opera fan groups is discussed in Nancy K. Baym, "Interpreting Soap Operas and Creating Community: Inside an Electronic Fan Culture," *Culture of the Internet,* ed. Sara Kiesler (Mahwah, NJ: Lawrence Erlbaum, 1997), 103–20.

22. See, for example, Ien Ang, *Watching Dallas* (London: Methuen, 1985); S. Elizabeth Bird, *For Enquiring Minds: A Cultural Study of Supermarket Tabloids* (Knoxville: U of Tennessee P, 1992); John L. Caughey, *Imaginary Social Worlds* (Lincoln: U of Nebraska P); David Morley, *Family Television: Cultural Power and Domestic Leisure* (London: Comedia, 1986); Andrea L. Press, *Women Watching Television* (Philadelphia: U of Pennsylvania P, 1991); E. Graham McKinley, *Beverly Hills, 90210: Television, Gender, and Identity* (Philadelphia: U of Pennsylvania P, 1997), and others.

23. Interview with Jim Hogshire, March 13, 1992.

24. For a detailed discussion of this process, see Bird, *For Enquiring Minds,* Chapter 5.

25. Article in *The Star,* 27 Feb. 1990: 32.

26. S. Elizabeth Bird, "What a Story! Understanding the Audience for Scandal," *Media Scandals: Private Desire in the Popular Culture Marketplace,* eds. James Lull and Steve Hinerman (Cambridge, UK: Polity P, 1997), 99–121.

27. Schechter, *The Bosom Serpent.*

28. George Lipsitz, *Time Passages: Collective Memory and American Popular Culture* (Minneapolis: U of Minnesota P, 1990), 18.

29. Ibid., 14.

30. Ibid., 115.

31. Martin-Barbero, *Communication, Culture, and Hegemony,* 102.

32. Ibid., 119.

33. Ibid., 119.

34. Walter Ong, *Orality and Literacy: The Technologizing of the World* (London: Methuen, 1982).

35. See John J. O'Connor, "It's Jane Seymour, M.D., in the Wild and Wooly West," *New York Times,* 4 Feb. 1993: B5; Richard Zoglin, "Frontier Feminist," *Time* (1 March 1993): 63–64.

36. S. Elizabeth Bird, "Chatting on Cynthia's Porch: Building Community in an Internet Fan Culture," *Southern Communication Journal* (forthcoming).

37. S. Elizabeth Bird, "Not My Fantasy: The Persistence of Indian Imagery in *Dr. Quinn: Medicine Woman,*" in *Dressing in Feathers: The Construction of the Indian in American Popular Culture,* ed. S. Elizabeth Bird (Boulder: Westview).

38. Stuart Hall, "Notes on Deconstructing 'the Popular,'" *People's History and Socialist Theory,* ed. Raphael Samuel (London: Routledge, 1981), 228.

39. Some types of jokes and legends, for example, are still largely circulated orally. An example would be the local legends I discuss in S. Elizabeth Bird, "Playing with Fear: Interpreting the Adolescent Legend Trip," *Western Folklore,* 53 (1994): 191–209. Nevertheless, even folk activities like the legend trip have been partly shaped and structured by media narratives such as horror movies, which in turn draw on teenage legends for their stories.

40. Anna-Maria Siikala, "The Praxis of Folk Narratives," ed. Bengt R. Jonsson, *ARV: Scandinavian Yearbook of Folklore,* 40 (1984): 152.

41. Stuart Hall, "Culture, the Media, and the Ideological Effect," in Curran et al. *Mass Communication and Society,* 315–48.

42. William Bascom, "Four Functions of Folklore," *Journal of American Folklore,* 67 (1954): 333–49.

43. Jay Mechling, "On Sharing Folklore and American Identity in a Multicultural Society," *Western Folklore* 52 (April 1993): 271–89.

44. This lack of consideration for ideology has been criticized from within folklore studies by, for example, Archie Green, "Interpreting Folklore Ideologically," in Richard Dorson, ed. *Handbook of American Folklore* (Bloomington: Indiana UP, 1983), 351–58.

45. John Fiske, "Meaningful Moments," *Critical Studies in Mass Communication* 5 (1988): 247.

46. Mechling, "On Sharing Folklore," 281.

VII.
Popularity

POPULARITY:
THE *SINE QUA NON* OF POPULAR CULTURE

Harold E. Hinds, Jr.

Harold E. Hinds, Jr., finds many previous conceptualizations of popular culture too broad and/or vague to provide the necessary basis for theory and methodology building. He suggests that defining popular culture as "those aspects of culture . . . which are widely spread and believed in and/or consumed by significant numbers of people" can provide a better foundation for development of the field.

Popular culture studies are thriving—and yet they disappoint. The Popular Culture Association's annual conventions thrive on ever larger numbers of participants and ever greater diversity. So many new monographs devoted to some aspect of popular culture appear each year that it has become impossible to delve into them all. And the flagship journal, the *Journal of Popular Culture,* has been joined by a number of other scholarly journals devoted at least partially to examination of the field. Popular culture studies are "in" and increasingly respected.

Why, then, the disappointment? Because there is still no widely accepted, basic definition of "popular culture"; and therefore no focus for theoretical considerations. Ray Browne's early suggestion that definitional inclusiveness is preferable to exclusiveness[1] has been taken so literally that popular culture's umbrella now shelters an extremely disparate group of subjects and borrowed methodologies. Indeed, the development of a general theory or set of theories of popular culture and a methodology or methodological approach unique to it may have become impossible without a sharper focus. In 1972 even Browne noted that early, broad definitions might need to be pared a bit.[2] This essay, after reviewing a number of current, competing definitions of popular culture, will suggest a considerably pared-down definition, which should allow for the development of popular culture theories and methodologies.

Harold E. Hinds, Jr., "Popularity: The Sine Qua Non *of Popular Culture," in Ray B. Browne and Marshall W. Fishwick (eds.),* Symbiosis: Popular Culture and Other Fields *(Bowling Green, OH: Bowling Green State University Popular Press, 1988), 207–16.*

359

A recent (1987) flyer from Cambridge University Press illustrates just how inclusive the term "popular culture" has become. Among the "Recent Books in Modern European and British History" that the Press advertised were the following: (1) *Power in the Blood: Popular Culture and Village Discourse in Early Modern Germany,* by David Warren Sabean, which reveals "peasant life" through the examination of a series of episodes in village life, such as "a peasant's refusal to celebrate church ritual, a prophet who encountered an angel in his vineyard . . ."; (2) *Lay Theology in the Reformation: Popular Pamphleteers in Southwest Germany, 1521–1525,* by Paul A. Russell, which examines the case made in printed Protestant tracts, a by-product of the invention of movable type, for a lay theology and greater lay piety; (3) *Fascism in Popular Memory: The Cultural Experience of the Turin Working Class,* by Luisa Passerini, which uses the oral recollections of workers to recall the fascist period and their resistance and/or acquiescence to *Il Duce.* Clearly, to Cambridge University Press, the phrase "popular culture" and the adjective "popular" are readily accepted and salable commodities, and can be applied indiscriminately to folk culture, mass culture, and working-class culture.

These three very different cultures are often the subject of popular culture investigations. Raymond Williams noted in 1976, in an etymology of the word "popular," that its most recent connotation is "culture actually made by people for themselves" and is largely synonymous with the term folk culture.[3] And indeed, folk culture has increasingly been incorporated into the academic discipline of popular culture. In reviewing the state of the discipline and the *Journal of Popular Culture* in 1980, Christopher Geist advocated further broadening of the field, and added that whatever broadening had occurred was due in large part to Ray Browne's vigorous solicitation for the *Journal* of In-Depth Sections which broke new ground.[4] Some of these sections devoted to such new turf as Bulgaria[5] have indeed included significant articles clearly labeled "folk" culture. Other areas of expansion which have carved out a more comfortable niche for folk culture within the field include: (1) Alvar Carlson's In-Depth Section on Cultural Geography, a field which devotes considerable attention to the origin and diffusion of folk cultural artifacts and traits; (2) Fred E. H. Schroeder's In-Depth Section on "Popular Culture Before Printing," which focused attention on a largely folk world, a world characterized by traditional oral culture, performer-audience interaction, direct communication, and isolated and self-sufficient small cultural groups.

The discovery by historians of ordinary people has also contributed to a greater incorporation of the folk. In particular, the *Annales* school of French historians set out to rewrite pre-nineteenth-century European history from the point of view, not of the literate elite, but of the illiterate, subordinate classes, of the folk.[6] The best summary in English, to date, with an *Annales*-type emphasis, Peter Burke's *Popular Culture in Early Modern Europe,* makes it clear that he considers popular culture to be culture of the non-elite, the folk.[7]

Internationalization of the popular culture field has also, largely through semantic confusion, aided in the incorporation of folk culture studies into popular culture. In the foreign culture with which I am most familiar, Spanish-speaking Latin America, the English-language term "*popular culture*" is often translated as "*cultura popular,*" which in Spanish literally means folk culture. And as an editor of the annual journal *Studies in Latin American Popular Culture,* I frequently receive submissions from Latinos on some aspect of folk culture, and far less frequently manuscripts on mass culture. Books with "*cultura popular*" in the title almost always treat folk, not mass, culture.

If folk culture has gained increased incorporation into popular culture, the prominent role of mass culture has never been in doubt. Initially, the *Journal of Popular Culture* was largely devoted to popular culture transmitted by the mass media, i.e., mass culture.[8] And Geist found that in the late 1970s mass culture still predominated, especially popular literature, although some other mass media, notably television, were represented.[9] Despite Ray Browne's efforts to plow new ground with In-Depth Sections, both the *Journal* and most works published with the phrase "popular culture" somewhere in their title still are overwhelmingly devoted to mass culture.

Popular culture as working-class culture is not well represented in the *Journal* and owes its development largely to European and Latin American scholars. Basically, these scholars argue that the hegemonic sector who own or control mass culture industries attempt to impose their capitalist world view through media products; and that this mass culture is not true popular culture because it does not reflect the people's culture and values. Rather, popular culture is that which springs directly (unmediated by elite culture) from the people, the working class, or combines this proletarian culture with mass-mediated culture which is creatively subverted by the working class for its own uses. Numerous Third World media scholars and pundits take the former view,[10] and British scholars, being less inclined to see the people as passive consumers of media and culture, have increasingly adopted the latter point of view.[11]

At times one or more, even all, of these types of popular (folk, mass, working-class) culture are combined in popular culture studies. Ray Browne argues for an inclusive approach, excluding only the "narrowly intellectual or creatively elitist."[12] Recently he states in "Popular Culture as the New Humanities" that by popular culture "we generally mean all aspects of the world we inhabit . . . It is the everyday world around us . . . [it] is the voice of the people."[13] Arthur Asa Berger states "As far as I'm concerned, it is everything that is not high or 'unpopular' culture."[14] Marshall Fishwick posits that any " 'intellectual or imaginative work' " that is "not narrowly elitist or aimed at special audiences" constitutes popular culture.[15] Michael Schudson, in two recent surveys of the growth of popular culture studies, defines popular culture as including both mass and folk culture, but excluding elite culture.[16] And finally, in a provocative new study Peter Narváez and Martin Laba argue that there is a folklore-popular culture continuum, and that at times either contains elements of the other; e.g., folk songs can be transmitted via modern media.[17]

What is offered then is a hodgepodge of definitions of popular culture. It may be as broadly defined as everything but elite culture, and as narrowly as a culture created by the mass media. Given this vagueness it is not surprising that popular culture studies have not spawned a unique set of theories and/or methodologies. In fact, those theories and methodologies which have been associated with the field are derived from other disciplines and are not specific to popular culture studies. The Fall 1975 special issue of the *Journal of Popular Culture* devoted to "Theories and Methodologies in Popular Culture" mentions content analysis, structuralism, formalism, and myth-symbol-image types of analysis, among others. Michael Schudson's recent surveys of new approaches to popular culture offer an extensive listing: for example, studies which stress the role of markets and organizations; Clifford Geertz and Victor Turner's anthropology of performance and the idea that virtually anything is a "text" that can be read; Claude Levi-Strauss' notion that the human mind reorders reality into binary oppositions; Roland Barthes' semiotics; and Janice Radway's focus on the act of reading. Now that the "concept of textuality has been applied to materials not previously regarded as textual at all,"[18] especially commonplace, non-literary objects, what these approaches have in common is that they can be applied to any text, whether elite, folk, popular, working-class, or whatever. For example, Levi-Strauss' binary oppositions can be applied not only to folk totems and myths, but to Shakespeare, or fashions, or horror films. Therefore, while these theories and methodologies have deepened our understanding of culture, they have not helped distinguish popular culture from culture in general.

One definition, however, does offer some promise of providing a basis for the development of theories and methodologies unique to popular culture studies. Gary Fine has observed that the *sine qua non* of popular culture is popularity.[19] This notion is at least partially echoed by others. Jack Nachbar, et al., in *The Popular Culture Reader,* write: "In general . . . the definition of popular culture as mainstream or mass culture is a useful one . . . There is, after all, a logical pattern established by assuming a kind of formula for the study of popular culture in which the more popular a thing is, the more culturally significant it is likely to be."[20] For Leslie Fiedler, popular culture is simply "'Majority' Culture."[21] Fred Schroeder, in *Outlaw Aesthetics,* observes that the popular arts are subject to competition in the market place and it is the vote of the consumer that makes them popular.[22]

I believe, then, that the definition of popular culture ought to be: those aspects of culture, whether ideological, social, or material, which are widely spread and believed in and/or consumed by significant numbers of people, i.e., those aspects which are popular.[23] Why has this common-sense definition, while agreed to by some, failed to gain acceptance and why does it offer a possibility of spawning a theoretical and methodological base when other definitions have failed this test?

The failure of adoption, I believe, relates to the history and sociology of the popular culture movement. Ray Browne's call for inclusiveness, not exclusiveness, has both nurtured exciting growth and led to a reluctance to do any pruning. Indeed, many, if not most, candidates standing for election to an Executive-level office in the Popular Culture Association have taken a stand for diversity, plurality, and inclusiveness. None, if memory serves, have run on a platform of stepping back and assessing where the movement is headed or have argued for the development of theories and methodologies especially appropriate to popular culture studies.

The membership of the Popular Culture Association and the authors of articles in the *Journal of Popular Culture* are predominately from the humanities, especially English and history.[24] Popularity, to be demonstrated, demands a willingness to use, at a minimum, crude statistical and quantitative techniques and measures. Unfortunately, most academicians in the humanities are poorly trained in such analytical tools, even hostile to them, and schooled in valuing the uniqueness of each cultural idea and artifact more than in measuring them in quantity. Indeed, when Gary Fine, a sociologist, edited a special issue of the *Journal* devoted to "Sociology," he assured the journal's largely humanities readers that "For this interdisciplinary journal, an attempt was made to refrain from incorporating tables and statistics."[25] And a perusal of the *Journal's* contents over the years will quickly demonstrate that not only are numbers avoided, but that an overwhelming percentage of articles do not bother to offer any proof of popularity other than a simple assertion; or the implication that since, for example, films are a mass medium, then the film under discussion must be popular. The reader has no idea whether the idea or product under discussion is consumed by 1 or 5 or 50 or 95 percent of a regional, national, or international culture.

If popularity is the key factor in popular culture, it is surprising that the concept has not been systematically analyzed and debated, especially within the *Journal of Popular Culture*.[26] Even if we can agree that to qualify as popular an idea or artifact or product must be accepted or consumed by lots of people, we still must ask, how many is lots? Should the geographical distribution be greater than just one local culture or subculture, or the demographic distribution extend beyond a single narrowly defined socio-economic group? Should the basic geographical unit of measure be the modern nation state or at least a complex society? Discovering a threshold, even an elastic one, for popularity will demand the careful collection of data and examples. But I would argue that popularity at a minimum demands adoption/consumption in more than one regional culture and by more than one narrow socio-economic group.

Popularity demands numerical data. In the first, and even in the second world, such data is often available.[27] It may not be as complete as one would like, or free from errors and inconsistencies of collection or recording. For the most part contemporary data is more complete, more reliable than that for earlier periods. Careful attention to such issues and problems can still produce meaningful statements about an idea's or product's extent of acceptance. If one works in the third or fourth world, or on periods which are largely free of numerical data, then, of course, even qualified statements as to popularity are extremely difficult. In such cases, scholars should at least note that a meaningful statement cannot be made, and state why, despite the absence of statistical data, they believe their subject to merit the label of popular. But above all, whether because of math anxiety or imperfect data, we must not throw the baby out with the bath water. Given the centrality of popularity, it must always be demonstrated, even if imperfectly.

If popularity is the *sine qua non* of popular culture, notwithstanding that very little systematic thought has been given to just what popularity means and entails, why might this central concept spawn theories and methodologies unique to popular culture? First, inclusiveness has not produced the hoped-for theories. Evidently, sweeping so many disparate elements into the popular culture grab bag has made this task well-nigh impossible. And even those approaches which do manage to embrace everything within the broadest of popular culture definitions, can be applied just as well to elite culture, which even the broadest definitions exclude.

Second, those areas in popular culture studies which have been the subject of considerable theoretical development and debate, aesthetics and formula, have not led to the generation of general theories or methodologies of popular culture and/or are seriously flawed. Can there be a philosophy of taste, an aesthetics, of popular culture? John Cawelti, Leslie Fiedler, David Madden, and especially Fred Schroeder, in *Outlaw Aesthetics,* have proposed such an aesthetics. Roger Rollin has countered with a devastating critique, that it is "an impossible mission—to devise an aesthetics of Popular Culture which will incorporate a value-theory." For in popular culture, the only authority on beauty, excellence, or value is the people, those who elect to accept or consume something. "In popular culture, the rule is 'one person-one vote.' "[28]

John Cawelti's seminal "The Concept of Formula in the Study of Popular Literature" is perhaps the most important article ever published in the *Journal of Popular Culture* which attempted to provide a basic theoretical perspective on the discipline.[29] Cawelti states that "In general, a literary formula is a structure of narrative or dramatic conventions employed in a great number of individual works."[30] The concept of formula has been extended to incorporate nearly all of popular culture. In the most recent edition of *The Popular Culture Reader,* Christopher Geist and Jack Nachbar write: "Whatever approach you choose to take toward the study of the popular arts and culture . . . the concept of formula will be an essential part of your study. For in almost all of the popular culture, repetition, imitation and familiarity are key principles of understanding."[31] Regrettably, there is a major flaw in the notion of formula being nearly synonymous with popular culture. The concept is too inclusive. It includes every member of a set (genre, formula), *even* if a member of that set is a failure, that is, even if no one or a mere handful of people consumes it. We have not argued for a given percentage of adoption by the public being equivalent to a significant threshold of popularity, for this will necessitate much research and may well differ for different cultures, for different ideas, products, etc.; but to include failures within popular culture just because they attempt to imitate successful ideas or works in a particular popular genre, as Geist and Nachbar argue, would subvert the notion that popularity is the key concept in popular culture, an idea which Geist and Nachbar accept.[32] It may be worth asserting that failures, rarely the subject of popular culture analysis, should be studied. Such analysis would perhaps give us greater insight into why others in a similar group or genre succeeded.[33]

Third, even though popular culture studies have very rarely used the criteria of popularity carefully and systematically, such an effort can be very productive for theory building. Will Wright's *Sixguns & Society: A Structural Study of the Western* is an excellent example of this. Wright found that including films in his study that the public failed to respond to means that "few clear patterns will emerge;" but if only the films which were box office hits are analyzed, then patterns of narrative and symbolic structure are discernible. Selecting only popular western films for analysis, Wright is able to "develop a cognitive theory of myth structure," which in turn allows "the structure of the Western . . . [to] be formally analyzed with respect to how its social meanings are communicated by its symbolism."[34] Regrettably, this model study which treats popularity as the *sine qua non* of one type of popular culture has had little impact on other popular culture studies.

Fourth, if popularity is the *sine qua non* of popular culture, then ideas, products, or whatever of similar popularity can be compared, those of different popularity contrasted. How are ideas and items of similar levels of popularity alike? What do they have in common in terms of creation, content, dissemination, and consumption? How do they differ? At what threshold level, if any, does popularity become a distinguishing, dominant factor? How do different economic, industrial, cultural, and social systems correlate with various levels of popularity? Are similar types of products and ideas adopted at comparable levels of popularity in such disparate countries as the U.S., U.S.S.R., and Mexico? In short, by a systematic examination of the essential variable, popularity, we will be able to build a theoretical base and adopt or create appropriate methodologies. By holding popularity relatively constant and discovering patterns, or the lack of them, we should unveil just what is unique about popular culture.

Fifth, by selecting one key variable, popularity, as the essence of our discipline, we can delete older analytic conceptualizations which have mystified, not aided, in discerning the basic elements and characteristics of popular culture. Popular culture commentators have subdivided culture into folk, elite, and mass;[35] or into high, folk, mid, and mass;[36] or high and popular;[37] and so on. Popularity demands that it alone be considered as a criterion, not categories imposed by some extraneous value or social system. Popular culture studies have been unable to deal with the anomaly of "why certain creative texts can and do become popular,"[38] or why the popular becomes elite, or the folk popular. By not prelabeling ideas or products, we avoid forcing the popular into conceptual straight-jackets which may have little to do with popularity. Only that which is demonstrably popular will be categorized, and then only in terms of levels of popularity. Whether elite, folk, or mass in origin, its adoption by a certain level of the population will determine its association with popular culture. Ridding the discipline of categories which have obstructed theory building and methodological creativity should allow for a fresh beginning, one which holds the promise of being more fruitful.

Sixth, periodization has been a major problem. Russel Nye, in his classic of 1970, *The Unembarrassed Muse,* argued that

The term 'the popular arts' cannot be used accurately to describe a cultural situation in Western civilization prior to the late eighteenth century. Certainly large numbers of people before that time found pleasant and rewarding ways of cultural diversion, but not until the emergence of mass society in the eighteenth century—that is, until the incorporation of the majority of the population into society—could either popular culture or popular art be said to exist.[39]

This view has been explicitly criticized, although not mentioning Nye by name, in Fred Schroeder's In-Depth Section on "Popular Culture Before Printing" and by Joise Campbell's Section on "Popular Culture in the Middle Ages," both in the *Journal of Popular Culture.*[40] Personally, I remain skeptical of Nye's critics. But the jury is definitely out on the question of just when popular culture began, precisely because, despite provocative essays in the *Journal,* no general test, such as popularity, has been systematically applied.

Lastly, a large number of general assertions have been made over the years about popular culture which are based only on an episodic examination of data which may or may not be relevant. If they were critically examined by a uniform across-the-board test, popularity, those which survived might well provide fundamental building blocks for popular culture theories and methodologies. Examples of such assertions are far too numerous to be listed, but a few selected examples will be given.

(1) Wilma Clark: "popular art *protects* the audience from what may be a painful exploration of the nature of reality."[41]
(2) Russel Nye: "popular culture is the most visible level of culture."[42]
(3) Tom Kando: popular culture is "the study of everyday life."[43]
(4) Fred Schroeder: "Popular works are not self-sustaining, because their meanings are thinly layered and tied to the moment."[44]
(5) Peter Prescott: "the novels most widely read tend to be innocent of just those qualities that make novels worth reading."[45]
(6) Jack Nachbar, et al.: "the more popular a thing is, the more culturally significant it is likely to be."[46]

This essay has argued that popularity is the *sine qua non* of popular culture, and that cultural elements which cannot demonstrate a sufficient level of popularity should be excluded from popular culture. It is acknowledged that the central concept of popularity needs to be further examined and refined, and that a threshold level for popularity may well differ in different societies and time periods. Indeed, developing a sufficiently sophisticated analytic tool will test traditional humanists. This effort should provide the field with a better theoretical and methodological grounding, something that has eluded popular culture studies to date.

Notes

1. Ray B. Browne, "Popular Culture: Notes Toward a Definition," in *Popular Culture and Curricula,* eds. Ray B. Browne and Ronald J. Ambrossetti, rev. ed. (Bowling Green, OH: Bowling Green U Popular P, 1972), 1–12. The first edition, which also contained Browne's essay, appeared in 1970.

2. Ibid.

3. Raymond Williams, *Keywords: A Vocabulary of Culture and Society* (New York: Oxford UP, 1976), 199.

4. Christopher D. Geist, "Popular Culture, the *Journal* and the State of the Study: A Sequel," *Journal of Popular Culture,* 13.3 (Spring 1980): 391–93.

5. *Journal of Popular Culture,* 19.1 (Summer 1985).

6. Chandra Mukerji and Michael Schudson, "Popular Culture," *Annual Review of Sociology,* 12 (1986): 51–53.

7. Peter Burke, *Popular Culture in Early Modern Europe* (London: Maurice Temple Smith Ltd., 1978).

8. Norman L. Friedman, "Mass Communications and Popular Culture: Convergent Fields in the Study of Mass Media," *Mass Comm Review,* 4.1 (Winter 1976–1977): 22.

9. Geist, 391–400.

10. For example, see Guillermo Bonfil Batalla, et al., Culturas populares y política cultural (Méxican: Museo de Culturas Populares, SEP, 1982); Herbert Schiller, et al., Foro internacional de comunicación social (México: El Día, 1982); and Ludovico Silva, et al., Medios de comunicacion, ideologia y estrategía imperialista, Cuadernos ol Centro de Estudios de la Comunicación, 5 (México: UNAM, 1979); Luís Ramiro Beltrán and Elizabeth Fox de Cardona, Comunicación dominada: Estados Unidos en los medios de América Latina (México: Editorial Nueva Imagen, 1980).

11. John Fiske, "Television and Popular Culture: Reflections on British and Australian Critical Practice" paper presented at the Iowa Symposium and Conference on Television Criticism, The University of Iowa, April 1985. Fiske ably reviews recent research by students of British television and its audience.

12. Browne, "Popular Culture: Notes Toward a Definition," 11.

13. Ray B. Browne, "Popular Culture as the New Humanities," *Journal of Popular Culture,* 17.4 (Spring 1984): 1.

14. Arthur Asa Berger, "The Poop on Pop Pedagogy," in Browne and Ambrosetti, eds., 75.

15. Russel B. Nye, "Notes on Popular Culture," quotes Fishwick. See excerpts from Nye's key essay in George H. Lewis, *Side-Saddle on the Golden Calf: Social Structure and Popular Culture in America* (Pacific Palisades, CA: Goodyear, 1972), 18. See also Marshall W. Fishwick, *Seven Pillars of Popular Culture* (Westport, CT: Greenwood, 1985).

16. Michael Schudson, "The Validation of Popular Culture: Sense and Sentimentality in Academia," *Critical Studies in Mass Communication,* 4 (1987): 51–52; and Mukerji and Schudson.

17. Peter Narváez and Martin Laba, *Media Sense: The Folklore-Popular Culture Continuum* (Bowling Green, OH: Bowling Green State U Popular P, n.d.).

18. Schudson, 56.

19. Gary Alan Fine, "Popular Culture and Social Interaction: Production, Consumption, and Usage," *Journal of Popular Culture,* 11.2 (Fall 1977): 453.

20. Jack Nachbar, Deborah Weiser, and John L. Wright, eds., *Popular Culture Reader* (Bowling Green, OH: Bowling Green State U Popular P, 1978): 5.

21. Leslie Fiedler, "Giving the Devil His Due," *Journal of Popular Culture,* 12.2 (Fall 1979): 197.

22. Fred E. H. Schroeder, *Outlaw Aesthetics: Arts and the Public Mind* (Bowling Green, OH: Bowling Green State U Popular P, 1977), 8, 13–14.

23. A somewhat similar definition is used by the editors of *Studies in Latin American Popular Culture.* See "Editors' Letter to Future Contributors," contained in each volume's front matter.

24. Friedman, 22; Geist, 390–91, 395, 398–99.

25. Gary Alan Fine, "Popular . . . Culture: Sociological Issues and Explorations," *Journal of Popular Culture,* 11.2 (Fall 1977): 382.

26. Promising beginnings are found in Richard A. Peterson, "Where the Two Cultures Meet: Popular Culture," *Journal of Popular Culture,* 11.2 (Fall 1977): 388–90; Peter Nagourney, "Elite, Popular and Mass Literature: What People Really Read," *Journal of Popular Culture,* 16.1 (Summer 1982): 99–107.

27. For a partial listing of data sources, see the "Appendix" to David Byron McMillen and Marilyn M. McMillen, "The Analysis of Popular Culture Through Social Indicators," *Journal of Popular Culture,* 11.2 (Fall 1977): 506–26.

28. Roger B. Rollin, "Against Evaluation: The Role of the Critic of Popular Culture," *Journal of Popular Culture,* 9.2 (Fall 1975): 355–65; and Roger B. Rollin, "Son of 'Against Evaluation': A Reply to John Shelton Lawrence," *Journal of Popular Culture,* 12.1 (Summer 1978): 113–17.

29. Cawelti's article appeared in 3.3 (Winter 1969): 381–90. See also his *Adventure, Mystery, and Romance: Formula Stories as Art and Popular Culture* (Chicago: U of Chicago P, 1976).

30. Cawelti, *Adventure, Mystery, and Romance,* 5.

31. Christopher D. Geist and Jack Nachbar, eds., *Popular Culture Reader,* 3rd ed. (Bowling Green, OH: Bowling Green State U Popular P, 1983), 304.

32. Ibid., 4. For another critique of the concept of formula, see David N. Feldman, "Formalism and Popular Culture," *Journal of Popular Culture,* 9.2 (Fall 1975): 384–402.

33. For two recent studies of failures, see Steven Back, *Final Cut: Dreams*

and Disaster in the Making of "Heaven's Gate" (New York: New American Library, 1987); Christopher M. Byron, *The Fanciest Dive* (New York: New American Library, 1987).

34. Will Wright, *Six Guns and Society: A Structural Study of the Western* (Berkeley: U of California P, 1977), 12–13, 15.

35. Browne in Browne and Ambrosetti, eds., 10.

36. Dwight MacDonald, *Against the Grain: Essays on the Effects of Mass Culture* (New York: DaCapo, 1983), 3–78.

37. Herbert J. Gans, *Popular Culture and High Culture: An Analysis and Evaluation of Taste* (New York: Basic, Harper Colophon, 1975), 14.

38. See Janice Radway, "Phenomenology, Linguistics, and Popular Literature," *Journal of Popular Culture,* 12.1 (Summer 1978): 98, n20.

39. Russel Nye, *The Unembarrassed Muse: The Popular Arts in America* (New York: Dial, 1970), 1.

40. These In-Depth Sections of the *Journal of Popular Culture* are found in 11.3 (Winter 1977): 627–753; and 14.1 (Summer 1980): 33–154.

41. Wilma Clark, "Four Popular Poets: A Century of Taste," in *New Dimensions in Popular Culture,* ed. Russel B. Nye (Bowling Green, OH: Bowling Green State U Popular P, 1972), 209.

42. Nye in Lewis, ed., 19.

43. Tom Kundo, "Popular Culture and Its Sociology: Two Controversies," *Journal of Popular Culture,* 9.2 (Fall 1975): 440. See also flyer for 1988 PCA national meeting, where popular culture is "the culture that most people enjoy . . . and all . . . phenomena of everyday life."

44. Schroeder, *Outlaw Aesthetics,* 40.

45. Peter S. Prescott, "The Making of a Best Seller," *Newsweek* 25 May 1961: 77.

46. Nachbar, Weiser, and Wright, eds., 5.

POPULARITY:
HOW TO MAKE A KEY CONCEPT COUNT
IN BUILDING A THEORY OF POPULAR CULTURE

Harold E. Hinds, Jr.

In this essay, Harold E. Hinds, Jr., further explores the idea that popularity is the sine qua non necessary to construct a theory of popular culture and also one approach which might salvage popular culture as a distinct category. It more completely probes the complexities and difficulties of defining popularity, and then, taking these into consideration, suggests both a minimal and an ideal standard for applying the concept to popular culture studies.

What approach or approaches should be adopted in the study of popular culture? The first generation of theorists believed that popular culture was especially characterized by formulas and its own aesthetics. Although both of these conceptual approaches have been subjected to a convincing critique (Rollin, "Against"; Rollin, "Son"; Feldman), they continue to enjoy currency among those, mainly critics writing for the popular media, who believe there are fundamental differences between "elite" and "popular" works of art, and by some scholars, e.g., Thomas J. Roberts' 1990 *An Aesthetics of Junk Fiction* and Arthur Asa Berger's 1992 *Popular Culture Genres*.

In my 1988 essay "Popularity: the *Sine Qua Non* of Popular Culture," I argue that popularity was the most promising concept for future theory building in popular culture studies. While the essay's main emphasis was on demonstrating that prior definitions of popular culture were too inclusive and that alternative conceptual approaches, e.g., those of aesthetics and formula, were seriously flawed, the concept of popularity itself was minimally developed. As a point of departure for theory building I suggested "that popularity at a minimum demands adoption/consumption in more than one regional culture and by more than one narrow socio-economic

Harold E. Hinds, Jr., "Popularity: How to Make a Key Concept Count in Building a Theory of Popular Culture," in Marilyn F. Motz, et al. (eds.), Eye on the Future: Popular Culture Scholarship into the Twenty-First Century in Honor of Ray B. Browne *(Bowling Green, OH: Bowling Green State University Popular Press, 1994), 43–53.*

group" (211). This essay will further explore the complexities and difficulties associated with defining popularity, and then, in light of these, suggest both a minimal and an ideal standard for applying the concept to popular culture studies. One basic question concerning popularity is: what exactly is to be counted, and how?

What constitutes a "text"[1] is a critical problem for any approach involving quantification. What is it exactly that will be counted? In one sense, a text would not appear to be problematic. Tonight's television sitcom, this morning's sports page, the local movie theater's current feature film, a new country LP that is number one on this week's *Billboard* charts, and Monday's chapter of the comic strip *Doonesbury,* all are easily identifiable texts. Or are they? For each might well appear, not in a single format, but in several, and if so, which one (or ones) should be considered the unit of study? For example, the film will eventually be seen not just as a feature movie in a movie theater, but on Home Box Office, and then as a video that can be purchased or, most likely, rented. And the movie originally shown at a cinema may well differ from the video release, for at a minimum most videos significantly crop the rectangular movie to make it fit the squarish television screen. Content, perhaps significant, is lost. Today's *Doonesbury* strip will appear on the comics page in some papers, but on the editorial page in others, and some papers will elect not to run it at all, if the paper's editors deem it's content too objectionable, and might well substitute an older episode in its place. And at a later date it will be collected in one, perhaps many, collections of Gary Trudeau's work. In general, though, the problems here are not of too great a consequence, for the "same" text is presented "relatively unaltered" in either a different format or a different context.

Many texts, however, *are* significantly altered when presented anew. Subsequent editions can be quite different. Illustrations may be added to a print text, as when Big Little Books transformed pulps into lavishly illustrated novels; consequently the text was both enhanced and expanded. Paperback editions, on the other hand, not infrequently delete most, or even all, of the original hardback's illustrations. Bowdlerized texts, *Reader's Digest* novels, and children's editions can even more radically alter by deleting original text. Altered texts also result from translations into other languages; from the modernization of archaic language, e.g., The Revised Standard version of the King James version of the *Bible* or high school editions of Shakespeare plays; and from the addition of explanatory text or annotations to another period's classics. Syndicated television programs, or later rebroadcasts, use different ads, creating a new text. Many types of popular texts, when presented in alternate mediums, result in quite different texts, e.g., the novelization of movies, postcards of famous vistas, Classics Illustrated comic books based on established literary works, and radio ads using only the audio part of television ads.

In addition, the very act of consumption alters the text. A text does not inject meanings into its consumer, rather there is a complex set of interactions, a give and take between a reader/viewer/consumer and the popular text. The consumer's values, opinions, beliefs, and the like interact/collide with those of the text to create a new text, one potentially quite different from that intended by the text's author(s). And these new texts may resemble those of other consumers with similar cultural and socio-economic backgrounds, or they may be highly individualistic (Fiske 62–83).

Incidentally, the problem of what constitutes a text applies not only to individual works, but to groups of texts, such as a popular author's complete corpus or a genre. But to the problems of how to count different editions or translations or appearances in new formats or mediums is added that of the degree of inclusiveness: just how similar to the prototype of a modern, adult Western, the *Virginian,* must a work be to be counted? Is Louis L'Amour's origin novel for the Sackett clan, *Sackett's Land,* which is set in Elizabethan England, a Western? Or are the adventures of a flying cowboy, Sky King?

What then is to be counted, if a title's, or a category's, popularity is to be summed up? All appearances by an individual title, despite its being abridged, condensed, modernized, illustrated, or censored, should be added together. Also counted, but separately, should be all appearances in alternate mediums, such as movie novelizations. It seems reasonable to be at least this inclusive, even if noting the difference between the above two categories. In addition, it would be useful to also at least note appearances which in some sense model or mold themselves upon the original text, e.g., parodies such as Mel Brooks' movie *Young Frankenstein.* One might also conceptualize these three groups as a text's field of popularity, with the original and near original texts occupying the center, with appearances in other mediums occupying an inner ring just beyond the center, and with an outer ring being composed of works bearing a strong family resemblance to the original.

If it can be decided what to count, how should the text's popularity be reported? Basically when stating that a given text is most popular or ranks X or Y on a given list, one of two variables is used: how many were bought, viewed, etc., or how many dollars, pounds, etc. were spent on sales and/or rentals. Both of these measures, when given as crude figures, can be highly misleading. If a bestseller sells one million copies, or the Superbowl draws an audience of 100 million plus, *and* both are labeled popular culture, as is often the case, *both* are *not* equivalent in popularity. One reaches less than half of one percent, the other about half, of the United States' population.

Likewise, if a movie grossed $50 million in 1928, and another movie in 1990 grossed $100 million, and one simply listed movies in rank order of total receipts, with ticket sales not given in constant units of currency; i.e., if inflation is not taken into account, then one would incorrectly list the 1990 movie as more popular than the 1928 flick. Popularity, whether stated in terms of total audience or gross income, should always be stated both as raw figures *and* either as a percentage of total population or in terms of constant units of currency.

Furthermore, available data on sales or consumption may not always agree or be reliable. Competing surveys using different definitions and measurement techniques, or surveying different populations or even questioning the same population but at different times and/or under alternate circumstances, can produce data which range from confirming each other to differing significantly. For example, there does not exist an agreed-upon set of criteria for how many copies a hardback or paperback book must sell to be placed on a "best-seller" list, or even which book sellers or publishers should be consulted in determining sales (Atlas). Frequent discrepancies between such lists should, then, come as no surprise. To cite another example, the Nielsen ratings for television programs can produce estimates of popularity different from those of the Gallup polling organization. Gallup, unlike Nielsen, does not produce an estimate of who is watching which programs, but asks a statistically valid sample of viewers which programs they enjoy. Both rank their findings, but in 1992 Nielsen rated the new television comedy *Home Improvement* sixth, while the show did not even make Gallup's list of top comedy programs, and the new comedy *Davis Rules* ranked 56th according to Neilsen but topped Gallup's list in the new-television-comedy category (Dorsey). The fact that statistics are neither as complete as desired, nor always consistent, nor gathered for the purpose(s) scholars wish to use them for, should not deter cautious, judicious use of what is available. Failure to do so will only perpetuate the confusion of marginally popular texts with those texts that do reach far greater audiences.

If total audience or sales for a text, or group of texts, can be ascertained, some attention, if possible, should also be given to who bought, who consumed the text. Assuming for now that the basic geographical unit of consumption is the modern nation state (see discussion on geography and popularity below), the "who" is generally stated, if addressed at all, in terms of a typical or average consumer, or as a demographic profile of all consumers, or as a statistically valid sample of consumers. Since consumers of a product or category of goods are a highly varied lot, a profile of an average or typical consumer may seriously distort the demographic basis of popularity. When data permit, a portrait of consumers should be given in terms of the variables of race, ethnicity, gender, and class/income, and a description of a typical consumer should be balanced by attention to the range of consumers. For instance, my sample of the purchasers of the Mexican superhero comic book *Kalimán,* revealed the average buyer to be a subteen lower-middle-class urban boy, but the age ranged from 12 to 60, and the socio-economic status (SES) from an illiterate shoeshine boy to lawyers practicing before a state supreme court (Hinds and Tatum 32–34). Unfortunately, data sufficiently abundant and reliable to enable popularity to be stated in terms of a demographic profile often either are proprietary, and thus not accessible, or simply have never been collected.

A number of caveats, however, are in order about demographic profiles of consumers. First, in at least some cases, purchase, possession, or presence does not mean the text is in fact consumed. Too many books litter my own study, bought with the best of intentions, but only partially read, or awaiting some never-to-be parallel life with a surfeit of reading time, for me to ever confuse purchase with consumption. Some consumers just enjoy shopping, but cannot limit themselves to window shopping: such purchases often end up in attics or yard sales. Some purchases function more as status symbols, used only for display, than as vehicles for either knowledge or entertainment, e.g., coffee-table books. The Italian semiotician, Umberto Eco, believed his first novel, *The Name of the Rose,* would appeal to about a thousand readers, yet it sold nine million copies, most of which probably remained unfinished. Indeed Eco has become the master of "a trend in modern publishing: the unread best seller." He followed his first novel with *Foucault's Pendulum,* a volume so dense and intellectually complex that he hoped 500 of the millions purchased would ever really be read (Stille 125, 128)! And is everyone really listening to all those turned-on radios and televisions? Evidently, at least many Americans and Britons use these media as background noise or pay only nominal attention until something is broadcast of "real" interest (Morley). Are all those books purchased for prospective readers by your local public librarian ever read by more than a few, or always read when checked out? The British scholar, Peter Mann, argues that most literary, i.e., "serious," novels are not purchased by individuals, but by libraries, and probably have multiple readers, but he also notes that very little is actually known about "what use is made of . . . [a purchased book] when it gets into the public libraries" (12). Finally, some purchases force the consumer to accept an entire package or collection when he or she is in fact only interested in one or two stories, songs, etc. For example, the Book-of-the-Month Club's offering of a special package deal which the consumer cannot resist, but which leaves that extra "bargain" unopened, points to selectively realized consumption.

Second, consumption is not always by choice. Sales of Shakespeare's more popular plays, *Hamlet* and *Macbeth,* are probably in the main to high schools and to college bookstores. Assigned texts should not be confused with those purchased and consumed by choice. Items purchased as Christmas or birthday gifts are not always received by choice, or even necessarily freely consumed. And, of course, every family has its collection of gifts relegated to a back closet, never consumed, but which no one will risk not having at hand should they be needed for display to the giver.

Third, pass-along consumption often goes unrecorded, or its being recorded depends a great deal on the delivery medium. Purchased books often are passed along to family and relatives, fellow workers, or neighbors. For example, a Mexican comic book, it is estimated, may on average be reread by ten additional readers other than the original purchaser. They either acquire it on the used market, rent a reading, hear it read aloud, or borrow it. These consumers largely remain uncounted. Samples of home TV audiences, on the other hand, do attempt to factor in entire households, and to account for just who does watch.

The above examples strongly suggest that in at least some cases a demographic profile of consumers based on "official" data may well provide only a partial picture of actual consumption. Sophisticated counts, and discussions of available data, should take into account such inadequacies and anomalies, even if the issue(s) cannot be satisfactorily resolved.

Demographic profiles of consumers, however, need to be placed within a geographical and historical perspective. A strictly regional culture would not qualify as popular, any more than one restricted to a narrow socio-economic group, e.g., recent Ph.D.s. The concept of a "region," however, has not been easy to define even for geographers. Peter Haggett in *Geography: A Modern Synthesis,* the most widely adopted college-level introductory geography textbook in the English-speaking world, simply states that "a region is any tract of the earth's surface with characteristics, either natural or of human origin, which make it different from the areas that surround it" (262). Cultural regions have both physical and cultural characteristics, and are the products of diffusion of generally multiple characteristics from a cultural hearth outward. For example, Donald Meining in a classic essay envisioned a region composed of three concentric areas: core, domain, and sphere; the core being the cultural hearth and having the highest concentration of the region's signature characteristics, the sphere being farthest removed from the regional center of diffusion and including the places where the defining characteristics have not yet been generally adopted. Regions may be rather small, as are those pockets of America targeted by nine-digit ZIP code mailings. Michael Weiss has identified some 40 neighborhood types based on the target mailing system developed by the

Claritas Corporation, e.g., working-class row house districts or small towns based on light industry and farming.

Regions of interest to popular culture scholars will undoubtedly be considerably larger than Weiss' neighborhood types which incorporate about one to five percent of the population. Wilbur Zelinsky's cultural areas, broadly inclusive cultural regions, number only five for the entire continental United States: New England, the Midland, the South, the Middle West, and the West, although he is not certain just where to place Texas, much of Peninsular Florida, and Oklahoma. When data is available for the United States on a state-by-state basis, aggregates of data can provide a good approximation of Zelinsky's cultural areas and even reveal cultural hearths. Most sources of data available on popular culture use the predominant geographical statistical unit of the modern world, the nation state. Of course, some cultural regions embrace supranational areas of the world, e.g., the Islamic world, but data at this level is generally less available. Whenever statistical data for the popularity of some text is available and is broken down into sub-national regions, the fact that consumption is not restricted to a narrow cultural region should be demonstrated. When data is only available at the national level and only a small percent of the population is reached on a first-hand basis, e.g., the case for a "bestseller" novel with sales of one million, the fact that this might represent consumption for only a quite limited cultural area and/or socio-economic status group should be acknowledged. That is, the study may really belong to regional, not popular, culture. In any case, the geographical scope of adoption/consumption should always be given, if known.

My 1988 minimal conception of popularity ignored the temporal or historical dimension, a serious deficiency in the original essay. Clearly different popular texts have very different life spans. Much of popular culture is ephemeral, throwaway culture. Pet Rocks, individual Harlequin romance titles, Hula Hoops, and the like are only momentary blips on the cultural scene.

Some previously ephemeral popular culture, due to new technologies or a multiplication of delivery channels, has gained a second life: rebroadcast of vintage television programs on superstation channels or on cable has given life to programs such as *Dragnet* or *Andy Griffith*. New video technologies have vastly expanded the temporal range of our choices for an evening's cinema entertainment: older movies which many of us might never have had the opportunity to see are now readily available, whether an Academy Award Winner, a critic's favorite, or a trashy "B" film. Indeed, "new" editions can significantly prolong the popular life of a text. Reissuing a hardback in a paperback edition, adoption as a *Reader's Digest* Condensed Book, selection by the Book-of-the-Month or Quality Paperback Clubs, for example, can significantly boost sales and extend the longevity of a text.

Some texts may never, if the time unit used is a month or even a year, appear on "bestseller" or such lists. Yet they are slow, steady sellers whose lifetime sales may well top even the most attention-getting short-term success stories: *The Bible* is easily *the* all time best seller in the United States. Many category books (Westerns, Romances, Mysteries) are slow, steady sellers. And in some of these cases, it will make more sense to count the lifetime sales of the entire category, e.g., Harlequins, or the entire corpus of an author, e.g., Louis L'Amour, than sales of individual titles. Classics frequently sell especially well when first introduced, then sell at modest levels indefinitely, e.g., James Frazer's *The Golden Bough* (Beard 216–23, 227).[2] Since the periodicity of popularity is so variable, popularity should always be expressed in terms of a specific period, whatever is appropriate and provides the fullest and most accurate portrait, whether the temporal unit is a month, season, decade, year, century, or even millennium. And if possible, it should also be expressed in terms of periodic totals or periodic averages.

If attention to popularity may be necessary for building theories and methodologies unique to popular culture studies, then popular culture scholarship should incorporate estimates of popularity. As a *minimum* those estimates should include the total number of consumers as a percentage of total population, attempt to determine who the consumers are and their geographical distribution, and be sensitive to just when an item is popular. If figures are given not for consumers, but for total sales, then sums should always be corrected for inflation (e.g., given in constant dollars). *Ideally,* consumer profiles will include information on typical consumers, as well as the diversity of consumers in terms of gender, race, class, and income; geographical data will attend to sub- and supra-national distributions of consumers; all appearances, regardless of format or medium, of a text or a group/category of texts will be taken into consideration; and the conditions under which consumption takes place, or fails to take place despite purchase, will be considered.

A perusal of the articles appearing in the flagship journal of popular culture studies, the *Journal of Popular Culture,* reveals that often not even the minimum is attended to, and the ideal almost never. This undoubtedly reflects the lack of confidence that popular culture scholars, overwhelmingly either literature or history professors, have in working with statistics. Yet the rewards for such attention could be considerable. Imagine a data base which gives at least minimal attention to popularity. Popular culture could then be presented not as a crude, homogeneous whole or as divided only along the lines of genres or categories of goods, but as stratified, with strata composed of texts of similar degrees of popularity, and within a stratum clusters of texts with distinct demographic, geographical, and temporal characteristics. Such information on, and organization of, popular culture might well allow sufficiently meaningful comparisons and conclusions to be drawn to build theories, models, and methodologies unique to popular culture. Perhaps with such a comparative base popular culture studies might yet suggest plausible answers to such questions as when, under what conditions, in which versions, and by whom do texts become accepted and consumed by some, a majority, or nearly all of a culture.

Finally, the model outlined in this article both incorporates recent theoretical concerns in humanities scholarship *and* transcends them. Any careful treatment of a text and its adoption/consumption, I argue, must reflect the concerns of post-modernist critics and social science scholarship: texts are not stable, often appear in multiple forms and mediums, and are appropriated by diverse audiences rather than by average consumers. The process of appropriation, which this essay has not focused on, in turn fashions new texts.

Then my argument parts company with these theorists, as this newer scholarship also posits that in the post-modern world traditional cultural hierarchies, such as elite vs. popular art, have dissolved. It also states that whether culture as a whole, or particular aspects of it, is the subject of study, the analytical method(s) used should be applied symmetrically (Collins, Sarchett, Mukerji and Schudson). Thus, while older approaches based on formula and aesthetics failed to establish the distinctiveness of popular culture, and while at least some post-modernist analytical models, e.g., semiology, can be profitably applied to a wide range of texts, including those commonly labeled popular or elite, my approach promises to salvage popular culture as a distinctive category. A great deal of empirical research, with careful attention to degrees of popularity, will first be necessary, but rather than resulting in the dissolution of popular culture into culture in general, it might yet provide an analytical foundation for this important category.

Notes

1. In this essay "text" refers to concrete physical objects, e.g., books, television programs, movies, print ads, and children's toys; to mental thoughts or images, e.g., beliefs, values, myths, lore, customs, and common knowledge; to events, e.g., the assassination of a political leader and rituals; and to experiences, e.g., watching the Superbowl and eating a Big Mac.

2. In particular see Beard (216–23, 227) where she makes a case for *The Golden Bough*'s "extraordinary and immediate popularity" upon publication, and

its contemporary popularity which "rests on the undeniable fact that it is so rarely read," as indeed are many classics.

Works Cited

Atlas, James. "Making the List." *The Atlantic* 252.6 (Dec. 1983): 108–12.

Beard, Mary. "Frazer, Leach, and Vigil: The Popularity (and Unpopularity) of *The Golden Bough.*" *Comparative Studies in Society and History* 34.2 (1992): 203–24.

Berger, Arthur Asa. *Popular Culture Genres: Theories and Texts.* Newbury Park: Sage, 1992.

Collins, Jim. *Uncommon Cultures: Popular Culture and Post-Modernism.* New York: Routledge, 1989.

Dorsey, Tom. "People Choose Favorites Tonight." *Courier-Journal* (Louisville) 17 Mar. 1992: C1–2.

Feldman, David N. "Formalism and Popular Culture." *Journal of Popular Culture* 9.2 (1975): 384–402.

Fiske, John. *Television Culture.* London: Methuen, 1987.

Haggett, Peter. *Geography: A Modern Synthesis.* Rev. 3rd ed. New York: Harper & Row, 1983.

Hinds, Harold E., Jr. "Popularity: The *Sine Qua Non* of Popular Culture." *Symbiosis: Popular Culture and Other Fields.* Eds. Ray B. Browne and Marshall W. Fishwick. Bowling Green, OH: Bowling Green State U Popular P, 1988: 207–16.

Hinds, Harold E., Jr., and Charles M. Tatum. *Not Just for Children: The Mexican Comic Book in the Late 1960's and 1970's.* Westport: Greenwood, 1992.

Mann, Peter H. "The Romantic Novel and Its Readers." *Journal of Popular Culture* 15.1 (1981): 9–18.

Meining, Donald W. "The Mormon Culture Region: Strategies and Patterns in the Geography of the American West, 1847–1964." *Annals of the Association of American Geographers* 55.2 (1965): 213–17.

Morley, David. *Family Television: Cultural Power and Domestic Leisure.* London: Comedia, 1986.

Mukerji, Chandra, and Michael Schudson. "Popular Culture." *Annual Review of Sociology* 12 (1986): 47–66.

Roberts, Thomas J. *An Aesthetics of Junk Fiction.* Athens: U of Georgia P, 1990.

Rollin, Roger B. "Against Evaluation: The Role of the Critic of Popular Culture." *Journal of Popular Culture* 9.2 (1975): 355–65.

———. "Son of 'Against Evaluation': A Reply to John Sheldon Lawrence." *Journal of Popular Culture* 12.1 (1978): 113–17.

Sarchett, Barry W. "The Joke Is On Us: The End of 'Popular' Culture Studies, and It's a Good Thing Too." Paper presented at "The Future of Popular Culture

Studies in the Twenty-First Century." Bowling Green State University, Bowling Green, OH, 4–6 June 1992.

Stille, Alexander. "The Novel as Status Symbol." *The Atlantic* 264.5 (Nov. 1989): 125–29.

Weiss, Michael J. *The Clustering of America.* New York: Harper & Row, 1988.

Zelinsky, Wilbur. *The Cultural Geography of the United States.* Rev. ed. Englewood Cliffs: Prentice-Hall, 1992.

THE DEVELOPMENT AND STAGES OF POPULAR CULTURE: A CASE STUDY OF TOKUGAWA AND MEIJI JAPAN

Ling Chan Becker and Harold E. Hinds, Jr.

If popular culture is understood as that culture which is widely dissemi-nated and consumed, then what are the historical conditions under which it emerges? Some have assumed its appearance is one result of industrial-ization, others have associated its emergence with urbanization. Becker and Hinds study early modern Japan as a test case, and conclude by sug-gesting a three-stage development for widespread and widely adapted culture or popular culture. Ling Chan Becker is a former student of Hinds. This essay began as an Honors Project. Becker earned an M.A. in Public Administration, and today is a "full-time mom."

The conditions under which popular culture, understood as that culture which is widely disseminated and consumed, emerges have only begun to receive considerable scholarly attention. Two pioneering scholars, Russel Nye and Fred Schroeder, independently suggested factors which led to the development of popular culture. For Nye, critical factors included urban-ization, dominance of the middle class, education and literacy, as well as in-dustrialization. In the United States and Europe, these factors began to emerge about 1750 and were definitely in place by 1850.[1] Schroeder offered several different critical factors in his analysis. His included the develop-ment of a metropolitan culture, in which the extension of a city's influence, not its size, was most important. In addition, he discussed the importance of replication, dissemination, efficient communication and effective, cen-tralized political control.[2]

Tokugawa and Meiji Japan provide an interesting test case in deter-mining the origins of popular culture, for several major reasons. In Toku-gawa Japan (1568–1867), we find a highly urbanized, but non-industrialized, society. We can look at popular culture development at the time of the Toku-gawa regime, while controlling for the variable of industrialization, which does not occur until the Meiji regime (1867–1911). In addition, a better as-sessment of popular culture origins would take into account both Nye's and Schroeder's factors, while re-evaluating popular culture origins by separat-ing it into two distinct stages of development. The first stage of popular culture development can be termed the "proto-popular culture" stage, which in our case study emerged during Tokugawa Japan. The second stage is a "popular culture" stage, which becomes evident following the emergence of Meiji Japan.[3]

Our case study is important for two additional reasons. The first is that Tokugawa and Meiji Japan provide an interesting non-Western test case in contrast to the Western bias of Nye's and Schroeder's theses. Moreover, this research adds further support to recent revisionists' analyses of Tokugawa Japan, in which it is revealed to have played a vital role in the eventual industrialization and modernization of Japan. In particular, since the case for the Meiji period is well known, but that of the "proto"-stage remains understudied, the latter will receive greater attention in this article.

There are several key factors associated with Tokugawa Japan which facilitated the development of a proto-popular culture stage, that foreshadowed the full emergence of popular culture. These include the following: (1) the high rate of urbanization; (2) the ability to widely diffuse culture; (3) periodic migrations to areas where culture could be directly experienced; (4) the development of a centralized state; (5) the growing capacity for replicating various cultural forms; (6) the gradual emergence of a class system, which allowed for some social mobility; (7) an integrated and commercialized market structure; (8) the ever more widespread attainment of the economic and educational means to consume culture. Each of these factors will be examined individually, and then in a discussion of a key cultural system, Kabuki. Then, focusing on these same key factors, we will selectively illustrate Japan's movement into the developed popular culture stage, during the Meiji period. Finally, we will outline a three-stage model (antecedent, emerging, and developed) for the development of popular culture.

Urbanization

The Tokugawa era represented nearly three hundred years of peace and stability for Japan, which allowed for prosperity and growth.[4] Its population of thirty million people lived in a highly urbanized society.[5] This was reflected by the country's capital, Edo, which around 1721 surpassed two other large Japanese cities, Kyoto and Osaka, in population. By that time, Edo was the most populous city in the world, with a population of about a million inhabitants.[6]

In comparison to Europe during the same period, Japan's urbanization rate was very high indeed. While only two percent of Europe's population lived in cities greater than 100,000, about five to seven percent of the Japanese population did so. Even Osaka and Kyoto were easily comparable to London and Paris in population, the largest cities in the West at the time.[7] In addition, there were other highly urbanized areas, castle towns, scattered throughout the Japanese countryside. For example, the castle town Kanazawa had a population of over 100,000.[8] The Tokugawa government, centered in Edo, developed these castle towns into a highly integrated network which became a key mechanism for maintaining control over the rest of the country. In addition, as these castle towns grew at an unprecedented rate, they became both strong administrative and economic centers which fostered innovation and spread changes to surrounding provincial areas.[9]

Within the largest Tokugawa urban metropolises of Edo, Osaka and Kyoto, there were sectors designated solely for entertainment purposes.[10] An example of one of these entertainment quarters was Yoshiwara on the outskirts of Edo, a place where townsmen, known as *chonin,* flocked and various commoner cultural forms were created. Entertainment quarters offered a wide range of activities. Within the sector were found courtesan pleasure quarters, Kabuki theaters, teahouses and independent street entertainers.[11] These districts were created by the Tokugawa government as a means of separating them from the rest of the city. These entertainment sectors were often relegated to the urban outskirts, in an attempt to limit their influences upon the general population,[12] but this was only partly successful, since many smaller entertainment sectors emerged throughout the city in response.[13]

Around the middle part of the seventeenth century, the urban townsmen began to frequent the entertainment quarters.[14] As a reaction to occupying the lowest rung on the official Confucian social scale, urban merchants created in the pleasure and theater districts a world which they could command with their growing economic prosperity.[15] The popularity of entertainment districts paralleled a period of rising income for many of these urban commoners.

In particular, the Genroku period (1668–1704) can be noted for its economic prosperity as well as for the development of a commoner culture within the urban centers. At this time, there was a tremendous rise in status of the urban middle class, as both commercial bourgeoisie and merchants prospered.[16] The merchants especially began to gain substantial profits between 1650 and 1660. These years also mark the growth of new popular art forms and the period in which Kabuki theater matured.[17]

Consumption patterns of the period reflect the new wealth which was accumulated by the urban commoner class. Their rise in income created an increased demand for goods and services within the urban centers. In addition, these individuals now had sufficient time and money to engage in leisure-time cultural activities.[18] "Buoyed by the support of wealthy *chonin,* both the Yoshiwara prostitution quarter and the theater district reached their zenith as the two great central fixtures of Edo culture."[19] For the first time, commoners became culturally very important.[20] Previously, elite cultural forms such as ink painting and noh theater had dominated.[21]

The Tokugawa government attempted to restrict conspicuous consumption on the part of the upwardly mobile urban townspeople. It was believed by the government that proper class relationships within Tokugawa society should be maintained not only by their functions, but also by material aspects of life such as food, dress and housing, and by cultural and intellectual activities.[22] Despite these attempts at restricting various aspects of conspicuous consumption, it was to little avail in most cases.[23] Instead, the pleasure quarters became the source of wide spread urban fads, e.g., kimono styles and hair styles.[24]

Cultural Diffusion

Culture flourished within the urban centers of Tokugawa Japan, and then diffused across the countryside. In particular, the popular culture of Edo became extended to other areas within the entire country. An example of this was traveling entertainment troupes who performed Kabuki and Bunraku (puppet) theater.[25] Often, the materials which were used by these troupes were re-worked from urban theatrical performances.[26] In castle towns both townspeople and samurai swarmed to theaters which were outdoors even though ticket prices were at times presumably quite high. Also, these cultural forms were diffused through provincial visits and tours by the same professional actors who performed in the great urban theaters; these tours often included circuits which enabled these well-known actors to simultaneously visit and perform at popular pilgrimage centers.[27]

Another mechanism for diffusion of cultural knowledge was itinerant merchants and craftsmen who traveled throughout the countryside. They not only peddled much needed commercial goods and services, but were also bringers of news and stories to the villages they visited.[28]

Likewise, books in the Tokugawa period, widely available to commoners, were important mechanisms for cultural diffusion. Before the 1600s, printed books were entirely of a religious nature and were quite expensive, and the literacy rate was low, but these hindrances were removed during the Tokugawa period, beginning around 1620.[29]

Rental libraries best reflect the importance that books played in the dissemination of culture throughout the country. One important element for diffusion was access, and rental libraries were essential in giving commoners access to a wide array of books. While books were in general quite expensive to buy, rental libraries would lend them for up to five days at only 1/10 of the general selling price, allowing even lower-class urban commoners access. In addition, the growing number of lenders during the Tokugawa period made books particularily easy to obtain in urban areas. For example, in Edo during the beginning of the seventeenth century, there were well over six-hundred rental libraries and by 1830 there were close to eight hundred. Similarily, Osaka with a population of about 400,000 in 1830 had close to three-hundred rental libraries.

During the Tokugawa period, books were not only available to those living in the urban metropolises of Edo, Kyoto and Osaka. There were also peddlers who travelled with packs of books on their backs through the neighborhoods at the outer edges of the cities and itinerant book peddlers who also helped disseminate works beyond the city limits,[30] who journeyed the countryside much like the wandering merchants and craftsmen, distributing books throughout Tokugawa Japan.[31]

Books were available on a wide range of topics, giving commoners a great deal of choice in reading materials. Some lenders had collections of close to ten-thousand volumes.[32] A popular genre of books was the *kusazoshi,* which were extremely popular with the *chonin.* In these illustrated texts, authors and artists cooperated in production. *Kusazoshi* were printed using wood blocks and large quantities were circulating by 1720.[33] As early as the 1660s, books with large illustrations and a minimum amount of text dominated the industry[34] and allowed even the illiterate to have access to cultural information.[35] The various genres of books available had a wide variety of subject matters, but themes centered around life within the pleasure and entertainment quarter predominated.[36]

Undoubtedly, the number of books and lending libraries were a reflection of the growing publishing industry of the period. Amazingly, by the 1650s the publication of books had expanded so rapidly that Kyoto dealers began publishing lengthy lists of the works which were available. "Starting with 1,600 titles in twenty-two subject categories, the classifications expanded to seventy-two as more and more different kinds of books were published. The fourteenth of these lists, published in Edo in 1696 . . . ran to 674 pages and listed author, number of volumes, publisher, and price for its 7,800 titles."[37] During the Genroku period, there were about 180 new titles each year. With initial printing, reprintings and revised editions one can estimate that each year, beginning around the end of the seventeenth century, there were close to 100,000 to 200,000 volumes printed.[38]

Another mechanism which facilitated the movement of culture was the local Ise confraternities which travelled each year to parishes throughout the Tokugawa countryside. They gave away religious souvenirs and in turn promoted a common knowledge through encouraging pilgrimages to Ise, the most important Shinto shrine in Japan.[39] Finally, the alternate residence system (*sankin kotai*) set up a means for cultural diffusion as well. This system forced daimyo (hereditary feudal noblemen) to spend part of each year in Edo and the remaining part of the year in their respective domains.[40] One example of this system assisting in the diffusion of urban culture to rural areas is that in order to keep up with changing cultural information, daimyo hired Rusuiyakus, whose tasks included disseminating news from urban centers to the daimyo while they were residing in their respective domains and away from Edo.[41]

Migration and Cultural Contacts

Moreover, during the Tokugawa period, people engaged in periodic migrations to areas where opportunities to consume popular culture were readily available. The primary example of this was the pilgrimage, an activity which included people from various classes converging on a variety of shrine sites during the year. Pilgrimages increased in popularity as road conditions were improved and pilgrimage restrictions were reduced, reflecting a renewed emphasis on such travel's religious merit. The numbers of pilgrims each year during the Tokugawa period was quite high by most standards.[42] "Ise Fever" or periodic crazes swept Japan from the sixteenth century on as people from various walks of life journeyed on pilgrimages to the Ise Shrine.[43] It has been estimated that as many as 4.3 million people went to the Ise Shrine in 1830.[44] While the primary purpose of pilgrimages was religious, for many it became an acceptable excuse to travel and in turn to sight see. Whenever people travelled, there was a tendency to spend the night in castle towns and other places where there were opportunities to experience an array of entertainments.[45]

While at the Ise Shrine, visiting pilgrims had countless cultural opportunities. For instance, near the shrine there was Furichichi Street, on which travelers could find brothels, eating houses, souvenir shops, Kabuki and puppet theaters and other places of entertainment that were similar to those found in the entertainment quarters of larger cities.[46] There were other large and popular shrines and shrine circuits, such as the Kompira Shrine and the Shikiku Circuit, but none were as frequented as the Ise Shrine.[47]

As was briefly discussed earlier, the alternate residence system allowed for a yearly migration to Edo by daimyo and their retainers. This movement produced opportunities for exposure to cultural activities emerging in the cities, particularily Edo. While daimyo were not supposed to go to Kabuki plays or visit the pleasure quarters, many did attend or at least did what they could to catch a glimpse.[48] While restrictions were in place prohibiting aspects of cultural consumption, in general the restrictions were not particularily effective in preventing any class from consuming aspects of urban culture.

In addition, frequent travel for recreation, especially by the latter half of the Tokugawa period, became more common and more multi-destinational as the country experienced continued peace and stability. When people went on pilgrimages, they often attempted to catch glimpses of sights along the way; many attempted to return home using different routes than they had previously traveled in order to see new attractions and to take part in a wider variety of experiences.[49] "The shrine visit itself was actually only one highlight in a long sequence of excited planning, drunken send-offs, adventures on the road, and a debilitating round of welcome-home parties."[50]

In addition, during the Tokugawa era many increasingly travelled to urban centers for visits or in search of employment opportunities.[51] "The Japanese have always been a traveling people . . ."[52] and clearly travel became a true cultural experience at this time. Undoubtedly, this growing contact with other Japanese gradually brought about a greater cultural unification of Japan.

Political Centralization and a More Common Culture

Tokugawa Japan became a highly centralized state. For example, the alternate residence system worked to reduced the local and regional power bases of the daimyos. In order to make the alternate residence system feasible[53] the centralized state developed an effective communication network, which in turn, assisted in the distribution and formulation of a common national culture.

The limits of centralized power also played a role in cultural unification. The ability of the merchants and peasants to experience even limited upward mobility indicates the inability of the government to maintain an absolute and rigid feudal state. And the rising incomes of Japanese commoners helped create a common culture which was in direct opposition to the power elite and to the restrictions which were placed on commoners at the time. In addition, the government was ineffective in using sumptuary restrictions to regulate consumption within Tokugawa society. For example, the government failed to control the movement of people even though it continually attempted to regulate travel on the Tokugawa roads.[54] Lastly, the centralized government was even limited in its ability to prevent the upper classes of Tokugawa society from taking part in urban commoner cultural activities. Court ladies and daimyo alike were curious about and even attended the worlds of pleasure and theater.[55]

Replication

The replication of cultural forms was also a key factor in the proto-popular culture development of Tokugawa Japan. Replication was not a recent phenomenon. For centuries monks and laypeople gathered at speical sites, scriptoria, to copy Buddhist texts by hand and thereby gain religious merit.[56]

Although movable type was briefly introduced in early Tokugawa times, it was soon replaced by woodblock printing. "As publishing became increasingly a commercial enterprise, the more economical method of printing from woodblocks, used in Japan for at least six hundred years, soon replaced movable type. Of the five hundred works known to have been printed between 1593 and 1625, eighty percent were printed by movable type, but movable type accounted for less than 20 percent of printing occurring during the next quarter-century, and for virtually none after 1650."[57] And thereafter, the principle vehicle for printing remained the woodblock until the Meiji period.[58]

During the Tokugawa period, woodblock printing became widespread as a method for replicating both books and prints, especially, *ukiyo-e* prints, which were picture prints that became widely disseminated throughout Tokugawa society.[59] With the onset of the seventeenth century, print blocks were made in large quantities and at more affordable prices.[60] While it did take about a decade before prints became inexpensive enough to be widely affordable, woodblock prints continued to increase in popularity among all classes until the mid-1800s.[61]

Ukiyo-e prints extensively depicted two popular subjects. Wood block prints captured the colorful and lively worlds of the theater and the pleasure quarters.[62] In particular, prints were done of actors and prostitutes. While the government saw both of these groups as outcastes, they were idols among the general populace.[63] "Pictures of famous courtesan beauties and portraits of actors in famous scenes attained great popularity, in part because they often depicted actual persons."[64] Actor prints became highly popular among a wide public; their popularity had no age limit as even young children bought and collected them.[65] These themes provided the basis for about two thirds of all *ukiyo-e* art during the seventeenth and eighteenth centuries.[66]

Prints were used in a wide variety of ways. As previously mentioned prints were used as illustrations for popular books; they were also used for calendars, greeting cards, etc.[67] In addition, prints were also sold separately and were often distributed by street hawkers and peddlers. In addition, *Ukiyo-e* pictures were used to advertise both Kabuki and the pleasure quarters.

Elements of *chonin* culture, or at least imitations of it, gained wide popularity. *Ukiyo-e* prints illustrate this phenomenon. On one hand, since a visit to the pleasure quarters was quite expensive, pictures of courtesans and actors could be bought by lower classes as a substitute for the actual experience.[68] On the other hand, prints also became souvenirs for wealthy individuals who lived far from Edo and could not visit the entertainment quarters as regularly as they would like. And of course, for those wealthy individuals living nearby, prints, as for others, could be used much as pin-ups are today. In response to these demands, these cultural centers became the prime topic for print artists and "printing techniques were rapidly devised to meet the popular demand. . . ."[69]

Alternatives were especially widely sought after by those whose access to the entertainment quarters was financially limited. For instance, the pleasure quarters and courtesans within them were undoubtedly a main social attraction for most commoners. While many could not afford to go into the quarter and pay for a courtesan, it was possible to take part vicariously in various forms of entertainment which were associated with the quarter. For example, in the Yoshiwara district girls often sat outside the entrance as a means of advertising the quarter and those passing by could catch a glimpse free of charge.[70]

A More Open Social Structure

The emergence of a class system from one based on caste assisted in the rise of a proto-popular culture stage by promoting a more accessible common culture. In Tokugawa society, an individual's status was based on his occupation, and there were four such status categories. These included, in rank order: samurai, peasants, artisans and merchants. However, there were significant deviations from this status system. Individuals could be included in more than one group, e.g., some were artisans as well as merchants. In addition, as was previously mentioned, there was a tremendous amount of social mobility between status levels, especially among the lower three groups, and some samurai even chose to become merchants.[71] The social structure was basically rigid, but fluid enough to foster the spread of a more common culture, and especially that connected with the dynamic merchant sector.

For those who lacked the economic means of elites or the emerging middle class, cheaper imitations were significant. Poorer sectors developed cheap versions of elite culture. Kabuki and Bunraku were available in low-cost editions for the less affluent. This spread of culture across a segmented society facilitated a movement toward a mass society.

Economic Exchange

The Tokugawa period witnessed a general movement toward a more integrated and commercialized market structure. Economic growth and development were not confined to the urban centers of Japan, but instead moved from the cities to the castle towns, infiltrated the countryside and eventually penetrated the villages.[72] "The sankin kotai system, which had many samurai traveling to Edo and living there for part of the time, the growing trade, regional specialization, and increasing participation by villagers in the national economy all contributed to [these patterns of] economic growth."[73] And the commodification of popular culture within this market structure facilitated wide dissemination.[74]

Nearly everywhere goods could be bought for a price. In the urban centers, there flourished markets and also stores which sold speciality items such as prints.[75] Even peasants shopped in castle towns and other regional markets,[76] or purchased commodities at small traveling fairs which often made regular circuits through various communities.[77] In castle towns such as Kanazawa, there were peddlers who also criss-crossed the city hawking a wide range of products.[78] Purchases were also frequently made on pilgrimages.[79] Such heightened and more widespread commercial activities made the development and diffusion of a common culture both more feasible and more acceptable.

Economic exchange was also facilitated by the further development of a network of roads, post towns and inns. The roads were cited by many European vistiors as comparable to those found in Europe and were efficient as well as being very well maintained.[80] Road maintenance was a high priority for the Tokugawa government. Roads were frequently improved throughout the period and were heavily traveled. The improving conditions of roadways during the period allowed for more efficient communication and an increased movement of goods and people around the country.[81]

Affluence and Literacy

Increasingly, many in Tokugawa Japan gained the means to obtain or consume popular culture. In particular, the urban merchants and an emerging middle class gained more discretionary income to spend on nonessentials. Moreover, education became more widely available and in turn led to increases in literacy among all classes of society. Much of the push for education arose with the development of a highly bureaucratic state which forced many to become educated in order to fulfill their administrative duties.[82] The need for education was substantially met by the spread of the *terakoya,* a small one room school often found in cities and villages throughout the Tokugawa period; often these were located within religious temples. It is estimated that the number of these schools for commoners located within both cities and villages increased dramatically during the Tokugawa period.[83] The number of *terakoya* by 1867 may have been as high as ten thousand.[84] Furthermore, teachers were plentiful and relatively inexpensive to hire.[85]

"In cities and towns . . . it is a fair presumption that a majority of the children, at least the boys, attended school for some period or other."[86] By mid-1800, in Edo, school attendence for commoners was close to eightysix percent.[87] This is reflected by the literacy rates. For even the least affluent village peasants, by the end of the Tokugawa, the literacy rate can be estimated as having been as high as forty percent for male commoners.[88] Certainly, the literacy rates of Japan by the mid-1700's were not inferior to those of Europe.[89] "Clearly education levels were rising, and the literacy skills needed to obtain the most basic knowledge and information had extended to even the lower levels of Edo society."[90] Through literacy, many gained the ability to "receive" culture through books, which, as we have already discussed, became widely available.

In additon, there developed the means for those without either the economic resources or the necessary knowledge to engage in cultural activities and experiences. To compensate for a lack of funds, local travel lotteries were set up for pilgrimage excursions. In many villages, there were Ise associations in which people pooled their money and sent representatives each year on journeys to Ise; for many this was their only opportunity to take part in a pilgrimage experience.[91] Another mechanism to ease financial shortfalls was the custom of *settai,* which involved giving alms to pilgrims. Villagers would give items such as free food or lodging to pilgrims. It was believed that pilgrims could actually be deities in disguise and through the giving of alms good fortune could be gained. In some instances, pilgrims arrived home richer than they had been prior to their pilgrimage.[92]

Aids were developed for those who lacked the necessary knowledge to participate in cultural activities such as travel. "The market for guidebooks and pictorial maps intended for those planning the trip, as well as prints and paintings for those who could not go, grew increasingly."[93] There was an increase in the amount and types of travel literature, including travel guides and books and printed itineraries and maps, all designed to guide even the novice traveler.[94] A specialized system of travel services was also developed to help Tokugawa travelers. An example of this was the lodging associations which can be compared to contemporary AAA agencies. The associations issued identification cards which authorized free lodging and travel information from member lodges.[95] All of the above made accessible the necessary knowledge for travelers to consume culture via their adventures.

Kabuki: A Case Study

Kabuki theater offers a wonderful synthesis of the factors we have discussed above which illustrate the development of a proto-popular culture stage. Kabuki's popularity flourished throughout the Tokugawa period, in particular, during the last several decades of the seventeenth century. The popularity of Kabuki and its actors can only be compared to our own cinema and movie star obsession of today. Without a doubt, Kabuki was one of the essential centers of social and cultural life in Tokugawa Japan that could only be paralleled in popularity and influence by the pleasure quarters.[96]

Kabuki theater, similar to puppet theater, was designed particularly for urban townspeople. Kabuki and the pleasure quarters both represented a key response by commoners to the elite culture. They were an expression of the emergent middle classes' frustration with their political and social powerlessness despite their growing economic independence. This affluence allowed the *chonin* to develop a cultural independence, which prominantly included Kabuki theater.

While the centralized government wanted to curb the spread of Kabuki and its perceived negative influences, it was generally difficult for it to do so. Throughout the Tokugawa period, the government made various attempts to enforce restrictions which were designed to regulate theater life. Laws were set up to restrict everything from who could act in plays and what actors could wear, to the subject matter of the plays and where plays could be held. Regardless, the appeal of Kabuki among the masses could not be checked.[97] In time, although it was never entirely accepted, the government increasingly saw it as a necessary evil, for it occupied commoners and channeled their new found material wealth away from more serious forms of mischief.[98] The government's distate was further weakened, for not only did urban townspeople become obssessed and fascinated by Kabuki, but samurai and members of their families also patronized the theater, often inconspicuously, in order to see performances.[99] Consequently, Kabuki theater became the stage upon which culture was disseminated to the wider urban population and its influence was uncontainable.

Popular demand for Kabuki and information about theater life was insatiable and widespread. Throughout the eighteenth and nineteenth centuries Kabuki was promoted and discussed in several mediums: novels set in the theatrical world,[100] critical guide books to theater districts and actors,[101] colorful *ukiyo-e* billboards which graced the entrances of Kabuki theater, smaller *ukiyo-e* woodblock prints sold as souvenirs of performances,[102] and pinup-like prints of famous actors.[103]

Kabuki, because of its vast popularity, was used to further the spread of the emergent commercial culture and as a means for cultural diffusion. Popular Kabuki actors endorsed commercial products. These products included items such as cakes, cosmetics, and clothing which were sold in urban shops.[104] As a result of having their names used for product advertising, the fame of actors extended to most urban homes.[105] Kabuki was also a socializing mechanism. It was ". . . a peculiar classroom of etiquette, the arts, fashion, and music. It fed the curiosity of the commoners with an approximation of the dress and deportment of their betters. And it provided, too, an example of the proper way for persons of every station and both genders to walk, sit, bow, and speak in different social situations."[106]

Particularily influential were *onnagata* (female impersonators) who played female roles on stage. *Onnagata* strongly influenced ladies of the city and were imitated by the courtesans of the pleasure quarters.[107] "Not least important, the stage became a showroom for the display of what was new in fashion—clothing, design and fabrics, weaving, dyeing, embroidery, hairstyles, combs, bodkins, makeup, and personal ornamentation."[108]

Kabuki in general did not exclude any socio-economic class in society. Instead, it embraced all levels of society, from the very lowest outcastes to the grandest daimyo.[109] While ticket prices did increase during the Tokugawa period, lower priced mediums evolved to insure accessibility. Theaters had a wide range of seats available. Those with very limited incomes could buy a seat in what was known as the deaf gallery, where one could not see or hear the performance, but could attend, i.e., ". . . just breathe the air of the playhouse."[110] There were also a wide assortment of lower-level playhouses,[111] which were cheaper than the grand theaters. In addition, summer performances were cheap because parts were played by amateur actors, and the opening shows of the grand theaters were even cheaper, being free.[112] For those unable to avail themselves of physically attending the theater, there were a large number of published guidebooks which allowed the average person to participate vicariously in this entertainment world.[113]

Another prime example of a cheap subsition can be found in the art of comic storytelling, know as *rakugo*. Several permanent storytelling halls were established and storytellers also entertained in market places and on street corners. The storytellers' main form of entertainment was imitating popular stage heroes, thus providing a cheap substitute readily available to the lower classes.[114]

There was an entire social culture which surrounded the Kabuki theater experience. Teahouses were popular places where urban townspeople gathered before or after a performance and the numbers of teahouses increased rapidly throughout the period. While in Osaka theater teahouses served the patrons of a number of theaters in the district, the Edo teahouses were affiliated with a particular theater.[115]

The Kabuki cultural experience was not limited to urban theater districts or shrines, for it was brought to people all over rural Japan. This penetration of provincial areas occurred through traveling troupes, establishment of local playhouses, *ukiyo-e* prints of actors and books about the theater world. In addition, some villages formed Kabuki or puppet theaters for their own entertainment.[116] "Most [Kabuki playhouses] were found in castle towns of daimyo or before the gates of major temples or shrines, yet their popularity reached even remote farming and fishing villages."[117] Clearly, Kabuki was popular culture for it was widespread and widely consumed, and it is an example par excellence of the stage of pre-industrial or proto-popular culture.

Meiji Japan

The Meiji period (1867–1911) witnessed dramatic change. Most importantly, following the forced opening to the West during the late Tokugawa period and the restoration in 1876 of the emperor as the central figure of its political system, Japan rapidly industrialized and modernized. These changes were so successful, that by the time of the Russo-Japanese War (1904–1905) Japan had emerged as a great power. This transition was also characterized by the transition from a proto-stage to that of a full-blown popular culture. Most of the features we have associated with the proto-stage were intensified; and those traditionally associated with mass culture, especially industrialization, mass production and dissemination, and a consumer culture, came to characterize Japan.

The population of Meiji Japan grew substantially, reaching about 51,000,000 by 1912.[118] But the population of Edo, which was renamed Tokyo, initially declined in the 1860s, due to the abandonment of the alternate residence system which had forced elites and their retainers to reside in the city periodically.[119] However, these losses were quickly recovered by about 1871, and for the remainder of the Meiji period the population of Edo grew at an annual rate of approximately 3.6 percent.[120]

Urbanization accelerated during the Meiji Era, and not only in the largest metropolitan areas, even reaching more than three percent annually between 1893 and 1898.[121] Towns and villages consolidated into cities.[122] Urban growth in smaller centers was especially dynamic.[123] Urbanization became even more pronounced after the Russo-Japanese War, as there was a substanatial shift from villages to cities throughout the country.[124]

Greater urbanization accelerated the movement toward a more common culture.[125] The flow of information within the urban centers increased, and eventually spread outward as well through newly established communication networks such as the railway and postal system. New cultural items and ideas, increasingly influenced by the West, were generally first introduced into urban centers or port cities and then quickily spread to provincial areas of the country.

New means of cultural diffusion were created and many of those already in existence during the Tokugawa period were further perfected. Ideas and material goods were spread from cities to the rural population during the Meiji years with what at the time seemed like astounding speed.[126] Rapid and widespread dissemination of cultural information became one key to the further creation of a national identity.[127]

"A modernizing society requires channels through which those at the helm can provide information about their destination and thus win over the mass of the population that must be drawn into the national endeavor."[128]

Book publishing intensified during the Meiji. Newspapers, which appeared for the first time in 1872, became a new disseminating channel. Twenty years later, six hundred newspapers and magazines were being published on a regular basis.[129] And over time newspapers became reader oriented.

The government came to view newspapers as essential to the wide dissemination of its ideas and programs.[130] Newspapers were expected to aid the administration's high-priority goal of making knowledge which would lead to an enlightened civilization accessible.[131] And to this end, newspapers did provide information about up-to-date developments at home and abroad.[132] In order to encourage the publication of newspapers, the Meiji government reduced their postal rates. And "public reading facilities were established in towns and villages where newspapers were made available, usually free of charge, for those who could not afford to purchase them."[133]

Another new means by which information was disseminated was the postal system. With the development of railway and steamship lines during the Meiji period, mail circulation increased steadily.[134] By 1901 there were as many as five thousand post offices throughout the country. Even the volume of foreign mail being handled rapidly increased. In 1900, eleven million pieces of foreign mail were handled and by 1908 fifty-six million pieces.[135]

The creation of an integrated postal system facilitated the spread of mass culture. For example, by 1887 picture postcards were the largest category of mail, and shops which previously had sold woodblock prints now sold picture cards. On the front these cards depicted standardized scenes, while on the back personalized messages could be written.[136]

Unlike the postal service, the telegraph system grew slowly because of the high cost of equipment. To help establish a system, "in 1903 a Petitions System for the Establishment of Telegraphic Offices was set, by which a community, a town or a village could start a telegraph office if it bore the cost of installation of the equipment and a part of the operation expense."[137] The telegraph network did eventually connect the important areas of Japan, which allowed for a greater diffusion of information.

People increasingly had a much greater opportunity to visit various areas of the country than had been the case in Tokugawa Japan. Increased geographic mobility allowed for additional cultural contacts, as many of the travel barriers in place during the Tokugawa period were abolished.[138] In addition, the government avidly encouraged travel through increased construction of roads and the creation of a railway system.

The railway played a key role in the movement of people and goods during the Meiji years. Construction of the railroad began in 1870, and "by 1887 . . . the spirit of railway enterprise had become almost a mania."[139] The first lines connected Tokyo and Kyoto. By 1893, 558 miles of track had been laid.[140] Railway mileage increased steadily during the Meiji Era.[141]

The development of a railway system allowed more individuals access to popular destinations, near and far.[142] Ordinary people used trains to travel to temple and shrine festivals. One major benefit of travel by train was that less time was needed to go even greater distances.[143] In addition, people began to use the railway for daily commuting. While at first only the wealthy could afford daily commuting by train, this use of the railways also expanded. More than 15,000 commuters a day were using the Shibuya Station in Tokyo by 1903. "Clearly the Japanese people became more mobile during the Meiji period, and they had not been nontravelers in earlier centuries; rather, the pace of travel quickened."[144]

Increased travel was not restricted to internal destinations. The government increasingly sent people abroad to learn about Western industries. In addition, business trainees were stationed in industrial countries and reported their findings to the government.[145] Students were also sent abroad in the hope that they would assimilate the advanced knowledge of the West and then share it upon their return to Japan.[146] Travel of all types to other parts of the world became a key mechanism for the diffusion of Western culture into Japan.

Increased political centralization was a central feature of the Meiji period. Power was further concentrated in the central government, which facilitated the government's role in creating conditions which facilitated the emergence of a more widely diffused and accepted culture. Industrialization was state led. The demise of the old feudal order was hastened when the government outlawed feudalism. And the state championed and ensured the creation of an economic infrastructure necessary to support industrialization and the modernization of the transportation and communication systems.

Industry and technology introduced new means to replicate cultural forms, making the creation of a common culture increasingly more feasible. The main means of replication during the Tokugawa period was woodblock printing. However, at the end of the nineteenth century movable type, which had been tried briefly about 1650, was reintroduced and completely replaced block printing.[147] Newspapers offer an excellent example of the greater efficiency of movable type. Around the mid-1870s the old technique of woodblock printing was abandoned and the Western printing press adopted. This improvement in ". . . printing technology made it possible to reduce printing time and to increase press run; hence, more copies were available for sale at lower cost per unit."[148]

The Meiji government adopted the policy goal of a more open social structure and of equal opportunity for all.[149] "Between 1871 and 1872, the caste system based upon the four classes of society was abolished and the freedom of choice in employment by all classes of people was recognized, thus permitting full play to the creative genius of the nation."[150] Individuals were freer to enter the occupation of their choice and to take part in experiences which they were previously barred from or had to engage in illegally. The resulting increase in social mobility and mixing of classes increased the potential for a more common culture.

The further integration and commercialization of the market struture inherited from theTokugawa period was seen as essential in order for Japan to industrialize. Some of the groundwork necessary for this transition had already been laid during the previous period. For example, by the end of Tokugawa, wage labor increased, new commercial networks emerged and even a few Western style industrial plants were established.[151] Clearly, the Tokugawa government had recognized the need for a progressive attitude toward economic endeavors.[152] In general, the internal barriers to trade were reduced, but not eradicated.[153]

The Meiji government intensified this trend. Part of its motivation for the removal of ". . . feudal restrictions, such as the monopoly on shareholding, stemmed from the consideration that free and unhampered activity of the people was the key to economic development."[154] Weights and measures were standardized,[155] and by the 1890s there developed a modern banking system which included a nationally integrated structure of interest rates.[156] The result of these and numerous similar changes was, ". . . the penetration of a money economy and the commercialization of economic life [which] led to the dissolution of the peasantry, the impoverishment of the feudal aristocracy, the rise of the merchant class and eventually to the establishment of capitalism."[157] And, it should be added, this resulted in the further standardization of Japan's consumer culture.

The Tokugawa era was characterized by a rising standard of living and increasing levels of educational attainment. Both of these factors were intensified during the Meiji years. Because of the numerous *terakoya* schools, people had a high regard for education by the onset of the Meiji period. This may have been ". . . the greatest legacy inherited by modern Japan in its process of modernization. . . ."[158]

During the Meiji period, education was a high priority which was linked to modernization. The 1872 Code of Education stated that "education is for all classes."[159] To achieve this, the government established schools throughout Japan and made attendence compulsory. By the end of Meiji, ninety-eight percent of all children were attending elementary school,[160] and nearly the entire Meiji population had achieved functional literacy.[161] The government "sought to disseminate education in order to change Japan fundamentally."[162]

And as with so many fundamental changes accelerated or initiated by the Meiji, educational reform linked modernization and a more widely diffused and acceped common culture. Education was intended to increase social mobility and equip the Japanese for life in the new industrial order. And

"[Meiji leaders] viewed uniformity as an essential value in the new [educa-tion] system . . ."[163] and thus worked toward a nationwide standardization of curricula and texts.[164]

Conclusion

Based on our research on Tokugawa and Meiji Japan, we suggest a three-stage development for widespread and widely adopted culture or popular culture. The first, not examined in this article, is a pre-popular cul-ture stage. Few, if any, of the features associated with the proto-stage ap-pear to have antedated the Tokugawa period in Japan. But the origins of some factors did precede the onset of the proto-popular culture period, e.g. replication through the appearance of Scriptoria and the widespread copy-ing by hand of religious books.

The proto-stage's appearance is probably marked by the emergence of several key factors: significant urbanization coupled with a strong central state that can project its culture outward; fewer restrictions on the move-ment of people; some pre-industrial means of replication; income levels sufficiently high that most sectors of the general populace can afford to adopt a common culture; significant movement toward a fluid class, rather than a rigid caste, social system; and the emergence of more integrated and commercialized market structures. One factor which appeared in Toku-gawa Japan that may not be a necessary one, is literacy. Clearly a common culture could be merely visual, e.g., *ukiyo-e* prints, or aural, e.g., story telling (although before radio, the aural was generally combined with a vi-sual medium as it was in comic storytelling). In addition, as Schroeder sug-gests, a high level of urbanization may not be necessary, if there exists a strong polity actively engaged in the spread of culture; but since Tokugawa Japan combined both of these features, it does not provide a test of this as-pect of Schroeder's hypothesis.

The final stage, that of popular culture, now appears to be one in which the factors identified for the proto-stage are intensified. And the main means of intensification is industrialization. Industrialization introduces new means which allow the proto-factors to be far more efficiently achieved. Culture becomes even more widely spread and adopted.

Notes

1. Russel Nye, *The Unembarassed Muse: The Popular Arts in America* (New York: Dial, 1970), 1–3.

2. Fred E. H. Schroeder, ed., *5000 Years of Popular Culture: Popular Culture Before Printing* (Bowling Green, OH: Bowling Green State U Popular P, 1980), 1–2, 4–13.

3. See *Tokugawa Japan: The Social and Economic Antecedents of Modern Japan*, eds., Chie Nankane and Shinzaburo Oishi (Tokyo: Tokyo UP, 1991).

4. Garrett Droppers, "The Population of Japan in the Tokugawa Period," *Transactions of the Asiatic Society of Japan*, 22 (Yokohama 1894; Kraus Reprint Limited. Vaduz, Liechtenstein, 1964), 257.

5. Droppers, 262; see also James L. McClain, "Castle Towns and Daimyo Authority: Kanazawa in the Years 1583–1630," *Journal of Japanese Studies* 6 (1980): 267.

6. Gilbert Rozman, "Introduction to Part Three," *Japan in Transition*, eds., Marius B. Jansen and Gilbert Rozman (Princeton, NJ: Princeton UP, 1986), 274.

7. James L. McClain, "Castle Towns and Daimyo Authority: Kanazawa in the Years 1583–1630," *Journal of Japanese Studies*, 6 (1980): 267–68.

8. Rozman, "Introduction to Part Three," Jansen and Rozman, 274; Takeo Yazaki, *Social Change and the City in Japan: From the Earliest Times Through the Industrial Revolution* (San Francisco, CA: Japan Publications, 1958), 131.

9. C. Andrew Gerstle, "Flowers of Edo: Kabuki and Its Patrons," *18th Century Japan: Culture and Society*, ed. C. Andrew Gerstle (Sydney: Allen and Unwin, 1989), 55–56.

10. Masakatsu Gunji, "Kabuki and Its Social Background," *Tokugawa Japan: The Social and Economic Antecedents of Modern Japan*, eds. Chie Nankane and Shinzaburo Oishi (Tokyo: Tokyo UP, 1991), 192.

11. Donald H. Shively, "Popular Culture," *The Cambridge History of Japan: Vol. 4, Early Modern Japan*, ed. John Whitney Hall, asst. ed., James L. McClain (Cambridge: Cambridge UP, 1991), 749.

12. Donald H. Shively, "Bakufu Versus Kabuki," *Studies in the Institutional History of Early Modern Japan*, eds. John Whitney Hall and Marius B. Jansen (Princeton, NJ: Princeton UP, 1968), 242.

13. Shively in Hall and McClain, 748.

14. Teruoka Yasutaka, "The Pleasure Quarters and Tokugawa Culture," *18th Century Japan: Culture and Society*, ed. C. Andrew Gerstle (Sydney: Allen and Unwin, 1989), 16.

15. C. Andrew Gerstle, Introduction, *18th Century Japan: Culture and Society*, ed. C. Andrew Gerstle (Sydney: Allen and Unwin 1989), xiii.

16. Kenneth P. Kirkwood, *Renaissance in Japan: A Cultural Survey of the Seventeenth Century* (Rutland, VT: Tuttle, 1970), 141.

17. Yasutaka in Gerstle, 16–17.

18. Shively in Hall and McClain, 663; see also Constantine Nomi Vaporis, Overland Communication in Tokugawa Japan (Ph.D. Dissertation, Princeton University 1987), 325.

19. Gunji in Nankane and Oishi, 205.

20. Shively in Hall and McClain, 706.

21. Emil Lederer and Emy Lederer-Seidler, *Japan in Transition* (New Haven, CT: Yale UP, 1938), 60–61; see also Shively in Hall and Jansen, 231.

22. Shively in Hall and McClain, 711. The government attempted various sumptuary regulations in hopes of curbing extravagant lifestyles. See Kirkwood, 145–66.

23. Shively in Hall and Jansen, 249–53.

24. Charles David Sheldon, *The Rise of The Merchant Class in Tokugawa Japan, 1600–1868: An Introductory Survey,* Monographs of the Association for Asian Studies, No. 5 (Locust Valley, NY: Augusin, 1958), 94; Yasutaka, 3.

25. McClain in "Castle Towns and Daimyo Authority," 295; Bunraku troupe performances were very popular, including among illiterate farmers. Tickets tended to be cheaper than for Kabuki. See Donald Keene, *No and Bunraku: Two Forms of Japanese Theater* (New York: Columbia UP, 1990), 148.

26. Gunji in Nankane and Oishi, 193.

27. C. J. Dunn, *Everyday Life in Traditional Japan* (London: Bradford 1969), 82.

28. Dunn, 88; Sheldon, 151.

29. Richard Lane, *Images from the Floating World: The Japanese Print* (Hong Kong: Konecky & Konecky 1978), 34.

30. Katshuhisa Moriya, "Urban Networks and Information Networks," *Tokugawa Japan: The Social and Economic Antecedents of Modern Japan,* eds. Chie Nankane and Shinzaburo Oishi (Tokyo: Tokyo UP, 1991), 117.

31. David Chibbett, *The History of Japanese Printing and Book Illustration* (Tokyo: Kodansha, 1977), 84.

32. Moriya in Nankane and Oishi, 117.

33. James T. Araki, "The Dream Pillow in Edo Fiction," *Monumenta Nipponica,* 25.1–2 (1970): 45.

34. Lane, 96.

35. Chibbett, 85.

36. Chibbett, 82.

37. Shively in Hall and McClain, 731.

38. Dunn, 116.

39. Vaporis, 343.

40. Toshio G. Tsukahira, *Feudal Control in Tokugawa Japan: The Sankin Kotai System,* Harvard East Asian Monographs, No. 20 (Cambridge: Harvard UP, 1970), 1.

41. Dunn, 99. As a result of the yearly migrations by daimyo with their processions, the Tokaido road became the most traveled route, see Vaporis, 33.

42. Vaporis, 299. People could travel because of economic growth and the development of a transportation system which was well maintained. As a result, pilgrimages became more than just religious, they became a form of recreation.

43. Vaporis, 357; McClain, "Castle Towns and Daimyo Authority," 295.

44. Vaporis, 320.

45. Vaporis, 371.

46. Dunn, 81; the most important theater group outside the three large metropolises was located in Ise, see Dunn, 81. In addition, some aspiring actors performing in the countryside might be spotted by actors from the great urban theaters while they visited pilgrimage circuits. See Dunn, 142.

47. Vaporis, 342–53. Travels to pilgrimage sites were not necessarily over long distances. For instance, replicas were created of both the Saikoku and Shikoku Circuits so that people in the east and north could travel closer to home. See Vaporis, 352–353.

48. Shively in Hall and Jansen, 248–49.

49. Vaporis, 374.

50. McClain in "Castle Towns and Daimyo Authority," 295.

51. Rozman, Introduction, 275. In general, there were few restrictions on individuals travelling into Edo unless they seemed suspicious, see Vaporis, 246.

52. Lane, 16.

53. Tsukahira, 2. Once the alternate residence system was set up, the Tokugawa roads became increasingly more congested as daimyo traveled to Edo and back again to their domains, see Vaporis, 82; see also Paul Varley, *Japanese Culture: A Short History* (Tokyo: Tuttle, 1973), 115.

54. Vaporis, 298. For example, during the large pilgrimage movements in 1651, 1705, 1771 and 1803, travel permit requirements, a system created to restrict travel, were waived. See Vaporis, 250. In general, peasants were less restricted than the townsmen because they were required to maintain land productivity; see Vaporis, 303.

55. Tatsuro Akai, "The Common People and Painting," *Tokugawa Japan: The Social and Economic Antecedents of Modern Japan,* eds. Chie Nankane and Shinzaburo Oishi (Tokyo UP, 1991), 189–91. The government particularly did not want samurai to endulge in leisure activities such as theater-going or patronizing brothels, see Dunn, 35.

56. Chibbett, 40.

57. Shively in Hall and McClain, 726–27.

58. Chibbett, 33.

59. Akai in Nankane and Oishi, 179–91.

60. Lane, 34.

61. Lane, 187.

62. Lane, 24; also Dunn, 186 who discusses the use of prints as publicity materials for the pleasure quarters and courtesans. Prints of actors could be bought in specialty shops and were used as decoration in homes.

63. Lane, 64.

64. Sheldon, 94.

65. Arai in Nankane and Oishi, 187–88.

66. Lane, 21.

67. Ukiyo-e Society of America, *Life and Customs of Edo as Portrayed in Woodblock Prints of the 17th through 19th Centuries* (produced in cooperation with Pratt Graphics Center New York City, 1978), 2; Lane, 63.

68. Lane, 61.

69. John Whitney Hall, "The Visual Arts and Japanese Culture," *Twelve Doors to Japan,* eds. John Whitney Hall and Richard K. Beardsley (New York: McGraw Hill, 1965), 289.

70. Dunn, 185

71. Sheldon, 25–27.

72. Lederer and Lederer, 60–61.

73. Susan B. Hanley, "Tokugawa Society: Material Culture, Standard of Living, and Lifestyles," *The Cambridge History of Japan: Vol. 4 Early Modern Japan,* ed. John Whitney Hall, asst. ed. James L. McClain (Cambridge: Cambridge UP, 1991), 663.

74. Hanley, 663.

75. Gerstle, Introduction, in Gerstle, xii.

76. Akai in Nankane and Oishi, 184–85.

77. Sheldon, 151,

78. McClain, "Castle Towns and Daimyo Authority," 287.

79. Sheldon, 151.

80. Vaporis, v, 384–95. Road conditions were also easy to maintain as a result of the absence of wheeled traffic. See Vaporis, 64.

81. Vaporis, 3, 82–83; "Daimyo improved transport facilities in order to promote the flow of goods into urban markets and to establish the castle town as the economic center of the domain. Road systems were devised with main highways connecting the castle town and all important points of communication, both within and outside the domain; secondary road systems branched off the main routes to reach even remote villages." Vaporis, 38; see also Moriya, 106.

82. Herbert Passin, *Society and Education in Japan* (New York: Columbia UP, 1965), 28.

83. Sheldon, 169.

84. Shively in Hall and McClain, 719.

85. Moriya in Nankane and Oishi, 120.

86. Passin, 28.

87. Passin, 45.

88. Passin, 47.

89. Gerstle, Introduction in Gerstle, xii.

90. Moriya in Nankane and Oishi, 120.

91. Dunn, 80–81; see also Lane, 16.

92. Carmen Blacker, "The Religious Traveller in the Edo Period," *Modern Asian Studies,* 18.4 (Oct. 1984): 606; Vaporis, 358.

93. Vaporis, 336–37. One example is a book entitled *A Collection of Travel Precautions* which was available in 1810. Vaporis, 339. Service areas were also created in response to the increases in traffic. Establishments were set up between post towns which were essentially rest areas for tired travellers. Vaporis, 325.

94. Lane, 176.

95. Vaporis, 333.

96. Gerstle, "Flowers of Edo" in Gerstle, 33; Edward Seidensticker, *Low City, High City* (New York: Knopf, 1983), 21.

97. Shively in Hall and Jansen, 258. The battle between Kabuki and the Tokugawa government lasted more than 250 years. Shively in Hall and Jansen, 231.

98. Shively in Hall and Jansen, 241.

99. Gunji in Nankane and Oishi, 197–98.

100. Gunji in Nankane and Oishi, 200; Gerstle, 34.

101. Shively in Hall and McClain, 760; Yazaki, 45.

102. Lane, 59 and 65.

103. Lane, 145–46.

104. Shively in Hall and McClain, 759.

105. Gerstle, "Flowers of Edo" in Gerstle, 34.

106. Shively in Hall and McClain, 759.

107. Gerstle, "Flowers of Edo" in Gerstle, 38; Gunji, in Nankane and Oishi, 195.

108. Gerstle, "Flowers of Edo," 34.

109. Jacob Raz, "The Audience Evaluated: Shikitei Samba's Kyakusha Hybanki," *Monumenta Nipponica,* 35.2 (Summer 1980): 217.

110. Gunji in Nankane and Oishi, 193.

111. Yasutaka in Gerstle, 18.

112. Gunji in Nankane and Oishi, 197.

113. Yasutaka in Gerstle, 18.

114. Susaki Miyoko and Morioka Heinz, "Rakugo: Popular Narrative Art of the Grosteque," *Harvard Journal of Asiatic Studies,* 41–2 (1981): 418–19. The number of Rakugo halls (known as *yose*) grew rapidly. The first one appeared in 1798 in Edo and by 1855 there were 172 storytelling halls in existence, see Miyoko and Heinz, 419.

115. Yazaki, 27.

116. Dunn, 83.

117. Gunji in Nankane and Oishi, 193.

118. Shibusawa Keizo, *Japanese Life and Culture in the Meiji Era* (Tokyo: Obunsha, 1958), 332.

119. Gilbert Rozman, "Castle Towns in Transition," *Japan in Transition,* eds. Marius B. Jansen and Gilbert Rozman (Princeton, NJ: Princeton UP, 1986), 322.

120. Henry D. Smith II, "The Edo-Tokyo Transition: In Search of Common Ground," *Japan in Transition,* eds. Marius B. Jansen and Gilbert Rozman (Princeton, NJ: Princeton UP, 1986), 356.

121. Rozman, "Castle Towns," Jansen and Rozman, 322.

122. Irokawa Diakichi, *The Culture of the Meiji Period* (Princeton, NJ: Princeton UP, 1985), 28.

123. Rozman, Introduction, Jansen and Rozman, 279.

124. Shibusawa Keizo, *Japanese Life and Culture in the Meiji Era* (Tokyo: Obunsha, 1958), 336.

125. Dakichi, 28.

126. Shibusawa Keizo, *Japanese Life and Culture in the Meiji Era* (1958), 337.

127. Ministry of Foreign Affairs, *Japan in Transition: One Hundred Years of Modernization* (1968), 24.

128. Albert A. Altman, "The Press," *Japan in Transition,* eds. Marius B. Jansen and Gilbert Rozman (Princeton, NJ: Princeton UP, 1986), 231.

129. Bolitho, 37.

130. Okubo Toshiaki, "Change of Social Conditions," *Japanese Society in the Meiji Era,* ed. Shibusawa Keizo (Tokyo: Obunsha, 1958), 62.

131. Altman, 237.

132. Altman, 240.

133. Ministry of Foreign Affairs, Japan, 24.

134. Kajinishi Mitsuhaya, "Development of Transportation and Communication Systems," *Japanese Society in the Meiji Era,* ed. Shibusawa Keizo (Tokyo: Obunsha, 1958), 394.

135. Mitsuhaya, 396–97.

136. Shibusawa Keizo, *Japanese Life and Culture in the Meiji Era,* 5, translated and adapted by Charles S. Terry (Tokyo: Tokyo Bunko, 1969), 250–51.

137. Mitsuhaya in Keizo, 397–98.

138. Francis Trevithick, "The History and Development of the Railway System in Japan," *Transactions of the Asiatic Society of Japan,* 22 (Yokohama: 1894; Vaduz, Liechtenstein: Kraus Reprint Limited, 1964), 124.

139. Trevithick.

140. Trevithick, 116–22.

141. Bolitho, 40.

142. Bolitho, 41.

143. Shibusawa Keizo, *Japanese Life and Culture in the Meiji Era* (1969), 226–29.

144. Hanley in Jansen and Rozman, 463.

145. Shibusawa Keizo, *Japanese Life and Culture in the Meiji Era* (1958), 137–38.

146. Ministry of Foreign Affairs, Japan, 57.

147. Chibbett, 78.

148. Altman, 240.

149. Ministry of Foreign Affairs, Japan, 32.

150. Ministry of Foreign Affairs, Japan, 28.

151. Crawcour, 114.

152. Ministry of Foreign Affairs, Japan, 27.

153. Sheldon, 18.

154. Ministry of Foreign Affairs, Japan, 44.

155. Ministry of Foreign Affairs, Japan, 24.

156. Crawcour, 123.

157. Crawcour, 114.

158. Ministry of Foreign Affairs, Japan, 31.

159. Ministry of Foreign Affairs, Japan, 28.

160. Passin, 55.

161. Ministry of Foreign Affairs, Japan, 32.

162. Ministry of Foreign Affairs, Japan, 31–32.

163. Passin, 4.

164. Richard Rubinger, "Education: From One Room to One System," *Japan in Transition,* eds. Marius B. Jansen and Gilbert Rozman (Princeton, NJ: Princeton UP, 1986), 228–29.

VIII.
Selective Bibliography
of Additional Work
on Popular Culture Theory and
Methodology

BIBLIOGRAPHY

Allen, Robert, ed. *Channels of Discourse, Reassembled: Television and Contemporary Criticism.* 2d ed. Chapel Hill: University of North Carolina P, 1992.

Ashley, Bob. *The Study of Popular Fiction: A Source Book.* Philadelphia: U of Pennsylvania P, 1989.

Barber, Karin. "Popular Arts in Africa." *African Studies Review* 30.3 (Sept. 1987): 1–78. See also Commentaries, 79–112.

Bennett, Tony, Colin Mercer, and Jane Woollacott, eds. *Popular Culture and Social Relations.* Milton Keynes, England: Open UP, 1986. See especially Preface and Section 1, vii–68.

Berger, Arthur Asa. *Popular Culture Genres: Theories and Texts.* Newbury Park, CA: Sage, 1992. See especially Part 1, 3–78.

Bigsby, C. W. E., ed. *Approaches to Popular Culture.* Bowling Green, OH: Bowling Green State U Popular P, 1976.

Browne, Ray B. "Up from Elitism: The Aesthetics of Popular Fiction." *Studies in American Fiction* 9.2 (Fall 1981): 217–31.

Browne, Ray B., and Marshall W. Fishwick, eds. *Symbiosis: Popular Culture & Other Fields.* Bowling Green, OH: Bowling Green State U Popular P, 1988.

Browne, Ray B., and Pat Browne, eds. *A Guide to U.S. Popular Culture.* Bowling Green, OH: Bowling Green State U Popular P, 2001.

Browne, Ray B., Sam Grogg, Jr., and Larry Landrum, eds. "Theories & Methodologies in Popular Culture." In-Depth Section. *Journal of Popular Culture* 9.2 (Fall 1975): 349–508.

Cawelti, John G. *Adventure, Mystery, and Romance: Formula Stories as Art and Popular Culture.* Chicago: U of Chicago P, 1976.

———. "Notes Toward an Aesthetic of Popular Culture." *Journal of Popular Culture* 5.2 (Fall 1971): 255–68.

Chambers, Iain. *Popular Culture: The Metropolitan Experience.* London: Methuen, 1986. See especially "Popular Culture, Popular Knowledge," 3–13, and "Theoretical Exposures: Framing Culture," 200–21.

———. "Rethinking 'Popular Culture.'" *Screen Education* 36 (1980): 113–17.

Collins, Jim. *Uncommon Cultures: Popular Culture and Post-Modernism.* New York: Routledge, 1989.

Cullen, Jim, ed. *Popular Culture in American History.* Malden, MA: Brockwell, 2001.

Demning, Michael. "The End of Mass Culture." *International Labor and Working-Class History* 37 (Spring 1990): 4–18. See also commentaries, 19–40.

Easthope, Anthony. *Literary into Cultural Studies.* London: Routledge, 1991. See especially Part 2, 65–103.

Fiedler, Leslie. "Beyond What Was Literature?: Looking Backwards and Forward." *Studies in Popular Culture* 7 (1984): 1–13. See also the Afterword, 14–17, by Gary Harmond.

———. *What Was Literature? Class Culture and Mass Society.* New York: Simon & Schuster, 1982.

Fine, Gary Alan, ed. "Sociology and Popular Culture." In-depth section. *Journal of Popular Culture* 11.2 (Fall 1977): 377–526.

Fishwick, Marshall W. *Seven Pillars of Popular Culture.* Westport, CT: Greenwood, 1985.

Fiske, John. *Reading the Popular.* Boston: Unwin Hyman, 1989.

———. *Understanding Popular Culture.* Boston: Unwin Hyman, 1989.

Fluck, Winfried. "Fiction and Fictionality in Popular Culture: Some Observations on the Aesthetics of Popular Culture." *Journal of Popular Culture* 21.4 (Spring 1988): 49–62.

———. "Popular Culture as a Mode of Socialization: A Theory about the Social Functions of Popular Culture Forms." *Journal of Popular Culture* 21.3 (Winter 1987): 31–46.

Forbes, Bruce David, and Jeffrey M. Mahan, eds. *Religion and Popular Culture in America.* Berkeley: U of California P, 2000.

Franco, Jean. "What's in a Name? Popular Culture Theories and Their Limitations." *Studies in Latin American Popular Culture* 1 (1982): 5–14.

Freccero, Carla. *Popular Cultures: An Introduction.* New York: New York UP, 1999.

Friedman, Norman L. "Mass Communications and Popular Culture: Convergent Fields in the Study of Mass Media?" *Mass Comm Review* 4 (Winter 1976/77): 20–28.

Frow, John. "The Concept of the Popular." *New Formations* 18 (Winter 1992): 25–38.

Gans, Herbert J. *Popular Culture and High Culture: An Analysis and Evaluation of Taste.* 2nd ed. New York: Basic, 1999.

Grimsted, David. "The Purple Rose of Popular Culture Theory: An Exploration of Intellectual Kitsch." *American Quarterly* 43.4 (Dec. 1991): 541–78.

Hall, Dennis R. "The Study of Popular Culture: Origin and Developments." *Studies in Popular Culture* 6 (1983): 16–25.

Hedges, James S. "Towards Formal Boundaries for the Act in Popular Culture." *Studies in Popular Culture* 4 (Spring 1981): 9–15.

Hinds, Harold E., Jr. "Boundaries and Popular Culture Theory." *Studies in Latin American Popular Culture* 12 (1993): 243–49.

———. "Folklore and Popular Culture: Theoretical Reflections and Latin American Applications." *Studies in Latin American Popular Culture* 11 (1992): 225–32.

Hudson, Harriet E. "Toward a Theory of Popular Literature: The Case of the Middle English Romances." *Journal of Popular Culture* 23.3 (Winter 1989): 31–50.

Jameson, Fredric. "Ideology, Narrative Analysis, and Popular Culture." *Theory and Society* 4 (1977): 543–59.

Kammer, Michael. *American Culture, American Tastes: Social Change and the 20th Century.* New York: Knopf, 1999.

Kurlansky, Mark J. "Pop Goes the Culture." *Change* 9.6 (June 1977): 36–39.

Lee, Robert G. *Orientals: Asian Americans in Popular Culture.* Philadelphia: Temple UP, 1999.

Levine, Lawrence W. "The Folklore of Industrial Society: Popular Culture and Its Audiences." *American Historical Review* 97.5 (Dec. 1992): 1369–99. See also Commentaries, 1400–30.

Lipsitz, George. *Time Passages: Collective Memory and American Popular Culture.* Minneapolis: U of Minnesota P, 1990. See especially "Popular Culture: This Ain't No Side Show," 3–20.

Lowenthal, Leo. *Literature, Popular Culture, and Society.* Palo Alto, CA: Pacific, 1961. See especially Introduction, "Popular Culture in Perspective," and "The Debate over Art and Popular Culture," xi–108.

MacCabe, Colin, ed. *High Theory/Low Culture: Analyzing Popular Television and Film.* New York: St. Martin's, 1986. See especially, Preface, vii–x; "Defining Popular Culture," 1–10; and "Popular Culture: Notes and Revisions," 156–71.

Maltby, Richard, ed. *Passing Parade: A History of Popular Culture in the Twentieth Century.* Oxford: Oxford UP, 1989. See especially Introduction, 8–19.

McCracken, Ellen. "Demystifying Cosmopolitan: Five Critical Methods." *Journal of Popular Culture* 16.2 (Fall 1982): 30–42.

McGuigan, Jim. *Cultural Populism.* London: Routledge, 1992. See especially Part 1, 9–85.

Mukerji, Chandra, and Michael Schudson. "Popular Culture." *Annual Review of Sociology* 12 (1986): 47–66.

Mukerji, Chandra, and Michael Schudson, eds. *Rethinking Popular Culture: Contemporary Perspectives in Cultural Studies.* Berkeley: U of California P, 1991. See especially "Rethinking Popular Culture," 1–61.

Narváez, Peter, and Martin Laba, eds. *Media Sense: The Folklore-Popular Culture Continuum.* Bowling Green, OH: Bowling Green State U Popular P, n.d. See especially Introduction and "Popular Culture and Folklore," 1–18.

Nye, Russel B. *The Unembarrassed Muse: The Popular Arts in America.* New York: Dial, 1970. See especially "The Popular Arts and the Popular Audience," 1–8, and "The Popular Arts and the Critics," 417–20.

Rosenberg, Bernard, and David Manning White, eds. *Mass Culture: The Popular Arts in America.* Glencoe, IL: Free, 1957. See especially sections 1, 2, and 8; 3–110, 457–561.

Ross, Andrew. *No Respect: Intellectuals & Popular Culture.* New York: Routledge, 1989.

Samson, John. "The Desire of the Unconsciousness: Julian Jaynes and a Theory of Popular Culture." Paper presented at Popular Culture Association, Toronto, March 29–April 1, 1984.

Schechter, Harold. *The Bosom Serpent: Folklore and Popular Art.* Iowa City: University of Iowa Press, 1988. See especially 1–24.

Schroeder, Fred E. H., ed. *5000 Years of Popular Culture: Popular Culture before Printing.* Bowling Green, OH: Bowling Green State U Popular P, 1980. See especially Forward and Introduction, 1–15.

———. *Outlaw Aesthetics: Arts and the Public Mind.* Bowling Green, OH: Bowling Green State U Popular P, 1977. See especially "The Aesthetics of Popular Culture," 1–15.

Schuetz, Arnold. "The Frankfurt School and Popular Culture." *Studies in Popular Culture* 7.1 (1989): 1–14.

Shiach, Morag. *Discourse on Popular Culture.* Stanford: Stanford UP, 1989.

Stern, Jerome. "Highbrow Taste as Popular Culture." *Studies in Popular Culture* 1.1 (Winter 1977): 1–6.

Storey, John. *An Introduction to Cultural Theory and Popular Culture.* 2nd ed. Athens, GA: U of Georgia P, 1998.

Strinati, Dominic. *An Introduction to Studying Popular Culture.* London: Routledge, 2000.

Wagnleitner, Reinhold, and Elaine May Taylor. *"Here, There, and Everywhere": The Foreign Politics of American Popular Culture.* Hanover, NH: UP of New England, 2000.

White, David Manning, and John Pendleton, eds. *Popular Culture: Mirror of American Life.* Del Mar, CA: Publishers, 1977. See especially Section 1: 2–93.

A Ray and Pat Browne Book

Murder on the Reservation: American Indian Crime Fiction
Ray B. Browne

Profiles of Popular Culture: A Reader
Edited by Ray B. Browne

Goddesses and Monsters: Women, Myth, Power, and Popular Culture
Jane Caputi

Mystery, Violence, and Popular Culture
John G. Cawelti

Baseball and Country Music
Don Cusic

Popular Witchcraft: Straight from the Witch's Mouth, 2nd edition
Jack Fritscher

The Essential Guide to Werewolf Literature
Brian J. Frost

Popular Culture Theory and Methodology: A Basic Introduction
Edited by Harold E. Hinds, Jr., Marilyn F. Motz and Angela M. S. Nelson

Rituals and Patterns in Children's Lives
Edited by Kathy Merlock Jackson

Images of the Corpse: From the Renaissance to Cyberspace
Edited by Elizabeth Klaver

Dissecting Stephen King; From the Gothic to Literary Naturalism
Heidi Strengell

Walking Shadows:
Orson Welles, William Randolph Hearst, and Citizen Kane
John Evangelist Walsh

Spectral America: Phantoms and the National Imagination
Edited by Jeffrey Andrew Weinstock

King of the Cowboys, Queen of the West: Roy Rogers and Dale Evans
Raymond E. White